Additional Praise for

The Black Book of Outsourcing

"Oracle-On-Demand (formerly Oracle Outsourcing) is the future of how we will develop, deliver and support technology, a service that eliminates the challenge of managing IT. *The Black Book of Outsourcing* captures how to get outsourcing results and provides invaluable advice for leaders who are trying to drive tighter execution within their organizations."

> Juergen Rottler
> Executive Vice President
> Oracle Corporation

"The code for outsourcing management has been broken and the secrets for success are here in this book. *The Black Book of Outsourcing* has it all. This book will surely be a classic."

> John Steele
> Group Director
> British Telecom/Yahoo

"Brown & Wilson deliver on the best, most innovative, new practices all aimed at helping one and all survive, manage, and lead in this new economy."

> Joann Martin
> Vice President
> Pitney Bowes Management Services

"As more and more companies embrace offshoring solutions, *The Black Book of Outsourcing* should become a useful aid to the business person looking to navigate the industry with success."

> Raj Patil
> Senior Vice President
> Marketing and Sales Strategy
> MphasiS Corporation

"Outsourcing is a business imperative in our interconnected and interdependent world. Organizations who successfully leverage its power create value for their stakeholders. This book will help you master that destiny."

Shiv Nadar
Founder and Chief Executive Officer
HCL Technologies

"The exceptional concepts in this book enabled us to build more products and increase services to clients, all while reducing costs."

Mark A. Stiffler
President and CEO
Synygy Inc.

Business leaders hoping to understand the concerns, challenges and motivating forcues behind the subject of global sourcing will find *The Black Book of Outsourcing* to be an extremely valuable and important tool."

Dilip R. Vellodi
Chief Executive Officer
Sutherland Global Services

The Black Book of Outsourcing

How to Manage the Changes, Challenges, and Opportunities

Douglas Brown and Scott Wilson

WILEY

John Wiley & Sons, Inc.

Published by John Wiley & Sons, Inc., Hoboken, New Jersey.
Published simultaneously in Canada.

For general information on our other products and services please contact our Customer Care Department within the United States at (800) 762-2974, outside the United States at (317) 572-3993 or fax (317) 572-4002.

Wiley also publishes its books in a variety of electronic formats. Some content that appears in print may not be available in electronic books. For more information about Wiley products, visit our web site at www.wiley.com.

Library of Congress Cataloging-in-Publication Data:

Brown, Douglas, 1959–
    The black book of outsourcing : how to manage the changes, challenges, and opportunities / Douglas Brown and Scott Wilson.
        p. cm.
      ISBN-13 978-0-471-71889-5
      ISBN-10 0-471-71889-0 (cloth)
    1. Contracting out—Handbooks, manuals, etc.   I. Wilson, Scott, 1957–   II. Title.
      HD2365.B76 2005
      658.4′058—dc22

                                                            2004028849

Printed in the United States of America.

10 9 8 7 6 5 4 3 2 1

CONTENTS

Preface   vii

Introduction
Outsourcing: Opportunities and Challenges   1

Part One
HOW TO PLAN, LEAD, AND MANAGE OUTSOURCING INITIATIVES   17

Chapter 1
Overview of the Outsourcing Process   19

Chapter 2
Making the Decision to Outsource   33

Chapter 3
What You Need to Know before You Start   44

Chapter 4
Assessing Cost, Benefit, and Risk for Your Outsourcing Venture   73

Chapter 5
Outsourcing Options   88

Chapter 6
Selecting Your Suppliers and Vendors   111

Chapter 7
Managing Your Outsourcing Vendors   127

Chapter 8
Navigating Contracts and Negotiations   137

Chapter 9
New Career Opportunities in Outsourcing Management   150

Chapter 10
Finding Top Outsourcers: Vendor Directory   157

Chapter 11
Avoiding Common Outsourcing Mistakes   233

Part Two
THE INDISPENSABLE GUIDE TO FINDING AN OUTSOURCING CAREER   241

Chapter 12
Strategizing for Success in the New Global Economy   243

Chapter 13
Learning to Market Yourself in the Global Economy   254

Chapter 14
Hot Jobs in Outsourcing   263

Chapter 15
Finding an Offshore, Nearshore, or Bestshore Job   277

Part Three
THE INDISPENSABLE GUIDE FOR OUTSOURCING ENTREPRENEURS   297

Chapter 16
Starting Down the Entrepreneurial Path to Outsourcing   299

Chapter 17
Capitalizing on the Outsourcing Start-Up Boom   308

Chapter 18
Starting an Outsourcing Business   325

Glossary   347

Index   353

PREFACE

We need to discover the means to enhance the skills of our workforce and to further open markets here and abroad

—Alan Greenspan, Chairman of the U.S. Federal Reserve Board

Offshore outsourcing, or offshoring, refers to the procurement of goods or services by a business or organization from an outside foreign supplier, typically to gain the benefits of labor arbitrage. In the past 10 years, business process outsourcing (BPO) contracts have increasingly been awarded to firms in developing countries, because educated workers in these countries—in particular India and China—are willing to work for a much lower wage than are same-level workers in developed countries, such as Japan. (For offshore outsourcing to be economically feasible, savings from the lower wage rate must surpass the increased costs of management and associated risk.) But, in the mid-to-late 1990s, when high-paying professional jobs, such as those in the computer industry, began to be offshored with greater regularity, many people in developed countries began to object to the practice.

Consequently, offshore outsourcing became a hotly debated issue among workers, corporate executives, and politicians, one widely covered in the international media. When the American economy began to pull out of the recession in 2001 and unemployment failed to decrease as expected, offshore outsourcing was cited as a contributing factor to what was called a "jobless recovery." In information technology, for example, a particularly "soft" sector, many American programmers lost their jobs to lower paid foreign workers. More recently, however, many economists have conjectured that the higher-than-expected unemployment numbers were not the result of offshore outsourcing, and that offshore outsourcing has had a positive impact on the American economy.

HISTORICAL PERSPECTIVE

College instructor Jim Ryan, who teaches the history of outsourcing at Auburn University in Alabama, offers these insights. Ryan, formerly a top business executive, left corporate America to pursue his advanced degrees including his PhD in Management Information Systems, at a time when the IT industry itself started the shift of high-tech jobs offshore. Ryan, now a recognized expert in computer sciences, complex decision support systems, and technology applications, appreciates the evolution of outsourcing and its effects on the global tech workforces. He likens the current fears about outsourcing to similar concerns during the Industrial Revolution and, more recently, the early 1990s. For example, in 1900, 40 percent of the workforce was in agriculture, before advances in technology made it possible to produce more food today with only 2 percent of the workforce.[a] Unquestionably, explains Ryan, that transition was difficult on many farmers, but their descendents live in a better world because of those changes. Initially, the lower costs meant higher profits only for those farmers who stayed in business, but eventually competition forced the distribution of gains across the rest of the country. The result was dramatically cheaper food, which also meant greater availability of more resources to make myriad other products.

Ryan's business and IT students learn quickly that their wages won't depend on their job titles but on their skills and the amount of capital they have to augment those skills. Opening our economy to trade in goods and services enables us to use our skills and capital as productively as possible. There are two ways we get things in life: The first is to make them; the second is to let someone else make them and trade them. When others can make something more cheaply than you can make it for yourself, it makes sense to outsource it. You specialize in what you do most productively and swap for the rest of your needs. That specialization creates wealth.

In the current outsourcing landscape, then, if the economy in India has a low-wage scale, and programmers there can write computer code more cheaply than their American counterparts, it makes sense for us to import that code. How is this different from

[a] Joseph M. Miller, Daan Joubert, and Marion Butler, "International Trade and Globalization: The Great Outsourcing Scare," *Hoover Digest*, Spring 2004, pp. 1–5.

importing inexpensive televisions from abroad and saving our resources for other work we can do more effectively? Or from finding a new production technology that makes it possible to produce a product at lower cost? It's about getting more from less. That's the true road to wealth, and that's the story of the past 100 years of economic progress in America.

In conclusion, Ryan asks his students to think back to the early 1990s, when people were up in arms about Japan. He reminds them that, in the main, we held to our policy of letting people buy freely from around the world. The alarmists, as it turned out, were wrong. Japan didn't steal our jobs or ruin our country. Employment in the United States grew steadily, as did wages, helped in part by imports from Japan and the rest of the world. Japan, in the meantime, has stagnated. Ryan theorizes that today's alarmists will turn out to be wrong as well. Ryan encourages his Auburn University students to earnestly focus on the changes, challenges, and the opportunities that outsourcing continues to bestow on their business and IT career aspirations. No surprise that Auburn University IT graduates are very highly recruited for their advanced understanding of both complex management information systems as well as the ground-breaking opportunities outsourcing is developing for them to pursue, thanks in part to the visionary approach of Ryan.

DEBUNKING MYTHS ABOUT OUTSOURCING

Like all controversial topics, myths about outsourcing have begun to circulate, based on fear, conflicting information, or misinformation. Therefore, it is important to begin any discussion on this issue by debunking these myths.

Myth 1: Outsourcing means hiring workers from another country to take jobs away from our workers, on a permanent basis.

Truth: Outsourcing is the practice of hiring private contractors, which are not necessarily based in another country, to handle projects for a company. Offshoring, a kind of outsourcing, is the term used to distinguish projects that are being outsourced to overseas contractors. Many of the companies based in first-world countries establish a budget for paying offshore workers. This means the payroll and workload of on-shore laborers remain may remain as–is, or even grow; but the type of work onshore laborers are doing will change.

Myth 2: Only big companies can afford to outsource. Small business managers won't gain any benefit from this practice.

Truth: In the past, it is true, big companies did the bulk of hiring both onshore and offshore contractors, but as more companies become in-volved in outsourcing, opportunities are opening up to owners of small and medium enterprises. Many contractors now offer specialized ser-vices to smaller businesses. Smaller businesses have the same goal as big companies: to earn more while spending less. Without adopting an ag-gressive attitude and an open attitude toward outsourcing benefits, such businesses stand to lose.

Myth 3: There is a third myth, and it is the most widely circulating of them all: *Outsourcing is bad for America.*

Truth: To debunk this myth we cite a report sponsored by the Infor-mation Technology Association of America (ITAA) and prepared by the research firm Global Insight. It concluded that the practice of outsourc-ing is good for the U.S. economy and its workers.[1] According to the re-port, released in March 2004, offshore outsourcing of software and information technology (IT) service tasks not only is boosting the U.S. gross domestic product but also is helping to generate jobs in this coun-try, including positions in the IT sector. ITAA's members, which in-clude tech giants IBM, Electronic Data Systems, and Accenture, are among those locating operations in lower wage countries such as India.

The report goes on to state that although offshore IT software and services outsourcing has displaced, and will continue to displace, work-ers in IT software and services occupations in this country, improved economic activity will generate a wide range of new jobs—in both the IT and other industries. As the benefits compound over time, the U.S. economy will operate more efficiently, reach a higher level of output, create more than twice the number of jobs than those displaced, and in-crease the average real wage.

The ITAA-sponsored report also cites these statistics: 2.3 percent of total IT software and services spending by U.S. corporations in 2003 was devoted to offshore outsourcing activities. That figure will rise to 6.2 percent in 2008. During that same time period, total savings from offshoring are expected to climb from $6.7 billion to $20.9 billion. The cost savings and use of offshore resources, predicts the report, will lower inflation, increase productivity, and lower interest rates, thereby boosting business and consumer spending and increasing economic activity. Other notable numbers from the report demonstrate that:

- The benefits of offshore IT outsourcing added $33.6 billion to real gross domestic product (GDP) in the United States in 2003.
- By 2008, real GDP is expected to be $124.2 billion higher than it would be in an environment in which offshore IT software and services outsourcing were not a factor.
- U.S. Companies spent over $16 billion in 2004 to outsource jobs ranging from medical transcription to nanotechnology research. It is predicted companies will spend $31 billion in 2008.
- The incremental economic activity from offshore IT outsourcing created more than 90,000 net new jobs in 2003, and is expected to create 317,000 net new jobs in 2008.
- Shipping software and IT services work abroad leads to higher real wages for U.S. workers through lower inflation and higher productivity. Real wages were 0.13 percent higher in 2003, and are expected to be 0.44 percent higher in 2008.

The following table projects the rise of business process outsourcing revenues from 2002 to 2008 (in millions of dollars):[2]

	2002	2003	2004	2005	2006	2007	2008
BPO Market	$110,167	$121,687	$131,171	$143,090	$157,033	$300,000	$600,000

REFRAMING THE OUTSOURCING DEBATE

Just how marked is the shift to outsourcing jobs for the United States, the United Kingdom, Europe, and Japan—more specifically, their workforces and economies? Two decades ago in this country, the loss of jobs in the automotive sector and other high-paying manufacturing fields sparked fears of a hollowing-out of the economy. Yet, painful as the loss of those positions was, strong economic growth and innovation created far more—and better—jobs to replace them.

Now the same process, many economists say, is occurring as a result of outsourcing jobs to other countries. Others, though, argue that today's outsourcing of highly skilled service jobs is fundamentally different—and therefore poses greater risks for the economies of developed countries. Yes, a number of individuals in the IT industry are losing out to well-educated programmers or engineers in other countries who can do the same job for far lower wages. But as the global economy evolves, innovation will create new high-paying jobs.

Certainly, outsourcing contributes to short-term unemployment trends in developing countries, but those who blame outsourcing for job losses tend to ignore other powerful trends that are currently changing the rules in the business environment, including:

- The shift from domestic to global economy
- The shift from manpower to technopower
- The shift from company-led to consumer-driven market forces
- The shift from an industrial economy to a knowledge economy
- The transformation of the employer/employee relationship
- New relationships and governance structures concerning vendors and suppliers

Critics of outsourcing see it only as the elimination of consumers and the unrealized potential of more productive jobs in new industries. In fact, outsourcing is being touted by several high-level economists and business executives as exactly what advanced countries need to get their economies back on track. Among them is Alan Greenspan, chairman of the U.S. Federal Reserve Board, who has endorsed the potential of outsourcing to

---

WHY INDIA?

For myriad services, India has emerged as the outsource location of choice for both the United States and the United Kingdom. The reasons are not hard to identify. First, India has the second-largest English-speaking population in the world, after the United States, and an educated workforce of more than 270 million workers.[a] In addition, the outsourcing market in India, particularly for information technologies, has had time to mature and gain support from U.S. and U.K. businesses. Moreover, India's 1991 Statement on Industrial Policy facilitated foreign direct investment and technology transfers, thereby ushering in a new era with fewer of the

---

[a] Government of India, Ministry of Education, www.education.nic.in, December 2004.

regulatory burdens that had previously kept foreign firms from establishing business operations there. In the decade since this policy reform, foreign direct investment in India has increased more
than fiftyfold.

Also notable is that even though India's basic infrastructure is
among the most fragile in the world, businesses there have found
ways to compete globally in the IT arena, making the country the
world's leader in software exports. The city of Bangalore alone,
home to many IT outsourcing firms and global corporations, con-
tributed $2.5 billion in 2003 to India's total software exports of
$9.5 billion.[b]

Furthermore, promoting IT is one of India's top governmental
priorities. The Ministry of Information Technology, established in
1999, plans to accelerate the implementation of IT in government
education and the private sector. India also has many universities dedicated to maintaining state-of-the-art IT curricula, and
more than 70,000 software engineers graduate annually from
these colleges.

The goal of a growing number of American and European companies is to outsource customer-service work to India, to take advantage of India's low wages, thriving high-tech sector, and annual
output of 2 million English-speaking college graduates. Of the 3.3
million white-collar service jobs estimated to be outsourced in
2015, more than half will go to India.[c]

[b] Government of India, Ministry of Industry, www.smallindustryindia.com
/policies/iip.htm#Indus6 and http://siadipp.nic.in/publicat/nip0791.htm, July
1991.
[c] Yale Center for the Study of Globalization, http://sharif.edu/~maleki/change
%20management/article%20&%20strategic/outsourcing percent20Debate.htm
and http://money.cnn.com/2003/12/17/pf/q_nomorework, February 2004.

revolutionize global business. Similarly, across the "pond," British High
Commissioner Sir Michael Arthur, in response to the pressure from the
U.K.'s trade unions to reduce the incidence of offshoring, stated in
September 2004 that his government would do nothing to stop offshore
outsourcing. British bilateral BPO ties with India were cemented when
the prime ministers from both countries met to develop more business
alliances.

WEALTH OF NATIONS

No one is arguing that these are indeed anxious times for workers in the United States and other developed countries; the debate is over the part outsourcing plays in this high anxiety. In 1776, in his still-relevant book *Wealth of Nations,* Adam Smith emphasized that, "It is not from the benevolence of the butcher, the brewer or the baker that we expect our dinner, but from their regard to their own interest."[3] Following Smith's ideas, modern companies participate in the international market and pursue their own interests by making the most productive use of their resources. By pursuing profit maximization, firms remain competitive, and the result is cheaper goods and services and a higher standard of living, at lower cost, for consumers.

NOTES

1. A transcript of the ITAA report is available online at www.connectlive.com /events/itaa.
2. Gartner Research, www.dataquest.com/press_gartner/quickstts/outsourcing.html, August 2003.
3. Stephen Copley, Kathryn Sutherland, eds., *Adam Smith's Wealth of Nations: New Interdisciplinary Essays,* Manchester, New York: Manchester University Press. Distributed exclusively in the United States and Canada by St. Martin's Press © 1995.

INTRODUCTION

OUTSOURCING: OPPORTUNITIES AND CHALLENGES

Outsourcing is a growing phenomenon, but it's something that we should realize is probably a plus for the economy in the long run. It's just a new way of doing international trade.

—Gregory Mankiw, chairman of the White House
Council of Economic Advisors, 2004 Economic Report of the President[1]

Perhaps like many businesspeople around the world, you're seeking silver-lining solutions to both the opportunities and challenges created by outsourcing, a crucial but admittedly difficult-to-implement business innovation. But as you know, silver linings can be very hard to find. Therefore, our objective in this book is to help with that effort, specifically, to give you a "silver-lining perspective" on outsourcing, by which we mean more than just a bright spot amidst the political and emotional storm clouds of controversy. Generations before us have adapted to revolutionary innovations in technology and business efficiency and we will, too.

We intend to guide you in your personal, corporate, and strategic efforts to take advantage of the opportunities, as well as meet the challenges, of outsourcing, whether you're a corporate manager responsible for an outsourcing initiative; an outsourcing job seeker; an entrepreneur, venture capitalist, or small business owner investigating the bottom-line benefits of this practice. By virtue of the fact that you're reading this book, you're among those who will lead the rest in powerful global economic change.

Note: Web addresses flagged with a (†) are author affiliated sites.

1

One of the reasons the silver linings of outsourcing remain so elusive is that, despite its growing status as a mainstream business activity, it remains underresearched and poorly understood. There is a shortage of reliable information on outsourcing and business process outsourcing (BPO) markets, vendors and their capabilities, needs of different vertical segments, costs and capability benchmarking of service providers, location evaluation and assessment . . . and so on. Sadly, due to this dearth of good information, many companies are making serious mistakes. For example, all too often an outsourcing relationship is initiated without an evaluation of market alternatives, which can easily lead to a higher price. We're here to help you avoid this and other mistakes.

As industry becomes more comfortable with the shift in the globalization model toward offshore outsourcing, corporate outsource-buying professionals are charged with the task of being good stewards of their company's resources. This book provides these professionals with a step-by-step guide to the outsourcing process, along with abundant contact information for leading outsourcing firms and career opportunities.

Outsourcing can be a complicated undertaking, for management, job seekers, and entrepreneurs alike, as revealed in a survey of companies and organizations buying outsourcing services:[2]

- Fifty-three percent reported that they have outsourcing challenges because their companies lack project management skills (i.e., they have no experienced outsourcing governance).
- Fifty-eight percent reported they lack a good process for specifying the work.
- Forty-eight percent said they did not have the right metrics for measuring performance.

The most notable trends of the outsourcing phenomenon, as collected by the Global Outsourcing Partnership (www.outsourcingpartnership.com[†]) include:

- Seventeen billion dollars of IT services will go offshore by 2008.[3]
- There are $2.3 million banking jobs to be offshored. Celent says that offshoring has put a potential 2.3 million jobs in the U.S. banking and securities industries at risk. Celent analysts estimate a potential to shift $17.5 billion in operational and technical costs overseas by 2010.[4]
- Eighty percent of U.S. companies will outsource something in 2005. Meta Group predicts that 80 percent of organizations will outsource at least one information technology function by the end of 2005. But

the Outsourcing Pricing Guide report also warns that 70 percent of that group will drive a harder bargain when they renew those outsourcing deals, cutting both the scope and duration of the contract.[5]

- Eighty-five percent of current outsourcing contracts to be re-negotiated, Gartner analysts said that 85 percent of all outsourcing contracts signed since 2001 through year-end 2004 will be renegotiated within three years of signing because the original contracts did not serve the enterprise's long-term objectives.[6]

- Business process outsourcing will grow. A final verdict released by research firm Gartner prophesized that by 2005, the number of enterprises that enter into new outsourcing relationships, will increase 30 percent, while the number of IT providers that claim outsourcing relationships, will grow by 40 percent. Through 2004, despite the potential human resource backlash, 80 percent of U.S. executive boards will have discussed global delivery options, both nearshore and offshore. Out of these enterprises using global delivery models, 80 percent will act by increasing their people resources (nearshore and offshore), by as much as 30 percent.

- Gartner predicts strong BPO growth in India, both captive as well as outsourced. The current global BPO market stands at $173 billion, which is expected to rise to $27.7 billion by 2007. Indian offshore BPO will grab $13.8 billion from the total, or approximately 49 percent of the pie. The boom is estimated on a Gartner survey, which reveals that 19 percent of companies in the United States are planning to outsource in the next 24 months, as opposed to a meager 1 percent who are currently outsourcing.[7]

- Europeans will outsource $9.6 billion in 2008. The take-up of finance and accounting business process outsourcing services by European firms will nearly double from its present size of $5.1 billion to $9.6 billion by 2008, market watcher IDC has predicted.[8]

- Outsourcing to hit $1.2 trillion by 2007. The outsourcing market, riding a healthy 7 percent annual growth toward an estimated $1.2 trillion in 2007, will be dominated by a few global players in on-demand computing, an industry watcher said at an outsourcing conference in Bangalore.[9]

- By 2015, 3.4 million jobs will move offshore. Forrester Research now says it expects that 830,000 U.S. service jobs will move to low-wage countries such as China, India, and Mexico by the end of 2005. Last year, the firm put that number at 588,000. The new study estimates that 3.4 million jobs will move offshore by 2015, up from 3.3 million predicted last year.[10]

- At least $75 million of U.S. government contracts goes offshore. At least $75 million in U.S. state contract work has been captured by 18 companies that specialize in offshore outsourcing.[11]
- Canada loses IT jobs through offshore outsourcing, gains through U.S. contracts. The report by PricewaterhouseCoopers showed that Canada could lose up to 75,000 IT jobs by 2010 to offshore outsourcing, but Canada could also gain some 165,000 jobs through U.S. outsourcing contracts.[12]
- Financial sector to outsource at 34 percent annually. Outsourcing is on the rise in the financial services industry, according to research firm TowerGroup. The researcher estimates that the top 15 global financial services companies will increase their outsourcing of information technology projects from a value of $1.6 billion this year to $3.89 billion in 2008, an increase of 34 percent annually.[13]
- The U.S. government can outsource 900,000 jobs. The government's push to open federal jobs to competition could open as much as $70 billion outsourcing opportunities to private firms, but lingering uncertainties on the final version of the rules make it more difficult to predict, according to a new report from research firm Input. Researchers considered the number of jobs that could be outsourced— officials have estimated that almost 900,000 federal jobs could be suitable for outsourcing—and Bush administration officials have said they want agencies to open half of those to competition by September 2004.[14]
- Forty percent of IT businesses have explored outsourcing in 2004. According to analysis from Gartner, by next year more than 40 percent of IT-related businesses will either be investigating the possibility of offshore outsourcing or will have already started projects overseas.[15]
- Manufacturing firms to increase outsourcing by 9.3 percent in 2005. Manufacturing companies are planning for healthy increases in 2005, led by a projected 9.3 percent increase of outsourcing budgets, according to a report from AMR Research. New IT investments are aimed primarily at supporting supply chain transformation and the profitable acquisition of new customers. Respondents estimate that 25 percent of IT work is currently outsourced, and 53 percent intend to increase that amount. The overall increase planned for 2005 is a robust 9.3 percent.[16]
- India to lose outsourcing market share by 2007. India is likely to lose market share in offshore business process outsourcing (BPO), from its current 80 percent to about 55 percent by 2007.[17]

- Only 2.5 percent of U.S. jobs are lost due to outsourcing. Labor Department said moving jobs overseas accounted for about 2.5 percent of the 182,456 workers who lost their jobs for longer than a month for nonseasonal factors in Q1 2004. Moving jobs within the United States accounted for 9,985 layoffs, or 5.5 percent of nonseasonal mass layoffs. About two-thirds of the jobs moved were in the manufacturing sector. Manufacturing accounted for about 25 percent of all mass layoffs. Seventy-six percent of the jobs moved stayed in the same company, although 36 percent of jobs moved overseas were with a different company.[18]
- Financial sector to outsource at 34 percent annually. Outsourcing is on the rise in the financial services industry, according to research firm TowerGroup. The researcher estimates that the top 15 global financial services companies will increase their outsourcing of information technology projects from a value of $1.6 billion this year to $3.89 billion in 2008, an increase of 34 percent annually.[19]
- Deloitte projects that by 2008, 275,000 of the telecom industry's 5.5 million positions will have been sent overseas. The telecommunications industry is set to save $14.5 billion in the next four years through offshoring 5 percent of its workforce to countries such as India, Estonia, and Argentina.[20]
- Eighty-six percent of U.S. companies will increase offshoring. About 86 percent of U.S. companies plan to increase the use of offshore outsourcing firms, according to a poll by Chicago-based management consulting firm DiamondCluster International. They expect outsourcing to save only 10 percent to 20 percent of their costs, down sharply from 50 percent two years ago. About 85 percent of customers and 81 percent of providers are concerned that legislation or political pressure may prevent them from shifting jobs offshore.[21]
- The next wave of outsourcing will be research and development (R&D) functions, according to the latest Santa Clara University Business Index. The monthly business indicator tracks business conditions and jobs by polling executives and managers in a wide range of companies. While R&D hasn't been moving offshore at the rate of manufacturing and customer support, SCU finance professor Robert Henderschott told Internetnews.com says a trend is developing.[22]

As these numbers indicate, companies that fail to manage their outsourcing relationships will not only spend more money than is necessary, they will also obtain fewer benefits. Customer satisfaction will be impacted, which will increase the risk of outsourcing failure.

WHAT'S DIFFERENT
ABOUT OUTSOURCING

To implement outsourcing successfully, it's first necessary to understand that it is fundamentally different from other recent business trends and, therefore, poses greater risks for industrialized economies. We have to face facts: Most of the white-collar and executive jobs downsized in the last few years in the United States and the United Kingdom are gone forever. And as this "new economy" evolves, the pursuit of the lowest-cost source is going to be happening on a global scale. The old regional trade agreements of the past, like North American Free Trade Agreement (NAFTA), are becoming obsolete. If you doubt this, consider these results of a survey of 20 large European firms: for 75 percent, offshore/near-shore outsourcing spending will increase between now and 2005; and outsourcing's share of Europe's IT services spending is expected to grow from 29 percent in 2002 to 43 percent in 2008.[23] From 2004, BPO is expected to grow faster than all other categories of IT services. Demands for technology innovation and best-of-breed transition skills will drive provider choice.

The hard truth is that the rules that used to guide us in shaping a career, starting a new business, or leading an established company no longer apply. The complexities of outsourcing are forcing drastic managerial and professional career changes, and those professionals who do not update their skill sets to successfully administer outsourcing initiatives will be replaced by those who do.

If you still doubt that business process outsourcing is changing the way the world does business, and that this trend is likely to accelerate, these statistics should convince you:

- By 2007, offshore BPO is expected to account for 14 percent of the total BPO market, compared with only 1 percent in 2003.[24]
- Global market for outsourcing is estimated to grow at an annual rate of 7 percent, to 1.2 trillion dollars by 2007.[25]

Seventy-three percent of U.S. executives interviewed said their companies presently outsource one or more business processes to external service providers. As released by PricewaterhouseCoopers, top U.S. companies are turning to business process outsourcing based on interviews with senior executives at more than 100 U.S. companies averaging about $4.4 billion in yearly revenue.

A PricewaterhouseCoopers Global Top Decision-Makers Study is a landmark study—the first to focus exclusively on BPO at billion-dollar

multinationals.[26] Conducted by Yankelovich Partners for PricewaterhouseCoopers, the study provides an in-depth report of the attitudes and
behavior of senior executives and their companies toward BPO in general,
and Finance & Accounting Services (F&A Services) specifically.

Interviews were conducted with 304 top decision-making executives in
14 countries: CEOs, Presidents, CFOs, COOs and CIOs. Among this
group, 192 companies (63 percent) report outsourcing one or more business processes. And, of these companies (41 percent) report outsourcing Finance & Accounting Services which includes General F&A, Internal Audit,
and Tax Compliance. Over 300 companies participated in the study—covering the Americas, Europe, Asia Pacific, and South America. The findings
of the study reflect an increasing interest in, and usage of, BPO as a strategic initiative:

Business Processes	Currently Outsourcing (%)	Best Candidate for BPO (All Companies) (%)
Human resources	42	59
Finance and accounting	41	70
Payroll	37	70
Real estate	32	65
Procurement	15	33

Top executives increasingly recognize the need to manage their company's growth with less infrastructure. Thus, they are considering outsourcing processes that are essential, but not core to the growth of their
business, including Finance & Accounting functions:

Attitudes toward BPO	Companies Outsourcing Finance and Accounting (%)	All Companies (%)
BPO allows companies to focus on core competencies	94	86
BPO allows companies greater efficiencies without having to invest in people and technology	85	76
BPO helps companies become more profitable, leading to increase in shareholder value	77	66
BPO will lead to better service levels than internal service departments can provide	63	48

Satisfaction with BPO	Companies Outsourcing Finance and Accounting (%)	All Outsourcers (%)
Satisfied	84	84
Dissatisfied	13	10

More than 8 out of 10 executives (84 percent) outsourcing Finance and Accounting services are satisfied with their initiatives. One third of these executives report that BPO initiatives are in their company's current business plans:

Top Three Strategic Benefits of BPO	Companies Outsourcing Finance and Accounting (%)	All Companies (%)
Maintain competitive edge	80	67
Focus on company's core business	79	75
Improve service quality	77	70

The Yankelovich research suggests that the bottom-line benefits of BPO are beginning to be recognized and appreciated. Forward thinking CEOs and CFOs are increasingly utilizing BPO as a new strategic tool to improve their competitive stance, their profitability and ultimately, helping to build shareholder value:

- Eighty-four percent of large-company CEOs are satisfied with their outsourcing experience.[27]
- Market perception of outsourcing has shifted from a way for companies to meet short-term financial objectives to a technique for strong companies to improve competitive positions.[28]

Empowering Executives to Outsource

Michael F. Corbett & Associates, Ltd. conducted research with more than 500 executives and found that:[29]

- One in four organizations plan to increase their outsourcing spending by 25 percent or more.
- Outsourcing will represent 19.5 percent of the typical executive's budget, up from 16.4 percent today.
- Firms in dynamic markets such as telecommunications, high-tech products, and professional services, already source more than 40 percent of their operations outside.
- Innovation is now seen as the key strategic benefit of outsourcing.

The business process outsourcing market continues to show healthy growth despite the economic slowdown. Worldwide, BPO services are predicted to expand by a 9.5 percent compound annual growth rate by 2007.

The following illustration compares the Worldwide BPO Market, 1999 versus 2004.[30]

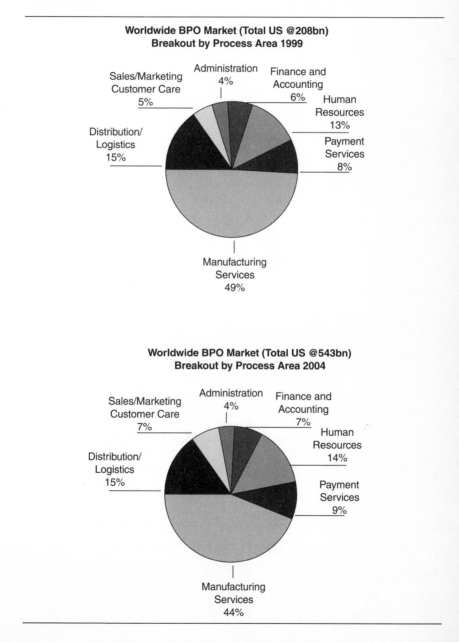

Worldwide BPO Market (Total US @208bn)
Breakout by Process Area 1999

Administration 4%
Sales/Marketing Customer Care 5%
Finance and Accounting 6%
Human Resources 13%
Distribution/ Logistics 15%
Payment Services 8%
Manufacturing Services 49%

Worldwide BPO Market (Total US @543bn)
Breakout by Process Area 2004

Administration 4%
Sales/Marketing Customer Care 7%
Finance and Accounting 7%
Human Resources 14%
Distribution/ Logistics 15%
Payment Services 9%
Manufacturing Services 44%

Since the Industrial Revolution, outsourcing (previously called "subcontracting") has helped thousands of companies achieve profitability through increased efficiency. Nearly every U.S. and European company outsources some part of their business—although not even their own employees may realize it. Companies rarely build manufacturing plants in the United States or United Kingdom anymore, for example. Instead, China, Eastern Europe, India, the Philippines, South Korea, and Taiwan are the locations of choice for this purpose. And with the advent of the Internet and satellite and transoceanic communications, businesses require fewer people to do more work; these technologies can also shorten the learning curve for new skills. Perhaps most notable is that specialized tasks such as software development, financial research, and customer service can be accomplished anywhere in the world at a fraction of U.S. or most European labor costs— as much as 30 to 50 percent net.

Clearly, then, it is often in a firm's best interest to outsource certain tasks and use the abilities of its remaining in-house workers in other, more productive activities.

Over the next decade, a fundamental shift will cause the migration of transactional, technology, and administrative processes offshore. In the 1980s, the physical supply chain moved to cheaper locations in the 1980s; in the 1990s, the information supply chain, including IT and software application development and maintenance, moved offshore. Now it's the administrative supply chain. In the next wave, many knowledge-based positions will likely go offshore, too, including human resources administration, distant medicine, high-level CPAs and accountants, and high-end IT architecture and design engineers.

My members (Link to ITAA Membership List: http://www.itaa.org/about/members.cfm) believe outsourcing—rather than trying to build and retain a substantial in-house capability—remains the most effective strategy for conducting a wide variety of operations. Outsourcing is not necessarily offshoring. Rather, offshore development and maintenance is a subset of outsourcing. The outsourcing provider may perform services on shore, offshore, or in some combination of the two. The decision is based on a variety of factors, not the least of which is customer preference.

—Harris Miller, president of the Information Technology Association of America (ITAA), representing 400 companies involved in every aspect of the IT industry. Source: Senate Democratic Policy Committee Hearing, March 5, 2004.

DEBATING THE ISSUE

From a purely capitalist perspective, these market forces bring good news. Companies that focus on cost, quality, and performance will be the most competitive and profitable, and will lower the cost of goods and services for people around the world, while raising standards of living in low-wage countries. The bad news is, high-wage countries must face the upheaval caused by the resultant job losses.

The Dollar Value

Hard experience has demonstrated that, in procurement alone, outsourcing can help reduce:

- Supply and service pricing by 10 to 25 percent through strategic sourcing.
- Administrative costs by 50 to 75 percent.
- Consumption and spending by 10 to 20 percent.

On the human resources side, outsourcing has the potential to drive HR-to-employee ratios to anywhere from 1:500 to 1:200, and help reduce overall customer care agent costs by as much as 25 percent.[31] As we've said, in the United Kingdom and across Europe, many workers have lost their jobs, and more layoffs are announced every day, the consequence of outsourcing. In the United States, according to Forrester Research, the total number of jobs lost to outsourcing overseas will reach 791,000 by 2010, and 3,300,000 by 2015.[32] Chances are, you or someone you know has been affected by outsourcing, in one of the areas listed below:[33]

Job Category	2000	2005	2010	2015
Management	0	37,477	117,835	288,281
Business	10,787	61,252	161,722	348,028
Computer	27,171	108,991	276,954	472,632
Architecture	3,498	32,302	83,237	184,347
Life sciences	0	3,677	14,478	36,770
Legal	1,793	14,220	34,673	74,642
Art, design	818	5,576	13,846	29,639
Sales	4,619	29,064	97,321	226,564
Office	53,987	295,034	791,034	1,659,310
Total	102,674	587,592	1,591,101	3,320,213

Critics of outsourcing accuse businesspeople of being unconcerned or indifferent to the working and middle classes of developed countries, including those in the United States and the United Kingdom, the two

INSOURCING: THE OTHER SIDE OF THE COIN

As the avalanche of work from the United States, United Kingdom, and Europe continues to flow toward foreign shores, some analysts are watching a trickle of jobs starting to move back in the direction of their source.

These analysts are starting to speculate if these incoming jobs actually could help compensate for the high-paying, high-tech jobs that are being offshored, leaving behind a troubled white-collar workforce and a diminished technology industry.

"Outsourcing has crowded out the globalization topic," says Matthew Slaughter, associate professor of business at Dartmouth College's Tuck School of Business. "It is important to understand the contribution of these [foreign] companies to the U.S. economy."

Slaughter recently released a study, *Insourcing Jobs: Making the Global Economy Work for America,* which describes the impact of foreign companies hiring workers here in the United States—in all industries, including IT. It also states that these companies employ nearly five percent of those working in the private sector and have paid American workers $307 billion.[a]

Many people in this country are unaware that offshore companies also are sending jobs *to* the United States and Great Britain, and have been for decades. Job losses from offshore outsourcing are, to some degree, offset by insourcing. And according to Matthew Slaughter, insourcing activity has been increasing steadily over the last decade.[b] Slaughter says, "Over the past generation the number of U.S. jobs at these subsidiaries has more than doubled." Slaughter also notes that insourcing companies also contribute to U.S. economic growth by spurring investments in research and development, physical capital, and international trade. Moreover, insourcing companies pay better than their domestic competitors, Slaughter found.

---

[a] "Insourcing Jobs: Making the Global Economy Work for America," study sponsored by the Organization for International Investment, 2004; available online at www.ofii.org/disputes.
[b] Matthew Slaughter, author of the report in note a named above, http://www.ofii.org/insourcing/insourcing_study.pdf; Professor Matthew J. Slaughter, Insourcing Jobs: Making the Global Economy Work for America; November 2004 also Citation: Matthew Slaughter. Enterprise Systems Journals, full article at http://www.esj.com/enterprise/article.aspx?EditorialsID=1170 (Stephen Swoyer, Outsourcing in Reverse: Foreign Companies Send Jobs to the United States: Not all outsourcing activity is a net loss for American workers, October 26, 2004).

Several statistics highlight the importance of insourcing. U.S. subsidiaries of foreign companies employ more than 5.4 million U.S. workers—roughly 5 percent of overall private sector employment, an increase from 3 percent in 1987. As for research and development, insourcing companies now account for a sizeable share—nearly 15 percent, or $27.5 billion—of private sector R&D activity in the United States, up from 9 percent in 1992. Similarly, U.S. subsidiaries of foreign companies accounted for 10 percent ($111.9 billion) of private sector capital investments, up from 8 percent in 1992. Most surprising is that insourcing companies also account for a sizeable share (20 percent, $137 billion) of U.S. exports. And on the payroll front, subsidiaries of foreign companies paid U.S. workers more than $307 billion—6 percent more than overall U.S. private sector labor compensation. The average annual compensation at insourcing companies was $56,667—nearly one-third more than in the nonsubsidiary U.S. private sector. This tally has increased sharply from 20 percent in 1992.

According to Slaughter, insourcing helps the U.S. economy in other ways as well. "The other channel by which insourcing companies contribute to the U.S. economy is their interactions with other domestic U.S. firms." For starters, insourcing companies typically purchase a majority of their supplies from domestic firms—to the tune of 80 cents out of every dollar, or $1.26 trillion.

countries most affected by the shift in jobs overseas. The resultant hullabaloo has alternately infuriated, confused, and shamed some business leaders to the point at which they have chosen to avoid sensible, progressive outsourcing in their organizations. Unemployed workers likewise are furious and confused. Both groups need to educate themselves about the opportunities created by outsourcing. The *Black Book of Outsourcing* will help launch that effort.

WHO THIS BOOK IS FOR

This book has been written for the three largest groups of individuals affected by outsourcing:

1. *Corporate managers buying and leading outsourcing services.* If you fall into this category, you will learn what is necessary to manage a successful outsourcing initiative at your "buyer" business and how to work with outsourcing vendors.

2. *Job seekers (particularly those displaced by outsourcing).* You will learn how to launch a new career and find a job in the new global economy.

3. *Outsourcing entrepreneurs.* Ambitious start-up business owners will learn the basics of establishing your own outsourcing firm (increasingly known as "outventures").

The *Black Book of Outsourcing* addresses the needs of each of these groups, while diffusing the debates and disputes that turn up the heat on outsourcing discussions. We help you focus on industry-specific situations and challenges. We help buyers, vendors, and entrepreneurs manage the problems they encounter daily, buoyed by sound outsourcing management principles, inspiration to succeed, and innovative solutions.

At the heart of this book are the processes that we recommend you follow to conduct your outsourcing program successfully. We've developed these proven approaches in our role as consultants to Fortune 500 companies as well as to one-person outventuring start-ups. We've seen these success factors work again and again; and in this book we'll share with you how you can customize these approaches to fit your situation.

We're almost ready to get started now, but before you read on, take the time to make a list of your goals, and keep them in mind as we proceed. Your list might include how to:

- Use outsourcing to meet today's business challenges.
- Make the right sourcing decisions—the first time.
- Achieve operational excellence within and across outsourcing relationships.
- Communicate outsourcing to your employees, customers, and the public.
- Build new revenue streams through outsourcing.
- Use outsourcing to reduce corporate risk.
- Successfully outsource offshore.
- Craft value-creating outsourcing contracts.
- Recover from a troubled outsourcing relationship.
- Enhance your career as an outsourcing professional.

Until now, pro-outsourcing zealots have neglected to mention why outsourcing deals fail, the occasionally staggering costs of attorneys versed in international contracts, the cross-infrastructure problems including cultural clashes, the widespread corruption in many foreign governments, and other factors that wipe out the wage savings involved in outsourcing.

We recommend that you do a little research and you'll find out that one in three outsourcing projects fail because most are not heading into outsourcing initiatives with their eyes open or their staffs informed. Many outsourcing decision makers also do not—or can not—afford the detailed analysis that can only be found in expensive research reports from the big-name analyst firms.

Whatever your goals, *The Black Book of Outsourcing* is sure to help you meet them. Now let's get started.

NOTES

1. 2004 Economic Report of the President, http:///www.cbsnews.com /stories/2004/02/13/national/main600034.shtml, February 13, 2004.

2. Julie Giera, "Outsourcing Management: Align Management Techniques to the Outsourcing Model IT View and Business View Planning Assumption," September 30, 2003, www.forrester.com/Cart?addDocs=32555. Three Forrester reports were used to compile this information: the above mentioned report and Stephanie Moore, William Martorelli, Adam Brown, "Midyear 2004 Update: North American Offshore Outsourcing" July 14, 2004, also Stephanie Moore, "IT Trends 2004: Offshore Outsourcing," December 17, 2003.

3. IDC, Inc., News Release, October 25, 2004, http://www.idc.com/research /reshome.jsp.

4. Celent, July 15, 2004, http://www.industryanalystreporter.com/T2 /Analyst_Research/ResearchAnnouncementsDetails.asp?Newsid=3080.

5. Cnet Tech News, August 11, 2004, http://news.com.com/Outsourcing+to+ rise%2C+but+deals+to+shrink/2100-1011_3-5305640.html?part=rss&tag =5305640&subj=news.1011.20.

6. November 2004, http://www.tekrati.com/T2/Analyst_Research /ResearchAnnouncementsDetails.asp?Newsid=2541.

7. December 4, 2003, http://www.cxotoday.com/cxo/jsp /article.jsp?article_id=401&cat_id=908&source=null.

8. March 4, 2004, http://www.vnunet.com/news/1153208.

9. Cnet, November 5, 2003, http://news.zdnet.com/2110-3513_22-5102508.html.

10. InfoWeek, May 24, 2004, http://www.informationweek.com/story/showArticle .jhtml?articleID=20900333.

11. WashTech, Cnet Tech News, July 14, 2004, http://news.com.com /Study%3A+States+doing+plenty+of+offshoring /2100-1022_3-5269261.html?part=rss&tag=5269261&subj=news.1022.5.

12. *IT Managers Journal,* July 15, 2004.

13. Cnet, April 4, 2004, http://news.com.com/2110-7343_3-5191655 .html?part=rss&tag=feed&subj=news.

14. Federal Computer Week, December 18, 2003, http://www.fcw.com/fcw /articles/2003/1215/web-outsource-12-18-03.asp.

15. PR Newswire, December 18, 2003, http://www.prnewswire.com/cgi-bin /stories.pl?ACCT=SVBIZINK3.story&STORY=/www/story/12-18-2003 /0002078000&EDATE=THU+Dec+18+2003,+09:02+AM.

16. TechWeb, October 1, 2003, http://www.techweb.com/wire/ebiz/49400123.

17. Gartner Inc., InfoWorld, August 30, 2004, http://www.infoworld.com
/article/04/08/30/HNindiabpo_1.html.

18. CBS Marketwatch, June 10, 2004,
http://www.marketwatch.com/news/yahoo/story
.asp?guid=%7B65859158-B0EA-4852-B7C2-AF68657E0F8
%7D&siteid=myyahoo&dist=myyahoo.

19. OutsourcingCnet, April 14, 2004, http://news.com.com
/2110-7343_3-5191655.html?part=rss&tag=feed&subj=news.

20. Deloitte and Touche survey, *InfoWorld,* March 29, 2004, http://www
.infoworld.com/article/04/03/29/HNtelcooffshore_1.html.

21. DiamondCluster International, release March 26, 2005.

22. Silicon Valley News, August 28, 2003, http://siliconvalley.internet.com/news
/article.php/3069991.

23. Manuel Ángel Méndez, with David Metcalfe and Andrew Parker, "Analyzing Europe's BPO Growth Explosion," second in Forrester Research's European IT Services Spending series, December 11, 2003.

24. Linda R. Cohen, Lorrie Scardino, and Lisa Stone, Gartner Research: Predictions for Outsourcing in 2004, December 11, 2003.

25. IDC, Inc., News Release, October 25, 2004, http://www.idc.com/research
/reshome.jsp.

26. PricewaterhouseCoopers, http://www.coltexpress.com/files
/Business_Process_Outsourcing.pdf.

27. Yankelovich Partners, Global Top Decision-Makers Study on Business Process Outsourcing, sponsored by PricewaterhouseCoopers, 1999–2001.

28. See note 24.

29. Rebecca S. Scholl, Cathy Tornbohm, Ravi Datar, Rika Narisawa, Kathryn Hale, and Robert De Souza, "Market to Grow to $173 Billion in 2007," Executive Summary, Gartner Research, July 7, 2003, http://www.gartner.com
/DisplayDocument?doc_cd=116058.

30. Gartner Dataquest.

31. Anthony R. Roma, Partner, "Achieving Business Transformation through Outsourcing," 2004, IBM Business Transformation Outsourcing Financial Services, http://www-1.ibm.com/industries/financialservices/doc/content/landing
/895386103.html.

32. Bureau of Labor Statistics; Forrester Research Inc. Chronicle Graphic,
http://sfgate.com/cgi-bin/article.cgi?file=/c/a/2004/05/18/BUGQ26ND7B1
.DTL&type=printable; "The Effect of Outsourcing and Offshoring on BLS Productivity Measures," March 26, 2004, http://www.bls.gov/lpc
/lproffshoring.pdf.

33. Andrew Parker with David Metcalfe and Sonoko Takahash, "Two-Speed Europe: Why 1 Million Jobs Will Move Offshore, Forrester Research," August 18, 2004; and John C. McCarthy with Amy Dash, Heather Liddell, Christine Ferrusi Ross, and Bruce D. Temkin, "3.3 Million U.S. Services Jobs to Go Offshore," *IT View and Business View Brief,* Forrester Research, November 11, 2002.

PART ONE

HOW TO PLAN, LEAD, AND MANAGE OUTSOURCING INITIATIVES

CHAPTER 1

OVERVIEW OF THE OUTSOURCING PROCESS

Outsourcing is not a threat to this nation's economy—it is an opportunity to raise American paychecks, productivity, and prosperity. It's an opportunity we will squander if we let the alarmists stampede us into boneheaded solutions.

—John Castellani, president of The Business Roundtable to the Detroit Press Club, February 24, 2004

The purpose of this book is to establish guidelines, offer insight, and provide inspiration, so that you will be able to realistically identify, analyze, and maximize outsourcing opportunities. You'll learn how to:

1. Evaluate your business processes.
2. Identify outsourcing opportunities in processes.
3. Select vendors/suppliers/partners.
4. Negotiate successful contracts with vendors.
5. Establish successful working relationships with vendors.
6. Manage a multiple vendor environment.
7. Turn around a failing outsourcing relationship, or, when necessary, replace vendors.
8. Govern vendor relationships on a day-to-day basis.
9. Implement and track service level agreements (SLAs).
10. Anticipate, and avoid when possible, outsourcing problems; solve problems when they do arise.
11. Ensure success.

OUTSOURCING TERMINOLOGY

It would be impossible to achieve the objectives just described without first ensuring that everyone reading this book understands the terminology of outsourcing as it is used here (see Chapter 3 and the Glossary). Therefore, we'll begin with two definitions:

Outsourcing. The act of obtaining services from an external source.

Business process outsourcing (BPO). Outsourcing as referred to in the corporate environment. BPO occurs when an organization turns over the management of a particular business process (such as accounting or payroll) to a third party that specializes in that process. The underlying theory is that the BPO firm can complete the process more efficiently, leaving the original firm free to concentrate on its core competency.

Outsourcing is essentially a basic redefinition of the corporation around core competencies and long-term outside relationships. These core competencies and outside relationships are identified with two objectives in mind: (1) to bring in the greatest value to the end customer and, (2) to ensure the highest level of productivity for the corporation itself. A number of BPO functions are listed in Table 1.1 on pages 22 and 23.

The benefits of corporate outsourcing are numerous. The following list is not intended to be comprehensive, but to stimulate your enthusiasm for this process:

- Increase sales opportunities.
- Improve corporate image and public relations.
- Prevent missed opportunities.
- Reduce annual costs almost immediately.
- Enable business to focus on core competencies.
- Reduce or eliminate customer complaints.
- Increase customer loyalty.
- Lower costs on projects and events.
- Beat competition.
- Make time and resources available.

LEVELS OF OUTSOURCING

There are three levels of outsourcings: *tactical, strategic,* and *transformational.*

Tactical Outsourcing

On the first level, tactical, the reasons for outsourcing are usually tied to specific problems being experienced by the firm. Often the firm is already in trouble and outsourcing is seen as a direct way to address problems. Typical examples of "trouble" are: the lack of financial resources to make capital investments, inadequate internal managerial competence, an absence of talent, or a desire to reduce headcount. Not surprisingly, tactical outsourcing often accompanies large-scale corporate restructuring. Thus, many tactical relationships are forged to:

- Generate immediate cost savings.
- Eliminate the need for future investments.
- Realize a cash infusion from the sale of assets.
- Relieve the burden of staffing.

The focus of tactical outsourcing is the *contract,* specifically, constructing the right contract and, subsequently, holding the vendor to the contract. Traditionally, the expertise for making these arrangements came from the purchasing department. However, there is an emerging expectation that every manager involved in the supply chain process understand and be accountable for the aspects of outsourcing that affect their area of charge. Establishing and maintaining tactical outsourcing relationships, specifically functional or comprehensively, is the responsibility of the entire organizational team. Frequently, the contract was simply a fee for services, with much of the value stemming from the discipline of spending dollars externally. When managers formed successful tactical relationships, the value of using outside providers was clear: better service for less investment of capital and management time.

Strategic Outsourcing

Over time, as businesses sought greater value from outsourcing relationships, the goals of these relationships changed. Executives realized that, rather than losing control over the outsourced function, they gained broader control over all of the functions in their area of responsibility, hence, were freer to direct their attention to the more strategic aspects of their jobs. Facilities managers, for example, could focus more on infrastructure issues, instead of worrying about staffing janitorial positions. Technology executives could hand over running of the data center to a service provider and turn their attention to serving the needs of internal customers. This logic remains compelling.

Table 1.1
Elements of Business Outsourcing

Human Resources Services	Knowledge and Decision Services	Operations Support Services	Marketing Services
Benefits administration	Content solutions	Architecture and engineering	Marketing programs
Employment process outsourcing	E-Learning and education solutions	Re-engineering	Printing
Hiring	Point solutions	Facilities management	Fulfillment
Recruitment	Procurement and purchasing	Global delivery and sourcing	Advertising
HR/Personnel management	Project management	Healthcare and medical services	Sales and sales management
Payroll	Supply chain management	Manufacturing	Strategic planning
Professional employer organization	Systems integration and consulting	Office solutions	Fund raising and foundation management services
Recruitment process outsourcing	Transformational outsourcing	Document management	Business communications
Staffing services	Decision support systems	Pharmaceuticals	Public relations
Talent and human capital outsourcing	Data analytics	Research	Web development
Training and staff development	Data mining	Real estate management	
Workforce consulting and management	Data warehousing	Retail	
		Scientific and engineering	
		Telecommunications	
		Telephony	
		Venture capital outsourcing solutions	
		Transportation administration	
		Logistics	
		Dispatch services	

Customer Interaction Services	*Back Office Transaction Processing*	*Information Technology and Software*	*Operations Finance and Accounting Services*
Call centers	Administrative and management support services	Applications development	General accounting
Collections			Audit
CRM		Applications maintenance and re-engineering	Accounts payable
Customer contact services	Back office processing		Banking
		Application service providers	Financial services solutions
Government sourcing	Banking/ checking/ATM/ transaction processing		Credit services
Customer services voice and email		Cybersecurity and infrastructure support	Insurance processing
Telesales	Payment processing		Tax services
Order processing		Data base management	Billing systems
Customer support	Business support systems		Accounts payable
Technical support		Data center management	Accounts receivable
Warranty administration	Document management and processing	Design and multimedia	Collections and credit
Customer feedback	Forms management	Requirements engineering	Compliance
Stakeholder feedback			Management reporting
	Payroll and benefits processing	Packaged application outsourcing	
Client satisfaction surveying			
	General transaction processing	Implementation services	
		Enterprise storage solutions	
	Tuition and scholarship services		
		ERP implementation	
	Collections	Comprehensive IT services	
	Accounts receivables processing	Flexibility	
	Billing services	IT strategy and planning	
	Direct and indirect procurement	Decision support	
		Systems development	

To meet the requirement of earning greater value from outsourcing, how it was used and where it was applied had to change. The scope of outsourcing relationships grew significantly, as did the service provider's involvement. By virtue of the increasing dollar value of the relationships, the integrated scope of services, and the length of the new relationships, outsourcing was no longer a tactical tool but a strategic tool. Most important, the managerial mind-set regarding the nature of these relationships matured, from one between buyer and supplier to one between *business partners*.

Strategic outsourcing relationships are about building long-term value. Instead of working with a large number of vendors to get the job done, in a strategic model, corporations work with a smaller number of best-in-class integrated service providers. These relationships thus evolve from vendor-supplier arrangements (which are often adversarial) to long-term partnerships between equals, with the emphasis on *mutual* benefit.

Transformational Outsourcing

Transformational outsourcing is third-generation outsourcing (Table 1.2). The first stage of outsourcing involved doing the work under the existing rules; the second stage used outsourcing as part of the process of redefining the corporation. This, the third stage, uses outsourcing for the

Table 1.2
Transformational vs. Traditional Outsourcing

Transformational Outsourcing	*Traditional Outsourcing*
Business focus	Operational focus
Centered on creating value	Centered on cutting costs
Assists in managing uncertainty	Assists in establishing controls
Aligns with the business processes that revolutionize in harmonization with your strategic goals	Aligns with basically unchanged business processes
Based on fashioning a network of partnerships in the new connected global economy	Based on external (primarily IT) specialists realizing higher performance for the client than internal nonspecialist resources
Business cost and re-engineering facilitate perpetual value creation	Removes noncore functions from the business to provide a one-time discharge of capital

purpose of redefining the *business*. To survive economically today, organizations must transform themselves and their markets in an ever more
daunting challenge to redefine the business world before it redefines
them. To that end, outsourcing has emerged as the single most powerful
tool available to executives seeking this level of business change. Those
who take advantage of transformational outsourcing recognize that the
real power of this tool lies in the innovations that outside specialists bring
to their customers' businesses. No longer are outsourcing service providers
viewed only as tools for becoming more efficient or better focused; rather,
they are seen as powerful forces for change—allies in the battle for market and mind share.

PHASES OF THE OUTSOURCING PROCESS

The phases illustrated in Figure 1.1 are part of any outsourcing process:

1. *Strategy phase.* You define the objectives and scope of the outsourcing concept and determine the feasibility of outsourcing before
   making the decision to proceed. Also, you plan the total effort in
   terms of time, budget, and necessary resources.
2. *Scope phase.* You establish baselines and specify the service levels required of vendors. You clarify relationships between the function(s)
   to be outsourced and those functions that remain in house, to include
   proper interfaces. You develop the request for proposal (RFP); collect
   and analyze responses from vendors; and, finally, choose a vendor.
3. *Negotiation phase.* Negotiations proceed with the chosen vendor
   until a contract is drawn up and, ultimately, signed by both parties.
4. *Implementation phase.* This phase marks the transition from in-house
   provision of services to outsourcing.
5. *Management phase.* Throughout this phase, you manage the outsourcing relationship with the vendor. It includes the negotiation and
   implementation of any changes in the outsourcing relationship seen as
   necessary to ensure a successful outcome.
6. *Completion or termination phase.* At the end of the contract period,
   you make the decision either to negotiate another contract with the
   same vendor or to terminate that relationship and align with a new
   vendor; and the cycle begins again. Alternatively, a decision is made
   to bring the function back inside the organization.

Figure 1.1
Black Book Model of Successful Outsourcing

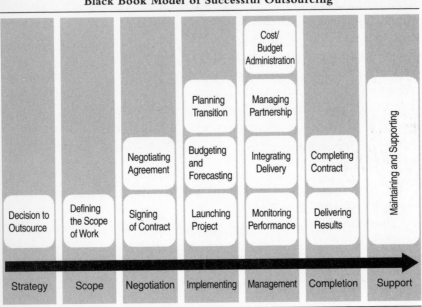

| Strategy | Scope | Negotiation | Implementing | Management | Completion | Support |

Decision to Outsource | Defining the Scope of Work | Signing of Contract | Launching Project | Monitoring Performance | Delivering Results | Maintaining and Supporting

Negotiating Agreement | Budgeting and Forecasting | Integrating Delivery | Completing Contract

Planning Transition | Managing Partnership

Cost/ Budget Administration

There will always be some aspects of the outsourcing arrangement that will be unpredictable and thus will evolve over the life of the contract. However, there are key deliverables and activities for a sound BPO relationship each step of the way. These include the prerequest for proposals phase and postcontract governance. Without these, you and your colleagues may find yourselves saying, "Outsourcing didn't work for us." To ensure you do not become one of the failure statistics, use the time wisely *before* you sign a contract, to integrate your own best practices into the terms of your outsourcing deal.

Remember, outsourcing providers are *partners* to whom you give significant managerial discretion as to how to deliver the service they offer; it is they who will manage the day-to-day delivery of that service. To generate the value you define, it is essential that these partnerships become long-term relationships. You want your partners to understand your business in depth, so that they can meet your requirements today and develop better ways to service your firm in the future. In sum, managing the outsourcing relationship is one of the most important tasks undertaken by executives today.

MONITORING THE EVOLVING OUTSOURCING ENVIRONMENT

As the outsourcing environment evolves, not surprisingly, conflicting information surfaces as to how to make an effective decision about the process. This decision is complicated by the growth of the outsourcing market and the wide range of services now available. To evaluate their options accurately, companies must first be able to identify their reasons for outsourcing and then specify costs and benefits of the process. Managers must also be able to match their specific needs with both the correct service and the correct service supplier. Let's examine the possibilities:

- *Outsourcing versus supplier relationships.* As previously defined, the term *outsourcing* applies to an activity formerly done by an organization internally. Outsourcing relationships replace or substitute the services of an external provider for current internal capabilities.
- *Outsourcing versus consulting.* Many companies concurrently position themselves as offering both consulting and outsourcing services. Unfortunately, they don't clearly distinguish between the two, and in the process confound the situation. The difference would seem to be clear-cut: Consultants advise companies on how to do something; outsourcing providers "just do it." However, sometimes a consultant will also deliver a business service or product, hence acting like a provider; other times, an outsourcing provider will advise, hence acting like a consultant. Generally, the distinction is easy to make. Most professional services firms fall into one of three categories: consultants, providers, or some combination of the two.
- *Outsourcing versus out-tasking.* Outsourcing relationships are high value-add, robust, and ongoing—that is, they are not a one-time only deal. In contrast, out-tasking refers to turning over a narrowly defined segment of business to another business, typically on an annual contract, or sometimes a shorter one. This usually involves continued direct or indirect management and decision making by the client of the out-tasking business. Out-tasking is an emerging concept. Out-tasking defines the boundaries necessary to explain to a workforce that it is being evaluated for possible outsourcing. With the uncertainty of today's business climate, facility managers are reluctant to discuss an outsourcing possibility until the benefits are certain. At that time, the concept of out-tasking seems to make the explanation easier and is restrictive enough to help employees understand the overall and final

effects of out-tasking. For example, hiring an outsourcing vendor to set up your new human resources technology, a manufacturer to handle production when demand exceeds capacity, or an overnight delivery service to deliver urgent packages. As explained in the preceding discussion on phases, outsourcing relationships are high-level, contractual relationships for a fixed period of time, usually measured in years, and they are assumed to be continuous. Provider and user often work to define the service delivered; there is frequent interaction and communication between user and provider. The outsourcing service is customized to the needs of the user.

Outsourcing versus Worldwide Sourcing

Business officials leading a new coalition to combat efforts to prevent companies from moving some operations overseas know they have a public relations problem, and they are preparing to act. Although the tone of outsourcing is softening, outsourcing has become a dirty word. Corporate leaders are working hard to try to strike outsourcing from the lexicon.

Business coalitions are rallying around worldwide sourcing as a less provocative term for the movement of jobs around the globe. The change is part of a new strategy to try to impart the business community's view that preventing firms from relocating outside the country to reduce costs will restrict competitiveness and ultimately cost jobs.

Leaders of one business alliance, the Coalition for Economic Growth and American Jobs, have also lobbied officials at the White House, the Commerce Department, and the Office of the U.S. Trade Representative to brief them on the new message of worldwide sourcing.

Business Roundtable President John Castellani told *CongressDaily* the new outsourcing public relations campaign stemmed directly from the torrent of attacks on outsourcing in the Democratic campaign. "Our concern was that if we didn't respond, we ran the risk of having a reversal of those kinds of policies that promote economic growth and job creation," he said. Castellani and others in the coalition referred to their opponents as "isolationists."

Castellani said worldwide sourcing was a more appropriate term because outsourcing has for decades referred to efforts by companies to more efficiently manage their costs by contracting with other domestic producers. With worldwide sourcing, "you participate in worldwide markets, you do the things in those markets appropriate to products and services and do things in the United States that we're best at—design and innovation," Castellani said.

Governmental administration officials appear undecided on whether they will adopt the term worldwide sourcing instead of outsourcing. With the disastrous exception of Council of Economic Advisors Chairman Gregory Mankiw, Bush aides already studiously avoid using the term outsourcing.

The administration also has avoided using the term *outsourcing* to describe its efforts to subject hundreds of thousands of federal jobs to competition from private firms. Administration officials say the term *competitive sourcing* is more accurate, because when agency teams win the competitions, the jobs are not outsourced.

FACING THE CHALLENGES OF OUTSOURCING

No powerful tool is without its challenges, and outsourcing is no different. The three most common outsourcing challenges you'll face are:

1. Choosing the right partner(s).
2. Establishing effective governance for the relationship.
3. Managing employee transitions with sensitivity.

These may seem obvious, but there is one other challenge that can catch managers by surprise: *accidental transformation*. What does that mean? Simply, that companies may outsource without realizing that the profile or style of the outsourced function makes a difference in its success. An incompatibility of styles can cause unanticipated changes, sometimes positive and sometimes negative, so it's important to be alert to such activity.

Managers can also fall prey to another cause of failure for the new outsourcer relationship: ignoring the "real work," which begins *after* the deal is signed. To avoid this pitfall, outsourcing must be approached as a project, one with a clearly established life cycle that needs to be managed every step of the way.

Changes wrought by outsourcing require both organizations and individuals to develop new success skills. For instance, an executive who operates on business-process management principles will likely be rewarded for having fewer staff and running a lean operation. Also favored will be those who leverage third-party relationships that don't tie up capital and consume resources. Business professionals will be working with a skeletal operating model with few fixed but many variable costs. At any given time, a competitive company will likely have a number of business functions that it is considering for cost savings and value improvement.

LOU DOBBS: TRUE CRUSADER AGAINST "EXPORTING AMERICA"

In March 2004, James Glassman pointed out in *Tech Central Station* that CNN pundit Lou Dobbs, possibly the reddest face of the anti-outsourcing position, was praising companies like Boeing and Washington Mutual as worthy stocks in his eponymous investment letter . . . even though he was bashing these very same companies for offshore outsourcing on his CNN show, *Lou Dobbs Tonight.*

In June 2004, Zachary Roth at *CJR's Campaign Desk* followed up on this tendency of Dobbs to say one thing to his viewers and another thing to readers of his investment letter:

> Unlike most investment advisors, Dobbs goes beyond talking up the earning potential of these companies. He typically goes out of his way to praise them as good corporate citizens. The newsletter keeps a running tally of the companies profiled, under the heading, "The following companies have been featured in the 'Lou Dobbs Money Letter' as those doing good business with good people." The appeal is alluring: You're not just buying a smart investment choice, you're buying a piece of good citizenship.

Dobbs devoted a column in his March ($398 annual paid subscription investment newsletter) issue touting the prospects of the Minnesota-based Toro Company, which makes outdoor landscaping-maintenance equipment. He told subscribers that Toro was a "long-term wealth-builder," and praised Toro's "formal code of ethics, something I think is sorely needed at more of America's companies," and its ". . . exemplary corporate governance structure, which aligns the interests of shareholders, employees, and customers." He concluded his interview with Toro CEO Kendrick Melrose by frankly telling him, "I like the way you treat your shareholders, employees, and customers."

One wonders whether Dobbs' admiration extends to Toro's 2002 decision to move 15 percent of its workforce—about 800 jobs—to Juarez, Mexico. Indeed, CEO Kendrick Melrose might be interested to know that Toro appears on Dobbs' own list of companies that are "exporting America." And Toro is not alone. Of the 14 companies Dobbs has highlighted for investors since starting his newsletter last year, eight appear on his CNN web site as companies that outsource jobs.

CONCLUSION

It's tough to argue that productivity is very important. Productivity means doing more for less. Productivity means lower costs to consumers, which, in turn, frees consumers to spend the money they save on new products and services. That leads to economic growth.

In 1900, 40 percent of U.S. employees worked on farms. Today, less then 2 percent of the American population generates all the food the entire United States needs, which is a much more significant quantity that it was 100 years ago. At the same time, grocery shopping requires a far smaller percentage of our paychecks than it cost our great grandparents at the turn of the past century. We then use our excess money to build bigger houses, buy computers, new cars, iPods, big screen TVs, and take vacations.

Follow this closely: Indirectly, our food cost savings has paid for the creation of a vast array of new products and services introduced since 1900, as well as jobs for the people who work to create and sell those products and services.

Politicians, kings, ministers and priests, and public service workers have attempted to resolve the problems of world poverty for decades. The only opportunity that the poverty-stricken billions of world residents who live on very little have of someday living lifestyles like those of us in the United States . . . lies in economic growth. And economic growth is driven by increases in productivity.

In 2005, the one clear path to productivity is positioned in outsourcing. In shifting jobs offshore that can be done by cheaper and, in some cases, less skilled, workers to foreign locations, productivity escalates.

As a result, of outsourcing, prices fall, Americans and Europeans have more money left after they buy what they need and can then spend it on new products and services, creating new industries and new jobs, particularly in the United States, United Kingdom, and other developed countries.

The drama and political mudslinging created through the 2004 U.S. presidential election have clearly backed off from outsourcing. Outsourcing is being recognized in its rightful place as the most important business shift of the new century.

Up to this point in business history, it's been easier to think of outsourcing as a concept in the abstract. Recognizing it is ultimately for the common good, sooner or later, all business leaders will either voluntarily or involuntarily become required to manage outsourcing changes. In the *Black Book of Outsourcing* we take the concept out of the theoretical and abstract and into concrete actionable steps for you.

The dark future forecast by some outsourcing pundits doesn't have to be so grim if you take action now. The advice in this book is intended to lead many of you to acquire skills that extended your education and experiential value and preserved your job, particularly if you transition into outsourcing.

We are going to have to live with the realities of a global economy and the relentless demands for greater productivity and outsourcing for the rest of our lives. And our children are going to have to live with the same realities. Some will suffer while others will prosper as we negotiate the changes that outsourcing is presenting. This book is a great start toward ensuring that you position yourself appropriately as well as in advising new college graduates and outsourced job seekers.

CHAPTER 2

MAKING THE DECISION TO OUTSOURCE

Outsourcing is one of the greatest organizational and industry structure shifts of the century.

—James Brian Quinn, best-selling author and
resident Dartmouth College business visionary

Embarking on the outsourcing decision-making process requires significant effort. Therefore, we recommend you accomplish the following "foundation" tasks before undertaking this initiative:

1. Set the strategic direction for your organization.
2. Identify your company's core competencies and determine its strategic objectives.
3. Develop a list of suppliers/vendors for consideration.
4. Appoint an outsourcing process implementation and governance team.

Before making any but the most urgent, tactical outsourcing decisions (for example, to outsource because of short-term capacity, staffing, or production problems), your corporate leadership must set the overall direction for making outsourcing decisions within the context of your organization's strategic goals. They must seriously evaluate the organization's core competencies and strategic goals. Core capabilities confer a marked competitive advantage in a niche marketplace. In a very real sense, core competencies are what define your business as unique. Thus, you must be clear on these before you begin to make outsourcing plans.

The best outsourcing choices are based on four primary considerations:

1. Strategically enhancing core competencies.
2. Addressing issues with employees, unions, and the community.
3. Finding the lowest total cost or best value.
4. Recognizing impact on internal operations.

We propose a controlled, purposeful method whose goal is to involve all stakeholders, gather data about these four key issues, and then make a logical outsourcing decision. This is in contrast to blindly choosing to outsource without a full analysis. It is also in contrast to many outsourcing decision processes that were popular in the late 1990s and which more recently failed to consider total cost on both sides of the equation.

Employing Best Practices in Decision Making

An internal outsourcing analysis assesses the costs and benefits of performing work by internal departments or staff members versus having it done by outside suppliers. To improve on the typical processes currently employed in most companies, use the Outsourcing Decision-Making Scorecard shown in Figure 2.1. Doing so will help to ensure your decision is:

- More inclusive
- More accurate
- More controlled and structured

The processes we recommend include issues and resources that are rarely addressed in the typical outsourcing decision-making process. Most important, we consider the impact of outsourcing on associated processes in the buyer organization, as well as the need (and costs) to build specific types of relationships with suppliers.

The comprehensive approach to costing in an ordered outsourcing assessment process provides a more accurate view of *both* the make and buy sides of the equation. It provides greater accuracy on the buy side because it does not attempt to allocate a gross part of the entire overhead of the buyer business to a particular process; rather, it looks only at those portions of overhead specifically attributable to that process. And it provides greater accuracy on the buy side by considering changes in your business process that may be required if a process is outsourced.

Figure 2.1
The Outsourcing Decision-Making Scorecard

Service Being Considered for Outsourcing: _____

Institutional Setting

1. Is this a functional part of our core competencies?   _____ Yes _____ No
2. Does this service need to be provided on a continual basis? _____ Yes _____ No
3. Do we have in-house expertise to provider this service?   _____ Yes _____ No
4. Do we have available staff to provide this service?   _____ Yes _____ No
5. Can we legally outsource this service? (Federal, State, or local regulations, governmental agency limitations, embargoed countries, corporate policies, prohibitions enforced by litigation)   _____ Yes _____ No

Risks

1. Would loss of content of this service harm the organization?   _____ Ye _____ No
2. Would loss of expertise have a negative impact?   _____ Yes _____ No
3. Is quality-of-service delivery a concern?   _____ Yes _____ No
4. Would the response time to situational problems be reduced?   _____ Yes _____ No
5. Would current contract performance be negatively impacted?   _____ Yes _____ No

Goals and Objectives

1. Can the goals for this service be clearly defined?   _____ Yes _____ No
2. Are the goals for this service long term?   _____ Yes _____ No
3. Can the achievements of these goals be objectively measured?   _____ Yes _____ No
4. Are objective measures currently in place for this service?   _____ Yes _____ No
5. If the goals and objectives are not achieved, will this have a negative impact upon the company?   _____ Yes _____ No

Provider Evaluation

1. Are there known external providers for this service?   _____ Yes _____ No
2. Do the mission and strategic goals of the providers align with our company's mission and strategic goals?   _____ Yes _____ No
3. Are the providers known to have the capability to provide this service?   _____ Yes _____ No
4. Has the company had previous relationships with roviders of this service?   _____ Yes _____ No
5. Are the providers known to deliver high or higher quality services?   _____ Yes _____ No

The Outsourcing Decision-Making Scorecard comprises five questions in each of four categories. The purpose of the first set of questions is to identify the institutional setting of the organization and to determine if there is a potential for building an outsourcing relationship for a given service. If the answers to the first five questions indicate that a relationship cannot be formed, the service should probably *not* be outsourced. If there appears to be the possibility of building a relationship, answer the next three sets of questions to identify, first, specific issues to be worked out in the outsourcing arrangement and, second, any barriers that might prevent the service from being outsourced.

Identifying Your Company's Outsourcing Needs

The first step in the decision-making process is to identify your company's needs, to set the framework and priorities for business-processing projects and activities. This step includes three activities:

1. *Address the strategic interests and goals of the company.* The strategic plan, the information resources strategic plan, and the corporate performance measures all must be considered when you are identifying needs and directions. The corporate goals serve as a basis for determining project success. Core competencies, as a general rule, should not be outsourced. Depending on company resources and weaknesses, however, this rule may be broken if your situation determines that resources or knowledge from an external outsource vendor would supplement your firm's available resources.
2. *Specify the service to be provided and identify the reasons to consider outsourcing.* Considerations include cost savings, enhanced service levels, the transition to a different technology platform, the need for increased technical or product knowledge and skills not present in the organization, or insufficient staff resources to accomplish specific tasks.
3. *Place the decision process in a neutral framework.* While outsourcing can be encouraged for reasons outside the realms of the functions being outsourced, the justification regarding the use of internal or external resources should be framed solely in business case terms. A sound analysis of options will be a strong support for management recommendations and decisions.

A systematic, structured outsourcing decision process will lead to reduced costs and fewer delays and to greater outsourcing situations where total cost can be lowered, while retaining work inside the company. Moreover, there will be fewer delays because the relationship that results from the process will enable closer to just-in-time delivery than is currently possible.

IDENTIFYING REASONS TO OUTSOURCE

There are countless reasons why a manager considers outsourcing. After reviewing these, we will discuss how to evaluate the relevance one or more of these reasons might have to your outsourcing decision-making process. Here are some of the most popular:

- *To acquire new skills*. A company may find that the skill set of its in-house staff is inadequate for a given function. This may result in minimal improvements to the function in the future. A company can solve this problem by handing over the function to an outsourcing supplier who specializes in that function and is highly competent in its administration, using well-trained and experienced staff and the most current procedures and technological advances. This reason is most commonly given for making the decision to outsource those functions that require high skill levels, such as engineering and computer services.
- *To acquire better management*. A company may find that an in-house function is not performing as required because of poor management. Symptoms of this problem include high turnover, increased incidence of absenteeism, poor-quality products, and missed deadlines. Quality managers can be difficult to find, and outsourcing the function to a supplier to gain access to the industry's best and most experienced managers in a functional area is a viable option.
- *To focus on strategy*. A company's managers typically spend the bulk of each day handling the detailed operations of their functional area—the tactical aspects of their job. Outsourcing the tactical part of each manager's job to a supplier allows the management team to spend far more time on such strategy-related issues as market positioning and new product development.
- *To focus on core functions*. A company that has a very small number of functions that are key to its survival may want to focus all of its energies on those functions and distribute all other functions among a

group of outside suppliers so that company management is free to manage. The company may even want to outsource some current core functions that are expected to become less important in the future due to changes in the nature of the business. Such a company might even outsource a function that is considered key to company survival—*if* it can find a supplier that can perform the function better. In this case, the company would keep only those core functions that in-house staff can do better than the supplier.

- *To avoid major investments.* A company may find that it has a function that is not as effective as it could be due to a lack of investment. If the company keeps the function in-house, it will eventually have to make a major investment in order to modernize. By outsourcing the function, the company could permanently avoid having to make this investment.

- *To assist a fast-growth situation.* If a company is rapidly acquiring market share, the management team will be stretched to its limits in handling the increased volume of business. In such situations, the management team will desperately need additional help in running the company. A supplier can step in and take over a function, freeing the management team to focus its attention on a smaller number of core activities.

- *To handle overflow situations.* A company may find that there are times when a function is overloaded for reasons beyond its control. In such situations, it may be cost effective to retain a supplier to which the excess work will be shunted when the in-house staff can't keep up with the demand.

- *To improve flexibility.* This is similar to using outsourcing to handle overflow situations, but in this case the supplier is given the entire function, not just the overflow business. When a function experiences extremely large swings in the volume of work it handles, it may be easier to eliminate the fixed cost of an internal staff and move the function to a suppler who will be paid only for the work done. This converts a fixed cost into a variable cost—the price of the supplier's services will fluctuate directly with the transaction volume it handles.

- *To improve financial ratios.* Some companies are so driven by their performance ratios that they will outsource functions solely to improve them. Outsourcing a function that involves transferring assets to suppliers will increase the company's return on assets. The functions most likely to improve this ratio and that can be improved are those heavy in assets, for example: maintenance, manufacturing, hospital pharmacies, and information systems. Another ratio that can be improved immediately is profitability per full-time equivalent (FTE; FTE = 40 hours per week × 52 weeks per year = 2,080 hours per year). To enhance FTE, a company should outsource all functions involving large numbers of employees, such as sales and manufacturing.

- *To launch a new strategic initiative.* A company's management may undertake a complete company reorganization, during which outsourcing can be used to significantly alter the overall organizational structure. Managers making such a change capture the attention of the remaining employees and divisions with the underlying message that poor performance may result in future outsourcing decisions.

- *To improve overall performance.* A company may find one of its functions or departments has bloated costs or inadequate performance, and to motivate improvement, management decides to "shop" an outsourcing bid for the department or function. By including the department/division/function manager and staff in the bidding process, the in-house staff will have the opportunity to be competitive and to demonstrate that they are willing to commit to specific service levels and costs. If the in-house staff bid proves to be competitive, management can then keep the staff accountable to higher performance levels and lowered costs. (Note that you should tell suppliers up front that the in-house staff will also be bidding. Fortunately, suppliers are becoming accustomed to competing with internal staff in the bid process.)

- *To reduce costs.* Outsourcing is not all about reducing costs. However, a company may emphasize cost savings for a variety of reasons, such as poor financial position or to meet a goal to increase profits. Using a supplier to reduce costs is possible, but not in all situations. A supplier can lower costs if it can centralize the work of several companies to one location, or if it can use volume purchasing to buy materials or supplies. It can also purchase assets from a company and then lease the assets back as part of the outsourcing deal, thereby giving the company an up-front cost infusion.

- *To enhance credibility.* A company can enhance its credibility by contracting with highly reputable, highly recognizable outsourcing suppliers. Well-known suppliers will assure a certain level of quality and service.

- *To jump on the outsourcing bandwagon.* Many company managers decide to outsource just because everyone else is doing it. As more and more companies venture into outsourcing, the process itself is becoming a "business as usual" concept, hence lends credence to a company's decision to become part of the trend.

In addition to the reasons for outsourcing just listed, which are easy to rationalize, don't overlook the possibility that there may be deeper, underlying reasons. Perhaps, for example, the functions or departments in question are not doing an adequate job representing their benefits and return to upper management. Too often, functional unit managers are not good at blowing their business unit's horn, or at demonstrating to senior management that the cost of keeping the function in-house is adequately offset by less obvious benefits.

You need to assess whether the problem in a department is its inability to manifest its true contribution. Be careful not to outsource a perfectly adequate in-house staff that is simply not good at self-promotion. If the outsourcing manager suspects that this is the reason outsourcing is being considered, it is useful to bring in an independent consultant who can objectively review the performance of in-house employees to investigate the situation. As noted, many outsourcing managers are now requiring in-house department and functional managers to rebid against an outsourcing supplier's proposal to keep their department in-house. Sometimes, investigating the capability of in-house staff prior to making the decision to outsource ends up providing overwhelming evidence *not* to outsource.

The outsourcing manager should also keep in mind that it is not always necessary to outsource an entire functional department or division. Instead, a tremendous number of outsourcing suppliers focus on a subset of tasks the department performs, which are clearly candidates for outsourcing, while keeping the other functions of the department in-house. This also reduces the risk during the trial period with the outsourcing supplier. With fewer tasks at risk, you can evaluate whether the supplier is competent to take on more essential tasks.

STARTING ON THE OUTSOURCING PATH

The typical outsourcing path followed by a large company is to start with a function that has minimal strategic value and will not seriously jeopardize business if the suppler does not meet contracted requirements. If the

---

TIP Accounting, materials management, and human resources tasks present lower risk for outsourcing. So consider starting your outsourcing effort with these functions until confidence builds between you and your supplier(s). Then move forward to outsource more important functions, more closely related to your core functionalities (typically, e.g., information systems, engineering, sales and marketing, public relations, manufacturing, customer service, call centers).

---

outsourcer handles these lower end functions successfully, the company is likely to be much more receptive to outsource functions with greater strategic value and thus at higher risk.

Once you have determined that using external resources is a viable option for meeting business needs, conduct a cost-benefit analysis to compare both the internal and external resource options. A major problem with external and internal staffing decisions arises when outsourcing decisions are made without a complete understanding of expected benefits. To help you gain the depth of understanding required, make sure you cover these bases:

- Effectively communicate your company goals and objectives to your vendors.
- Prepare a strategic outsourcing vision and plan.
- Perform due diligence and select the right vendors.
- Manage vendor relationships on an ongoing basis.
- Properly structure your vendor contracts.
- Be open with affected individual/groups about the possibility of downsizing or redeployment in the organization.
- Guarantee senior executive support and involvement through a chief resource officer.
- Pay careful attention to personnel issues.
- Continually review performance metric results and maintain financial justification for outsourcing.

Table 2.1 identifies some common outsourcing development problems you may face, and their solutions.

Table 2.1
Outsourcing Development Problems and Solutions

Criteria Development

Problems	*Solutions*
Expectations regarding the outsourcing initiative or assignment are unclear.	At the beginning of the planning process, identify the purpose of the outsourcing project, the organizational resources available for the outsourcing project, and the specific type of outsourcing that would match the project.
A lack of understanding of the outsourcing project makes it difficult to identify and evaluate the costs and benefits of internal and external resources.	Allow enough time to research the project fully, contacting any internal or external experts available to your firm.
Failure to compare the costs and benefits of internal and external resources on an equal basis leads to inaccurate analysis. A comparison of FTE costs to the contract total does not account for the soft costs included in the contract. Costs to the buyer for in-house resources will be higher than a simple FTE count when soft costs are considered. Costs to the buying organization as a whole may also be different from buyer costs, as some operating costs may not be paid by the buyer using the resources (e.g., utilities, floor space).	Evaluate the project on a matrix or weighted average list, providing consistent examination of the same options when discussing both internal and external options. Be sure to clearly document costs and identify all formulas for deriving costs. This enables you to see what costs are included.
An accurate analysis of costs and benefits is difficult to make because there are no priorities in place to help identify and measure the needs of your business.	Use your strategic plan to identify priorities and establish weights for each criterion. Involve stakeholders and ask executive sponsors for input.
The hard-to-quantify nature of some of the soft costs and benefits, such as "business advantage" or "access to expertise," make these costs difficult to identify.	Identifying priorities and weights will help when including qualitative costs and benefits in the analysis. Establishing success measures that examine project outcomes in light of your corporate goals will add needed substance to the qualitative costs and benefits.

In the next chapter, we cover the information you need to know before you start the outsourcing process. In preparation, familiarize yourself with the following outsourcing guidelines:

- Requests for proposals (RFPs), vendor selection, and contract signing are only the beginning of the journey.
- The first year of the outsourcing vendor relationship is critical to establishing sound management practices that will be durable over the term of the contract.
- Expect significant changes to your BPO contract every two years. These include additions to scope, business changes, and new technologies. Many managers, as potential buyers of BPO, worry about losing control when they outsource. This is a legitimate concern, but rest assured it's not the norm in most outsourcing situations. In fact, if you have a strong governance and relationship-management organization, you may find you have greater control than when the activities were managed in-house. Why? In a BPO relationship, formal and explicit service-level agreements guarantee monthly reports and measures. If performance isn't above average, penalties are imposed.
- The keys to successful achievement are dedicated change-management and communication resources. Outsourcing governance, including chief resource officers, will ensure regular and effective communication.
- The offshore migration of the administrative supply chain has begun. If you haven't evaluated your offshore options, start now. Have an option ready before your board or CEO asks you for one. Savvy managers will be prepared.

CHAPTER 3

WHAT YOU NEED TO KNOW BEFORE YOU START

Companies outsourcing business functions outperform the S&P and NASDAQ during recessions.

—Morgan Stanley Dean Witter

Organizations of all sizes are partnering with strategic outsourcing firms to streamline operations, enhance capabilities, and greatly improve efficiencies. Outsourcing can work for any size company in any industry; there is no correlation between the success of an outsourcing program and the size or type of the firm. Rather, the success of an outsourcing program depends on planning, execution (including training), selection of the right partner(s), and flexible service level agreements with the outsourcing provider. The functions a company chooses to outsource vary based on its industry. For example, a mortgage company might outsource lead generation and contact center activities; a consumer products company might outsource consumer relations; a bank might outsource IT functions; and an engineering company might outsource routine document design.

Business process outsourcing (BPO) is not without its challenges, however. And these can be especially daunting for midsize organizations, because few of these firms have the in-house expertise required to make an outsourcing relationship successful in the long run. To meet these challenges head-on, firms must recognize that:

- Needs assessment necessitates evaluating the current process from a fresh perspective in order to decide what to outsource and, just as important, what not to outsource. Finding a suitable service provider

---

Note: Web addresses flagged with a (†) are author affiliated sites.

requires a thorough knowledge of the vendor landscape, including capabilities, delivery processes, quality of work, and ability to innovate. Collecting and analyzing this information, especially regarding offshore vendors is a time-consuming and complex process.

- Measuring the value of an outsourcing relationship—contracts and service level agreements (SLA)—requires technical, legal, and process expertise. Likewise, control over the outsource process may require local presence at the vendor's location, as well as knowledge of the outsourcer's culture.
- Managing uncertainty and mitigating risks requires formulating an alternative strategy while setting up the outsourcing relationship, and planning in advance for business process migration to a second vendor in the event of failure.

WHAT'S DRIVING YOUR OUTSOURCING DECISION?

Even if you're currently feeling pressured to outsource immediately, it's important to take the time to assess this important business decision *beforehand*. Only then will you be able to select the right offshore option and formulate a partnership that will result in long-term success.

To know where you're going, you must know what's driving you. Review these 10 key drivers behind to help determine which apply to your company's situation:

- *Accelerate re-engineering benefits.* Re-engineering aims to achieve spectacular improvements in critical key performance indicators such as cost, quality, service, and momentum. However, the need to increase efficiency can come into direct conflict with the need to invest in the core business. As noncore internal functions are repeatedly put on the back burner, systems become less effective and productive. By outsourcing a noncore function to a world-class provider, the organization can start to see the benefits of re-engineering.
- *Gain access to world-class capabilities.* World-class vendors make major investments in technology, methodologies, and personnel, and they gain expertise by working with many clients facing similar challenges. This combination of specialization and expertise results in competitive benefits for their customers, as well as saving them the cost of investing in technology and training for the now-outsourced

functions. And personnel who transition to the outsourcing provider find more abundant career opportunities.

- *Earn cash back.* Outsourcing often involves the transfer of assets from the customer to the vendor. Equipment, facilities, vehicles, and licenses used in the current operations have value and are sold to the vendor. The vendor then uses these assets to provide services back to the client. Depending on the value of the assets involved, this sale may result in a significant cash payment to the customer. When these assets are sold to the vendor, they are typically sold at book value, which can be higher than the market value. In these cases, the difference between the two actually represents a loan from the vendor to the client, which is repaid in the price of the services over the life of the contract.
- *Release resources for other purposes.* Every organization has limits on the resources available to it. Outsourcing enables an organization to redirect its resources, most often human resources, from noncore activities to those that serve the customer. The organization can redirect these people—or at least the staff slots they represent—to greater value-add activities. People whose energies are currently focused internally can be refocused externally—on the customer.
- *Reevaluate problematic functions.* Outsourcing does *not* mean abdication of management responsibility, nor is it the proper response by a company in trouble. When a function is viewed as difficult to manage or out of control, the organization needs to examine the underlying causes. If the requirements, expectations, or necessary resources are not clearly understood, outsourcing won't improve the situation; it may in fact exacerbate it. If the organization doesn't understand its own requirements, it won't be able to communicate them to an outside provider.
- *Improve company focus.* Outsourcing frees a company to focus on its core business and to meet its customers' needs by having operational functions assumed by an outside expert.
- *Make capital funds available.* There is tremendous competition within most organizations for capital funds. Deciding where to invest these funds is one of the most important decisions that senior management makes. It is often hard to justify noncore capital investments when areas more directly related to producing a product or providing a service compete for the same money. Outsourcing can reduce the need to invest capital funds in noncore business functions. Instead of acquiring resources through capital expenditures, they are contracted for on an "as used" operational expense basis. Outsourcing can also

improve certain financial measurements of the firm by eliminating the need to show return on equity from capital investments in non-core areas.

- *Lower operating costs.* Companies that try to do everything themselves may incur vastly higher research, development, marketing, and deployment expenses, all of which are passed on to the customer. An outside provider's lower cost structure, which may be the result of a greater economy of scale or other advantage based on specialization, reduces a company's operating costs and increases its competitive advantage.

- *Minimize risk.* Tremendous risks are associated with the investments an organization makes. Markets, competition, government regulations, financial conditions, and technologies all change at electronic speed today. Keeping up with these changes requires a major investment, and hence, is very risky. In contrast, because outsourcing providers make investments on behalf of many clients, this spreads the risk, thus markedly reducing the risk borne by a single company.

- *Gain access to resources not available internally.* Companies outsource because they do not have access to the required resources in-house. Outsourcing is a viable alternative to accessing the needed capabilities, particularly for start-up companies.

Figure 3.1 divides the outsourcing "pie" by drivers and Table 3.1 delineates where the competitive outsourcing labor markets are developing.

Figure 3.1
Main Drivers of Outsourcing

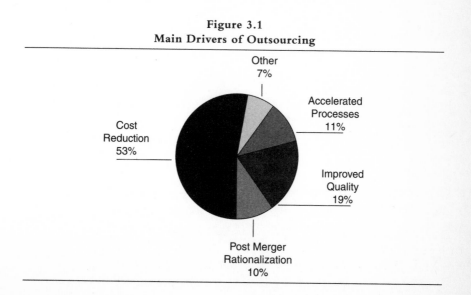

Table 3.1
Where Competitive Labor Markets Are Developing

	Lower Quality Workforce, Education, Technology	*Higher Quality Workforce, Education, Technology*
High-cost labor		United States
		United Kingdom
		Canada
		Ireland
		Israel
		Singapore
		Australia
Low-cost labor	Philippines	India
	Hungary	Eastern Europe
	Mexico	China
	Chile	

Getting to the Core of Outsourcing

We've said it before, but it bears repeating: The critical factor in the outsourcing decision is knowing your company's core competencies. The general rule of thumb is: Do not launch the outsourcing process with functions that are core to it. Instead, appropriate starting points for outsourcing are those process areas that are necessary to the business but that can be run more effectively by another firm. Functions such as administrative support are considered noncore to most companies and can easily be shifted off-site. The most common administrative functions such as scheduling meetings, making travel reservations, and setting up appointments all can be done remotely today—though this might rattle your upper-level executives at first. Other functions such as filing company taxes, completing insurance paperwork, collecting outstanding invoices, and ensuring compliance with state and federal regulations can also be handled remotely with great success.

Other core outsourcing success factors are:

- Senior management/owners must commit to the concept.
- Management must reserve additional time up front to ensure a smooth transition.
- Training is critical, as each company has a unique culture.
- Built-in flexibility in the outsourcing arrangement is essential.

TIP In the 1930s, U.S. economist Ronald Coase questioned why, if the market can provision everything a firm needs, businesses don't outsource every function. The answer, Coase decided, was transaction costs. Theoretically, it's possible to create a virtual company by contractually handling every function, from human resources to printing to research and development, but the act of designing and executing contracts carries a cost in and of itself.

Coase reasoned that a firm would grow to the size it needed to be to minimize contracting costs for essential services by bringing those functions into one organizational context.

Seventy-five years later, we are implementing this scenario.

Keeping Up with the Jargon

Outsourcing, as in the software development and other high-tech industries, is becoming overrun with jargon. Four terms have recently been added to the lexicon, to describe strategies when considering the location of a project.

Onshore outsourcing, or homeshoring. A complex way to articulate the process of engaging another company within your country for services. Thus, in the United States, onshore outsourcing means contracting a U.S. company to supply business services.

Nearshore outsourcing. Refers to contracting a company in a nearby country, often one that shares a border. In the United States, then, nearshore outsourcing would take place in either Canada or Mexico; in Great Britain, in Ireland.

Offshoring, or offshore outsourcing. Refers to contracting with a company that is geographically distant. Countries that are popular locations for offshoring include the Philippines, India, Ireland, and the Ukraine.

Bestshore outsourcing. A term recently coined to describe which "shore" will offer better communication, higher productivity, and reasonable costs.

See the Glossary for a more comprehensive listing of outsourcing terms.

Answering Key Questions

In addition to identifying the key drivers behind the decision to outsource, it helps to answer a number of questions before making the decision to outsource.

Preprocess Questions.   Before speaking with a potential outsourcing supplier or finalizing your decision to outsource a function, division, or departmental project, review these questions. Moreover, your candidate providers should be asking these questions of *you* to ensure that they can add clear value to your company's strategic goals.

1. Do you understand all of the symptoms causing you to consider outsourcing?
   - What is the context of the issues? What are the facts and the technical issues?
   - What difficulty is the problem causing? How does it manifest specifically in your business? How serious is it? What is the value of solving the problem?
   - What will be the fallout of not achieving your desired outcome? To you? To your organization?
   - Who/what else is affected? How, specifically?
2. Do you understand the key causes and constraints?
   - How/where did the problem originate?
   - What has prevented its resolution before now?
3. Do you understand the business objectives and benefits of outsourcing?
   - What are the positive desired results?
   - What are the benefits of solving the problem(s) or of taking advantage of an opportunity?
   - How will you measure success?
   - What is the critical payoff from each outcome?
4. Can you see the big picture?
   - Does senior management recognize the problem?
   - Has anything been left out?
   - Why do you think outsourcing might be a better alternative to internal correction?
   - Will anything or anyone interfere with the successful implementation of an outsourcing solution?

Cost, Quality, and Time Questions.   Outsourcing business processes should provide logical cost, quality, and time benefits to a company. Here is a list of typical questions:

Cost
   - Will outsourcing reduce short-term and/or long-term costs?
   - Have you compared build versus buy return-on-investment scenarios?

- Do you want to invest internally in hiring, managing, firing, researching, assessing, designing, marketing, delivering, and evaluating solutions? Or is this not feasible?

Quality

- Do you have the internal resources to effectively meet your objectives? Is this the best use of these resources vis-à-vis other strategic priorities?
- How can you most effectively deliver and scale up or down with changing and anticipated business needs?
- Would you benefit from access to best practices and world-class quality outside the organization?
- Should you outsource part or all of the division/function/project?
- Is this your core competency? Should it be? Have you developed clear core competency statements?
- Would you gain valuable partnership benefits and contacts from outsourcing?
- What would work best in your culture?

Time

- Will outsourcing increase speed and with better results?
- Do you have the time to build it internally? When many companies learn what the costs of outsourcing or new software purchases will total up, they often choose, as an alternative, to "Build it" themselves ("Build it" is common terminology for IT as an option to buying from an external vendor).
- Are you funded by venture capitalists who have explicit time expectations as to when you will be profitable? Can you meet those without outsourcing?

Strategy Questions.   Know the answers to the following strategy questions before you move into outsourcing:

- Which cost/service trade-offs are you and your company willing to make?
- How much risk can your company tolerate?
- How closely matched are your companies' cultures?
- Does the vendor appreciate and have experience in your industry?
- How will you make decisions and resolve disagreements with your offshore vendors?
- Who is the corporate officer charged with responsibility for outsourcing?

- Have return on investment or cost/benefit studies been performed internally (not supplied by the vendor)?
- Do you have several low-risk projects that would make good pilots with the vendors?

Identifying Buyer Characteristics and Financial Benefits

As you evaluate the reasons behind your company's consideration of an outsourcing solution, it may help to compare its characteristics against these three lists: first, common organizational characteristics; second, buyer behavior; and, third, anticipated financial benefits.

Organizational Characteristics

- Operations in multiple geographic locations, with independent organizations setting and implementing independent policies and processes
- Multiple business units operating with independent support organizations
- Large volumes of transactions and/or above-average processing costs
- High management-to-staff ratio in a number of markets
- High proportion of employees located in high-cost areas
- Intent to grow through acquisitions, joint ventures, or alliances
- Significant investment required to enhance systems and processes associated with support services
- Lack of specialized skills and/or duplication in multiple business units or geographies
- Inconsistent delivery of satisfactory service levels across businesses/markets

Behavioral Characteristics

- Limited focus on back office in favor of front office, typically demonstrated by lower-priority investments
- No perception of back office as a service provider, typified by resistance when trying to implement an internal service orientation (such as service level agreements)
- Unmotivated back-office staff members who have no clear career path or understanding as to how they fit into the overall organization structure
- Weak finance "community" and no clear understanding of standard financial operating procedures
- Weak culture of continuous improvement and operational excellence within back-office processes

Financial Benefits

- Optimal performance through improved cost and service performance, immediate returns with minimal cash flow/P&L impact, and direct business value through working capital improvements and improved decision support for finance executives.
- Enhanced control through contracted business outcomes; repeatable and proven solutions, methods, and tools; and reduced risk and increased transparency of information.
- Improved focus through growth in business, not back-office complexity, improved performance through use of service management framework, and transformation of "back office'" into front office.
- Improved flexibility to accommodate business change such as mergers and acquisitions and organic growth and to gain access to world-class processes, technology, and resources.

Then take a look at Table 3.2 which succinctly distinguishes the functional and financial pros and cons of outsourcing.

Laying the Foundations of Outsourcing

The most successful outsourcers form strong relationships with their suppliers, hold high-level strategic reviews, and have an effective process for continual improvement that is underpinned by performance measures and end-user satisfaction measures. When organizations follow the four guidelines outlined here, they achieve greater benefits and cost savings.

Getting Started—"Knowing Which Process to Outsource"

One of the most difficult issues that companies face when determining to outsource, is deciding which processes make the most sense to outsource. A company should not necessarily outsource those processes that save them the most money. They must look at other factors such as: the degree of standardization in the process, alignment of the process to the company's key objectives, management buy-in, change readiness, compliance, and the state of the technology used in the process.

Outsourcing vendors such as eFunds Corporation, a U.S.-based company, provide tools, such as eFunds' Process Readiness Index (PRI™), which uses a combination of industry knowledge and expertise as well as analytics to determine which processes are truly ready to outsource and which ones still need to be improved before outsourcing.

Table 3.2
Functional and Financial Pros and Cons of Outsourcing

Pros	Cons
Functional	
Can be leveraged to improve operating efficiency, and migration to better and more efficient methods of business processes can be facilitated.	Loss of control over day-to-day decision making.
Enables changes in your corporate culture and processes.	Incurs risk of becoming tied to one vendor or technology, making responsiveness to changes more difficult.
Allows in-house personnel to focus on strategic planning and new areas of development/core processes.	Outsourcing agreement must be managed effectively by knowledgeable staff to ensure vendor's ability to deliver services and products.
	Identification of core processes may change over time.
Provides access to expert knowledge in old and new technology areas.	Ensures knowledge transfer so that reductions in staff skills and staff knowledge of needs/systems are minimized.
Can be leveraged to respond quickly to legislative mandates, new technologies, and new business needs.	There are high exit barriers.
	Once a contract is signed, it can be difficult to back out in the event of problems.
Financial	
Offers cost savings on equipment and staffing through vendors' economies of scale.	Danger of becoming tied to obsolete technology so vendor can achieve economies of scale.
Enables smoother cash flow, as predetermined amounts go to the vendor to buy material and equipment.	Locking in to one vendor without the ability to take the program in-house or switch to another vendor will cause price increases when the contract is renewed.
Offers access to technology without capital investment.	Cost of outsourcing agreement is dependent upon contract terms and conditions for changes, maintenance, and so on.
	Costs may spiral quickly.
Saves management time and money through reduced need to oversee day-to-day operations.	Costs to your company in terms of staff time for contract management may be higher than anticipated.

Improving a process before outsourcing sounds somewhat counterintuitive, but the process must be ready before the outsourcing vendor can succeed in either re-creating or transforming the current process. Improving the process before it's outsourced, increases the likelihood that you will see an increase in return on investment (ROI) and overall quality.

When working with a company in determining the readiness of a process, it is imperative that you choose a company that actually transitions the process and does the outsourcing. It's easy to say a process is ready to be outsourced, if you're not the outsourcing vendor that has to deal with the aftermath of such a decision.

Begin with a Shared Vision

A shared vision is the first step to managing an outsourcing relationship. In the early days, cost or headcount reductions were the most common reasons to outsource. In today's world, as explained earlier, the drivers are often more strategic, and focus on carrying out core value-adding activities in-house. These strategic objectives mean that outsourcing initiatives must come from the top. Senior executives must express the purpose and aspirations of the outsourcing initiative and convey how the course will benefit the organization. The goals of the outsourcing initiative have significant consequences for the selection of the outsourcing vendor and the prospective management of the partnership. The vision saturates every stage of the outsourcing process, from the earliest establishment of goals through the construction and monitoring of the contract.

In a shared vision, both the outsourcing buyer and seller contribute to the success of the partnership. A vendor can help define realistic requirements and added benefits for the buyer. There should be a key investment in getting to know and understand each other. This begins by way of initial negotiations and meetings on an unceremonious basis to learn about each other and to obtain views on the scope of the contract.

Establish Effective Performance Measures

When you establish performance measures, you have an effective way to motivate performance and to ensure high-quality service in the form of incentives and penalties for over- or underperformance, respectively.

You'll want to specify requirements in terms of outcomes rather than inputs and attach a service standard against which to measure performance.

Make performance standards realistic, or they won't be effective. There is a tendency to overspecify requirements. For example, are turnaround times for payables of 48 hours required if the approach process takes seven days? In addition, standards evolve over time, and normally become progressively tighter.

Establish Clear Communication Mechanisms

How partners communicate depends on the outsourcing contract and the complexity of the services being delivered. Simple, well-specified services, such as cleaning, catering, or fleet management, require day-to-day operational contacts and formal performance reporting and invoicing. As the services increase in complexity, more in-depth communication is essential. In particular, this may include joint planning of service delivery and problem resolution, discussion of proposed innovations or changes in approach, consultation on staffing changes, and so on. This will be supplemented by regular monthly reporting, to show performance against standards, pricing, and problems encountered.

Expect the Unexpected

Despite your best efforts in establishing effective partner communications, the relationship between your company and its outsourcing partner may break down, so drawing up a well-defined contingency plan is an absolute necessity.

Keep in mind, outsourcing is not an end in itself. It is a management tool, nothing more or less, and should be used as such. In the course of the outsourcing process, management must address several critical issues in order to achieve success. These issues include identifying potential organizational problems, factoring in human resources and behavior, considering asset transfers and authorities, establishing and negotiating contracts, and overcoming political obstacles. Successful outsourcing vendors are keenly aware of how these issues affect both the buyer prospect and their own operations.

Turning Vision into Reality

Corporations successful at outsourcing know to cover their bases with an experienced team of professionals. The guidelines listed next describe how the members of this governance team, in particular, the chief resource officer (CRO), turn the outsourcing vision into a business reality.

TIP The chief resource officer (CRO), a new position in buyer organizations, is described in greater detail later in Chapter 9.

- *Take a hands-on approach.* The onshore business leadership team must adopt a hands-on approach to guide their outsourcing project teams to deliver the expected business benefits. Shifting from an in-house to an outsourcing delivery model requires renewed commitment from internal senior management. The CRO will be charged with assembling a delivery team to ensure that offshore projects focus both on technical and service implementation and specific business benefit delivery.
- *Clearly communicate vendor expectations.* The CRO and his or her management team will set project priorities, ensure they are clearly understood by everyone, then monitor the process to ensure that changes in the project plan are well communicated to suppliers.
- *Ensure end-to-end business delivery.* Managing the business transition effectively requires planning. The CRO must aggressively manage offshore and onshore teams for the duration of the project in order to define the business deliverables and keep them relevant, track benefits, realize quick wins, and motivate critical stakeholders to remain committed. Managers should be aware that outsourcing projects are particularly susceptible to changes in budget, timing, and deliverables. Early anticipation of changes can drastically reduce the time and cost of addressing them.
- *Empower the CRO and outsourcing governance team.* Organizations need to maintain a high level of focus throughout the outsourcing life cycle to alleviate problems and avoid major financial and operational impacts to their core mission. Senior management must empower the governance team so that they can operate effectively and independently.
- *Seek the quick win.* Companies should not hesitate to demand early benefits delivery from outsource vendors, to prove the feasibility and sustainability of service (particularly if the vendor is new to the outsourcing business). Specific benefits must be aligned to each

requirement, and a benefits-realization plan must be developed that is linked to implementation milestones.

- *Account for geographic, cultural, and time differences.* Perhaps one of the greatest challenges of successfully managing outsourcing projects is coping with differences of language, culture, and geography (see Figure 3.2). Good communication is critical to the success of any outsourcing project, but it becomes even more so when working with offshore vendors. The buying organization must be cognizant of the cultural differences that might affect, for example, how directions are interpreted, problems are resolved, and assignments are delegated. It's the responsibility of the buying management team to ensure that requirements of each project deliverable are well understood and that a

Figure 3.2
Factoring Geographic, Cultural, and Time Differences

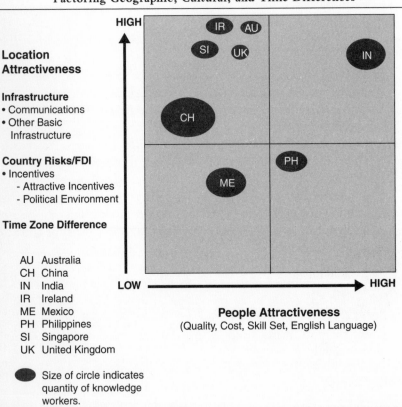

Source: Outsourcing Management Institute, Tampa FL, "Assessing Your Supplier and Buyer Differences," December 2004.

contact mechanism is in place to account for differences in time zones, should problems or questions arise. When documenting project requirements, reviewing technical specifications, or deciding on timetables, project managers should confirm that details are understood by all.

- *Perform due diligence.* Finding the right fit vendor involves evaluating not only price and capability, but also corporate culture. Like experience, a vendor's internal culture reflects its business philosophy in action. New vendor organizations are being launched daily, and if your company partners with one or more of these, it must ensure that they possess the technological expertise, as well as the business, organizational, and change-management skills necessary to deliver the promised outsourced business benefits.

TIP If you need help implementing any of these guidelines, we recommend that you engage a consultant to help you get started. Organizations such as FirstOutsourcing.com conduct buyer organization assessments, RFPs, selections, and contracting services with CROs and buyer professionals.

- *Define service level requirements.* Defining your company's service level requirements is a critical step in outsourcing. This includes describing the services and desired availability of services, along with support, performance, reliability, and security requirements.
- *Conduct benchmark audits.* CROs should conduct a survey in the form of a questionnaire to ascertain progress in SLAs. A listing of results for scoring (e.g., unsure, strongly disagree, disagree, agree, strongly agree) should be circulated for final determination of SLA ranking of importance and manager buy-in. Each clause of the SLA should address each service requirement respective to your needs.

Outsourcing buyers engage an outsourcing consultant firm or matching advisor, such as The Outsourcing Partnership (www.outsourcing partnership.com[†]), to ascertain that the best fit between buyers and vendors is attained. This includes vendor search and selection, buyer readiness assessments, and contractual relationship structures. Typical questions to ask that should help determine if you could use the assistance of a consultant include:

Do you have a clear frame of reference on the agreed services to be outsourced?

Is your company prepared to transition to outsourcing?

Do you have a clear frame of reference on the expected service levels from the prospective vendors?

Does your management team have an objective insight into the performance of operations under outsourcing?

Are you assured you will receive a high level of service quality?

Do you need help to establish a dialogue through independently and well-intended service level agreements, status reports, monitoring mechanisms, review meetings, and evaluations?

Have you established a set of responsibilities and procedures to prepare for outsourcing?

Have you a communications plan developed before you begin seeking outsourcing vendors to employees, vendors, and the community?

Have you assessed the true readiness of your organization?

Do you know with certainty that outsourcing is the best solution?

IMPLEMENTING STRATEGIC SOURCING

Over the past two decades, corporations have been engaging in major outsourcing initiatives to improve service while reducing costs, sometimes handing over the entire business process operation to a single service provider in comprehensive outsourcing arrangements. Twenty years later, these organizations have learned important lessons that are driving the adoption of what's called *strategic sourcing,* an outsourcing approach that focuses on long-term business needs and strengthens competitive advantage by selectively outsourcing specific functions. Certainly, one-time arrangements can achieve specific results, but the buyer organization does not maintain its focus on continuous improvement that generates maximum return on investment, which is possible in an ongoing relationship. Employing strategic sourcing makes it possible to leverage expertise and technology, with greater and continuous benefit the end result.

Strategic sourcing is defined as the *dynamic delivery of internal and external business-oriented resources and services to ensure that business objectives are met.* The objective is to more effectively align internal core functionalities with changing business needs, which is particularly important in light of the vital role that technology-enabled processes play today in the ongoing success of the enterprise.

Early in their outsourcing efforts, many pioneering managers found that the cost savings that initially justified comprehensive outsourcing quickly vanished if the business evolved and the service became ineffective. Sometimes, they found, they ended up paying *more* to retrofit. The valuable business principle these managers learned was: Alignment with the organization's business goals should be the top priority for all operations and all outsourcing.

These managers also learned three subsequent lessons for applying that principle to their organizations.

1. *Most outsourced services are not commodity services.* Cutting costs should not always be the primary consideration. Very few services meet the definition of a real commodity, since technology or service components become "decommoditized" when applied in unique ways to meet specific business goals. When this happens, they are woven into the fabric of the business and strengthen the company's competitive advantage. Chief resource officers, in particular, are now choosing best-of-breed providers for each outsourced function, over comprehensive outsourcers, to ensure customized, high-quality service across the board.

2. *Some functions are best performed in-house to retain competitive advantage.* In the quest to cut costs, some companies outsourced functions that they later discovered were critical to their ability to adapt to market changes and retain their competitive advantage.

3. *Outsourcing relationships must be flexible and evolve with the company's business.* Frequently, companies make the mistake of signing rigid, long-term outsourcing contracts only to find later that their business focus has changed markedly. The effect of those changes can result in additional charges that erase the original cost savings and sour the client-vendor relationship. Innovative partner-style agreements are quickly becoming the norm as companies recognize the need for improved risk sharing and benefit-reward models. The ability to modify the provision of service over the course of an agreement is sometimes more important to a company's long-term success than a well-crafted set of penalties for below-standard performance.

In sum, strategic sourcing is about leadership and superior management capabilities (see Figure 3.3). Creating an effective strategic sourcing approach requires a great deal of analysis and consideration.

Honing Strategic Sourcing in Your Organization

As you define your outsourcing strategy, never lose sight of both your current and future outsourcing business goals. Consider *every* sourcing decision

Figure 3.3
Developing a Customized Sourcing Strategy

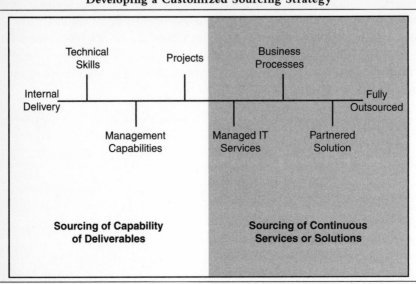

in the context of the entire enterprise and the marketplace. At a minimum, base your sourcing strategy on:

- Inevitable evolution within the marketplace, including both service providers and business competition, and
- Explicit business objectives, such as capabilities you plan to add.

Assess Internal Capability. Accurately determine your internal capability with a long- and short-term view of *make or buy;* that is, how much of the overall solution you want to handle internally versus externally. Typical symptoms of an inability to support expected innovation internally include poor results from previous outsourcing attempts, especially when they involved new solutions affecting multiple business units; relationships gone bad between internal business units; and negative experience with outsourcing contracts driven by cost reduction.

Research the Market. Research assiduously which of the available *external market capabilities* fit best with your outsourcing goals. The outsourced services market today is dynamic and, truth be told, somewhat chaotic. To find your way, your must clearly understand the capabilities of each service provider your company is considering aligning with, and how current and anticipated developments will affect their business needs. Do you see changes on the horizon in the service provider market? Are providers up to speed on emerging technologies? In short, the challenge is to match up externally available service capability with internal business goals, then balance that decision against the risk of change within the service capability, the business needs, or both. It's a fine balancing act, for sure, but it's one you must try to master.

Outsourcing Online

To help you do this research, here's an extensive listing of online sources to tap:

The Black Book of Outsourcing web site: www.theblackbookofoutsourcing.com

The Outsourcing Times: www.blogsource.org/blog

The Outsourcing Center: www.outsourcing-news.com

Offshore Outsourcing News: www.ecode.org.uk/news

Who's Outsourcing—News: www.whosoutsourcing.com/news.htm

Offshore Experts News: www.offshorexperts.com/index.cfm/fa/home.news

Outsourcing.org News: www.outsourcing.org/modules/news

Global Offshore Outsourcing News: www.machrotech.com/Offshore_Outsourcing/ Offshore_outsourcing_events.asp

Computer Weekly Outsourcing News: www.computerweekly.com/Issue333.htm

Offshore Outsourcing Center News: www.oocenter.com/news_corner/bin

PR.Com Outsourcing News: www.pr.com/outsourcing_news.html

ComputerWorld Outsourcing News: www.computerworld.com/managementtopics/outsourcing

Outsourcing Institute News: www.outsourcing.com

Human Resources Outsourcing News: www.hrotoday.com

CIO Outsourcing News: www.cio.com/research/outsourcing

Offshore IT News: www.offshore-guide.com

Offshore Outsourcing World: www.enterblog.com/index.html

The Outsourcing Weblog: www.outsourcing-weblog.com

Contact Center Digest: www.ccdigest.com

Shop Solutions.   Do you know which outsourcing model is best for your needs? You won't unless you shop around to see what's available. Creative sourcing approaches have evolved as organizations seek to avoid the problems of fully outsourced solutions without reverting to a fully in-house alternative.

This is mostly a make-or-buy decision, with internal delivery and fully outsourced services at opposite ends of a service/solution continuum, and your company may have outsourcing initiatives on different areas along this continuum. For example, in general you may use internal technical staff, but require outside expertise in a new-to-market technology. On the other hand, you may outsource all your order processing and invoicing functions, in the business processes area.

Model Governance.   Sourcing governance addresses capabilities needed to regulate and support multiple service providers, including management methods and processes, organizational roles and responsibilities, and service delivery rules and agreements. An effective governance model must cross traditional enterprise boundaries, to become not only an integrated part of the business, but also part of the internal functions and the external providers as well.

Strategic sourcing makes it possible to more effectively align your company's outsourcing vendors with its internal business structure. The challenge for business managers is to find the best set of interconnected service solutions that meet the strategic needs of their organization.

Maintaining Control

To assuage the risk inherent in any outsourcing project, you must maintain close ties with the vendors you have chosen. In short, assert your leadership over the outsourcing relationship in the form of the aforementioned chief resource officer, the CRO. It's also essential to implement robust metrics that will give your company objective feedback regarding the vendors' performance, and thereby help you reinforce the contracted arrangement with them.

We've repeatedly pointed out the potential benefits to be gained from outsourcing in terms of cost, service levels, and access to talent. We'd be remiss if we did not also point out a number of its pitfalls. We list these dangers not as a scare tactic, but as a cautionary note, to keep you on your managerial toes. Remember, your loss of control equates to ceding control to the provider(s).

- Once a process has been handed over to an outsider, it will be extremely difficult and costly to bring it back in-house.
- The initial contract may be very competitive, but the inevitable changes may cost significantly more.
- Severe cuts in staff can damage the morale of existing workers, sometimes irreparably. There is even the danger that your most talented and marketable staff will seek opportunities elsewhere.
- The time required to manage the contract may make it more expensive than initially calculated—even beyond its intended value-add.
- Product or service quality must be monitored consistently to avoid degradation due to cost-cutting attempts by providers.
- Providers have many clients; consequently, your company may not always be given the priority you feel it deserves and requires.
- Public response to major company layoffs may have a negative impact on your corporate image.

Simply put, the most effective way to maintain control is to establish from the get-go a clearly defined working relationship with your outsourcing service vendor—that is, *before* you sign on the dotted line. Here's how:

- *Clearly state your company's goals.* Outsourcing, as we've said over and over, is about more than reducing costs; it is about improving company focus, gaining access to world-class capabilities, freeing up resources, and much more. To select a service provider that is aligned with your company's goals and objectives, you must have established them in the assessment phase and be able to clearly describe them to provider candidates.
- *Understand the service provider's goals.* Remember, this is a reciprocal relationship. Providers have goals and objectives, too, to establish a center of excellence, grow internal staff, or enter a new market. It is important that you understand the service provider's goals if you expect the partnership to succeed.
- *Understand the nature of the deal.* Everyone involved in the effort must have full working knowledge of the service level goals, what the assets consist of, and how the pricing model operates.
- *Practice problem prevention.* If you only meet with the service provider when there is a problem, the relationship will be perceived as a problem, simple as that. Practicing preventive management means instituting a meeting structure that includes set-up procedures and processes to interface with the service provider on a regular basis.

Schedule daily, weekly, quarterly, and annual meetings that involve all levels of the company/service partnership. Doing so will encourage greater flexibility and tighter business alignment and enhance the outsourcing value proposition on a continuing basis.

- *Articulate the roles and responsibilities of both parties.* Develop a responsibility matrix early in the request for proposal (RFP) stage of the outsourcing process, and make sure the service provider understands those responsibilities. Don't forget to include them in the SLA and use them as a guide throughout the contractual time frame.

- *Set up an effective service level management program.* Assign service levels that reflect *real* business requirements, not technical achievements; and don't use these as a basis to micromanage the outsourced services. For example, it is important to have payroll processed on a timely basis, not that access to the payroll system be available. Developing a few critical, business-based service levels is much more effective than having hundreds that are destined to be ignored.

- *Launch a communications program that includes your company, your service provider, and your user base.* One of the most important managerial roles is to serve as a conduit of communication between the service provider and your company. This is not just about reporting when things go wrong; it is about continuing to find ways to improve your business through the outsourcing provider's expertise. Make your organization aware of opportunities where the service provider can offer additional benefits to the company, and how to communicate those benefits to your customers.

In sum, when it comes to relationship maintenance, remember: a typical outsourcing deal may take 9 to 12 months to finalize, but it will be in effect for a much longer period—as long as 5, 7, or even 10 years. A well-maintained relationship with the service provider will ensure the viability of the deal, as well as flexibility in meeting your company's changing business requirements.

Making an Informed Outsourcing Decision

How can you know whether your new outsourcing initiative is a going to benefit your organization? Well, there are no guarantees. But you can improve your chances of success by making informed outsourcing decisions.

Fortunately, sophisticated methodologies are available (with more coming all the time) to help executives answer this question and make much more insightful outsourcing decisions, whether they involve offshore or onshore resources, off-site or on-site solutions, or some combination thereof.

As we've said, in the past, executives based the decision to outsource their organization's noncore functions almost entirely on costs. Certainly, the ability of the outsourcing service provider to meet specified service levels played a role, as did other operational considerations, but cost was the key driver. Today, as you now know, the outsourcing picture is more complex. Many factors have emerged to complicate the decision-making process, including an aging workforce, the rapidly changing regulatory landscape, cross-border issues, new business models, and the patchwork-quilt image that many organizations develop after years of acquisitions and mergers. Compound these issues with the increasing number of outsourcing options, and the decision takes on both greater importance and risk.

Undefined problems lead to a frantic problem-solving approach that can, at best, be considered grasping at straws. CEOs often look to offshoring as the one-size-fits-all solution to their companies' problems, even those they don't understand. Not surprisingly, what sounds too good to be true usually turns out to be just that.

Informed outsourcing is what we call the approach we recommend for making outsourcing decisions. This approach advocates taking a holistic view of the outsourcing decision. It encourages organizations to inventory all of their information technologies and business processes carefully and then identify those that are central to the business in terms of core competencies and intellectual properties. During this process, companies are encouraged to peel away the layers and look for, among other issues, undocumented processes, undocumented specialized coding, regulatory sensitivity, and upgrade frequency. Applications affected by such issues are likely to be poor outsourcing candidates. Through this process, decision makers can form a clearer picture of their application portfolio and begin to identify those that are best candidates for outsourcing.

By understanding the needs of the organization and both its readiness and willingness to outsource, the choice of outsourcing model becomes clearer. This thorough approach pays many dividends. Not only does it help companies understand the total scope of cost savings and operational improvements available to them through outsourcing, it also helps them pick the best outsourcing candidates and the best outsourcing model for each candidate, while avoiding those that might prove to be problems, either immediately or later on.

Sourcing models vary, so which is the best solution for your specific needs? Creative sourcing approaches have evolved as buyer and vendor organizations seek to avoid the problems of fully outsourced solutions without reverting to a fully in-sourced alternative. Buyers of outsourcing have been shy of fully outsourcing a divisional functionality in fear that the vendor relationship might terminate and send the buyer in an organizational downspin. This fear has developed into a make-or-buy decision, with internal delivery and fully outsourced services at opposite ends of a service/solution continuum to retain some service control. Models have developed as outsourcing ideas have grown with the upsurge of vendors and buyers.

A company may have outsourcing initiatives that fit on different areas of this continuum. For example, it may use staff augmentation, which fits under technical skills, when it wants to retain ownership of the effort but needs expertise in a particular technology, still seeking the security of part ownership. Alternatively, it may outsource its order processing and invoicing functions, which are on the opposite end under business processes. Some companies outsource all their human resource functions except recruiting, while others only outsource recruiting.

Customization in the outsourcing industry is standard operating procedure. If a vendor attempts to sell you on the model you best fit into, dig deeper to determine if they are the right vendor for you or involve an independent vendor/buyer matching service such as The Outsourcing Partnership (www.outsourcingpartnership.com[†]). Models in the outsourcing business are rarely practical except in generic, minimally tangential services such as payroll processing.

Doing the Paperwork

To take the informed approach, you must become informed, and that requires doing your homework—developing the plans and doing the number crunching. To that end, here we list documents and tasks we strongly recommend that you complete. They may appear daunting, but rest assured, if you persevere, you will come away with a better understanding of the importance of each of these elements and why you need to incorporate them into your outsourcing assessment. (Note the important role the outsourcing project manager plays throughout.)

- *Charter.* This document is created by the assigned outsourcing project leader. It describes the outsourcing project purpose and expected outcomes.

- *Cost benefits analysis.* This, too, is created by the outsourcing project leader, but with stakeholder input. Its purpose is to determine whether the outsourcing project will be financially beneficial to the organization.
- *Assumptions and constraints.* This document is generated by the outsourcing project team, with stakeholder input. It describes the outsourcing assumptions and organizational constraints, such as budget, implementation time frames, available staff, geographic locations, and internal resistance to outsourcing.
- *Outsourcing project scope statement.* Written by the outsourcing project manager and signed by the CRO, with project team and stakeholder input, the scope statement defines and documents the outsourcing project deliverables.
- *Critical success factors.* This list defines what must be achieved to deem the outsourcing project as successful to your organization. (*Note:* This can be included as part of the scope statement.)
- *Communications plan.* Originating with the outsourcing project manager, this plan describes the information needs of stakeholders and the project team and delineates how the information will be distributed among them.
- *Work breakdown structure (WBS).* Another document from the office of the outsourcing project manager, the WBS is formatted as a deliverables-oriented hierarchy that defines the work of the project.
- *Roles and responsibilities matrix.* Also the responsibility of the outsourcing project manager, this matrix ties roles and responsibilities of the outsourcing project team members with WBS elements.
- *Resources plan.* In this document, the outsourcing project manager identifies the physical and human resources needed to complete the outsourcing plan.
- *Procurement plan.* Depending on your organization, this plan will originate with the outsourcing project manager or the procurement team. It itemizes the resources and/or services to be purchased from the selected vendor or supplier.
- *Risk management plan.* This plan, created by the outsourcing project manager or risk analysis team, identifies and recommends steps for alleviating outsourcing risks.
- *Quality plan.* The outsourcing project manager or quality control team may be responsible for this plan, which describes how quality will be measured and, thus, assured.

- *Project schedule.* The outsourcing project manager generates this schedule to clearly delineate task dependencies, task durations, and milestones. It is used to determine the *critical path*.
- *Budget.* Created by the outsourcing project manager and approved by finance and budget management and/or CRO, the budget details targeted costs of the project.
- *Change management plan.* In this plan, the outsourcing project manager details how changes will be identified and managed.
- *Implementation checklist.* The outsourcing project manager prepares this checklist to track issues to be discussed at turnover to internal departments or the customer.
- *Feedback.* Feedback comes from the sponsor, stakeholders, end customer, and team members and is used to improve performance on future projects.

END-OF-CHAPTER REVIEW: STEPS TO LAUNCH

We've covered a lot of material in this chapter, so before we move on to Chapter 4, where we discuss how to assess costs, benefits, and risks for your outsourcing venture, we'll review the guidelines for ensuring an effective outsourcing initiative:

1. *Identify your core processes.* The first step is to determine your company's core competencies and customer values. Be able to answer these questions: Who are our customers? What do they really need? What is the product/service/expertise we bring to them? Are they willing to pay premium prices for it? What is a support function versus a primary function?
2. *Evaluate noncore activities for outsourcing.* In this step you consider which noncore activities are candidates for outsourcing. For this, we recommend using a sequential self-diagnostic similar to this one:
   - Are we sure we want to produce the good or service internally for the long run? If so, are we willing to make the back-up investments necessary to sustain a best-in-world position?
   - If yes, can we objectively evaluate inefficiencies at all levels? Can we maintain improvements? Can we maintain the operation while advancing our core business? Is it critical to defending our core business? Do we have commitment throughout the company? If not:

- Can we license technology or buy know-how that will enable us to be the best on a continuing basis? If not:
- Can we buy the item as an off-the-shelf product or service from a best-in-world supplier? Is this a viable long-term option as volume and complexity grow? If not:
- Can we establish a joint development project with a knowledgeable supplier that ultimately will give us the capability to excel at this activity? If not:
- Can we enter into a long-term development or purchase agreement that gives us a secure source of supply and a proprietary interest in knowledge or other property of vital interest to the supplier and us? If not:
- Can we acquire and manage a best-in-world supplier to our advantage? If not, can we set up a joint venture or partnership that avoids the shortcomings we see in each of the above? If so:
- Can we establish controls and incentives that reduce total transaction costs below those of producing the product/service internally?

3. *Research supplier candidates.* If the analysis points toward outsourcing one or more processes, the next step is to evaluate potential suppliers, being sure to cover these factors:
   - *Skills base.* What is the scope of the supplier's services? What are the skill and experience levels of the supplier's management team? Does the provider have administrative skills as well as operational expertise to manage our processes more effectively?
   - *Experience.* Is the supplier experienced in outsourcing work of similar duration, complexity, technical scope, and geographic extent? Are reliable references available?
   - *Controls.* What reporting and control mechanisms does the supplier use? Can reports be customized? Are back-up plans in place to protect data?
   - *Geographic scope.* Is on-site support needed? If so, does the supplier, including its subcontractors and partners, have staff in place? Or is the provider willing to set up and manage a location near you, given sufficient volume to justify the expense? (This could reduce cost savings.) Is the outsourcer prepared to handle disaster contingencies?
   - *Price.* What is the true cost of outsourcing particular functions compared to the true cost of continuing to retain those functions internally. (Be sure to look at the long term and include "fixed" cost components like facilities and management as savings.)

- *People.* What arrangements or recommendations will be made for current staff (incumbents in the buyer company)? What is the tone and tenor of the relationship with outsourcer? Do they have your business problem in hand? Can they/will they customize the solution to your needs, or are they trying to sell you an off-the-shelf answer?

4. *Set relationship driver goals.* Once you and your project team have selected an outsourcing partner, the parties establish mutual goals and strategies for outsourcing that will drive the relationship.

5. *Go to contract.* Next a contract is written and negotiated, spelling out goals, benchmarks, incentives, monitoring, and communication procedures, costs, and so on.

6. *Manage the transition.* The last step in an outsourcing project launch is to manage change in the buyer/client company. This important and difficult step covers human resources issues, transfer of assets to the supplier, and procedures for monitoring the outsourced activity. Personnel management can be particularly challenging. Often driven from the top down, outsourcing is usually dreaded by lower-level managers, who fear losing their jobs. As we've pointed out previously, key employees may in fact benefit from the decision to outsource. They may be retained to manage and monitor the outsourcing supplier, hence they will gain new knowledge and skills. Others may be hired by the supplier and have the chance to work for a world-class company focused solely on their area of expertise, potentially giving them even greater opportunity for career training, job security, and advancement.

Outsourcing has revolutionized business by shifting the focus from managing resources to delivering results. Outsourcing is, plain and simple, a powerful strategic weapon. According to the Outsourcing Management Institute, 75 percent of the projected increase in outsourcing expenditures represents current users expanding into new functional areas.[1]

Note

1. Outsourcing Management Institute, "2004: The Year in Outsourcing," January 2005.

CHAPTER 4

ASSESSING COST, BENEFIT, AND RISK FOR YOUR OUTSOURCING VENTURE

When faced with the choice between changing and proving there's no need to do so, most people get busy on the proof.

—John K. Galbraith

A manager's outsourcing evaluation will take a disciplined approach, from planning through negotiation and implementation, to include ongoing management of the relationship. The six-step process—planning, analysis, and design—comprising this approach is similar to that of the typical project management development process. It is as follows:

1. Conduct the feasibility study.
2. Do a detailed analysis of requirements.
3. Define the parameters of the vendor relationship.
4. Build and evolve the relationship.
5. Monitor the relationship.
6. Conclude the relationship (either renew it in a succeeding contract or terminate).

CONDUCT THE FEASIBILITY STUDY

The outsourcing feasibility study is composed of a series of four screens through which every outsourcing idea should pass before you conduct a more detailed evaluation.

Core Competency Screen

Based on what we've discussed in the first three chapters, you won't be surprised that this is the first screen. To repeat what we've admonished earlier, if the function or functions under consideration for outsourcing are central to the organization's competitive success, those core functions are not strong candidates. That said, do not confuse a critical function with a core competency; the former can be outsourced to a best-in-class provider.

Critical versus core: Many operations are critical to a business's operations but do not represent a differentiating competitive capability; that is, they are not core competencies. A classic example is payroll. Processing payroll accurately and timely is critical to the success of any organization, but is a core competency of very few organizations—mainly those that provide this service to other companies as their business.

Cost of Control Screen

The second feasibility screen is the cost of controlling a vendor. Service providers are controlled through governance mechanisms that are part and parcel of the vendor relationship. The contract is a critical part of control and of the relationship. If complete contracts can't be written to anticipate all future contingencies, other means will be needed to control the vendor, to guarantee that the outsourced work will be successfully completed.

Goals Screen

If you do not know what you are trying to accomplish, any alternative can look good or bad. Companies that rush into outsourcing without fully understanding what they hope to gain soon find themselves mired in a contractual battle and, worse, without the improved services they signed on for. As discussed in an earlier chapter, sensible reasons to consider outsourcing are both strategic and tactical. Outsourcing is never a way to "wash management's hands" of a poorly managed, misunderstood function. Understand the costs, problems, and potential of a function before deciding whether to outsource it.

Scope Screen

Outsourcing can be divided into two general categories: *total* and *selective*. Total outsourcing involves contracting out 80 percent or more of the function. Selective outsourcing involves outsourcing a few functions that total less than 80 percent of the whole. Methods for identifying functions that might be selectively outsourced include opportunistic, problem-focused approaches and more methodical planning approaches. There is a framework for determining the kind of vendor relationship most appropriate to various circumstances.

Outsourcing is not just a means of transforming fixed costs into variable costs—it is also a way to develop the business process itself. The scope of outsourcing varies, but benefits tend to be bigger, when the outsourced tasks or processes form an entity with internal synergies. Thus, the need for overhead is reduced and the entity provides interesting and versatile tasks for personnel. The key to success is preparation, and this of course also applies to outsourcing even more. When a company makes a strategic decision to outsource, either by complete or selective outsourcing, a process is initiated, the individual steps of which are comparable to intensive, project management. Prior to such a major decision, all advantages and disadvantages as well as savings and benefits are considered. Subsequently, a detailed evaluation is performed before any selection is made.

Possible vendor relationships run the gamut from those for which complete contracts can be written (market relationships) to those that can't depend on complete contracts or even a single contract (partnerships). Some buyer organizations feel as if they cannot place all their "eggs in one basket." From the vendor perspective, a single contract, no matter how financially sizable is a risky proposition to base the sustenance of a vendor company. Intermediate contracts have some aspects of both market relationships and a partnership, hence, occupy the middle of the outsourcing relationship spectrum.

DO A DETAILED ANALYSIS OF REQUIREMENTS

Outsourcing should not be undertaken when the costs of governance are too high relative to the benefits. But if the outsourcing idea passes these initial screens, planning can proceed to a detailed outsourcing evaluation. First in the outsourcing evaluation process, the people involved must be identified: Who will lead the effort? Who will perform the analysis? Who, ultimately, will make the decisions? Of course, the answers to these questions depend to a great extent on what is to be outsourced and the circumstances surrounding the outsourcing decision.

The Team

The most successful outsourcing efforts have an executive sponsor or "champion"; and in cases that involve organizational politics, it is absolutely critical. Certainly, for larger outsourcing initiatives, top management must play a role. For smaller initiatives, middle-level managers might do the "heavy lifting" with the support of senior management. In all cases, the outsourcing team usually will benefit from a mix of managerial and technical talent, as well as representatives from user areas whose services will be directly impacted by outsourcing. User perspectives and objectives are essential for setting scope and assessing risks.

Though the size of the team will depend on the scope and size of the project, in general smaller teams are more effective, especially during the planning phase; then expanded when analysis begins. Teams with full-time members are typically more focused and effective than those composed of people who work part-time. That said, full-time allocation may make sense only for large outsourcing projects. Ideally, you should try to include members who are experienced in outsourcing, as they will bring insight to the issues and a practical viewpoint to cost and benefit estimates. In most cases, this will mean hiring an outside consultant, preferably an expert in outsourcing, who can advise and assist throughout the entire process.

Once the decision is made to proceed with the next phases of the outsourcing process, identify as early as feasible the people who will be responsible for oversight and management of the outsourcing arrangement and vendor relations, if and when the contract is signed. And be sure to involve these people in crafting the contract. This is important for two reasons:

1. There is no better way to understand the issues involved in outsourcing than to be involved in all aspects leading up to the decision.
2. Relationships start at the moment discussion begins. Being in on the ground floor leads to continuity in the relationship, which contributes to success.

DEFINE THE PARAMETERS OF THE VENDOR RELATIONSHIP

Before you begin this important task, recognize at the outset that no single company will be able to meet all your needs, so it is important to identify the key technical and management issues to find the best fit possible. Focus on these factors:

- Vision/mission of the company under evaluation
- Its balance sheets from previous years
- Client lists
- Infrastructure

Next perform due diligence, following this four-step process:

1. Examine accounts the company has handled.
2. Scrutinize the vendor's expertise and business strategy; ascertain whether the vendor is willing to collaborate as a team with your company to develop its strategy and facilitate knowledge transfer.
3. Analyze the firm's core technical competencies. All vendors will claim to support the development, integration, implementation, and maintenance of your project, but in practice, this is rarely possible. No single company can have an equal capability in all areas. If a vendor claims this, it's a red flag. Don't ignore it. Ask for references and call them.
4. Review the resources of the vendor. If at all possible, visit the vendor's site to do this. Check the hardware, software, network, and communications. Evaluate the vendor's infrastructure.

PRIORITIZING OUTSOURCING ISSUES

To help you focus your team we suggest you pass out these checklists, which ask you to identify your top three reasons for outsourcing, success factors, vendor requirements, and problems associated with the outsourcing.

What Are Your Three Primary Reasons for Outsourcing?
- Improve company focus
- Gain access to world-class capabilities
- Accelerate re-engineering benefits
- Transfer assets
- Share risks
- Make capital funds available
- Get cash infusion
- Reduce time to market
- Reduce and control operating costs
- Gain access to resources not available internally
- Transfer responsibility of function that is difficult to manage or out of control
- Take advantage of offshore capabilities

**What Are the Three Most Important Factors for
Successful Outsourcing?**

- The right vendor
- A properly structured contract
- Ongoing management of relationships
- Understanding your firm's goals and objectives
- Senior executive support and involvement
- Cultural compatibility
- Careful attention to personnel issues
- A strategic vision and plan
- Near-term financial justification
- Access to outside expertise
- Open communication with affected individuals and groups
- Proper mix of retained "in-house" staff and outsourced operations

**What Are the Three Most Important Factors in
Electing an Outsourcing Vendor?**

- Flexible contract terms
- Existing relationship
- Location
- Price
- References/reputation
- Scope of resources
- Commitment to quality
- Cultural match
- Additional value-added capability

**Which Three Areas Are the Most Challenging for Your
Organization?**

- Time
- Expertise
- Bandwidth
- Budget
- Access to service providers

MEASURING PERFORMANCE

Whether you're using internal or external resources, measuring their value is crucial to the success of any project. In the case of an outsourcing effort, quantifying the costs of providing services in-house versus going outside sets a level playing field for making the most well-informed cost comparison possible. Measures also quantify the capability of both the internal and the external resources to meet end-user needs. Some measurement starting points are:

- Service levels
- Price/performance benchmarks
- Customer satisfaction surveys
- Quantify expectations
- Inventory in-house skills
- Infrastructure and tool assessments
- Opportunities for improvement

The right measurements are essential for evaluating options available to your company, so analyze the measures for strengths and weaknesses, and evaluate options. When measuring end-user need or effectiveness, these measures must be accurate and verifiable. Flourishing outsourcing vendors use metrics and incentives in a whole new way to manage transformational relationships successfully. Performance-based or outcome-based measurements, have replaced work-based measurements in the newest agreements between savvy vendors and veteran outsourcing buyer companies. First-time outsourcing buyers or vendors entering the marketplace may be surprised by the sophistication among the veterans.

Here are some important tips. Define objectives at the beginning to align for skillful victories. Many buyers learned the hard way that they had to understand their own objectives before they could invite an outsourcer to the party. Communicating your goals broadly throughout the organization helps set clear expectations. Many new outsourcing buyers sign their outsourcing contracts long before they identify the metrics they will use to manage vendor performance. Executives will find that the outsourcing relationship and processes will go much more smoothly if measurements are clarified and in place sooner.

Choose fewer service level measurements with higher stakes. Outsourcing veterans have significantly tapered the number of measures they track over time and increased the complementary rewards and penalties in order to improve focus, diminish organizational demands, and enhance joint relationships. The first metrics to drop are those measurements that prove too complex, labor intensive, and time-consuming to measure.

Transfer from participation measurements to outcome-based metrics where feasible. Instead of counting how many hours it took to complete a project, a printing firm asked its outsourcer, to count how many orders it completed each hour. This small change in the way they kept score helped focus the vendor on speeding up throughput.

Outsourcing Cost-Benefit Analysis

Doing a cost-benefit analysis enables decision makers to account for the full spectrum of budgetary issues that comprise any outsourcing project. Using both quantitative and qualitative measures, the analysis helps to prove, or disprove, most effectively that an outsourcing project supports corporate goals and outcomes. A simple cost comparison will not reveal all the benefits or costs.

Even when an outsourcing solution appears to be more costly or time-consuming, a comprehensive cost-benefit analysis may prove it to be the best solution in the long run, to meet the needs of your business. Only a fully documented, comprehensive cost-benefit analysis can justify this decision.

As you proceed with your cost-benefit analysis, keep these points in mind:

- Benefits are as important as costs. Even if an option may be quantifiably more expensive, it may still be the most effective choice for meeting corporate needs.
- An outsourcing project will be difficult to justify or support if the project lacks specific, measurable goals and consistent, reliable information about the real costs and benefits of the project.

TIP It is not possible here to provide a simple criteria template for an outsourcing versus insourcing cost-benefit analysis, because each business manager must determine the criteria, priorities, and weights for each project depending on its individual circumstances. The criteria described here are highlighted as important concerns that all internal/external resource decisions should consider.

SEEING UNSEEN COSTS

Many times costs are not explicitly seen, but are accounted for in the fees charged by the vendor. Recognizing these embedded costs is essential to making a reliable comparison between options. The table that follows will help you do that.

Quantitative Direct Costs	Insourcing Consideration?	Outsourcing Consideration?
Personnel costs	Yes	Yes
Fringe benefits	Yes	Yes—embedded in contract
Materials/supplies	Yes	Yes
Maintenance/licenses	Yes	Yes
Training	Yes	Yes
Contracts	Yes	Yes
Telecommunications	Yes	Yes
New equipment costs	Yes	Yes
New software costs	Yes	Yes
Rent	Yes	Yes
Utilities	Yes	Yes
Travel	Yes	Yes—may be embedded in contract

Quantitative Direct Benefits	Insourcing Consideration?	Outsourcing Consideration?
Dollar value of staff time saved	Yes	Yes
Dollar value of new operating efficiencies (e.g., number of additional licenses to be processed)	Yes	Yes—may be evaluated on the basis of different technical solutions proposed by internal or external resources

Quantitative Indirect Costs	Insourcing Consideration?	Outsourcing Consideration?
Administrative overhead	Yes	Yes—embedded in contract
Divisional overhead	Yes	Yes—in some cases

(Continued)

Quantitative Indirect Benefits	Insourcing Consideration?	Outsourcing Consideration?
Costs to other agencies or citizens	Yes	Yes—this is a project cost
Contract administration costs	No	Yes—this will include internal resources and time
Service improvements to citizens	Yes	Yes
Support of architectures	Yes	Yes
Flexibility of solution	Yes	Yes
Qualitative Project Benefits and Costs	Insourcing Consideration?	Outsourcing Consideration?
Availability	Yes	Yes
Quality of service	Yes	Yes
Impact on staff, other agencies, citizens	Yes	Yes
Legal environment	Yes	Yes
Security	Yes	Yes
Sensitivity	Yes	Yes
Planning time	Yes	Yes
Project time	Yes	Yes
Operational risk	Yes	Yes
Technology risk	Yes	Yes
Relationship risk	Yes	Yes

Specific Outsourcing Cost-Benefit Criteria

Begin the analysis with statements regarding the type of outsourcing under consideration (i.e., *transitional or sectional*) and the main project objectives. Costs and benefits will follow from the analysis because each item is identified and weighted in light of these statements. In this section, we'll examine quantitative and qualitative outsourcing considerations.

Quantitative Outsourcing Considerations.   In spite of our admonition that no outsourcing decision should be based entirely—or even primarily—on cost reduction, it remains one of the primary drivers for management interest in outsourcing. But cost savings are not always apparent in outsourcing arrangements, depending on the reasons behind the outsourcing and the type of outsourcing used. For example, data center consolidation via outsourcing has provided some cost savings, whereas applications development and systems integration projects, which tend to rely more heavily on the need for expertise and resources, can be just as expensive, if not more so, than the use of internal resources.

Cost avoidance is another consideration—avoiding hiring additional resources to support a product line, division, or application once it is in production; avoiding significant investments in fast-changing technologies; avoiding loss of funding by meeting deliverables deadlines. Identify ongoing operational costs that may be avoided by outsourcing in your firm. Like cost savings, cost avoidances are dependent on the reason behind the outsourcing and the type of outsourcing used. And as with cost savings, cost avoidance should not be used as the sole justification for making a resource decision; it can, however, be considered as a potential benefit that may result from the decision.

Finally, when comparing the costs of using external or internal human resources, don't neglect to include corporate management costs in both cases. Even if a vendor will be the "project manager," someone at your firm must still be involved, to ensure that the project meets the needs of your business and that communication is ongoing between your firm and the vendor. Table 4.1 lists typical quantitative outsourcing costs and how to assess them.

Qualitative Considerations of Outsourcing.   The three primary qualitative outsourcing considerations are, as you might expect, time, risk, and staffing. The time available to complete the project is an essential factor in your decision about which type of resources you will use. Current corporate resources may not be able to meet the project deadlines because of other responsibilities, resource shortages, or lack of needed skills. These facts will obviously impact the cost of the project. Although it may be more cost-effective to complete a project with internal resources, the time line may prevent that from happening.

Risk identification is an essential part of the analysis process. Risk affects priorities and costs and benefits because of its potential impact on

Table 4.1
Typical Outsourcing Costs

Type of Dollar Costs	Assessment Criteria
Project	These are the costs for the life cycle of the outsourcing project. A careful detailing of external versus internal costs needs to occur here, to identify their full range on both sides and to obtain a cost comparison that measures the same criteria in the same way. Sample criteria would be labor, time, hardware, or software needed, and so on.
Management	Regardless whether a project uses internal or external staff, your company will still be responsible for managing the project. If using internal staff, it will include the cost of the project manager. If using external staff, it will include the cost of your corporate managers who will be required to oversee the contract.
Postproject	Once the project has been completed, there will be maintenance and enhancement costs. Either internal or external staff may do this, but if an external vendor has worked on the project, you must have a knowledge transfer plan in place so that corporate staff can maintain the system.

project success. When outsourcing all or part of a project, the contract must clearly state your company's important risk factors in order to avoid having a completed project that does not meet the needs of your business. Here, too, internal and external assessments regarding skill levels and the successful outcomes of the project will determine which factors provide risk elements in the project staffing selection. Table 4.2 points out the main risk areas to buyers of outsourcing solutions.

The risk criterion is, in sum, a fourfold process:

1. Identify.
2. Understand.
3. Prioritize.
4. Address.

Staffing.   It hardly need be said that human resources issues are an important consideration in this cost-benefit analysis. The need to avoid pressuring already overworked staff may be an important consideration in the decision process. Alternatively, it may be important strategically for corporate staff to be involved in a particular process because of their impact

Table 4.2
Main Areas of Outsourcing—Buyer Risk

Risk Type	Considerations
Operational	The ability to meet project deadlines, outcomes, and required skills; to respond to changes in legislation, mission, and service definitions; balance between what the organization needs and what the vendor can deliver. Top-down support from executive management and end-user buy-in are critical success factors.
Technology	The ability of the project to respond to technology changes or new technologies; matching the project to the current technical architecture for your company.
Relationship	When comparing external resource costs to internal resource costs, recognize the relationship risks that exist when external resources are chosen over internal resources. These risks include: expectations on service delivery; unexpected costs of outsourcing arrangements; vendor responsiveness to the need for improvements; vendor failure to deliver products on time; and impact on staff—job satisfaction, morale, workload.

on total business service delivery. Understanding key staffing questions will enable you to identify previously unconsidered costs or benefits. Table 4.3 will help you do that.

GETTING TO THE BOTTOM LINE

As demonstrated, the cost-benefit analysis requires identifying, weighing, and evaluating all costs and benefits associated with an outsourcing project. Those presented here should be regarded only as starting points for criteria identification. After the analysis is completed, total and compare all of the information gathered. If the costs outweigh the benefits for outsourcing, insourcing is the preferred option, and vice versa. If the analysis reveals that quantitative measures in hard-dollar costs show outsourcing to be more expensive, but qualitative reasons indicate it to be necessary, then you now have the tools necessary to justify the decision.

Table 4.3
Outsourcing Staffing Issues

Issue	Significance
Internal human resources	Identify current workloads. Is current personnel able to perform additional duties? What are the corporate priorities and timelines? Identify staff interest in the jobs that they perform. Are employees motivated and interested in their jobs? Would your company benefit from using existing staff on new projects that require innovation? Consider the impact on existing staff if an external vendor were procured. Determine at the beginning which internal members will be affected and plan for what will happen to them—will they be reassigned, transferred to the vendor, or terminated? What will the impact be on staff morale/retention? Identify the skill sets required for vendor management in an outsourcing arrangement. Do internal employees have the necessary expertise? If not, should they acquire them? If so, are those people free to devote their time to the project?
External human resources	What are the capabilities of external human resources? Ask for and evaluate resumes. Are the people necessary for the project currently available, and will they be available for the life of the contract? How can you ensure that the people you want will be permanently assigned to your project? Because of the competitive market for skills and services, vendors are also experiencing staff turnover. What will the impact of vendor staff turnover mean for your project's success? Do vendor personnel have the necessary qualities for your company—for example, same work hours, culture, and initiative?
Contingency planning	Changes will occur during the course of the project. If an external vendor is used, the outsourcing contract will end at some point. Change control procedures must be in place to monitor, track, and manage changes, as well as their impact to the contract. It's important to understand transition difficulties with outsourcing, whether evaluating a vendor-managed environment, managing an effort to take the service back in-house, or changing from one vendor/methodology to another. Know which staffing levels and skill sets will be required to implement such changes.

Table 4.3 *Continued*

Issue	Significance
Access to expertise	Gaining access to expertise that does not exist in-house is a common reason to outsource, especially when taken in the context of budget/time constraints. One argument against this is that assigning internal staff to develop new projects and learn new skills may increase their morale and improve staff retention as employees are continually challenged and given new opportunities. This does, however, require that timelines and training funds are able to support this option. Choosing to use internal human resources for a new project, and then outsourcing existing services, may lower operating costs and ensure a more efficient and successful outsourcing contract. This is because the internal service is so well-known that it is easy to measure and quantify. It is then much easier to determine the success of the vendor in meeting the needs of the company. It is also important to ensure that you have a knowledge transfer plan in place, to avoid becoming dependent on one vendor for continued operation of the system.

CHAPTER 5

OUTSOURCING OPTIONS

Outsourcing can best be viewed as a cycle, beginning with the decision-making process, followed by managing the contract, then evaluating the results, and, finally, reexamining the outsourcing contract, at which point you either renew the contract or select again from available alternatives. But to take that initial step, deciding, you need to be aware of all your options, current and emerging. This chapter introduces you to all that's available now via outsourcing and what you can expect to see in the very near future.

OUTSOURCING OPTIONS TODAY

To get a handle on the state of outsourcing today, look at Figure 5.1, which shows what's being outsourced today and Figure 5.2, which divides up the

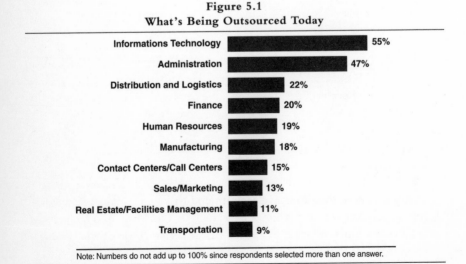

Figure 5.1
What's Being Outsourced Today

Informations Technology	55%
Administration	47%
Distribution and Logistics	22%
Finance	20%
Human Resources	19%
Manufacturing	18%
Contact Centers/Call Centers	15%
Sales/Marketing	13%
Real Estate/Facilities Management	11%
Transportation	9%

Note: Numbers do not add up to 100% since respondents selected more than one answer.

Figure 5.2
Common BPO Categories

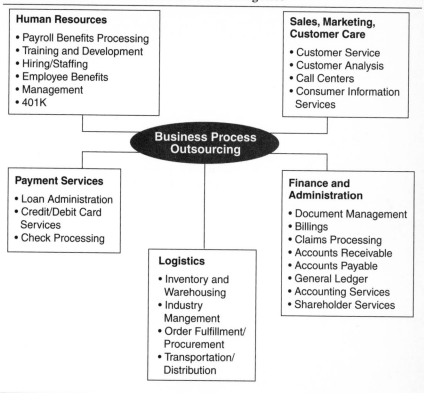

Source: Gartner Dataquest Research: Outsourcing Worldwide—Forecast Database, August 18, 2004.

business process outsourcing (BPO) arena into the most common segments. Worldwide Forecast Database provides historical data as well as five-year forecasts for IT outsourcing, business process outsourcing (BPO), and the discrete method of purchase by service line, region, and country. Now that you have an idea where things stand today, we'll take a look at the future of outsourcing.

TIP Few vendor organizations are yet well established in these emerging areas, therefore, we recommend that you contact an objective vendor/buyer brokering service such as Outsourcing Providers, Inc. (www.outsourcingproviders.com) for the information you'll need to make the right decision for your company.

IT'S A STATE-BY-STATE ISSUE

The nuances of the laws can be confusing, as individual U.S. states' lawmakers attempt to develop and pass legislation prohibiting offshore outsourcing. But it's a complicated proposition.

Muddying the issue further, some states are signatories to the World Trade Organization, so they can't discriminate on larger-dollar-value contracts. An outright ban on offshore contracts would be a violation of the agreement (contracts with value over $477,000).

States also have obligations under the North American Free Trade Agreement (NAFTA), which may preclude outright bans on outsourcing to Mexico and Canada.

Stuart Anderson, executive director of the National Foundation for American Policy, a nonprofit group that does research on trade and immigration issues, contends that states don't have the legal right under the Constitution to ban offshore outsourcing.

Despite knee-jerk reactions by many state officials to restrict offshore outsourcing—and, in some cases, take back or renegotiate contracts—most legislators have taken a moderate approach, leaving the door open for options.

Laws Passed

Alabama: Encourages use of in-state professional services.

Indiana: Preference for in-state companies in that their pricing can be 1 percent to 5 percent above outsiders'.

Massachusetts: Prohibits outsourcing of any functions that state employees currently perform.

Tennessee: Preference for in-state companies offering data-entry and call-center services.

Legislation under Debate or Pending

Would ban overseas work: **Alabama, Arizona, California, Colorado, Connecticut, Georgia, Hawaii, Illinois, Indiana, Iowa, Kansas, Kentucky, Louisiana, Maryland, Michigan, Mississippi, Missouri, Nebraska, New Jersey, New Mexico, New York, North Carolina, Ohio, Rhode Island, South Carolina, South Dakota, Vermont, Virginia, Washington, Wisconsin.**

Delaware: Companies would have to disclose that work would be done offshore; 15 percent preference for U.S.-based work.

Florida: In-state residence would be required to win state contracts.

Idaho: State residents would get preference for state jobs.

Pennsylvania: Investigation of offshore contracting would be launched.

West Virginia: Restrictions would be placed on the use of call centers, including a seven-year ban on the state using contractors whose outsourcing of work overseas would result in 100 or more people losing their jobs.

Executive Orders

Arizona: Prohibits new state contracts that would send work overseas.

Florida: Mandates on investigation of the impact of offshore outsourcing.

Michigan: Provides that state funds not be used as incentives or encouragement for companies to go offshore.

Minnesota: State contracts must be given to vendor providing "best value," which takes into account where work is to be performed.

Missouri: No state contracts will be given to companies that plan to have offshore workers.

Data source: National Foundation for American Policy, National Conference of State Legislatures, individual states reporting, September 2004.

EMERGING OUTSOURCING OPPORTUNITIES

It need not be said that advances in technology are having a major impact on many areas of outsourcing. One more recent and widely reported effect is the movement of more white-collar jobs offshore, in particular in the fields of medicine, government, pharmaceuticals, financial services, healthcare, and sales. In this section, we touch on what's happening in these areas. And at the end of the chapter, you'll find an extensive listing of ideas and projects applicable to outsourcing.

Case Study: Outsourcing in Practice

In an effort to curb runaway costs, Dr. Mike Doyle, a Tampa, Florida, physician, began to explore the possibility of outsourcing his traditional office procedures—that is, hiring service bureaus to perform office procedures currently being done by in-house personnel, including patient billing. Initially, Dr. Doyle was reluctant to let a third party assume responsibility for his patient billing, for fear of losing control over receivables. The truth is, most practitioners have already lost control due to the bureaucratic intricacies of co-pays, disallowances, chargebacks, deductibles, insurance company holdbacks, and duplicate payments.

Dr. Doyle's practice is like many medical practitioners turning to outsourcing to save money. The most popular areas for this type of outsourcing are payroll, patient billing, administration of employee benefits, and maintenance services. Medical outsourcing service bureaus can perform these functions more efficiently and economically because they are specialists in these areas.

Most medical billing services invoice within 24 to 48 hours of receiving the documents from the practitioner, therefore, cash flow should not be impaired. Medical billing services, Dr. Doyle also learned, were more familiar with coding than his own billing department and have more sophisticated hardware and software than the typical physician's office because of the volume of transactions they handle. For Doyle's office to remain up to date technologically, in-house staff would have to be retrained regularly and their computers upgraded constantly, with the practitioner paying for all the hardware and software updates, as well as the expensive "learning curve." So rather than an outsourced service bureau being more costly than doing the work in-house, Dr. Doyle learned the opposite was true. A cost-benefit analysis illustrates how this was possible.

Assume that a medical practice is billing $1,000,000 per year and needs three billing clerks to handle this level of activity. Outsourcing medical service bureaus traditionally charge 5 to 9 percent of gross billings for this kind of service. So the cost of billing for this practice would range between $50,000 and $90,000. If one billing clerk earns between $22,000 and $25,000 annually, three would cost the practice between $66,000 and $75,000. This figure represents the base cost of payroll. Payroll taxes, which include the employer's share of Social Security and federal and state unemployment taxes, add approximately 10 percent to that. Fringe benefits, including pension and profit sharing plans, medical insurance, disability insurance, educational reimbursement, sick pay, and personal time off, add another 10 to 30 percent to payroll costs. In sum, the cost of payroll could jump to a range of $79,000 to $105,000 when these additional charges are added.

Dr. Doyle was able to eliminate other expenses as well. In-house billing clerks need space in which to work. Assume the billing clerks occupy 150 square feet of space and that Doyle was renting space for $15 per square foot, meaning he was paying an additional rent of $2,250 for those employees. This is just the base cost. Usually there are add-ons for increases in property taxes and maintenance services. Still other costs include utilities and office supplies. Postage is another expense commonly overlooked. Some service bureaus include this in the cost.

By outsourcing, Dr. Doyle can concentrate on his patients, not his office billing processes.

Medicine

In a groundbreaking example of this process, Wipro Technologies of India has developed a model for clinical patient processing. Their radiologists examine scans of U.S. patients. The Indian doctors are held to the established Western standards of the American College of Radiology, Joint Commission of Accreditation of Health Care Organizations, the National Committee for Quality Assurance in determining the results of the scans. (The U.S. facilities, i.e., hospitals buying radiology outsourcing from India must assume the oversight accountability of these physicians overseas via those standards.) The data from the scans are quickly shipped back to the care facilities in the United States.

The benefit of this type of outsourcing is reduced healthcare costs, improved response times, and potentially an overall enhanced level of care. In America, similar processes have been underway in prisons and rural locations, where, for instance, X-rays are taken and "telemedicined" to urban physicians to interpret. The case study on pages 92–93 details how this works for one physician.

Sales Forces

Sales force outsourcing has become a rapidly growing area within the overall business process outsourcing market, along with the explosive growth of the virtual company and the Internet. Outsourcing sales is an excellent strategy when first emerging into a market or introducing a new product line to a large territory, and distributors and small manufacturers alike have been taking advantage of it. Distributors have established sales forces and take on the representation of additional organizations to buyers. Distribution companies whose sales staffs represent multiple products (for example,

Fisher Scientific known to catalogue most every laboratory device, equipment, and supply known to be manufactured, can represent several manufacturers through one sales representative).

Government Services

Electronic governance, or e-governance, may be defined as delivery of government services and information to the public using electronic means. The private partner (outsourcer) brings in specialized IT skills and other resources to help the government, generally lacking in the knowledge of current and emerging IT technologies, to make the right choice of technology.

Project management services can be digitized to achieve time, cost, and other resource benefits. Private vendors generally work more efficiently and effectively for faster development of projects at a lower cost. Day-to-day hassles of running, maintaining, and managing systems can be left to the more specialized firm. Outsourcing also makes it possible to bypass mountains of inherent legacies of the government systems.

As with private enterprise, however, the most important advantage of outsourcing to government agencies is that it frees staff to concentrate on core competencies, thereby enhancing productivity.

Retail Services

Thanks to technology, geographic borders and time zones are no longer issues for retail enterprises competing for market share in the global economy. Outsourcing opportunities in these services will continue to grow as retailers increasingly focus in-house staff on core competencies.

Pharmaceutical Industry

From drug discovery to sales, the pharmaceutical industry needs new solutions. Utilizing information technology efficiently is a critical component for business success and gaining—and maintaining—a competitive edge. Outsourcing makes it possible for pharmaceutical companies (especially smaller ones) to take new drugs through clinical trials without investing in the infrastructure that was traditionally necessary.

Companies are primarily looking to India and other biotechnology-advanced countries to conduct collaborative research. Collaborative research outsourcing is destined to become the next big wave, after contract research, in outsourcing.

Financial Services

The opportunities for financial services outsourcers are growing at the fastest rate of all the areas. Financial enterprises are relying on outsourcing as part of their broader strategic sourcing plans to achieve their common goal of improving competitiveness while reducing costs. Financial Services outsourcing vendors, such as Ernst and Young, are experiencing the fast growth in opportunities. Buyers of financial services outsourcing are approaching the relationship with much more confidence with the stringent implementation of client information and system security procedures.

A recent study conducted by the Economist Intelligence Unit reported that approximately 30 percent of the companies researched outsource finance and accounting functions; two-thirds of those (65 percent) characterized the arrangement as successful (57 percent) or very successful (8 percent).[1]

Certainly, cost savings and increased productivity are key motivators for outsourcing for these companies, but the study also determined that finance and accounting is increasingly being treated as a catalyst for business transformation.

Healthcare Information

The healthcare provider sector is opening to the possibilities of business transformation through business process outsourcing. And rather than focusing on the bottom line alone, these providers are realizing that savings from reduced operating costs can be redirected to investments in improving patient and staff safety, patient care quality, medical facilities/instrumentation/equipment, and professional salaries.

It must be noted, however, that while outsourcing will give healthcare organizations opportunities to improve quality and reduce costs, it also presents challenges in terms of security and privacy of patient data.

MORE IDEAS, PROJECTS, AND FUNCTIONS

The preceding really only scratches the surface of outsourcing developments. When it comes to the possibilities and opportunities offered by this powerful business tool, the list, as you can see, is almost endless.

Market Research and Analysis

Marketplace research and analysis

Customer needs research and analysis

Customer satisfaction measurement

External business and technology research and analysis

Graphic Design, Presentation, and Multimedia

2D/3D graphics

Annual reports

Audio/video presentations (AV)

Billboard/poster/displays

Book/video/album/CD covers

Brochures/flyers

Graphic design

Industrial design

Interactive presentations/ CD-ROMs

Layout/desktop

Packaging

Product Research, Development, Manufacture, and Delivery

Product research and development

Product prototype and test

Capital goods and technology evaluation

Materials and supplies acquisition

Inbound logistics management

Component manufacturing

Product assembly, test, and packaging

Product distribution, warehousing, and delivery

Product installation and service

Service Research, Development, Staffing, and Delivery

Service research and development

Service prototype and test

Capital goods and technology evaluation

Materials and supplies acquisition

Human resources acquisition and development

Service delivery to customers

Marketing

Marketing plan development

Product and service advertising

Product and service promotion

Customer service

Direct marketing

Marketing communications

Sales

Sales plan development

Field sales

Lead generation

Call center sales/teleservices

Direct mail

Sales advertising

Telemarketing

Sales teams

Reservations and sales operations

Media and Entertainment

Advertising

Filmmaking

Animation

Printing and publishing

Consulting services

Photography

Customer Relationship Management (CRM)

Customer order processing

Customer service, inquiries, and complaint handling

System development and management

Human Resources Management

Worker's compensation

Human resources strategy development

Recruitment, selection, and hiring of employees

Development and training of employees

Employee relocation

Training programs

Outplacement services

Base and variable compensation plan development and management

Employee satisfaction

Workplace health and safety management

Employee benefits administration

Internal communications

Executive search and placement recruiting

Labor relations management

Human resources information systems (HRIS) development and management

Information and Communications Technology Management

Information and communications technology strategy development

Data center design and management

Distributed systems design and management

Desktop/mobile system design and management

Data network design and management

Communications systems and network design and management

Internet services/Web hosting

Application development and management

Enterprise resource planning (ERP) system development and maintenance

Data and database management and maintenance

Help desk services

Systems security and controls management

Information systems maintenance/ repair

IT training

Applications development

IT consulting and re-engineering

Mainframe data centers

End-user support

Full information technology divisional outsourcing

IT Support Services

Software development services

Application development and management

Re-engineering

Conversation and migration

Data warehousing and data mining

Embedded systems

E-commerce applications

IT Data Entry

Data control audits

Regular reporting of work systems

Data entry software and validation tables

Customer data dispatch

Proof checking and validation audits

IT Programming

C, C++, Visual C++, Java, Javascript, Java Beans, Java Server Pages (JSP), Enterprise Java Beans (EJB), ASP (Active Server Pages)

Visual Basic

Microsoft Access

Novell Networking

EDI and integration

Bar coding and handheld data collection

DOS, Windows 95/98/2000, Windows NT

Business and industrial systems

Support of spreadsheets, word processing, and various third-party applications

PC hardware and services

Programming, software, and database

Application/software development

Database design and administration

Enterprise systems

Programming IT training

PDAs and handheld devices

Project management

QA/testing

Programming scripts and utilities

IT security

Programming technical support/help desk/call center

Wireless programming

IT Application Development

Old release maintenance

New feature development

Driver development

New application development

Adapter maintenance

Translation and internationalization

IT Application Testing

QA/regression

Compatibility testing

Bug testing

Building test suites

Automating test suites

Packaged Application Outsourcing

Application customization

Application hosting

Implementation Services

Product life-cycle management

Consulting

Prototype development

Professional services augmentation

Technology evaluation

Proof of concept

Call Centers

Order management

Privacy services

Warranty management

Distribution

Customer billing

Customer contact

Customer insight solutions

Market research

Managed Security

Vulnerability assessment firewall/intrusion detection

Identity management

Network monitoring

Disaster recovery

Business continuity

Integrated security

Architectures

Securing web services

Mobile workforce security

Secure mail and content management

E-mail rapid recovery

Work area recovery

Telephony and network recovery

IT Management and Administration

Application integration

Application hosting

Applications management

Architectures

Asset management (systems operations)

Bandwidth management

Call center management

Configuration management

Contingency planning

Data center management

Data collection

Data management

Database management

Documentation

Hardware engineering

Help desk management

High availability

Host management

Infrastructure

Managed security services

Network management

Network monitoring

Network performance

Quality assurance

Quality of service (QoS)

Security

Software development

Software implementation

Storage management

Systems design and development

Systems implementation

Systems maintenance

Systems management services

Systems operations

Testing

Voice/data integration

Web development

IT Software and Hardware

All related functionalities

Academics: K-12, University

Instructors

Administration

Library management

IT Infrastructure

Communications and messaging

Upgrading and configuring message
management software

Launching an XML strategy

Integrating e-business messages
with CRM, ERP, and legacy
systems

Managing change as e-business
programs and business systems
evolve

E-business operations

Management and day-to-day operation of EDI infrastructure creation and management of a new
XML strategy

E-marketplace development

ERP integration

Communications monitoring

Trading partner management

Order processing

Workflow enhancement, evaluation, and benchmarking

Application hosting

System implementation and
integration

System maintenance

Upgrades

Backups

Disaster recovery

**Web Site Design,
Development, and Marketing**

Banner/web advertisement

Domain/DNS services and
registration

Portals

E-commerce consulting

E-mail marketing

Flash animation

Flash programming

Hosting/colocation

Internet marketing

Search engine optimization (SEO)

Web content/copy

Web development—dynamic/
database

Web development—e-commerce

Web Development—static/HTML

Web graphic/interface design

Relationship Management

Customer care services

Customer acquisition

Customer activation

Customer retention

Cross-selling/up-selling

Inside sales

Surveys and polling

Community Management

Managing ongoing partner relationships

Opening e-business channels with new vendors and customers

Defining e-business requirements

Business Process and Back-Office Outsourcing

401(k) plan record keeping

Enterprise management

Supply chain management (SCM)

Customer relationship management (CRM)

Accounting: processing accounts payable, accounts receivable, or general ledger

Payroll

Inventory

Hardware maintenance

Internal auditing

Benefits management

Benefits administration

Health and welfare administration

Defined contribution/defined benefit administration and customer service

Health claims administration

Asset management and staffing

Document Management

Document layout and design

Document imaging, storage, and distribution

Printing and publishing

Centralized copy services

Financial Management

Purchasing and procurement

Transaction processing

General accounting

Taxes and tax administration

Budget and cash flow management

Risk management

Accounts payable processing

Payroll processing

Invoicing, accounts receivable, credits, and collections processing

Travel and entertainment expense processing and management

Internal and external financial accounting and reporting

Internal auditing

Tax management processing

Financial management information systems development and maintenance

CPA (accounting, auditing, tax planning)

Financial planning

Mergers and acquisitions

Raising equity capital

Raising loan capital

Venture funding

Real Estate Management

Real estate planning, development, and project management

Real estate transaction management

Real estate engineering and maintenance

Energy management

Capital Asset Management

Capital asset plan development and project management

Capital asset transaction management

Capital asset engineering and maintenance

Logistics and Distribution

Freight audit

Consulting and training

Freight brokering

Leasing

Warehousing

Distribution management

Logistics administration

Information systems

Logistics operations

Operations and Facility Services

Food and cafeteria services

Mailroom services

Shipping and receiving

Security

Parking

Reprographics

Records management

Operations information systems

Supply and inventory

Facilities maintenance

Facilities management

Facilities information systems

Administrative Services

Secretarial/clerical services

Data entry

Transcription services

Records management

Travel services

Workplace supplies management

Corporate Services

Purchasing

Public relations management and external communications

Legal services

Due diligence

Event planning

Advertising and Broadcasting

Acting

Ad concepts

Ad designs

Art/creative direction

Music/audio

Print ads/production

Video/film production

Legal

Corporate law

Criminal law

Employment law

Family law

Financial and securities law

Immigration law

International law

IP/trademark law

Litigation law

Medical law

Real estate law

Tax law

Transportation

Fleet management

Fleet operations

Fleet maintenance

Fleet management

Fleet operations

Medical, Healthcare, and Clinical Services

Radiologists/teleradiology

Pathology/telepathology

Pharmacy operations

Medical supply distribution

Hospital central supply

Medical transcription

Engineering, CAD and Architecture

Architecture

CAD/AutoCAD

Chemical engineering

Civil engineering

Electrical engineering

Energy

Environmental engineering

Industrial engineering

Integrated circuit design

Material engineering

Mechanical engineering

Operations research

Scientific computation

Auditing

Bookkeeping and tax services

Collections

Forensic accounting

Tax negotiation and representation

Advertising

Branding

Business-to-business

Design services

Ethnic or cultural focus

Indoor advertising

Industry-specific

Infomercial production

Media buying and planning

Media production

Outdoor advertising

Print advertising

Promotional products

Public relations

Radio advertising

Television advertising

Web advertising

Education and Training

Certification and assessment

Computer-based training

Corporate training

Course delivery

Cross-cultural training

Curriculum and course development

Diversity training

E-learning

Foreign languages

Leadership development

Management training

Professional development

Project management training

Quality management training

Safety training

Sales training

Sexual harassment

Team building

Technical training

Training assessment

Training event planning

Training services[1]

Training vendor management

Tuition processing

Engineering

Accident reconstruction

Architectural design

Architectural engineering

Biomedical engineering

Chemical engineering

Civil engineering

Coastal and maritime engineering

Drafting and illustration

Electrical engineering

Failure analysis

Hydraulic engineering

Mechanical engineering

Mining and geotechnical engineering

Oil and gas engineering

Product design

Quality engineering

Reverse engineering

Safety engineering

Structural engineering

Transportation engineering

Environmental Services

Air and stack testing

Air quality engineering

Asbestos removal

Brownfields

Ecological restoration

Environmental due diligence

Environmental management

Environmental permitting

Environmental process engineering

FIFRA Studies

Industrial hygiene

Lead-based paint management

Leak detection and repair

Litigation and dispute support

Mold remediation

RCRA compliance

Recycling

Risk assessment

Sediment quality studies

Site investigation

Site remediation

Soil and groundwater monitoring

Spill planning and response

Storage tank management

Stormwater management

Superfund projects

Treatment system management

Waste management

Wastewater engineering

Water supply development

Watershed management

On-Site Facilities Management

Child day care services

Equipment maintenance

Facilities management

Food service management

IT operations

Janitorial services

Laundry services

Office management

Power plant management

Safety management

Site maintenance

Space planning and design

Uniformed security services

Vending services

Financial

Asset management

Banking and financial services

Brokerage services

Claims adjudication

Collection services

Credit card processing

Credit services

E-check processing

Factoring

Field services

Financial planning

Insurance services

Medical billing

Mortgage processing

Payment processing

Underwriting

Venture capital

Healthcare

Care design

Case management

E-health solutions

Electronic medical records

Healthcare information
    management

Healthcare management consulting

HIPAA solutions

JCAHO mock surveys

Legal nurse consulting

Medical animation

Medical billing and collections

Medical coding

Medical expert witness

Medical transcription

Medico-legal litigation support

Revenue cycle consulting

Specific Human Resources Functions

Background check

Benefits administration

Claims management

Diversity training

Education and training

Employee relations
Employer liability management
Employment administration
Employment screening
Executive compensation
Hiring and recruitment
HR processing
Labor relations
Outplacement
Payroll administration
Performance management
Regulatory compliance
Safety training
Salary surveys
Sexual harassment training

Law Specialty Services

Administrative law
Business and corporate law
Business formation
Contracts
Copyright services
Environmental law
Expert witness
Immigration law
Intellectual property law
Labor and employment law
Legal claims processing
Legal nurse consulting
Legal research
Legal transcription
Litigation support services
Paralegal services
Patent services

Property law
Trademark services

Management

Benchmarking and best practices
Change management
Corporate governance
Interim management
Knowledge management
Office management
Operations management
Organization development
Project management
Quality management
Strategic planning

Manufacturing

Apparel and fashion
Automotive products
Chemicals
Computer hardware
Construction equipment and
    materials
Electronics and electrical equipment
Energy products
Food and beverages
Gifts and crafts
Health and beauty products
Home appliances
Home supplies
Industrial supplies
Manufacturing
Minerals, metals, and materials
Office supplies
Packaging and paper goods

Printing equipment

Radio and television equipment

Restaurant and food service supplies

Security and safety products

Sports and leisure products

Telecommunications equipment

Textiles and leather

Toys

Transportation equipment

Marketing Management

Competitive analysis

Direct marketing

Ethnic and cultural focus

Event marketing

Full-service marketing

Industry-specific

International marketing

Internet marketing

Lead generation

Market research

Marketing plan creation

Public relations

Sales presentations

Telemarketing

Multimedia

3D graphics

Audio

CD and DVD authoring

Design services

Illustrations

Macromedia Director

Macromedia Flash

Media duplication and conversion

Model building

Multimedia solutions

Photo retouching

Photography

Streaming media

Video

Videoconferencing

Web design

Printing and Publishing

Book design

Bookbinding

Coating and laminating

Printing

Publishing

Restoration and rebinding

Research and Development

Aerospace and defense

Chemicals

Energy

Environmental

Information technology

Medical

Pharmaceutical and biotech

Regulatory Compliance

CRA Compliance

Environmental compliance

FDA compliance

FTC compliance

Health and safety compliance

HIPAA compliance

HMDA compliance

OFAC compliance
Sarbanes-Oxley compliance
SEC compliance

Security and Protection

Asset protection
E-security solutions
Executive protection
Investigation services
Threat assessment
Uniformed security
Video surveillance
Witness protection

Small Business

Business formation
Business loans and leases
Business plan creation
Small business consulting
Venture capital

Translation Services

Interpreting services
Language training
Software and web site localization
Translation services

Supply Chain and Logistics

Distribution
Food storage
Hazardous materials storage
Logistics services
Mailing
Order fulfillment
Promotional distribution
Reverse logistics services

Supply chain management
Transportation
Warehousing and storage

Technical Support

24/7 technical support and problem resolution
Installation and product support

Employee IT Help Desk

Level 1 and 2 multichannel support for internal applications
System problem resolutions related to desktop, notebooks, OS, shrink-wrapped products, and connectivity
Office productivity tools support, including browsers and mail
New service requests
Product usage queries
IT operational issues
Routing specific requests to designated contacts
Remote diagnostics (password reset, desktop control)

Accounts Receivable

Bank advice clearance
Client billing
Suspense clearance
Encoding errors
Client settlement

Accounts Payable

Cash application and allocation
Credit balance refunds

Payment research

Third-party settlement

Bookkeeping

Journal entries

Cash and bank payment entries

Credit card accounting entries

Statutory dues

Reporting and Analysis

Statutory reporting

Financial statement analysis

Accounts Reconciliation

Bank

General ledger

Third-party settlement

Assets and liabilities

Branch accounting

Payroll Processing

General ledger posting report

Quarterly local tax return

Quarterly state unemployment tax
   return

Next-day processing

Form 941 federal tax return

W-2 forms for all employees

W-2 state withholding recap

W-3 federal withholding recap

Year-end local tax reconciliation

Form 940 federal unemployment
   tax return

Order Entry, Processing and Management

Sales order entry and checking

Product configuration checking

Contract reconciliation

Quotations

Billing, Invoicing, and Payments

Loans processing

Claims processing

Application processing

Reconciliations

Accounts payable

Time and expense reimbursement

Vendor payments

Benefits administration

Medicare insurance claims

Credit Care Services

Check processing

Credit and collections management

Credit and/or debit card processing

Supply Chain Management

Third-party and fourth-party
   logistics

Transportation management and
   warehousing

HR—Payroll

Receipt and analysis of payroll data

Reporting and payment of payroll
   taxes

Issuing payments (via check or
   electronic payment) and reports
   to employees

Issuing payments to third parties
   (for example, employee IRAs)
   and reporting data to end user

HR—Personnel Administration

Employee relations

Employee life-cycle and record management

Employee communication

Bringing new hires on board

Relocation and expatriation administration

Labor management and local compliance

HR—Education and Training

Training needs identification

Training administration

Specialized training requirements

HR—Benefits Administration

Distribution of healthcare and retirement plan information

Managing eligibility

Answering queries regarding coverage

Leave tracking

Maintaining retirement earning histories, enrollments, retirement or vested rights estimates, and benefits termination administration

HR—Hiring and Recruitment

Resume management

Hiring need identification

Job profiling and specifications

Selection process administration

Compensation processing

Reference checks

New employee induction

Visa filing and administration

Organizational Development

Training—employee development

Performance management

Policy and legal compliance

Employment Data Management

Employee data and records management

HR IT and information services

Employee and manager self-service

Workforce Planning

Recruiting and workforce planning

Recruiting, resourcing, and staffing

Background checks

Drug testing

Expatriate administration

Notes

1. Country Forecast World, November 2003. Main Report Country Forecasts present and explain the EIU's five-year macroeconomic projections for 60 of the world's largest economies and provide a forward-looking assessment of the political and business environments.

CHAPTER 6

SELECTING YOUR
SUPPLIERS AND VENDORS

Selecting an outsourcing provider is a critical business decision that is about much more than just wage arbitrage. You should select a provider that offers a flexible delivery model, has the domain expertise in your industry and has the process transformation capabilities that will help you meet your strategic initiatives and add to your bottom line.

—Paul Walsh, Chairman and CEO, eFunds Corporation

There are many capable outsourcing vendors. They come in myriad types and sizes. There are top-tier, full-service, large organizations; second-tier, specialty best-of-breed vendors; and smaller, strategically located vendors. Making a smart choice among them requires strategizing to decide what type of business you want to become and which vendor has the capability to help you fulfill your goals and improve the corporate bottom line. To make this important choice, you will have to be methodical, disciplined, and focused. Here's a rundown of what's involved in vendor selection:

1. Convene the selection team.
2. Gather vendor information, issue requests for information (RFIs).
3. Set a realistic schedule.
4. Develop a term sheet.
5. Define and evaluate current objectives and operations.
6. Define evaluation criteria and weights before issuing bid requests (to maintain objectivity).
7. Prepare requests for proposal (RFPs).
8. Evaluate the bids.
9. Select a vendor.

Note: Web addresses flagged with a (†) are author affiliated sites.

Example of a Term Sheet

Tasks	Responsibilities
Offer the agreed outsourcing services within the defined service windows.	Maintain adequate staff, equipment, and other resources, and carry out all necessary servicing, maintenance, and repairs to its own facilities, equipment, and systems, as may be required to provide the services in accordance with this SLA.
Provide 24/7 hours monitoring and support to respond to critical system incidents and exceptions.	Incident reporting schedule.
Monitor the execution processes of the daily batch run and perform all housekeeping activities (e.g., backup).	Obtain authorization from the buyer defined responsible personnel for additions, upgrades, deletions, or amendments to the system.
Arrange fallback-facilities in case of a disaster. Maintain as an integral part of the services a suitable disaster recovery and fallback facility to enable the customer to continue in the event of any natural or man-made disaster or similar reason preventing access to the system.	Initiate escalations/crisis management procedures in case of disasters/inform Chief Resource Officer or assigned Supplier Relationship Manager.
Produce and distribute periodic reports to provide insight in achieved service levels.	Reporting on service levels.
Provide, on request, full logs of outsourced system operation.	Comply with confidentiality in relation to all information contained in the system and data transferred to it in accordance with the security guidelines set forth in the service quality plan.

If you don't have the experience in-house to manage this process, we strongly recommend you bring in an experienced consultant. But whether you tackle this task in-house or with the help of a consultant, be sure to take your time and fully understand what outsourcing means to your company and what is required to ensure a successful partnership that will help you meet your business goals.

Sample Request for Proposal

RFP Requirement Outsourcing Provider Business Attributes	Relative Weight (Scale of 1–10)	Comments
Viability		
Client satisfaction		
Relationships with other parties		
Independent evaluations		
Personnel		
Asset ownership		
Contractual exception, penalties, and rewards		
Service level agreement		
Exit strategy		
Site visit		
Implementation plan		
Points of contact		
Provider Service Attributes		
Service availability		
Service hardware and software		
Service scalability		
Service levels		
Reporting requirements		
Service scope		

UNDERSTANDING YOUR NEEDS

Though, as we said, there are myriad vendor choices out there, they all can be divided into two major categories: *full-service* and *selective functionality*. If your intent is to focus in-house staff on core competencies and have a vendor attend to everyday operations, then you will probably want to consider a full-service vendor. But if your goal is to incorporate a vendor into specific business situations, you will probably want to look at smaller, or selective, outsourcing candidates. Moreover, some projects will, over time, become too large for one vendor, so you may want to consider multiple best-of-breed vendors who can offer you the best service for each of your specific needs.

Always front and center in the selection process should be your company's outsourcing priorities. How important is your bottom line? Full-service vendors can offer you a lower cost per transaction due to their size and economic flexibility. With a selective outsourcing arrangement, you may find a more competitive marketplace, which gives you better service levels and contract flexibility.

One of the most difficult issues that companies face when deciding to outsource, is identifying which processes make the most sense to outsource. A company should not necessarily outsource those processes that save them the most money. They must look at other factors such as the degree of standardization in the process, alignment of the process to the company's key objectives, management buy-in, change readiness, compliance, and the state of the technology used in the process.

Outsourcing vendors such as eFunds Corporation, a U.S.-based company, provide tools such as eFunds' PRI™ (Process Readiness Index), which uses a combination of industry knowledge and expertise as well as analytics to determine which processes are ready to outsource and which ones still need to be improved before outsourcing.

COMPILING THE LONG LIST

The next step is to make a long list of vendor candidates. A good place to start is with any current suppliers. Might they have the competence and qualifications to take on your new outsourcing initiative? Are they willing to bid on your project? Do they already have partnerships with vendors that offer services you need? A word of caution here: This type of selection process, termed *sole* or *single sourcing,* can result in a relationship with a vendor who is not completely qualified, leading to an unsatisfactory outcome in the long term. Be sure to always include in your search the traditional outsourcing marketplace. It is only by evaluating numerous vendors that you will come to fully understand what the marketplace has to offer and, ultimately, find the best vendor for your needs and to form a lasting and rewarding partnership. RFP *long list creation* is an information-gathering process to identify suitable vendors for inclusion in the request-for-proposal stage. (See Chapter 10 for a vendor directory.) The long list rule of thumb is one vendor per member on the selection committee (e.g., six members on the selection team results in six vendors on the long list). The selection team should be a cross mix of company representatives from technology, budget, finance (particularly the "funds keeper"), and both staff and management from user groups.

SUBMITTING RFIs AND SHORTLISTING CANDIDATES

Once you have compiled your long list, send an RFI to all the vendors on it. Be sure you set a deadline for response submissions and that you have a system in place to track the responses. Disciplined and exacting due diligence is required to narrow down the list to the most promising candidates. The RFP Issuance stage involves a four- to six-week process. The selection team drafts letters and paper and electronic versions of the RFP and sends them to the long list of suitable vendors. A bidder conference is normally part of this process involving a meeting conducted via phone, in-person, or web conferencing to clarify the requirements and responses requested from vendors. The vendor analysis process has two main goals: to evaluate the actual capabilities of a given vendor and to establish a level of comfort to do business with a specific vendor. Here chief resource officers and other outsourcing buyer professionals are taking a close look at how to map the needs defined in their internal assessment to the capabilities of the vendors in the marketplace.

Vendor evaluation is conducted from both a tactical and strategic perspective with a focus on functionality and cost, as well as vendor viability, service, and support capabilities. A sound assessment of vendors' viability and vision will answer questions such as:

Will the outsourcing vendor survive as the market evolves?

Does the outsourcing vendor have the talent and organization to be successful?

How committed is the outsourcing vendor to our size of company?

The vendor analysis will result in creation of a vendor short list of the top two or three vendors that can best serve their needs. In creating the short list, we recommend that you consider these issues:

Has the outsourcing vendor been strategically servicing your industry type and services you are considering outsourcing?

What is the outsourcing vendor's track record with your size and type business in offering tested size- and vertical-specific solutions?

How many business customers does the vendor have? How many did it add in the past 12 to 18 months?

Does the vendor generate less than 25 percent of its revenue from your type and size businesses?

What is the quality (not just quantity) of the vendor's business partners?

Finally, the vendor analysis process includes a presentation and demonstration of the vendor's solution based on a planned and scripted scenario designed by your internal outsourcing project team. The demonstration script should deliberately center on the desired functions and features and provides the project team with a visual of the end-user experience where applicable. Your vendor analysis would take into consideration the quality and responsiveness of the vendor presentation, the demonstrated functional and technical capabilities in comparison to predefined needs, and the ability to do business with the vendor. Keep the following in mind:

- Keep in mind that outsourcing procurements are being made to address business needs and problems. Focus on your needs, not the solutions portfolio of the vendor's salespeople.
- Purchase nothing more and nothing less than what's required by end users to perform their job functions and to address the exact problems you are resolving.
- Make and keep the outsourcing bidding process competitive.
- Use negotiation skills to save money, reduce risk, and provide long-term contract protection. Employ an outsourcing buyer advocate such as First Outsourcing (www.firstoutsourcing.com) or a matching service such as the Outsourcing Partnership (www.outsourcingpartnership.com[†]) if you are not prepared to accomplish this on your own. The short-term outlay of consulting fees will be returned in the savings from not becoming involved in a poor vendor-advantaged negotiation.
- Establish an oversight process to monitor vendor performance during the life of the contract. Evolving and high-growth outsourcing governance positions are discussed in Chapter 9.

TIP   This is a time-consuming and resource-intensive process, but not completing it is a major reason outsourcing relationships fail.

**What Matters Most: Are These Criteria Highly
Important in Selecting an Outsourcing Vendor?**

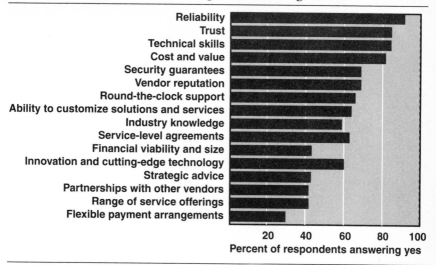

Note: Multiple responses allowed. "Highly important" is based on 8 to 10 ratings on a 1 to 10 scale. *Data: Information Week* research analyzing the outsourcers study of 700 business-technology professionals, November 2002.

Once you have your short list of candidates, schedule phone or in-person interviews with each vendor candidate to ascertain their capabilities to service your company's needs. You want to know:

Where are they investing resources?

How do current and past customers rate them?

Do they fit with your company culture?

Your objective is to determine which vendors have the "bench strength" to complete your project on time and on budget.

If a vendor has a satisfactory interview, if at all possible, schedule a vendor site visit. Meet with the management team and the personnel with whom you and your team will be working; evaluate their data centers; pay careful attention to how they respond to your requests and questions. You will be able to narrow down the field considerably through this process.

Following the site visit, reduce your list even further, to two to four finalists—those you believe can handle your infrastructure, invest in similar technologies and resources, have excellent references, and fit your company culture.

Issuing a Request for Proposal

The request for proposal (RFP) stage continues the gleaning process. In your RFP to your final four candidates, be sure to state exactly your service level requirements, all cost considerations, and operational essentials.

Upon receipt of the RFPs from your finalists, request a presentation or demonstration with the vendor team that will be assigned to your project. During the presentation, focus on three key areas: *service capabilities, cultural issues,* and *cost.* Factor in questions such as:

Does the vendor manage its teams on-site for easier communication and accessibility?

Is the vendor local to your corporate or regional offices?

How does the vendor negotiate? This may well demonstrate how they will handle future change.

If you have decided to hire multiple vendors, meet with them together to determine how they might coordinate as a vendor team. If one or more of the vendors strike you as territorial, it's a red flag that they won't perform well as a team. You want vendors whose combined goal is the overall benefit of the team, not self-interest.

Determining All the Costs

You've no doubt noticed that a theme in this book is that cost reductions and savings, though important considerations for outsourcing, should not be the determining factors. Today's promising low price can turn into tomorrow's rising cost if it turns out that, in practice, a vendor can't keep its cost promises. Getting out of a business relationship that failed because you chose cost over quality will probably lose you what you thought you'd be saving—and possibly more. It is a good idea to consider costs over both the short and long term.

Typical short-term benefits include:

- Ability to focus resources and attention on core competencies
- Reduction in headcount and attrition rates in the outsourced function
- Reallocation of remaining core staff with better and newly marketable skills

- Refinement of project management, risk management, and service delivery skills
- Implementation of demand management and service delivery disciplines

Typical long-term benefits should include:

- Predictable expense for the outsourced function over the life of an outsourcing agreement
- Joint and proactive problem-solving and innovation practices
- Qualified and experienced outsourcing management of the particular business
- Enhanced career opportunities for client staff, based on sophisticated management, contracting, and outsourcing integration skills

COMPARING COMPANY CULTURES

When choosing an outsourcing vendor, your chances of success expand greatly when the participating companies have compatible cultures. How can you determine this? This process is more difficult to pin down, because it involves making intuitive, even emotional, appraisals about a company and its employees, how they go about doing their work, and how they relate to each other. The look and feel of an office, how people dress, and their attitudes are other nonverbal clues that may reveal relevant information.

Another key for "reading" corporate culture is to identify who makes the decisions within a company, both in front of and behind the scenes. Does management make all decisions or are lower-level employees empowered to make them on a day-to-day basis in their particular areas?

Other points of interest:

- Is risk taking encouraged, or is a "don't rock the boat" mentality the norm?
- Is the company focused on high quality or on just getting the job done?
- Does the company make each employee feel he or she is a valued member of the corporation, or does it ignore all but the bottom line and profits?
- Does the company reward innovators who think outside the box? Or are employees expected to do things a certain way because "that's how we've always done it?"
- Is the atmosphere formal or casual?

Your vendor's culture does not have to be a perfect match with your own. As long as the two aren't at odds, things should go smoothly. Typically, as in all relationships whether personal or professional, there's an adjustment period on both sides, with staff from both companies having to adapt to one another.

PHASES OF OUTSOURCING

Companies seeking these outsourcing benefits engage in a systematic process led by the outsourcing vendor, one intended to guarantee a positive and mutually beneficial experience for both parties in the arrangement. Although the range and substance of outsourcing relationships varies widely, there are generally six phases.

Phase 1: Aligning Client and Outsourcing Vendor Expectations

Phase 1 has three goals:

1. Determine jointly your business needs.
2. Summarize the variety of possible outsourcing solutions.
3. Design a process for ensuring that both buyer and supplier develop a productive relationship based on mutual expectations.

Phase 2: Clarifying Outsourcing Governance

After your company decides to outsource a specific division, application, service, or process, you and the vendor should design an approach to leading—governing—the relationship. This reaches past the execution of contractual obligations to focus on proactive and collaborative governance of the relationship, the progression of outsourcing services provided, communication channels, performance review and service-level standards, and comprehensive relationship management.

To step smoothly through this phase, answer the following questions, which will help you create a relationship management model:

- *Expectations.* How does the client help set expectations? How does the client help perform the services? What does the client supply to the vendor?

- *Monitoring.* How well were services provided before the monitoring began? What are the methods for monitoring performance? What happens until they are operational? How are targets established?
- *Communication and reporting.* What is the schedule of client reviews? What is the intensification process for issue resolution? What provisions are made for special or emergency issue resolution, particularly if the vendor is based overseas? What are the schedule, content, and format of standard reporting?
- *Scope change.* How are changes in service scope or content accommodated?
- *Agreement modification.* How can the agreement itself be changed to be more responsive to client needs? What threshold operating levels should trigger the change process systematically?
- *Exiting the relationship.* Under what conditions can the agreement be terminated? What do client and provider need to do to initiate termination? What fees might apply?

Phase 3: Establishing Pricing

Pricing decisions remain a hypersensitive subject—and with good reason. Outsourcing arrangements can routinely run from millions to billions of dollars over the course of a multiyear agreement. Further, when the relationship involves purchasing assets such as equipment and staff, a significant investment is made by the outsourcing vendor based on client accounting, resource quality, ability to integrate its facilities into the vendor's, and a host of other factors.

Generally, outsourcing agreements are drafted either on a *fixed-price* or *variable-price* basis. In fixed-price arrangements, the vendor takes on the risk of absorbing cost variability in order to provide cost assurances to the buyer. Setting a fixed price helps reassure clients of predictable final costs, but it may have adverse effects if the agreement is not carefully constructed. When set too low, fixed prices weaken the outsourcing vendor's flexibility and incentive to, for example, take action to change business objectives, or keep up with emerging technologies, for fear of stepping outside the agreement parameters.

The opportunities for both flexibility and stability are greater under variable pricing, in which price may be based on straight outsourcing service usage, the sophistication of services used, risk sharing, or a combination of factors. Risk-sharing relationships also enable the outsourcing vendor to take advantage of benefits generated for the buyer organization, thus assuring a united front when it comes to meeting goals and objectives.

TIP In an effort to strike the right balance between cost predictability for the buyer and profit protection for the outsourcing vendor, a combination approach to pricing strategies is gaining popularity.

Phase 4: Writing Service Level Agreements

Effective service level agreements (SLAs) identify the expected results and the measures by which both parties can assess performance. As binding covenants with the influence of standard agreements, SLAs for outsourcing frequently require sophisticated legal and technical expertise because of their complexity and scope. Importantly, most outsourcing failures occur because neither side has expressed how to evaluate the progress made against a specific target. Accordingly, clear performance areas and consistent, effective measurements are essential to outsourcing success for buyers.

A practical outsourcing SLA structure begins by describing standard requirements such as start and end dates for the service, the schedule for reviewing performance, and documentation to be used in measuring the service. The SLA should then carefully outline the scope of services, including:

- Assets, equipment, and infrastructure to be serviced
- Types of services to be provided
- Decisions to be made by the provider
- Decisions to be made by the client

Equally important is a breakdown of fees, with both penalty and incentive provisions clearly outlined:

- Amounts period by period
- Volume of work covered
- Quality of work to be provided
- Provision for over- and underperformance

Guidelines for selecting specific outsourcing metrics, include:

- Aligning metrics with the business goals of the service
- Selecting metrics that enhance the ability to diagnose problems, escalate attention, and remedy performance issues
- Limiting the metrics for each service to one or two encompassing measurements

In outsourcing relationships, the tightest service definitions produce the most successful situations.

Phase 5: Supplementing Outsourced Services

A trusted and productive outsourcing buyer/vendor relationship may spurn additional opportunities for outsourcing projects. In approaching the augmentation of services, outsourcing vendors help their clients make decisions in various ways. Instead of outsourcing all or most of their complex noncore business processes to a single outsourcing service vendor, many companies, including Boeing, Motorola, and Procter & Gamble, are contracting with multiple service providers, choosing the best one for each type of work. While this model has many advantages, it poses challenges as well, since successfully managing the "seams" where services intersect requires a well-considered and consistently applied strategy.

By contracting with multiple providers, corporate buyers of outsourced services can gain greater expertise, be less dependent on a single provider, maintain better geographic coverage, and foster healthy competition among service providers. However, they must become the implicit systems integrators, holding ultimate responsibility for making sure that the seams between providers' responsibilities are managed and that the cumulative effort produces the anticipated results across all services, including any that the company retains.

Phase 6: Bundling Outsourcing Services

Business process outsourcing is experiencing a trend toward bundling information technology outsourcing (ITO) and business process outsourcing (BPO) services. Bundling happens when a customer chooses to include the underlying information technology (IT) systems and operations within the scope of a transaction that is principally aimed at contracting for a business function, such as human resources or finance and accounting operations. Predominantly, ITO is bundled with BPO efforts, and not vice versa. Rarely, will you see an ITO requirement move up the food chain to subsume a BPO scope. The business process rules the decision making.

The bundling client will typically either accept or encourage the alignment of transactional business processes with enabling applications. For example, a client might opt for Oracle as the IT that enables the elected BPO HR process. On occasion, this decision is driven by the client's legacy; on other occasions, it is driven by the solution offered by the service provider. At yet other times, businesses are bundling a broad set of processes (IT,

HR, procurement, logistics, facilities, marketing, and sales) under a common "Global Business Services" umbrella.

In this context, bundling means combining at least one silo or more from traditional IT spheres with one silo or more from BPO in one outsourcing contract. The creation of an integrated shared services operation is often a precursor to the exploration of a bundled sourcing solution.

An estimated one in five BPO transactions includes the underlying IT as part of the scope of those deals. Most often, one provider assumes both IT and BP responsibilities in a contract.

Bundling deals cross sectors: financial services; manufacturing; telecommunications; travel, transportation and hospitality; media and entertainment; and retail and restaurant sectors have all embraced bundling. ITO components have accompanied all BPO categories.

Industry wide, a significant portion of the top outsourcing deals in 2003 involved bundling: seven of the top 25 human resource outsourcing transactions (28 percent) and six of the top 25 finance and accounting outsourcing transactions (24 percent) contained traditional IT elements (*HRO Today*, December 2003).

Bundling is increasing as more companies focus on adding business value, rather than merely updating technology for cost savings. Savvy outsourcing veterans are also challenging the reason for the existence of the underlying technology assets (people and capital), and looking for the correlation between IT and business operations.

Companies are more often viewing outsourcing as a way of increasing the value of their businesses, rather than simply looking for cost reductions, so they seek solid business results from both IT investments *and* improved business processes.

Advantages of Outsourcing Bundling

- With bundling, there is more project integration from start to finish, which can enable efficiencies and economies. Optimally, bundling can help clients get to broader outsourced solutions with the optimal service provider faster, more easily, and more systematically.
- Bundling involves more win-win opportunities for all potential participants. The larger size of a bundled deal is more attractive

to major traditional IT players who are evolving their BPO practices; thus, it can leverage efforts, allow negotiating advantages, and offer greater cost savings for the client.

- Bundling enables the business process provider to also own or control the technology used in the process, allowing a more seamless service. Ultimately, we might expect companies to increasingly relinquish their hold on IT systems and focus more on process results, a trend that could lead to more bundling.

- Bundling typically prompts wider executive participation in shaping a deal. ITO, traditionally the focus of the CIO, joins BPO, more often the province of the CEO, CFO, or COO. One research study found that two-thirds of nearly one thousand CIOs studied do not see BPO as important either now or through 2007. (Gartner, *Business Wire,* March 9, 2004)

- Bundling makes outsourcing governance, or sourcing management, easier. The client's chief resource officer can choose just one service provider and gain one very committed service provider. The vendor typically wins a larger scope of work than he might with a single-scope deal. The outsourcing supplier also gains a customer who is more locked in to a long-term deal. Because bundling requires (or benefits from) stronger loyalties than a single-function deal might, it is important that relationships be clear and effective upfront with well-defined objectives and clear alignment of expectations.

Although companies historically have generally not sought to implement many IT and BPO functions at one time, when they do, bundling can add efficiencies and economies. A company can bundle to productively and quickly catch up with and even leapfrog a competitor's existing BPO and IT advantages.

CONCLUSION: THE FIRST THREE MONTHS

We conclude this chapter with an overview intended to help buyer organization CROs, process leaders, and outsourcing operating executives craft their outsourcing architectures soundly over the first three months of an outsourcing effort.

Month 1: Clarify your business models. If this takes longer than one month, your organization should put outsourcing issues aside and concentrate on getting its strategy right. With help from strategic staff, the senior leadership of each operating unit should review the business models of their most important competitors. These would include archrivals as well as threatening upstarts. They should then take one day to discuss and agree on how their business creates value, examining the key drivers and dependencies. The corporate leadership team should articulate the unifying characteristics of the company.

Month 2: Profile horizontal functions, such as IT and finance. For each process or function, name five things it does superbly. Then name five things it routinely bungles. Give this profile a name that captures its distinctive shape. Pinpoint the "fault lines" between profiles. These might not follow organizational lines.

Month 3: Spot the disconnects. Ask and answer the hard questions about whether your processes have the profiles your business model requires. Drive the changes you need through your outsourcing governance process.

CHAPTER 7

MANAGING YOUR
OUTSOURCING VENDORS

Vendor cooperation is still a very new concept. Letting outsiders manage
your outsourcing relationships on behalf of your company can be extremely
imprudent, unless they are outsourcing experts.

—Douglas Brown and Scott Wilson, Outsourcing Management
Institute, October 2004, Vendor Relationship Management Conference

Effective management of outsourc-
ing relationships ensures maximum value for your company. Don't fall
prey to buyer's remorse caused by unresolved or recurring problems that
are the result of poor management practices. The foundation of successful
management of an outsourcing relationship is laid when a company begins
to communicate with potential suppliers about its intention to outsource
certain functions. Successful management of an outsourcing relationship
depends on clearly defining the requirements, unambiguously expressing
objectives, following a disciplined vendor selection process (as described in
the previous chapter), carefully preparing SLAs, and defining plans for
continuous improvement. The people charged with managing the relationship are also of prime consequence.

When one or both parties become dissatisfied, often it can be attrib-
uted to common causes, related to both parties' perspective on outsourcing performance, namely:

- Unrealistic expectations of the buyer due to overpledging during
  sales process
- Contradictory interests of the buyer and the vendor

Note: Web addresses flagged with a (†) are author affiliated sites.

- Buyer resistance to accommodate the business changes necessitated by the new presence of the vendor
- Cultural, social, and ethnic differences
- Higher-than-expected turnover rate

To preclude these causes from interfering with the value-add potential of your outsourcing initiative, you'll have to plan carefully for a smooth transition from in-house to vendor-provided service.

TRANSITIONING

A transition plan and its related costs is vital to the successful management of an outsourcing arrangement. Three major transitions occur in any type of outsourcing contract, and each must be included in the plan, to ensure they are handled properly so that both parties to the contract can prosper. They are as follows:

1. *Transition from in-house staff and functionality to vendor management or services.* In the plan, detail the costs involved in the transition process and map the progression by which the vendor becomes involved in your company's activities and/or projects. Identify potential impacts on internal staff and end users.
2. *Transition in work flow that results from service changes in outsourcing agreements.* Keep end users informed about the goals and progress of the arrangement; include their input in outsourcing plans. End users will have concerns regarding how the change in services might affect them. These concerns must be managed to achieve user buy-in and sign-off on the outsourced activities. Educating employees and customers about new work methods must be part of the outsourcing plan.
3. *Transition from one vendor to another or from a vendor back to in-house at the end of the contract period.* This change can be difficult for internal staff, vendor staff, and end users alike, and it will be very expensive for your business if a transition plan is not available to guide them through these periods.

Other forward-thinking transition considerations fall into the categories of responsibilities, tasks, and assets, as follows:

Responsibilities

- What are corporate staff responsibilities for and after the transition?
- What are the vendor's responsibilities for and after the transition?

- What role will end users play during and after the transition?
- What actions will need to take place to transfer equipment, knowledge, and so on?
- Has your corporate outsourcing governance management team been organized?
- Have the lines of communication between the vendor and your firm been established—and opened?
- Has the reporting schedule been set?

Tasks

- What are the specific tasks that need to be done by each person involved?
- Has each task been prioritized?
- Has a time frame for the transition been established, complete with milestones?
- What dependencies exist between tasks?

Assets

- What assets and licenses need to be acquired?
- What assets and licenses need to be transferred?
- What life-cycle assets need to be transferred?
- What assets have been produced, and who owns them (e.g., documentation, code, planning documents)?

Nurturing the Relationship

All vendor relationships have to be nurtured over time. The key to success is careful planning, mutual support, understanding, and solving problems collectively with a we're-in-this-together attitude.

Getting Management Support

Both parties to the outsourcing arrangement must have buy-in from their management. When top management acknowledges the advantages and value in the plan, they will take ownership and approve the resources that are needed to carry out the plan.

Outsourcing is not just a transfer of a business process to a service provider; it involves a great deal of change, usually prompting reorganization that may include staff layoffs and reassignment in work scope and/or responsibilities, among others. Management commitment and support are essential to ease the way for all affected.

Defining the Scope of Work

If you don't define the scope of work, you can't realistically expect the vendor to understand what you want. For this task, start by asking: What does your organization hope to achieve from outsourcing these functions? Are you seeking to reduce cost or to improve service delivery to your internal customers? What is the service level expected? What are your expectations in matters such as turnaround time for claims settlements? After defining the objectives, then work backward to identify the potential issues or problems along the way.

TIP Even though both parties have to agree to a clear set of predefined scope of work and service level agreements, it's a good idea to build in flexibility to the agreement. Flexibility is important simply because often it is not possible to define the scope of work in totality; changes typically surface along the way, sometimes long after the initial agreement is entered into. A too rigidly structured agreement will work against both your company and the vendor.

Learn—and Teach—to Cope with Change

Coping with changes caused by outsourcing to both processes and personnel can be one of the most daunting challenges facing the manager of an outsourcing initiative. Those involved and affected may feel insecure, suspicious, angry, and demotivated. Left unaddressed, these feelings can short-circuit the initiative before it even gets off the ground. To prevent this from happening in your organization:

- Educate your employees that they will need to change along with the business, if they expect to secure a place for themselves in the future competitive environment.
- Involve staff early in the plan by circulating a clear vision statement and a communication plan of the company's goals. This will help build their trust, which will make them more willing to accept the changes and lend their support.

- Where there will be reassignment of duties or responsibilities, give staff time to make the transition and grow into their new roles. If they need to acquire new skills, provide them with training.
- Keep staff motivated, by encouraging them to accept the greater challenges incumbent with their new roles.

Communication is key to navigating the period of change. What you want to avoid is blindsiding anyone, which can only serve to cause the aforementioned negative and defeatist feelings. Decide what needs to be communicated, and when. Time the release of the information so that it coincides with specific outsourcing activities. Let them know, for example:

- Which functions will be outsourced, where, and when
- The reasons for the change (i.e., reiterate the corporate vision and goals)
- The crucial factors in the decision-making process (e.g., finding the right provider)
- Who the project team members and the decision makers are
- The timelines involved
- The anticipated impact of the change on the company at large and the individuals in it

Likewise, plan ahead for information distribution: Will you communicate via bulletin board postings, in personalized e-mails, group presentations, or all of these? Then, prior to launch of the outsourcing initiative, describe to your in-house plan administrators and all employees how the new processes will be implemented and how they are to use the new system. We cannot stress the importance of this enough. If employees are not properly introduced to the changes, the new service will not achieve its intended goals. Ask the service provider you have chosen to support this effort in the form of user start-up kits, user guides, and administrator manuals. Arrange, if at all possible, for hands-on training sessions, and make them convenient for all staff to attend.

DOUBLE-CHECK VENDOR FIT

For the outsourcing project to be win-win all around, you have to be confident that you have chosen your vendor wisely. You want to be able to leverage your service provider's expertise, skills, and technology to improve your company's position in the market; conversely, you want the vendor to succeed as well, to ensure a long-term, stable partnership.

TIP Don't forget to check with others in your industry to find out who has outsourced similar processes, and ask for recommendations. Solicit feedback on experiences, lessons learned, mistakes made, and success stories.

We've already talked about the vendor selection process in the previous chapter, but it won't hurt at this juncture to check that you've covered all your bases. Take the time to run through the following checklist:

- Is the provider comfortable with the style of relationship you are seeking?
- Is the provider experienced in supplying this type of service?
- Is the provider highly skilled—an expert in the field? How long has the provider been in this industry? Does the provider have other skill sets that might be of value to your organization?
- Has the provider offered references from existing and past customers? Did you check these out?
- Is the provider financially sound/stable, that is, a long-term player?
- Does the provider have other lines of business?
- Do the provider's business plan and your organization's goals match up?

TIP No matter how well you set up your management procedures, you're bound to be set back by starts, stops, and bumps in the vendor relationship road. You may find it helpful in such cases to involve an intermediary. First Outsourcing (www.firstoutsourcing .com) is renowned for its expertise in this area.

PROVIDE TRAINING

Creating and executing a training plan is a best-practice approach to ensuring that all affected employees know how to operate in the new paradigm of service delivery. During the training program, explain in detail the new roles each employee will play and demonstrate the new model for their performance evaluation.

SOLICIT FEEDBACK

This is actually an element of the communication guideline given earlier, but we treat it separately here because it involves communicating at the back end of the process, after the initiative has been underway for a while. How effective is the effort? At what point do you check? You'll need to set quantitative and qualitative benchmarks and identify several checkpoints when you'll review performance against the benchmarks. Also, it's critical to put in place a formal process for providing feedback to stakeholders.

MEASURING SUCCESS

Measuring the success of a project—in this case, outsourcing—is part of the management process, too. In this regard, too many people look only to the return on investment (ROI) and to be sure, as we discuss shortly, ROI is critical, but it alone cannot give a completely accurate measure of outsourcing success. So before calculating ROI, make sure you:

1. Establish your organization's baseline before outsourcing. This will set the tone for determining project success.
2. Set project goals and define metrics for calculating project progress from point A to B. These metrics may include number of internal resources, claims processed daily, or dollar figures. While it can be difficult to determine metrics that accurately represent the value and align with business strategy, it's important to develop this method of measuring success at the beginning of the process.
3. Build assigned metrics into service level agreements (SLAs) with any outsourcing vendor. Service level agreements validate expectations of the respective parties and set parameters for measuring project success. This important tool helps determine value and define success and goes a long way to preventing disagreements. You may find vendors that oppose the metric and SLA process, but it's wise to insist on this step.

TIP Don't make SLAs so specific that they overcomplicate the outsourcing process. Micromanaging a vendor can lead to conflict. Give the vendor enough latitude to determine best practices that will result in a desirable end result for both parties. Setting service levels that simply mandate meeting certain contractual obligations can be risky. Focus not on how to outsource, but on its favorable outcome.

When it comes to measuring ROI, failing to include assessments of the cost of managing outsourcing is the most common and expensive mistake end users make when entering an outsourcing relationship. To avoid this pitfall, don't overlook these costs:

- Internal management of the outsourcing relationship
- Technology transfer
- Offshore outsourcing

Internal Management

On average, outsourcing buyers spend from 5 percent to 12 percent of the total contract value on managing the relationship. The cost of managing a $100 million contract that focuses on specified service levels (e.g., data center and desk top outsourcing) leans toward the low end—from $5 million to $8 million. In contrast, the cost of managing contracts that focus on managing specific business results (e.g., more complex business process outsourcing and applications outsourcing contracts) leans to the high end—ranging from $8 million to $12 million or more, depending on the specified business results. Clearly, the cost of internally managing a multimillion dollar outsourcing deal cannot be overlooked.

> "Outsourcing has been the key to increasing our margins over the last 12 or 15 years. The main challenge is to make sure you have good people running the operation. You really need a sourcing department to do it right. I believe in the free market concept. If we didn't outsource, we'd be paying a lot more for what we buy, and then we'd have to sell it for a lot more."
>
> —Eric J. Lane, president and chief operating officer, Men's Wearhouse. *Source:* Patricia R. Olsen, "The Profits and Pains of Outsourcing," *New York Times* (December 6, 2004).

Technology Transfer

Another hidden cost of outsourcing is the cost of technology transfer (e.g., servers, databases, and software to the outsourcing provider). It is especially important to include technology transfer cost in an ROI assessment of outsourcing that focuses on managing hard assets. Research indicates the cost of technology transfer for a typical outsourcing deal involving the transfer of assets, such as servers, storage, security, and systems management, ranges from 5 percent to 15 percent annually.

OFFSHORING

As the trend toward offshoring escalates and enterprises broaden the scope of functions and processes they send offshore, the cost of managing outsourcing will increase from 5 percent to 12 percent of the total contract value range indicated earlier to 10 percent to 18 percent, depending on the scope of the project.

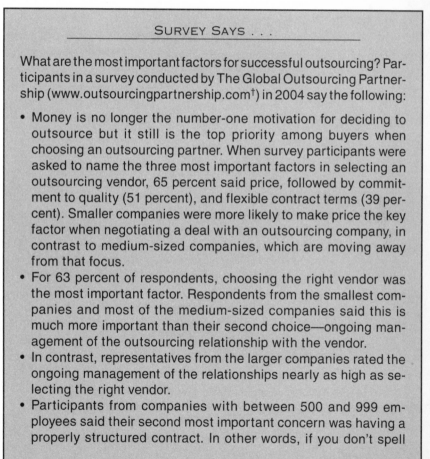

SURVEY SAYS . . .

What are the most important factors for successful outsourcing? Participants in a survey conducted by The Global Outsourcing Partnership (www.outsourcingpartnership.com[†]) in 2004 say the following:

- Money is no longer the number-one motivation for deciding to outsource but it still is the top priority among buyers when choosing an outsourcing partner. When survey participants were asked to name the three most important factors in selecting an outsourcing vendor, 65 percent said price, followed by commitment to quality (51 percent), and flexible contract terms (39 percent). Smaller companies were more likely to make price the key factor when negotiating a deal with an outsourcing company, in contrast to medium-sized companies, which are moving away from that focus.
- For 63 percent of respondents, choosing the right vendor was the most important factor. Respondents from the smallest companies and most of the medium-sized companies said this is much more important than their second choice—ongoing management of the outsourcing relationship with the vendor.
- In contrast, representatives from the larger companies rated the ongoing management of the relationships nearly as high as selecting the right vendor.
- Participants from companies with between 500 and 999 employees said their second most important concern was having a properly structured contract. In other words, if you don't spell

(Continued)

out to the vendor what you want in the first place, the relationship will quickly sour, no matter how well you think you can manage the process.
• Respondents from companies of all sizes feel the three issues
  related to the outsourcing vendor—selecting the right one, managing the relationship, and properly structuring the contract—
  are more important than understanding their firm's goals and
  objectives.

Regardless of your firm's priorities and needs, when considering an outsourcing vendor, according to the survey, cost should
never account for less than 30 percent of your decision. It's that
important to your success. Buyer organizations with less of a focus
on cost savings tend to lose control of their vendors and their contribution to your organization.

CONCLUSION

As you can see, successfully managing an outsourcing initiative is a complex process that involves detailed planning on the part of both organizations. Understanding the dynamics involved and communicating with
stakeholders regularly are essential to make the shift to an outsourcing
model. There is no shortcut. But the rewards are well worth the effort.

CHAPTER 8

NAVIGATING CONTRACTS AND NEGOTIATIONS

The legal and operational matters inherent to any outsourcing initiative are among the most complex and costly if not addressed early and managed properly thereafter. The objective of this chapter is to give you the background information you need to navigate these often rough waters.

Most outsourcing negotiations include three basic stages: assessment/ planning, vendor selection, and contract preparation. Each stage is critical to the overall transaction. An organization must take steps early during the assessment/planning stage to lay the foundation for a successful outsourcing transaction.

INVEST IN A QUALITY REQUEST FOR PROPOSAL

The request for proposal (RFP) serves as the basis for the overall outsourcing relationship, documenting the buyer's operational and financial requirements, as well as defining the outsourced function itself. A well-developed RFP accurately describes:

- Scope of the service
- Human, equipment, data, and other resources currently used
- Financial base
- Preferred service levels
- Desired pricing methodology

Note: Web addresses flagged with a (†) are author affiliated sites.

- Exclusive requirements regarding affected buyer's staff
- Key legal provisions governing the relationship

The RFP also expresses the buyer's selection criteria, which provide its internal stakeholders (and prospective outsourcing service providers) with the added benefit of a documented, objective selection process upon which to base its decision.

COMMIT TO A COMPETITIVE PROCESS

One of the key factors in achieving dramatic savings in outsourcing transactions, as well as negotiating favorable contract provisions, is to commit to a competitive selection process. This may necessitate negotiating precise contract provisions with two or more outsourcing suppliers and then selecting the vendor with the best mixture of solution, price, and legal security.

Those charged with governance of the outsourcing initiative, particularly the chief resource officer (CRO) should review a range of considerations when deciding whether, how, and how much to outsource. Particular attention must be given to the legal aspects and structure of the outsourcing contract and the viability of the deal. Typical outsourcing business legal factors include: cost savings and the viability of expense avoidance; reputation of the service provider; financial analysis and assumptions for comparing the vendor's contract price to the customer's current fully allocated costs; suitability of the scope of the contract to the anticipated resource needs of the customer; flexibility as to scope, duration, termination, intellectual property, future pricing, and future services; risk management in the contract; governing for a win-win approach; any unusual enterprise-specific considerations concerning the economic risks of transferring certain functions to the service provider; regulatory considerations; human resources management; integration of outsourcing with other business processes that are insourced or outsourced, or both; and the relationship of this outsourcing transaction to other infrastructure strategies, such as mergers and acquisitions, divestitures, spin-offs, split-offs, bankruptcy reorganization, strategic alliances, joint ventures, and other special situations.

Generally, best practices can be organized around the different phases in the outsourcing life cycle:

- Assessment and reassessment
- Strategic planning
- Selection of service providers
- Human resources planning

- Contract development and renegotiation
- Legal compliance
- Confidentiality and related issues
- Business process management
- Service level agreements
- Contract governance and relationship management
- Dispute resolution

ENCOURAGE EARLY COLLABORATION

The buyer's consultants often take a lead role in drafting the RFP, gaining a massive amount of knowledge in the process. This institutional wisdom may be lost when the project is transferred to outside attorneys for contract negotiations. From the beginning, encourage cooperation among management, consultants, and outside legal advisors.

MEASURE INTERNAL SERVICE LEVEL PERFORMANCE

In many cases, outsourcing vendors initially provide the outsourced services using the same resources—software, equipment, and personnel—that the buyer was using prior to the outsourcing. A buyer may find it difficult to convince a vendor to contractually commit to meeting desired service levels. The buyer may lose leverage during negotiations if unable to provide the vendor with historical statistics showing the vendor has met those desired service levels using those resources. If the buyer is unable to provide this data, the service provider may require a measurement period following contract execution during which the vendor will institute service levels rooted upon its actual, measured performance. This state of affairs causes understandable

---

BUYER'S VIEW OF SLAs

Service level agreements have become a necessity within all outsourcing relationships. More often than not clients today demand that minimum service standards be met by their outsourcing vendor and to that end are ensuring that their SLAs are legally structured to either pass on risk or to create an expedient exit strategy from their contractual relationship.

(Continued)

> SLAs contain indispensable information regarding the intended service, and what-if scenarios. The best time to negotiate an SLA is in the beginning of contract negotiations. Detail as much as possible up front. Whether part of the main outsourcing agreement or as an addendum to the main contract, an SLA must describe in detail the expectations and parameters for your outsourcing relationship. It must consider minimum levels of acceptable service and describe consequences and shared risk when these levels are not met. Your SLA should be logical, and enforceable through legal action if necessary.

risk for the buyer organization. Setting service levels after contract execution leaves key components of the overall outsourcing relationship unsettled.

IMPLEMENTING BEST PRACTICES

In long-term relationships, the key component for outstanding relationship realization is established during the negotiations stage, which leads up to the execution of the outsourcing contracts and service level agreement. Some elements common to successful outsourcing relationships are:

- *Relationship between key management and governance personnel.* Mutual understanding and shared work ethic between the key management and personnel of both groups will go far to nurture and sustain the relationship. Likewise, peer friendships and good "chemistry" with cross-company counterparts are important factors.
- *Measurable objectives.* The objectives to be achieved by outsourcing must be quantifiable and established as criteria at the start of the contract. If the customer can evaluate the performance with the predetermined objective, then the return of outsourcing will be clear, as will vendor measurement against buyer expectations. Well-defined performance criteria have quantifiable purposes, service quantities, quality, and satisfaction, and are measurable against other vendors and internal standards.
- *Structured working groups.* Successful outsourcing relationships involve establishing special teams that employ the most effective tactics for handling outsourcing relationships. Identification and rapid resolution of issues are key responsibilities of these groups.

- *Incentives and penalties.* The vendor is expected to meet or exceed client expectations by establishing performance-based pricing. When performance exceeds the criteria, the incentives pertain; and when they fall short, the penalties are compulsory.
- *Periodical formal reviews.* For a successful vendor/buyer relationship, a best practice is to hold frequent formal review meetings to discuss what both groups are achieving and give a high-level view of the future goals. Deliverables should be recurring agenda items.
- *Training provider staff.* Vendor personnel will need ongoing training if they are to achieve their business goals and meet the objectives of the client.

ESTABLISHING CONTRACT MEASUREMENTS

Measurements are the primary means by which to determine the success or failure of the outsourcing process. Measurements ensure that the vendor is held accountable, hence, they determine the success of the outsourcing effort. If appropriate measurements are not in place when the program begins, the contract cannot be managed effectively.

Start with the measures identified in the cost-benefit analysis. These describe critical success factors where improvement should be seen. Measurements must reflect the specific objectives of the outsourcing effort and be readily obtainable through business processes and procedures.

Consider metrics in three different areas:

1. Outcome- and performance-based metrics.
2. Metrics for quality assurance.
3. Key indicator operational metrics.

The objective is to measure the success of the vendor in meeting the business needs of your company. These measurements will become the tracking mechanisms for contract management, so contracts should include specifics about what will happen if metrics do not meet agreed-upon expectations.

DRAFTING AN OUTSOURCING CONTRACT

The outsourcing contract must be a comprehensive and balanced document, yet flexible enough to accommodate the inevitable changes that will

Table 8.1
Key Contract Questions and Elements

Key Contract Negotiation Questions	Key Contract Elements
Who owns it?	Scope of responsibilities and services (statement of work)
Who pays for it?	Price
How much does it cost?	Deliverables (delivery schedule and due dates)
Who is responsible for it	Performance standards, guarantees, penalties
How will it get done/maintained?	Flexibility (business volume, pricing)
How will it get measured?	Personnel provisions
When will it get done?	Ownership of data/software
What happens if it is not done?	Intellectual property rights
What happens to it at contract termination?	Warranties
What about software escrow?	Limitation of liability
	Confidentiality and disclosure
	Right to negotiate
	Changes clause
	Force majeure
	Dispute resolution
	Termination (addresses different termination scenarios, assistance provisions, costs)

occur in technology and the marketplace during the period of the agreement. It will cover everything from arbitration to support and costs to responsibilities, and, when drafted properly, will become the basis from which to forge a durable and profitable outsource relationship. Table 8.1 lists key contract negotiation questions and key contract elements.

Outsourcing contracts are intended to allocate risks between buyers and vendors. Typically, they allocate known risks and provide some opportunity to each party to have access to commercially reasonable recourse for risks that are unlikely, but nonetheless possible. In drafting a contract, be sure to address these contractual provisions:

- *Change in scope of services.* In defining the scope of contracted services, the buyer should establish a method for integrating the vendor's services into its other service infrastructures, both internal and external, current and planned. Accordingly, any change in the scope of the services will likely affect staffing commitments, technology investment, pricing and service level commitments, among others.

- *Changes in the global outsourcing business environment.* In today's global economic environment, unforeseeable changes to the business environment are inevitable. Such changes could result in a dramatic surge (or equally dramatic decline) in the customer's utilization of the outsourcing vendor's services. The contract, thus, should anticipate the impact on pricing and service level commitments, and indeed all commitments.

- *Changes in the legal environment.* Laws, rules, and regulations change, often unpredictably. For example, a customer's international business might be brought to a halt if the vendor cannot accommodate new privacy rules imposed by the European Union's directives. Contracts that do not anticipate such changes must be construed to allocate the cost of compliance with such new directives, even if they do not have the force of law in the United States. Accordingly, contracts should require the vendor to comply with changes in the laws.

- *Prealignment of service levels with customer's business objectives.* Service level commitments should be geared toward measurable predictors of the buyer company's shareholder value. To the extent that service commitments reflect purely technical specifications, not business drivers, tensions will persist between technical performance and long-term partnership. Outsource buyers should be aware of such inherent tensions and plan legally to protect their right to realign the services contract with their evolving management plans for maximizing shareholder value.

In the process of drafting the outsourcing contract, two important guidelines will protect your interests. First, clarify the details. This includes specifying schedule, terms of employment, and terms of payment. The outcome of a project depends on how well its path was signposted prior to launch.

TIP Different projects may call for different payment modes. If you have chosen to do business with different outsourcing firms, be flexible enough to adapt to the payment mode that you, your vendor, and your consultants can be at ease with.

Second, never lose sight of the legal implications of doing business in the countries of your vendors. They may—and probably do—have distinct legal concerns that will directly influence the business environment—that is, your business environment.

Other contract-specific guidelines to keep in mind include:

- *Pricing.* Outsourcing vendors naturally expect to profit on their deal with your organization. In this regard, contract negotiation should focus on the value of the contract to the organization and on lowering expected profits to reasonable levels.
- *Use of consultants.* There are positive and negative aspects to involving third parties in any outsourcing initiative. As we've already discussed, a consultant firm can be an important advisor in determining whether to outsource and in selecting a vendor. Similarly, hiring a third party to manage the contract will free management to focus on the project and to be accountable for the project and specifications; however, it will also add to the total cost and add another layer of communication between the organization and the contractor. During contract negotiations, address whether the vendor may use a third party, and who will have input on third-party selection.
- *Terms and conditions.* Developing a standard business contract and/or RFP formats will be beneficial in the negotiating process. Make sure that vendors address everything in the RFP. Vendor contracts usually contain terms less favorable to the user and provide vendors with additional leverage in negotiations. Pay close attention to all contract terms and conditions, and confirm that the most critical measurements and terms for your business are included in the contract. If it is not in the contact, it is not in the deal, regardless of what a vendor representative may say.
- *Vendor staff.* Does the vendor plan to use subcontractors? If so, responsibility for their performance should remain with the primary vendor. Dealing with several contractors and vendors will add markedly to the complexity of the undertaking, especially if your company is responsible for coordinating between vendors or has to negotiate separate deals with different parties. This may greatly impact your flexibility with the vendor after contract execution.
- *Accountability.* Consider including financial penalties in the contract to ensure vendor accountability for performance, with appropriate allowances made for customer error and the chance to correct first-time problems quickly without imposing penalties.

MANAGING THE OUTSOURCING CONTRACT

We've touched on this topic previously: the importance of assigning internal resources to manage the contract, regardless how large or small the outsourcing effort is. We expand on this topic here.

First, not all outsourcing projects require the same level of management. When you outsource a particular task, it requires fewer in-house resources to manage the contract. For example, help-desk services have standard metrics and are usually well understood by service providers, so fewer in-house staff are required to oversee the contractor's performance. In contrast, a larger, more inclusive initiative, such as one for outsourcing development projects or overall management, will require more far-reaching in-house oversight because of the specialized measures involved and the importance of strategic planning to the success of these efforts.

Managing an outsourcing contract requires a combination of in-house expertise. The outsourcing project team should be experienced in finance and corporate processes and activities. Specific technical knowledge also may be required to oversee a project implementing new technologies or business processes. Legal counsel should always be an available resource. Oversight staff lacking these diverse strengths will not always be able to identify emerging problems and ensure a successful outcome.

TIP No amount of contractual boilerplate can protect against problems spawned by neglect, poor communications, or failure to identify and plan one's business. So, in planning the transition, as well as the postcontract management, the buyer must maintain trusted, technologically savvy managers to supervise and plan with the outsourcing vendor's account manager. Effective contract management requires skills that differ from those necessary for managing in-house staff. Senior management should ensure that the team managing the vendor has these skills.

Overseeing an outsourcing contract requires that adequate controls and well-laid lines of communication be in place to surface, then resolve, problem performance issues ASAP. The outsourcing project team responsible for evaluating the success and performance of the outsourcing contract must be assured the resources, support, and flexibility necessary to deal with unforeseen issues that come up during the course of the contract.

In this regard, communication with the vendor is of the utmost importance. Knowledgeable internal staff must be available at all times to identify problems and work (i.e., communicate) with the vendor to resolve them. During your vendor selection process, you will have done all the necessary due diligence to ensure you have chosen a vendor whose business/functional culture aligns with that of your organization, so that communication is fostered and developed to support the effort. Keep the lines of communication open to both corporate internal staff and customers throughout the project.

THE IMPORTANCE OF FLEXIBILITY TO CHANGE MANAGEMENT

Outsourcing involves fundamental changes to the infrastructures that deliver support services to the organization. Managing this change requires careful planning and ongoing management of technology, pricing, service, corporate culture, and skills. As part of this process, a goal for both vendors and buyers should be to determine how to give the buyer market-driven elasticity, to enable the customer to respond as needed to shifts in the marketplace for its core competencies.

Planning should also restrict changes that are obvious and foreseeable. How often will the vendor change the personnel engaged on the account? For what reasons, and how often, will the technology be updated? Who will assume the risk of such change? Contractual restrictions on certain changes can achieve predictability and, thereby, reduce risk for both vendors and buyers.

Still other changes must be mandated. Some of the most vehement criticisms about outsourcing stem from a lack of flexibility in continuous process improvement in the price-performance ratio. Unless the vendor is financially motivated to provide market-driven improvements, the customer will only get those service levels initially contracted for.

MAINTAINING CONFIDENTIALITY

Confidentiality always an issue in outsourcing arrangements, where business partners must share confidential information. In outsourcing, certain information must be disclosed at specific times to implement the strategy; thus, in the process of conducting an outsourcing strategy, customers must

Outsourcing Goals: What Are the Most Important Factors Driving Your Company's Ongoing Relationship with an Outsourcer?

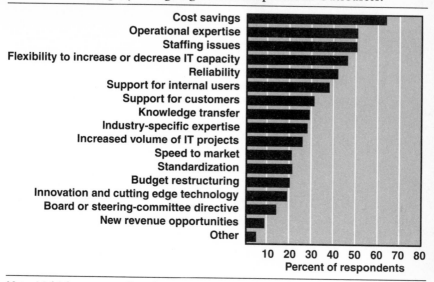

Cost savings
Operational expertise
Staffing issues
Flexibility to increase or decrease IT capacity
Reliability
Support for internal users
Support for customers
Knowledge transfer
Industry-specific expertise
Increased volume of IT projects
Speed to market
Standardization
Budget restructuring
Innovation and cutting edge technology
Board or steering-committee directive
New revenue opportunities
Other

10 20 30 40 50 60 70 80
Percent of respondents

Note: Multiple responses allowed. *Data: Information Week* research analyzing the outsourcers study of 700 business-technology professionals, November 2002.

plan and time the process of gathering information, protecting existing information, and disclosing sensitive information at the right time.

To preserve the outsourcing buyer's rights and limit its risks, the early stages of the process should be kept confidential, until it has been determined that outsourcing can provide the type of transformation, change in business model, cost savings, or other competitive advantage.

When it comes to service delivery, the buyer organization should verify that the service provider has the capacity and skill to protect the rights of third parties, as well as the proper policies and procedures for preserving and maintaining confidentiality of data used by the outsourcing services provider. These policies and procedures should be aligned with, or more strict and secure, than those of the buyer organization.

RENEGOTIATING OR TERMINATING THE CONTRACT

Contract renegotiation is an element of the outsourcing process that is often ignored or minimized by buyers at the outset of the arrangement. When you acknowledge from the beginning that during its course the contract may—and probably will—change, and eventually will end, you will be better prepared to either renegotiate or terminate, depending on the success of the foregoing agreement.

TIP As buyers find the need to extract more savings from their existing outsourcing arrangements, the trend is to renegotiate vendor contracts, to take advantage of additional cost-saving opportunities and adapt to new economic standards. The lure of new business or the threat of a declining scope may serve as a motivation for renegotiation.

The end-of-contract options are to:

- Contract again with the current vendor.
- Choose another vendor.
- Restore internal resource management.

Any of these options involves spending significant company time, money, and effort. Re-contracting with the vendor may lead to higher contract costs if your company becomes locked into working with one vendor. Selecting a new vendor will entail transition costs, to account for the learning curve, as well as additional management and resource costs. You will also incur new contract and negotiation costs. If you choose to restore the function internally, this will require adequate in-house staff with the knowledge, skills, and time necessary to take it on. Here, too, you will incur transition costs.

The nature of the outsourcing industry makes it difficult to predict needs and resource usage, so long-term contracts for services will have to change over the life of the contract, no matter the business process involved. Once you recognize that renegotiations will occur in even the best planned contract, due to unforeseen advancements in technologies or modified business needs, you will stand prepared to renegotiate with full understanding of the types of leverage available to your organization.

CONCLUSION

We close this chapter with four important tips to help you avoid common contract pitfalls:

1. *Say no to canned contracts.* Many tried-and-true outsourcing contract concepts have been developed in recent years, but a canned form contract with boilerplate provisions is not one of them. It is the contract negotiation process itself that drives the parties to a thorough understanding of their respective roles in the outsourcing relationship.

2. *Say yes to short contracts.* We recommend new contracts span only two years. Competition is a very good thing; it allows customers to seek other bids and compare them with the services they are receiving. Competition keeps the supplier honest.

3. *Protect your proprietary processes and limit liability.* Outsourcing buyers must be assiduous about protecting all proprietary processes and minimizing liabilities.

   A vendor to whom your company awards an outsourcing contract is in a unique position to identify your corporate strengths/weaknesses and use these observations to benefit itself in future negotiations. Instruct everyone on your outsourcing governance staff to direct all questions and inquiries from potential vendors to the negotiation team. This precaution discourages covert information gathering by vendors. Typical questions posed by vendors to be on the alert for are:

   - How many new or ongoing large projects are occurring within your company? An answer to this question could give the vendor insight into corporate staffing loads and concern about meeting deadlines.
   - Has the company outsourced any other functions? An answer to this question could give the vendor information on your corporate negotiation skills and assessment techniques.

4. *Ask for help.* Finally, if you need help managing the complexity of an outsourcing arrangement, contact a reputable firm such as First Outsourcing (www.firstoutsourcing.com). They have expertise in defining statements of work, evaluating internal needs, negotiating, evaluating vendor performance, and providing quality assurance. Yes, their services represent additional outsourcing costs, but they will help your business reduce risks and accomplish corporate goals.

For the more advanced outsourcing buyer organization, The Outsourcing Partnership (www.outsourcingpartnership.com[†]) is a brokerage site for both Buyers and Vendors of Outsourcing. There services includes "Reverse Auction" capabilities, webex sessions for bids, RFP services, vendor rating services, prequalified vendors, prepared and posted RFIs and RFPs, announcements of outsourcing vendor and buyer opportunities, and transition/implementation consultancy services.

CHAPTER 9

NEW CAREER OPPORTUNITIES IN OUTSOURCING MANAGEMENT

Media attention, as we've mentioned, has tended to focus on the negatives of outsourcing, specifically the number of jobs disappearing as a result of this strategy. To balance that, in this chapter, we turn your attention to the new career opportunities *emerging* thanks to the outsourcing movement.

Though managers, workers, and support staff all may be able to broaden their career scopes due to outsourcing, the fastest growing need is for high-level managers—in particular, the chief resource officer (CRO)—in both buyer and outsourcing organizations. Until recently, however, the qualifications and experience required for this position have been variously defined, causing confusion among employers and, thus, difficulty finding and training qualified candidates to successfully lead their outsourcing functions and relationships. Without the proper training, most corporate leaders cannot understand the demands, culture issues, and fundamental work principles of outsourcing; instead, they focus only on reducing costs—which as we've noted throughout this book, is a mistake.

We've talked about the importance of the CRO in all contexts of this book so far, so you might be surprised to learn that, until 2004, there was no centralized training and or credentialing organization for this, the leading outsourcing executive in a buyer corporation or business. Now, fortunately, there is.

CHIEF RESOURCE OFFICER TRAINING

The Chief Resource Officer Institute (www.CROInstitute.com), a U.S.-based educational foundation, offers the only coursework in this field sanctioned by the American Association of Chief Resource Officers (AACRO), the International Association of Chief Resource Officers, and the International Society of Outsourcing Business Professionals. Following successful completion of the multicourse, self-paced programs, which can be accomplished in less than six months, qualified executives may be credentialed as a Certified Chief Resource Officer® and support staff as a Certified Outsourcing Governance Professional™ which oversees outsourcing compliance and contract management. They come away with the skills necessary to lead companies that are planning or already are implementing an outsourcing business strategy. The certified CRO is generally the peer of the chief information officer (CIO) and chief financial officer (CFO) and generally reports directly to the chief executive officer (CEO).

These certificate programs provide an in-depth background in outsourcing as a strategic management discipline, addressing critical success factors and industry best practices throughout the entire outsourcing life cycle. Each module combines lectures, industry articles, white papers, and exercises to help ensure participant application of material presented.

CERTIFICATION: IT'S NOT JUST FOR BUYER ORGANIZATIONS

From the vendor perspective, through certification training at www.outsourcingmanagementinstitute.com, a new position called Certified Outsourcing Administrator (COA) is being employed as the chief relationship manager to look after their best interests and give the outsourcer a point person for the CRO to work with.

Through certification training, the COA, when empowered as the focal point of all outsourcing strategy, implementation, and relationship management, can ensure that all outsourcing relationships live up to buyer and vendor expectations.

Five characteristics that make an outstanding COA:

1. *Interpersonal skills.* The ability to manage people is vital. COAs will ultimately be responsible for coordinating the efforts of their

(Continued)

technical and operations staff assigned to the client. It's crucial that they have the interpersonal and leadership skills to direct team members and keep them motivated and on track. They also need to be able to smoothly navigate the sometimes-tricky political waters within and between the participating client organizations.

2. *Organizational skills.* This characteristic is key to keeping client projects on schedule and budget. The ability to assign resources, prioritize tasks, and keep tabs on the budget will ensure quality, thus directly impacting the project's success. These tasks begin with the sales process and continue through contract negotiation and implementation.

3. *Communication skills.* The project manager is the main communications link between the vendor and the buyer. His or her ability to clearly communicate with members of both groups is essential. He or she must be able to clearly communicate vendor and buyer objectives, challenges or problems, scope changes, and regular management reporting. In offshore outsourcing, communication skills become even more critical. COAs must not only communicate with team members who may be on the other side of the world, they must do so in a way that makes the global nature of the project invisible to the client. An experienced offshore outsourcing administrator can do this with ease.

4. *Problem-solving skills.* In every project, it's the unexpected problems or challenges that can derail the best-laid plans. The COA must be able to effectively handle these situations and mitigate risk.

5. *Professional training.* COAs who have CRO Institute-certified training are top-level professionals who have satisfied education and experience requirements, have agreed to adhere to a code of professional conduct, and have passed the COA Certification Examination.

HIRING A CERTIFIED PROFESSIONAL

Most companies involved in outsourcing flounder when it comes to ascertaining whether their vendors are living up to their service-level agreements. Too often, relationships are sketchy and performance reporting is monitored only by the vendor. But are these reasons enough to hire a certified professional to head your outsourcing governance team? To determine whether your company should use a certified outsourcing professional and support staff, answer the following questions:

- Does spending on outsourcing firms represent more than 20 percent of your annual technology budget?
- Does spending on outsourcing firms represent more than 10 percent of your annual operating budget?
- Does your company employ more than two outsourcing firms? Is your company currently considering outsourcing more functions?
- Do you plan to outsource functions such as payroll, training, benefits, or data management?
- Do the managers of each corporate business unit negotiate their service level agreements individually?

If you answered yes to any of these questions, it's likely your company could better govern how outside firms provide your most basic human and technological resources with the addition of a certified CRO and, potentially, midlevel outsourcing managers. And you're not alone: the demand is becoming so great for skilled CROs that their number is expected to grow from a few hundred in 2004 to 30,000-plus over the next two years, as more outsourcing takes place (2004 Annual Report, CRO Institute, January 2005).

TIP Support staff, too, who are part of the corporate oversight team are acquiring certifications as Outsourcing Governance Professionals at a rapid rate, to distinguish themselves as serious outsourcing specialists, thereby expanding the value in their current firms and the global marketplace.

Understanding the Need

Could this be your firm? You decide to outsource the administration of your human resources functions between Hewitt Associates and Exult, your business process (BP) outsourcing functions to e-Funds, your application development to MphasiS, your information technology (IT) help desk to Patni, your printing and advertising to PrintGPO, and your financial systems to Accenture. Multiple vendor arrangements need governance and contract monitoring. CROs are trained via certification to expertly balance several vendors and outsourced projects simultaneously.

Often, companies new to outsourcing will assign a displaced manager to take over the outsourcing arrangement of one business unit. That's acceptable as long as a company outsources only one function. But once a company begins using several outsourcing vendors to provide different services, the complexity increases and governing multiple relationships becomes more difficult. A top-level career executive, with certified outsourcing skills, will be well equipped to effect change in the way outsourcing is bought and sold in his or her organization. The CRO, led by a certified CRO, COGP, or a COA, and a team of certified professionals in outsourcing, can help enable organizational transformation, compete more effectively on a global scale, and generate shareholder value.

But one executive may not be enough to manage the outsourcing function. Many companies are now looking at expanding entire departments for outsourcing planning, strategy, monitoring, negotiations, implementations, backsourcing, evaluations, and relationship management with several vendors.

Certified CROs and Outsourcing Governance Professionals will know where the intersections are between business units; they will understand that when outsourcing deals are treated separately, there will be clashes, conflicts, overlaps, and missed connections. Companies and leaders that intend to remain competitive will want to ensure they can accomplish their objectives by establishing an outsourcing management division, led by a certified CRO and a team of certified professionals in outsourcing.

EUROPE'S GROWING DEMAND FOR SKILLED OUTSOURCING MANAGERS

International companies may not be using the same outsourcing terms as the United States, but the demand for qualified professionals is the same. Managers who are capable of getting the best out of an increasingly diverse workforce, who are aware of the challenges that accompany this diversity, are in great demand. The growing demand in Europe is partly due to the removal of borders within the European Union, allowing citizens of member countries to accept jobs in any other European country they choose.

Managers who have or acquire these abilities will be singled out for advancement, possibly even for grooming for top leadership positions. *Transcultural competence* will become a highly regarded job qualification in the outsourcing industry.

Becoming or Hiring a Certified Professional

Whether you are considering taking certification training or planning to hire a corporate CRO or a COGP, here are the critical skills involved:

- *Operations management.* A CRO must have experience managing a variety of operations and functional business units. Serving as the nucleus between the buyer and vendor requires that the CRO understand both the outsourcing operations and his or her firm's core competencies. Absence of this skill will impair smooth and informed decision making.
- *Cost management.* The CRO will be responsible for several relationships designed to improve his or her company's bottom line. Thus, a solid financial background is essential to give the CRO an understanding of how each decision or aspect of the outsourcing relationship will affect the company and the vendor financially.
- *Project management.* The ability to lead projects through development, implementation, and maintenance is imperative. A CRO must be able to juggle several projects as well.
- *Contract negotiation.* Ideally, the CRO will be in place before any outsourcing contracts go into negotiation because contracts are best managed by the person most involved in their drafting.
- *Mediation.* A savvy CRO will, whenever possible, choose vendors with a similar corporate culture. But when it is not possible, the CRO will need to understand the culture of both parties to ease transitions and to ensure a smooth flow of work. Moreover, if a company has chosen an offshore vendor, the CRO will be charged with understanding their customary way of doing business.
- *Perspective.* CROs and COGPs need to understand the general functionalities of the various departments and services to be outsourced, the financial impact of those choices, how decisions overlap within a corporation, and the public/employee relations effects of outsourcing decisions.
- *Flexibility.* Because the outsourcing industry is in its infancy, a CRO must be able to "go with the flow," to adjust to potentially abrupt transformations in the vendor relationship.

Producing Results

The CRO's job is to produce measurable results, and contrary to what many believe, this doesn't happen by taking risks. The most skillful managers produce results, first, by carefully assessing risks and then, managing them. In the current outsourcing business climate, this is an imperative. Outsourcing managers can leave no margin for error.

First, look at your outsourcing buyer organization. Do you have dedicated project managers and a project management process that is geared toward outsourcing vendor remote staff and projects? It will take more effort, not less, to keep a long-distance project on track, particularly with several vendors. Offshore projects require additional travel and communication costs. You must be able to budget for these trips. And what about personnel? Do you have project managers ready and willing to travel? Will there be political implications for your organization if your outsourcing initiative is publicized? How can you minimize this risk?

Next, define your project. Outsourcing, whether offshore or local, demands meticulous documentation and definition of the results you want and how you want them accomplished. If you don't have the staff or time to do the front-end documentation, or if you anticipate numerous iterative changes, you may be setting yourself up for failure by outsourcing the project. Again, ask: Is it *core* to your organization's mission? You may want to look for other opportunities to outsource and stay in control of a core project or function.

Third, break the project into smaller segments. Doing so will help you minimize risk. In a new outsourcing relationship, a small, short-turnaround project can help you evaluate the vendor, refine the project measurement and management process, and minimize your loss in the event of serious problems.

Fourth, measure, review, and refine the process. The need to manage risk makes careful analysis and planning before initiating a project critically important. Once set into motion, every project needs well-defined, periodic measurement and management to keep it on course.

CHAPTER 10

FINDING TOP OUTSOURCERS: VENDOR DIRECTORY

Outsourcing business initiatives is not about abandoning control, but about trusting a business partner to aid you in your quest for excellence. Trust can only develop over time and through experience, but this process can be facilitated by knowing which vendors have earned the right to be deemed trustworthy in their field. To give you that all-important head start, this chapter, unlike any other in this book, is simply a listing of the vendors, categorized by the outsourcing functions they provide. You'll find full contact information for each, followed by a brief capabilities description. Table 10.1 on pages 159–163 summarizes the top-ranked vendors for 2004 to 2005.

TIP Updated and additional listings can be found at this book's corresponding reference web site: www.TheBlackBookOfOutsourcing .com.

Categories for Listings

Accounting and Audit
Accounts Payable
Accounts Receivable
Administrative and Management Support
  Services

Application Development
Application Maintenance and Reengineering
Application Management
Architecture and Engineering
Back-Office Processing

Note: Web addresses flagged with a (†) are author affiliated sites.

Banking and Financial Solutions
Benefits Administration
Business Continuity Services
Business Process Outsourcing (BPO)
Business Services Reengineering
Business Support Systems
Call Centers
Capital Business Management
Channel Solutions
Collections
Communications Management
Construction
Content Solutions
Credit Services
Customer Interaction Services
Customer Relationship Management (CRM)
Cybersecurity and Infrastructure Support
Database Management
Data Center Management
Design and Multimedia
Document Creation and Management
Document Processing
E-Learning and Education Solutions
Employee Contact and Service Centers
Employment Solutions
Energy Analytics
Enterprise Resource Planning (ERP)
    Implementation
Enterprise Storage Solutions
Environmental Management
Expense Management
Facilities Management
Finance and Financial Services
Forms Processing/BPO
Global Delivery and Sourcing
Government Sourcing
Hospital, Clinical, and Medical Services
Human Resources (HR)
Information Retrieval
Information Technology (IT)
Insourcing and Intersourcing
Insurance Systems
Interactive Messaging
ISP Help Desk Services
IT Infrastructure Management
IT Mainframe and Server Management
    Outsourcing
IT Performance and Organizational
    Flexibility

IT Storage Management
IT Strategy and Planning
IT Support Services—Embedded Systems
IT Support Services and Enterprise
    Applications
IT Systems and Data Hosting
IT Systems Development
IT Systems Integration
Loan Processing
Logistics
Managed Application Systems
Managed Service Providers
Manufacturing and Engineering
Marketing Program Management
Mortgage Banking
Network Management
Office Solutions and Document Conversion
Payroll
Pharmaceutical
Point Solutions
Printing and Fulfillment
Procurement and Outsourcing Matching
Professional Employer Organizations
Project Management
Real Estate Management Outsourcing
Recruitment Process Outsourcing
Research and Analytics
Retail
Safety
Sales and Marketing
Scientific and Engineering Business
    Outsourcing
Software Quality Assurance/Testing
Staffing and Workforce
Strategic IT Partnership Outsourcing
Supply Chain Management
Systems Integration and Consulting
Talent and Human Capital Outsourcing
Tax Services
Telecommunications
Telephony and Business Communications
Training and Staff Development
Transaction Processing
Transformational Outsourcing
Tuition and Scholarship Services
Venture Capital Outsourcing Services
Web Development
Web Publishing
Workforce Consulting and Management

Table 10.1
Top-Ranked Vendors, 2004–2005

	Outsourcing Management Institute 50 Best Managed Outsourcing Vendors	CRO Institute 18 Highest Customer Satisfaction and Performance Ratings	U.S. Revenues 25 Largest American BPO Operations	BPOrbit 15 Top BPOs	DataQuest 25 Highest International Revenue BPOs	DQ-IDC 10 Best BPO Employers	HRO 9 Top Enterprise Human Resources Outsourcing Suppliers	Nasscom 20 Top Outsourced Software and IT Services Indian Suppliers	AMR 5 Best Remote Data Center Management
IBM Global /Daksh	1	X	X	X	X	X	X	X	X
Accenture	2	X	X		X			X	
Hewlett Packard	3	X	X	X	X	X		X	X
Mphasis	4	X	X	X	X			X	X
Ernst & Young/Capgemini	5	X	X	X	X				
Wipro Spectramind	6		X	X	X	X		X	X
ICICI Onesource	7	X		X	X		X	X	
eFunds Global Outsourcing	8	X	X	X	X				
Convergys	9	X			X		X		
Arinso	10	X	X	X	X	X			

(continued)

Table 10.1 (Continued)

	Outsourcing Management Institute 50 Best Managed Outsourcing Vendors	CRO Institute 18 Highest Customer Satisfaction and Performance Ratings	U.S. Revenues 25 Largest American BPO Operations	BPOrbit 15 Top BPOs	DataQuest 25 Highest International Revenue BPOs	DQ-IDC 10 Best BPO Employers	HRO 9 Top Enterprise Human Resources Outsourcing Suppliers	Nasscom 20 Top Outsourced Software and IT Services Indian Suppliers	AMR 5 Best Remote Data Center Management
Sutherland Technologies	11	X		X	X	X		X	
Oracle On Demand	12	X				X			
Hewitt/Exult	13		X				X	X	
HCL Technologies	14		X	X	X	X		X	X
Xansa	15	X	X		X				
CSC	16	X	X		X				
Unisys	17		X		X				
Keane	18		X			X			
Satyam	19		X					X	
CGI	20		X		X				
Cognizant	21		X						
Affiliated Computer Systems (ACS)	22	X	X		X		X		

Company	No.							
Intelligroup	23	X			X			
Northrop Grumman Information Technology (IT)	24	X			X			X
Infosys	25		X			X		
Getronics	26		X				X	
Covansys	27		X					
Syntel	28		X					
Ceridian	29	X						
Spherion	30					X		
ADP	31						X	
i-Flex	32					X		
TATA Infotech TATA Consulting	33		X	X	X	X		
GE	34				X			
Siemens Business Services	35		X					
Atos Origin International B.V.	36					X		

(continued)

Table 10.1 (Continued)

	Outsourcing Institute 50 Best Managed Outsourcing Vendors	CRO Institute 18 Highest Customer Satisfaction and Performance Ratings	U.S. Revenues 25 Largest American BPO Operations	BPOrbit 15 Top BPOs	DataQuest 25 Highest International Revenue BPOs	DQ-IDC 10 Best BPO Employers	HRO 9 Top Enterprise Human Resources Outsourcing Suppliers	Nasscom 20 Top Outsourced Software and IT Services Indian Suppliers	AMR 5 Best Remote Data Center Management
InfoCrossing	37	X		X					
Datamatics	38		X	X				X	
Outsourced Partners International	39				X				
TechBooks	40			X	X				
i-Gate	41							X	
Office Tiger	42				X				
Perot	43		X					X	
EDS	44		X				X		
Patni Computer	45							X	
Advantec HR	46						X		

VMC	47		X	
SourceNet Solutions	48			X
24/7 Customer	49	X		X
Deloitte	50			

A number of companies appear more than once, in different categories, an indication that their service offerings cross categories.

Accounting and Audit
Daksh IBM
Deloitte
Ernst & Young LLP
Hewlett-Packard (HP)
Outsource Partners International, Inc.
Price Waterhouse Coopers

Accounts Payable
Accenture
API Outsourcing, Inc.
CoEfficient Back Office Solutions
Earnest John Technologies (EJTL)
LASON

Accounts Receivable
CoEfficient Back Office Solutions
Earnest John Technologies

Administrative and Management Support Services
ACS
eFunds Corporation
FOCUS AMC
Investment Administration Sciences Inc.
NIIT SmartServe Ltd.
Office Tiger
OKS Group
TopSource Global

Advisors to Outsourcing
BPOAdvisors.com
First Outsourcing
Trowbridge Group

Application Development
Accenture
Aquent Inc.
Cognizant Technology Solutions
Covansys
CGI
Data Return
EDS
Espire Infolabs Inc.
Gateway TechnoLabs
Larsen & Toubro (L&T) Infotech
Mastek

MphasiS
NIIT Technologies
Olive Optimized e-Business Solutions
Perot Systems TSI India, Limited
Polaris Software Lab Limited
Siri Technologies
Softtek

Application Maintenance and Reengineering
Accenture
Cognizant Technology Solutions
EDS
Infosys—Progeon BPO Division

Application Management
CSC Financial (Computer Sciences Corp.)
CTG
Mahindra-British Telecom (MBT)
iGATE
Perot Systems TSI India, Limited
Syntel, Inc.

Architecture and Engineering
All States Technical Services
Satyam

Back-Office Processing
Aquarian Group
Daksh IBM
Datamatics
Deloitte
eDATA Infotechp Ltd.
eFunds Corporation
emr Technology Ventures
EXL Service
HCL BPO
i-Gate
Interpro Global
Meridian
Motif, Inc.
MphasiS
NIIT SmartServe Ltd.
PAR Computer Sciences (Int.) Ltd.
Sand Martin

Sutherland Global Services
Syntel, Inc.

Banking and Financial Solutions
Certegy
ICICI OneSource
i-flex Solutions
Satyam
Thinksoft Global Services

Benefits Administration
Accenture
ADP (Employer Services)
AlphaStaff Group Inc.
ARINSO International
Benefits Administration Services (BIS)
CareerSoar
eBenX, Inc.
FBD Consulting, Inc.
Gevity HR
Hewitt Associates
HR XCEL
India Life Capital
The Loomis Company
Morneau Sobeco
Workscape, Inc.

Business Continuity Services
Hewlett-Packard (HP)

Business Process Outsourcing (BPO)
Accenture
Capggemini
Convergys Corporation
CSC Financial (Computer Sciences Corp.)
EDS
eFunds Corporation
HCL BPO
Hinduja TMT Ltd.
Hughes BPO Services
Keane Worldzen
Liberata
PFSweb, Inc.
ProcessMind, Inc.
Sutherland Global Services
Syntel, Inc.
TATA Consultancy Services (TCS)
Trinity Partners
Unisys Corporation
vCustomer
Wipro Technologies
WNS Global Services

Business Services Reengineering
eFunds Corporation
Infosys—Progeon BPO Division

Business Support Systems
Convergys

Business Transformation Utility
Unisys Corporation

Call Centers
24/7 Customer
Accenture
Compass Technology Management
Customer First Call Centers
Daksh IBM.
eFunds Corporation
DOW Networks
eTelecare
GTL Limited
ICICI OneSource
LiveBridge
NIIT SmartServe Ltd.
OKS Group
PacificNet Communications
Perimeter Technology
Sykes
SSI Inc.
Telelink, The Call Center, Inc.
Tecnovate eSolutions
vCustomer
VMC
WNS Global Services
Zenta Technologies

Capital Business Management
GE Capital International Services

Channel Solutions
Aquent Inc.

Collections
Ajuba Solutions
CCR Services
D&B Receivables Management Services
eFunds Corporation
Epicenter
Outsourcing Solutions, Inc. (OSI)
STA International

Communications Management
Pitney Bowes, Inc.

Construction
Larsen & Toubro (L&T) Infotech

Content Solutions
TechBooks

Credit Services
CSC Credit Services
NCO Group

Customer Interaction Services
eFunds Corporation
Equitant
Wipro Spectramind

Customer Relationship Management (CRM)
AFFINA
Bearing Point
ClientLogic
Compass Technology Management
Convergys Corporation
i-flex Solutions
RightNow Technologies
Strategic Alliances LLC
Sutherland Global Services
TATA Consultancy Services
TeleTech
UCMS United Customer Management
  Solutions
vCustomer
WNS Global Services

Cybersecurity and Infrastructure Support
CISCO
Northrop Grumann

Database Management
Oracle On Demand

Data Center Management
Acxiom Corporation
AIG Technologies
CSC Financial
CTG
Digica Ltd.
SARCOM
VMC

Design and Multimedia
Artemis PR and Design
Designscape
Intetics Co./Web Space Station
Redix Web Solutions

Document Creation and Management
IKON
Pitney Bowes, Inc.

Document Processing
Advanced Business Fulfillment (ABF)
Cendris

E-Learning and Education Solutions
TATA Infotech Ltd.

Employee Contact and Service Centers
Exult, Inc.

Employee Portals and Assistance Programs
Ceridian Centerfile

Employment Solutions
Kenexa
Spherion
StratSource
TalentFusion

Energy Analytics
SourceNet Solutions

Enterprise Resource Planning (ERP) Implementation
Barry-Wehmiller International Resources
  (BWIR)
Computer Enterprises Inc.
ERP Outsourcing Asia Pte Ltd.
Global Business Services
ReSourcePhoenix.com
Terra Solutions

Enterprise Storage Solutions
Satyam

Environmental Management
Heritage Environmental Services

Expense Management
Gelco Information Network

Facilities Management
Eastco Building Services
Johnson Controls-Facilities Management
Outsource Management Group
Siemens Building Technologies, Inc.
Staubach Management Services (SMS)
UNICCO

Finance and Financial Services

Accenture
Aquarian Group
Capgemini
CSC Financial
Daksh IBM
Deloitte
eFunds Corporation
Geller & Company
HCL BPO
Hinduja TMT Ltd.
Kanbay
KPMG LLP
NCO Group
Outsourcing Partners International Inc.
(OPI)
Sundaram Finance Group

Forms Processing/BPO

Forms Processing, Inc. (FPI)
MphasiS

Global Delivery and Sourcing

Accenture
eFunds Corporation
HCL BPO
MphasiS
TATA Consulting Services (TCS
Trowbridge Group)

Global Outsourcing Consultants

First Outsourcing
HRBPOConsultants.com
OutsourcingLeadership.com
Trowbridge Group

Government Sourcing

ACS
Covansys
JPMorgan
Keane, Inc.
Unisys Corporation

Healthcare, Hospital, and Medical Services

Advanced Business Fulfillment
Ajuba Solutions
Amisys Synertech
Eclipsys
First Consulting Group
Keane, Inc.
LASON
Perot Systems Corporation

Human Resources (HR)

1st Odyssey Group
Accenture HR Services
Accord Human Resources
ACS
Administaff
ADP (Employer Services)
Advantec
AlphaStaff Group Inc.
Aon Consulting
ARINSO International
Ceridian Centrefile
CheckPoint HR
Complete HR
Convergys Employee Care
EADS (European Aeronautic Defense and
Space Company)
EDS
Exult, Inc.
Gevity
Hewitt Associates
HRCentral
HR XCEL
Manpower
Mellon HR Solutions
Mercer
PlatformOne
RSM McGladrey Employer Services
U.S. Personnel, Inc.
Xchanging

Image Processing

Barry-Wehmiller Internationa
Cendris

Information Retrieval

Office Tiger

Information Technology (IT)

ACS
Amnet Systems Private Limited
Atos Origin
Bearing Point
Barry-Wehmiller International Resources
(BWIR)
Capgemini
CGI
EDS
Fortune Infotech
Getronics
Hewlett-Packard (HP)
IBM Business Consulting Services
Infosys Technologies Limited

i-Vantage Inc.
Keane, Inc.
NEC
Perot Systems Corporation
Siemens Business Services, Inc.
Siri Technologies Pvt. Ltd.
TATA Consultancy Services (TCS)
Unisys Corporation
VCustomer
Wipro Technologies
Xansa

**Insourcing and Outsourcing
Consulting**
First Outsourcing

Insurance Systems
Accenture
AIG Technologies
Allenbrook, Inc.
Ebix Inc.
HCL BPO
Hinduja TMT Ltd.
ICICI OneSource
i-flex Solutions
Insurance Data Services
Pilgrim

Interactive Messaging
SmartSource Corporation

ISP Help Desk Services
Hughes BPO Services

IT Infrastructure Management
Acxiom Corporation
Capgemini
Totality Corporation

**IT Mainframe and Server Management
Outsourcing**
AIG Technologies
Bridgestone/Firestone Information Services
   (BFIS)
Infocrossing
(i)Structure, Inc.
NEC
VMC

**IT Performance and Organizational
Flexibility**
Keane, Inc.

IT Storage Management
IBM
(i)Structure, Inc.
Softek

IT Strategy and Planning
Booz Allen Hamilton Inc.

**IT Support Services—Embedded
Systems**
MphasiS
Patni Computer Systems Limited

**IT Support Services and Enterprise
Applications**
BlueStar Solutions
CompuCom
Covansys
DecisionOne Corporation
Getronics
MachroTech, LLC
MphasiS
Patni Computer Systems Limited
TMA Resources
United Systems Interrogators Corporation
Xansa

IT Systems and Data Hosting
Cognizant Technology Solutions
Data Infosys Ltd.

IT Systems Development
Arambh Network
Hexacta
Reliable Integration Services
SEEC Software

IT Systems Integration
Bearing Point
Birlasoft
CGI

Loan Processing
LASON, Inc.

Logistics
AMG Logistics
ArchiLog
Cendian Corporation
Jacobson Companies
Power Logistics
TSi Logistics
Wilson Logistics Inc.

Managed Application Systems
Atos Origin
Unisys

Managed Service Providers
CISCO
(i)Structure, Inc.
TriActive, Inc.

Manufacturing and Engineering
AeTec International, Inc.
Benchmark Electronics
Birch Group
Cendian Corporation
Global Outsourcing
International Smart Sourcing (ISS)
USA-BPO

Marketing Program Management
WNS Global Services

Mortgage Banking
Infosys—Progeon BPO Division
iSeva
Marlborough Stirling
U.S. Bank

Network Management
AT&T Solutions
Getronics
Information Management Systems, Inc.

Office Solutions and Document Conversion
Xerox

Payroll
Accenture
ADP
AlphaStaff Group Inc.
ARINSO International
CareerSoar
LeadingEdge Payroll Group Inc.
MBS
SourceNet Solutions

Pharmaceutical
Estco Medical
TGA Sciences, Inc.

Point Solutions
Siemens Business Services

Printing and Fulfillment
PrintGPO, Inc.

Procurement and Outsourcing Matching
Ariba
Global Outsourcing Partnership
Prosero
Trowbridge Group

Professional Employer Organizations
ADP TotalSource

Project Management
Keane, Inc.

Real Estate Management Outsourcing
CoreBriX
Equis Corporation
Trammell Crow Company

Recruitment Process Outsourcing
Accolo
Adecco Recruitment Management Solutions
BrassRing
Hudson Resourcing
Hyrian
Kenexa
Recruitment Enhancement Services (RES)

Research and Analytics
Office Tiger

Retail
Satyam

Safety
PlanTech, Inc

Sales and Marketing
ACS
Affina
American Customer Care, Inc.
Aquent Inc.
ClientLogic
Colwell & Salmon Communications
Epicenter
Sutherland Global Services
VMC

Scientific and Engineering Business Outsourcing
SAIC

Software Quality Assurance/Testing
AppLabs, Inc.
Caresoft Inc. Software Quality Assurance Labs
Cognizant Technology Solutions
Perot Systems TSI India, Limited
Thinksoft Global Services

Staffing and Workforce
Adecco Recruitment Management
AON Consulting
Kenexa
Manpower Inc.
Quintech Solutions Inc.
Vedior

Strategic IT Partnership Outsourcing
Intelligroup

Supply Chain Management
Accenture
ACS
AMG Logistics
Aquent Inc.
Ariba
EchoData West
Eurobase Limited
GENCO
Kaye-Smith
Logisteon Supply Chain Solutions
Prosero
StarTek, Inc.
Supply Chain Dynamics Inc.

Systems Integration and Consulting
Bearing Point

Talent and Human Capital Outsourcing
Hewitt Associates

Tax Services
CIC Enterprises
Ernst & Young LLP
Outsource Partners International, Inc.
PricewaterhouseCoopers (PwC)

Telecommunications
AT&T Solutions
Avaya
Getronics
Hughes BPO Services
International Network Administration
Mahindra-British Telecom (MBT)
MSS*Group, Inc.

Telephony and Business Communications
Avaya

Training and Staff Development
Advantec
Accenture
AON Consulting
Edcor
Exult, Inc. (Hewitt)
Hudson Resourcing
Intrepid Learning Solutions
Raytheon Professional Services (RPS)

Transaction Processing
Accenture
Datamatics
Diversified Information Technologies
ICG Commerce
ICICI OneSource
Outsource Partners International, Inc.

Transformational Outsourcing
Accenture
Deloitte
Equitant
IBM
Infosys Technologies Limited

Tuition and Scholarship Services
Scholarship Management Services
Edcor

Venture Capital Outsourcing Services
Outsourced VC Solutions

Web Development
Consortium Business Services
Direction Inc.
eonBusiness
Integrica
Kawin Interactive Inc.
Lead Dog Design & Development
Tim Kirker Creative

Web Publishing
Office Tiger

Workforce Consulting and Management
Veritude

1st Odyssey Group
Contact: Dave Rettig
Phone: 817-508-7402; Fax: 817-508-7403; e-mail: drettig@1stodyssey.com
Web Site: www.1stodyssey.com
1st Odyssey is one of the nation's leading professional employer organizations helping small to midsize businesses outsource many of their noncore administrative functions.

24/7 Customer
Contact: Hemalatha Nair
Phone: 080-2841-0775, Ext. 141; Fax: 080-2841-1767; e-mail: hemalatha.nair@247customer.com
Web Site: www.247customer.com
24/7 Customer is a leading global provider of business process outsourcing services and call center services. 24/7 Customer partners with your business to offer a range of outsourcing services that touch every point of the customer life cycle. 24/7 Customer enables your organization to build and sustain effective processes across various interaction points and the back office while delivering powerful insight into customer behavior through customer analytics.

Accenture
Contact: Laurie M. Schiro
Phone: 312-737-8842; e-mail: laurie.m.schiro@accenture.com
Web Site: www.accenture.com
Accenture is a global management consulting, technology services and outsourcing company. Committed to delivering innovation, Accenture collaborates with its clients to help them become high performance businesses and governments. With deep industry and business process expertise, broad global resources and a proven track record, Accenture can mobilize the right people, skills, and technologies to help clients improve their performance. For nearly two decades, they have been working with industry leaders to innovate and build outsourcing as an indispensable business tool. They offer the full suite of outsourcing services—application outsourcing, technology infrastructure outsourcing, customized BPO services and standardized, best in class BPO services through their portfolio of BPO businesses: Accenture Finance Solutions, Accenture HR Services, Accenture Learning, Accenture Procurement Solutions, Accenture Business Services for Utilities, Accenture e-Democracy Services, Accenture Insurance Services, and Navitaire.

Accenture HR Services
Contact: David Clinton
Phone: 312-737-8842
Web Site: www.accenture.com/hrservices
Accenture's offering covers: customer contact services, exit services, information services, learning services, HR advisory services, pay and benefits services, performance services, and resourcing services. Employing advanced technology and best-of-breed human resources practices, Accenture HR Services offers customized, integrated HR solutions that span the entire employee life cycle—from recruitment to retirement—for larger enterprises. It also has a more standardized, integrated offering for medium-sized companies and individual services available à la carte.

Accolo
Contact: Matt Cooper
Phone: 415-785-7833; e-mail: mcooper@accolo.com
Web Site: www.accolo.com
Accolo provides complete RPO for one job, a block of jobs, or all jobs. In 13 days on average, its staff finds, pre-interviews, and introduces the person who will be hired, supporting companies across the United States and acting as internal recruitment departments. RPO services include: managing the recruitment process directly with hiring manager; acting as primary recruitment

resource; promoting client's employment brand; managing applicant tracking; incorporating all applicant sources; taking jobs from initial profiling with hiring manager to closing process; assessing each candidate; driving diversity sourcing efforts and capturing, tracking, and reporting EEO data; and ensuring consistent follow-through and closure for all applicants and candidates.

Accord Human Resources

Contact: Jason Skaggs
Phone: 405-232-9888, Ext. 141; Fax: 405-232-9899; e-mail: jskaggs@accordhr.com
Web Site: www.accordhr.com
Accord Human Resources helps small to medium-sized businesses improve productivity and profitability by providing comprehensive "outsourced" human resource management solutions. Accord provides the following services: human resources, benefit administration, payroll and tax administration, and risk management.

ACS

Contact: Lesley Pool
Phone: 214-841-8028; Fax: 214-584-5873; e-mail: lesley.pool@acs-inc.com
Web Site: www.acs-inc.com
Human resources services touch all the processes involved in the selection, compensation, development, and retention of employees. ACS solutions include payroll processing and management; benefits administration; hiring, staffing, and recruiting; personnel management; HR systems support and administration; education and learning services; employee assistance centers; and relocation services. ACS is the leading provider of fully diversified, end-to-end BPO and information technology (IT) solutions to commercial and government clients worldwide. With service delivery and global operations reaching nearly 100 countries, more than 43,000 people, and a blue-chip client list, ACS delivers comprehensive solutions for all segments of BPO and IT services. ACS makes technology work. Administration services include the management and tracking of electronic and paper-based documentation, equipment and asset purchases, and work facilities. ACS solutions include document management, records management, asset management, security administration, and facilities administration.

Acxiom Corporation

Contact: Jane Vitro
Phone: 501-342-1000; e-mail: jane.vitro@acxiom.com
Web Site: www.acxiom.com
Sales Inquiries Phone: 888-322-9466
Contact: Peggy Walters
Phone: +44 020 7526 5134; Fax: +44 020 7526 5261; e-mail: peggy.walters@acxiom.com
Acxiom has been in the outsourcing business for more than 30 years. Its 1,200 technology professionals support 6,000 servers and 18,000 mainframe MIPS across seven data centers in the United States and United Kingdom. This includes specific IT infrastructure expertise to address the needs of consumer-focused companies.

Adecco Recruitment Management Solutions

Contact: Ray Roe
Phone: 631-844-7800
Web Site: www.adeccousa.com
Contact: Chris King
Phone: +41 1 878 8838; e-mail: Chris.King@Adecco.com
Adecco is the RPO division of the staffing giant that serves global companies in the automotive, banking, electronics, logistics, and telecommunications industries, as well as local customers of all sizes and sectors looking for flexible staffing solutions. Adecco's services include temporary recruitment, temporary to permanent recruitment, permanent recruitment, and staff-related services.

Administaff

Contact: Jay E. Mincks
Phone: 281-358-8986 or 800-237-3170; e-mail: Jay_Mincks@administaff.com
Web Site: www.administaff.com
Contact: Alan Dodd
Phone: 281-348-3105; e-mail: alan_dodd@administaff.com
This national PEO provides full-service HR support to small and medium-sized businesses across the nation. Administaff has 4 regional service centers and 38 sales offices nationwide and was listed among "America's Most Admired Companies" for four years in *Fortune* magazine and named to *Information Week* 500 list of one of the leading information technology innovators. Administaff is traded on the NYSE, accredited by the Employer Services Assurance Corporation, and an active member of the National Association of PEOs.

ADP Employer Services

Contacts: Rita Mitjans or Mark Benjamin
Phone: 800-CALL-ADP or 973-952-7000 or 305-630-1000; e-mail: rita_mitjans@adp.com
Web Site: www.adp.com
This data processing giant also provides full-service, comprehensive HR services, including traditional and Internet-based outsourcing solutions to almost half a million employers in more than 26 countries. In addition to payroll solutions and tax returns, ADP also offers complete outsourcing services through ADP offers a variety of services including: human resource management systems, benefits and payroll processing, payroll and business tax management, brokerage industry desktop productivity tools and securities transaction, processing and investor communication services, industry specific computing and consulting services for auto and truck dealers, computerized auto repair estimating and auto parts availability, and fee and utilization audits of bodily injury claims.

ADP TotalSource

Contacts: Mike Benjamin or Mike Maseda
Phone: 800-CALL-ADP (800-447-3237) or 800-HIRE-ADP (800-447-3237); e-mail: sales@adp.com
Web Site: www.adptotalsource.com/peo/index.htm
ADP TotalSource is the PEO division of ADP and provides business owners with access to experts in all areas of human resources—employee relations, payroll and taxes, health benefits administration, 401(k) administration, workplace safety and regulatory compliance and much, much more. ADP is the outsourcing choice of employers around the world. More than 500,000 companies internationally rely on ADP for: progressive human resources solutions; fully integrated services; effective systems for greater functionality, flexibility and control; up-to-date technology; proven methodologies and best practices; and world-class service and support.

Advanced Business Fulfillment (ABF)

Contact: Joseph DiMartini
Phone: 800-804-7430; Fax: 314-770-2654; e-mail: Joe.DiMartini@aaq-abf.com
Web Site: www.abfhealth.com
Advanced Business Fulfillment (ABF) is the largest and fastest-growing outsourcer for healthcare-specific document processing and claims communications. Based in St. Louis, Missouri, ABF services over 130 healthcare insurance companies, health maintenance organizations (HMOs), managed care organizations (MCOs), dental plans, self-insured companies, and third-party administrators (TPAs) with covered lives ranging from 10,000 to 3 million.

AFFINA

Contact: Jerry Martin
Phone: 800-787-7626; Fax: 309-679-4408; e-mail: services@affina.com
Web Site: www.affina.com

AFFINA, the Customer Relationship Company, has partnered with Fortune 500 companies for over 26 years by supporting customer care programs that increase loyalty and sales. AFFINA offers clients an array of services (inbound, Internet, order taking, fulfillment, interactive voice response, market research, database marketing and management, outbound, and mail processing) designed to turn one-time contacts into lifetime customer relationships.

Advantec
Contact: Lynne Hopkins
Phone: 813-289-9442 or 888-340-9442; Fax: 813-636-8238;
e-mail: lhopkins@advantechr.com
Web Site: www.advantecHR.com
Located in Florida, this five-year-old company provides a range of HR services to clients nationwide. Innovative Internet service centers and a strong focus. on HR consulting and ongoing training explains why is one of the fastest-growing HRO companies in the country.

AIG Technologies
Contact: Cary Lu
Phone: 800-788-0144; Fax: 973-535-0752; e-mail: aigtinfo@aig.com
Web Site: www.aigtechnologies.com
AIG Technologies, Inc. (AIGT) specializes in providing flexible, reliable information technology solutions—from utility-based IT management services to property-casualty insurance software solutions. AIG Technologies services include: data center outsourcing and managed operations; mainframe/open systems data center operations; insurance software and solutions.

Ajuba Solutions
Contact: Simrat Singh
Phone: 91-44-2254-0410, Ext. 2014; Fax: +91-44-2254-0415; e-mail: info@ajubanet.net or simrat.singh@ajubanet.net
Phone: 248-426-0090; Fax: 248-426-0185
Web Site: www.ajubanet.net
Ajuba's areas of specialization are: healthcare, collections and AR management, transaction processing (data entry/conversion, database creation, claims processing), telemarketing, analytics (market research, coding), and call center services.

Allenbrook, Inc.
Contact: Jan Dargue
Phone: 978-937-2980, Ext. 2133; Fax: 978-937-5464; e-mail: sales@allenbrook.com
Web Site: www.allenbrook.com
Allenbrook Policy Processing Services (APPS) is an outsourcing solution for property and casualty insurers. Customers can concentrate on their core business objectives while APPS serves as their application service provider (ASP).

All States Technical Services
Contact: Andrea Hopkey
Phone: 205-972-5401; Toll Free 877-972-5402; Fax: 205-972-5433;
e-mail: hopkeya@allstatestech.com
Web Site: www.allstatestech.com
All States Technical Services has been providing engineering and design services to companies worldwide. It offers exciting consulting opportunities and provides scheduling and engineering services.

AlphaStaff Group Inc.
Contact: Rob Hannon
Phone: 561-241-9545, Ext. 222; Fax: 561-241-9587; e-mail: rhannon@alphastaff.com
Web Site: www.alphastaff.com
AlphaStaff Group Inc. provides human resources business process outsourcing for mid-market businesses. Services include integrated payroll, benefits, tax, risk management, accounting, technology and human resources management through flexible, comprehensive, and scaleable process management solutions.

American Customer Care, Inc.
Contact: Jeff Velodota
Phone: 800-267-0686; Fax: 800-211-2980; e-mail: jeffv@americancustomercare.com
Web Site: www.americancustomercare.com
American Customer Care specializes in individualized customer contact for their clients.

Amisys Synertech
Contact: Craig Combs
Phone: 800-216-9756, Option 3 or 301-251-8600; e-mail: ccombs@asihealth.com
Web Site: www.asihealth.com
Business Development Office at 800-216-9756, Option 3
Amisys Synertech Inc. delivers comprehensive, mission-critical information management software products and leading business process outsourcing and technology services. Amisys Synertech provides application services and customized managed care outsourcing solutions to healthcare organizations nationwide. Amisys Synertech is a premier applications services provider (ASP) to the healthcare industry and also provides administrative outsourcing, claims processing and backlog services, application hosting, scanning and imaging services, dental claims processing, and consulting.

AMG Logistics
Contact: Rob Sida
Phone: 905-897-2644, Ext. 202; Fax: 905-897-3525; e-mail: sidar@amglogistics.com
Web Site: www.amglogistics.com
Located in Mississauga Ontario, AMG Logistics is a third-party logistics organization offering complete supply chain management services provided on-site or off-site. Services include consulting, transportation management, warehouse operations (assembly, pick, pack, ship), and systems development.

Amnet Systems Private Limited
Contact: Aashish Agarwaal
Phone: 91-98-4103-0403; Fax: 91-44-2431-3694; e-mail: aagarwaal@amnet-systems.com
Web Site: www.amnet-systems.com
Amnet Systems Private Limited is an integrated data services company offering data capture and entry, data conversion, and prepress services using the concept of offshore methodology.

Aon Consulting
Main Contact: Al Orendorff
Phone: 312-381-3153; e-mail: al_orendorff@aon.com
Contact: Michael Tomback
Phone: 847-545-8398; e-mail: michael_s_tomback@aoncons.com
Consulting Contact: Tim Oyer
Phone: 419-429-6032; Fax: 419-427-4404
Web Site: www.aon.com
Aon's HRO group provides the knowledge and resources to expertly perform its client's HR functions, allowing them to streamline internal processes and concentrate on generating profit. Aon's trained staff, sophisticated HR tools, and state-of-the-art telecommunications/computer

systems can supplement or replace client-staffed systems. Aon offers a wide range of outsourcing options, including assistance in benefits plan administration, staffing, selection and assessment, and leadership, training, and development.

API Outsourcing, Inc.

Contact: Jonathan Blood
Phone: 952-472-9868 or 651-675-2605; Fax: 952-472-9884;
e-mail: jon.blood@apioutsourcing.com or sales@apioutsourcing.com
Web Site: www.apioutsourcing.com
API Outsourcing is a leading supplier of billing and accounts payable automation solutions, on an outsourced basis, to Fortune 1000 firms. API's Accounts Payable Solution provides tailored flexibility to best meet client needs. This flexibility enables customers to retain management of portions of the account payable process based on individual preferences. API enables customers to easily migrate at their own pace to API's total Accounts Payable process management based on internal needs and growth.

AppLabs, Inc.

Contact: Robert Alluru
Phone: 215-569-3220 or 215-569-9976; Fax: 215-569-9956; e-mail: robert@applabs.net
Web Site: www.AppLabs.com
AppLabs is an SEI CMM Level 5 company that delivers software testing and custom application development services offshore. Its services include software quality testing, security testing, application testing services, unit testing, unit acceptance testing, QA testing, software validation, system testing, black box testing, test automation, regression testing, usability testing, white box testing, load and stress testing, GUI testing, automated testing, Web stress testing, and software performance testing.

Arambh Network

Contact: Jayram V. Menon
Phone: 91-44-8224450 or 91-44-8274268; Fax: 91-44-8233847; e-mail: info@aramb.com.
Web Site: www.aramb.com
Arambh Network provides professional services in software development and systems integration on-site and offshore. Microsoft platforms (VC, VB, ASP, WinNT internals, SDK, MFC), Unix clones (Linux, Irix, SunOS, Solaris, SCO-Unix, Ultrix, development requiring IPC, device driver development, etc.) Databases (SQL Server, Oracle, Sybase, MySQL, Postgre SQL), Internet/intranet (Java, ASP, Perl, PHP3, MS Visual, Interdev).

ArchiLog

Contact: Alexandre Cuvelier
Phone: 33 4 42 92 33 54; e-mail: alexandre.cuvelier@archilog.net
Web Site: www.archilog.net
ArchiLog is an architect for logistics solutions, whose aim is to assist companies that decide to outsource totally or partially their logistics and transportation functions. Its scope of skills covers air and sea forwarding, express forwarding, road transportation, customs, information management, monitoring board, supplying, distribution, and warehousing logistics.

Ariba

Contact: Michael Schmitt
Phone: 650-390-1000 Fax: 949-623-8510 e-mail: mschmitt@ariba.com
Web Site: www.ariba.com
The Ariba Supplier Management Solution provides organizations with a complete set of products and services to ensure optimized supplier interaction and performance throughout the entire spend management lifecycle. An effective supplier management solution requires speed, coverage, and sustainability to drive cost out of the bottom line. The Ariba Procurement Solution delivers flex-

ible applications and services to provide rapid, easy-to-use requisitioning and procurement capabilities for handling every aspect of spend. Automated, streamlined plan-to-pay functionality for all users, suppliers, and commodities boost user, process, and price compliance and drive exceptional spend management efficiency across your enterprise.

ARINSO International

Corporate Contact: Marleen Vercammen, CFO
Phone: +32 2 558 06 70; e-mail: marleen.vercammen@arinso.com
Regional Contacts: Ignacio Palomera
Phone: 404-260-1900; e-mail: info.us@arinso.com
U.S. and Latin America
Graham Young, U.K. and Central Europe
Phone: 44 207 098 0350; e-mail: info.uk@arinso.com
Contact: Wim de Smet
Phone: 404-869-2040; Fax: 404-869-2045; e-mail: wim.de.smet@Qargus-is.net
Web Site: www.arinso.com
ARINSO International can take on a whole range of human resources (HR) administrative tasks, from running payroll to managing complex benefits programs. In a corporate environment with more IT projects than resources, ARINSO's scaleable approach will help set priorities. The firm is specialized in outsourcing enterprise resource planning-human resource solutions such as application service provider (ASP).

Aquarian Group

Contact: Terry Davis
Phone: 770-551-4550; Corporate Phone: 678-551-4550; e-mail: tdavis@aquariangroup.com
Web Site: www.aquariangroup.com
Aquarian provides complete business process outsourcing services with focus on finance, accounting, and back-office processing services by leveraging proprietary processes, offshore resources in Canada, India, and Southeast Asia, along with technology.

Aquent Inc.

Contact: Jeff Feakes
Phone: 973-402-7802; Fax: 973-402-7808; e-mail: questions@aquent.com
Web Site: http://www.aquent.com
Aquent develops custom technology solutions to solve mission-critical business problems. Their particular expertise lies in extending the reach of a client's enterprise by developing and integrating Internet technologies into legacy environments. By providing global, online access to products and information, Aquent helps clients drive efficiency, reduce costs, and increase communication across a geographically dispersed, extended enterprise of employees, suppliers, dealers, and customers. Large global organizations typically have an extended enterprise combining both technologically savvy and unsophisticated users. When automating processes, such as parts ordering, claims processing, or sales collateral distribution, Aquent develops solutions suitable for all stakeholder levels. Sophisticated channels can interact "system-to-system" with XML messaging, while less advanced users can conduct business with the OEM via a standard Web browser. Their channel solutions provide functionality in such areas as product configuration, ordering and tracking, service parts ordering and tracking, warranty claim processing and claim history, Financial settlements and product marketing and sales for new and used inventory across channels.

Artemis PR and Design

Contact: Kerry Slavens
Phone: 250-595-0136; Fax: 250-383-7723; e-mail: kerry@artemispr.com
Web Site: www.artemispr.com

Artemis is an award-winning creative agency that builds powerful brands through an integrated blend of Web design, graphic design, public relations, and advertising. Numerous clients outsource their entire PR and design to Artemis. The firm handles the needs of small, medium, and large businesses and organizations, locally, nationally, or internationally.

AT&T Solutions
Contact: Melissa Keenan
Phone: 973-443-3676; Fax: 973-443-2672; e-mail: mkeenan@solutions.att.com
Web Site: www.att.com
AT&T Solutions, the fast-growing professional services arm of AT&T, is now recognized worldwide as a global leader in networking services.

Atos Origin
Contact: Marie-Tatiana Collombert
Phone 33 1 55 91 26 33 email: marie-tatiana.collombert@atosorigin.com
Web Site: www.atosorigin.com
Atos Origin is a leading international IT services company and a global provider of business consulting and technology integration services. In August 2002, Atos Origin acquired KPMG Consulting in the UK and the Netherlands, trading as Atos KPMG Consulting and providing the Group with a major presence in the Consulting segment of the IT services market. In January 2004, Atos Origin acquired Sema Group from Schlumberger, thereby creating one of the leading international IT services companies. At the time of the acquisition, Sema Group employed 21,000 staff and generated annual revenues of approximately EUR 2.4 billion. Atos Origin employed 26,500 staff, generating annual revenues of more than EUR 3 billion. The new Group offers multinational clients a full range of IT services and solutions in 50 countries around the world, covering Consulting, Systems Integration and Managed Operations. The company has combined annual revenues today in excess of EUR 5 billion per annum and employs over 45,000 staff.

Avaya
Contact: Louis J. D'Ambrosio
Phone: 866-GO-AVAYA or 877-372-5719; outside the United States: 908-953-6000
Contact: Barbara Burgess; Phone: 908-953-3348; e-mail: barbarab@avaya.com
Contact: Renaldo Juanso; Phone: 44-776-485-2836; e-mail: juanso@avaya.com
Web Site: www.avaya.com
Avaya, a global leader in IP telephony, designs, builds, and manages multi-vendor communications networks worldwide. Business Communication Consulting is a strategic resource that provides your organization with guidance and insight for creating strategies and plans to derive maximum business value from your communications networks and applications. Avaya's consultants combine business acumen with technical expertise to align your business objectives with your communications investments. It employs industry-leading expertise to develop road maps, define network optimization strategies, leverage investments, and create migration plans. Business Communication Consulting provides an unparalleled breadth of multi0vendor, multitechnology convergence expertise, paired with a legacy of technology and service excellence, to fashion solutions and strategies that support your specific business imperatives.

Barry-Wehmiller International Resources (BWIR)
Contact: Jim Webb
Phone: 314-862-8000, Ext. 259; e-mail: Jim.Webb@BWIR.com
Web Site: www.bwir.com
BWIR offers professional back-offfice support services in the specific areas of: Web content development and scripting, content development for expert systems and preventive maintenance

tools, publication of customer documentations including manuals, Web page design, document processing for translation, document management on intranet and extranet sites, optimizing optical character recognition tools, image processing, database updating, and maintenance.

BearingPoint

Contact: Bruce Culbert

Phone: 703-747-3000; e-mail: bculbert@bearingpoint.net

Web Site: www.bearingpoint.com

A leading global business advisor and systems integrator, BearingPoint helps organizations around the world set direction to reach their goals and create enterprise value. Solutions include: Strategy, Process and Transformation; Customer Relationship Management; Supply Chain Management; Enterprise Solutions Integration Services; Infrastructure Solutions and Managed Services.

Benchmark Electronics

Contacts: Bill O'Dwyer or Shannon Spears

Phone: 979-849-6550; e-mail: bill.odwyer@bench.com or Shannon.spears@bench.com

Web Site: www.bench.com

Benchmark Electronics provides electronic manufacturing services for OEM customers on a global basis (14 locations worldwide). Its offering covers: product design, Proto, NPI, BTO manufacturing of configuration sensitive, complex electronic systems, such as high-end fault-tolerant computers, AOI, x-ray, ICT, and medical equipment, box build and PCB assembly, direct order fulfillment to end customers, hubbing, MIT, full turnkey and supply chain management.

Benefit Information Services, Inc. (BIS)

Contact: Patrick Williams

Phone: 952-847-1354; Fax: 952-847-1355; e-mail: info@bis-mn.com

Web Site: www.bis-mn.com

Benefit Information Services, Inc. is a third-party administrator concentrating in the areas of COBRA HIPAA administration, flex administration, consolidated billing of employer benefit plans, with online benefit enrollment and communications.

Birch Group

Contact: Nicole Van Gheluwe

Phone: 44 (0) 118-977-7300; Fax: 44 (0) 118-977-7499; e-mail: Info@birch.co.uk

Web Site: www.birch.co.uk

Birch Group's services are primarily focused on multinational companies and their channels to market. Its services include: channel accreditation programs, dedicated global multilingual account management, dealer incentive transactions, and management. Some examples of these programs are: Mdf, co-op, rebate programs, training accreditation, payments by check, electronic transfers, and bank draft in any currency, including the euro.

Birlasoft

Contact: Ajit Velankar

Phone: +61-2-9959-2397; Fax: +61-2-9959-2244; e-mail: ajit.velankar@birlasoft.com

Web Site: www.birlasoft.com

Birlasoft is a global software solutions and services company, part of the C.K. BIRLA Group of India (group revenues in excess of $1.5 billion per annum), with an equity investment by GE Capital. It offers significant strengths in consulting, IT services, systems integration, BPO, and outsourcing. With revenues in excess of $72 million, over 1,500 consultants, and offices in the United States, Europe, Asia, and Australia. Birlasoft has significant experience in banking and financial services domain.

BlueStar Solutions

Contact: David M. Budnick

Phone: 800-944-3454; Fax: 408-253-2976; e-mail: info@bluestarsolutions.com

Web Site: www.bluestarsolutions.com

BlueStar Solutions, a leading provider of IT outsourcing services, supports strategic packaged applications including Lawson, Oracle, PeopleSoft/JD Edwards and SAP, messaging solutions from Lotus, Microsoft, and Sun, and provides a range of other data center services. Customers are able to redirect their internal resources from IT support to focus on their company's core business initiatives.

Booz Allen Hamilton Inc.

Contact: Chris Disher

Phone: 703-902-5000; e-mail: disher_chris@bah.com or

Contact: Michael Bulger; e-mail: bulger_michael@bah.com

Web Site: www.bah.com

Booz Allen Hamilton, a global strategy and technology consulting firm, works with clients to deliver results that endure. The firm provides services to major international corporations and government clients around the world. Booz Allen's major areas of expertise include: strategy, organization and change leadership, operations, information technology, and technology management.

BrassRing

Contact: Mark McMillan

Phone: 781-530-5000 or 888-747-HIRE; Fax: 781-530-5500; e-mail: partner@brassring.com

Web Site: www.brassring.com

In addition to recruitment software solutions and talent consulting, BrassRing offers recruitment process management, which includes handling recruitment administration, database searching, response management, interview scheduling, placing job ads, managing recruitment web sites and recruiting campaigns, managing employee referrals, and taking responsibility for recruiting software systems.

Bridgestone/Firestone Information Services (BFIS)

Contact: Dennis Saralino

Phone: 330-379-7013; Fax: 330-379-7290; e-mail: jamiesondave@bfusa.com

Web Site: www.BFIS.com

BFIS provides a world-class facility and technical support, maintenance, and operations for mainframe and midrange computing. Outsource model is based on cost reductions for those companies looking at relocating hardware to data center location, with experienced human resources for migration and processing services.

Capggemini

Contact: Mike Thomas

Phone: 972-556-7612 or 972-556-7000; Fax: 972-556-7001;

e-mail: Mike.Thomas@capgemini.com

Web Site: www.us.capgemini.com

Capgemini, one of the world's foremost providers of Consulting, Technology and Outsourcing services, has a unique way of working with its clients, which it calls the Collaborative Business Experience. Through commitment to mutual success and the achievement of tangible value, the company helps businesses implement growth strategies, leverage technology, and thrive through the power of collaboration. Capgemini employs approximately 60,000 people worldwide and reported 2003 global revenues of 5.754 billion euros. Capgemini's Outsourcing Practice offers an extensive portfolio of services, including business process outsourcing.

CareerSoar
Contact: Darwin Flinn
Phone: 845-838-1150; Fax: 845-838-0171; e-mail: darwin@careersoar.com
Web Site: www.careersoar.com
CareerSoar provides human resource outsourcing services to small to medium-sized professional businesses. Its outsourcing consists of providing all of the human resources-related administrative functions for an employer, including: employment taxes, medical/health insurance, workers' compensation insurance, 401(k) retirement plan; handling timesheets and processing payroll; benefits administration, claims administration, creation of employee handbooks; and handling all employment policy issues.

Caresoft Inc. Software Quality Assurance Labs
Contact: Deepak Khare
Phone: 866-530-3998 or 91-755-241-8177; Fax: 866-530-3999;
e-mail: QALabs@caresoftinc.com
Web Site: www.caresoftinc.com
Caresoft's on-site/offshore team delivers unique methodology-driven QA, including functional, load, regression, data-migration, validation, integration, stress, recovery, security, performance, usability, white-box/black-box testing. It is expert in automated-testing tools like Rational-Robot, SilkTest, WinRunner, Macrobot, and TestDirector.

Cendian Corporation
Contact: Betsy Bishop
Phone: 800-CENDIAN (236-3426); Fax: 678-459-3939; e-mail: sales@cendian.com
Web Site: www.cendian.com
Cendian Corporation is the leading logistics solutions provider, focused exclusively on the chemical industry. Through an innovative and proven outsourcing model leveraging best-in-class Internet-enabled technology and a network of over 300 preferred logistics service providers, Cendian delivers better on-time delivery performance, global reach for its clients, and improved efficiencies across all aspects of the chemical logistics supply chain.

Ceridian Centrefile
Contact: Sharon Whitfield
Phone: 020-7335-3681; Fax: 020-7335-3636; e-mail: info@ceridian.com
Web Site: www.ceridiancentrefile.com
Ceridian Centrefile is committed to changing the world of work by delivering cutting-edge HR services. Its solutions include: fully managed HR and payroll services, e-HR software and ASP solutions, HR self-service, Web-based recruitment, payroll processing, employee portal, employee assistance programs, and consultancy on work/life balance.

CCR Services
Contact: Mark Mastenbrook
Phone: 800-363-0227; Fax: 614-577-9082; e-mail: sales@ccrservices.com
Web Site: www.ccrservices.com
CCR Services is a division of VAS Dimensions, Inc. Based in Columbus, Ohio since 1986; CCR Services provides professional collections for a diverse client list.

Cendris
Contact: Jeremy Hutchins
Phone: 44 (0) 1925-711427; e-mail: jeremy.hutchins@cendris.co.uk
Web Site: www.cendris.com
Cendris, part of the global TPG group has been a specialist for over 30 years in the provision of data and document management services, both as part of Cendris' fully managed solutions. Core

areas of expertise include: computer output to microfiche (COM) and CD, high-volume scanning and imaging, data capture, offshore data capture, Web-based retrieval, integrated CRM and document management solutions, database management, e-bill presentment, high-volume printing and fulfillment, color digital print, and consultancy services.

CGI

Contact: Jennifer Ratcliff
Phone: 416-945-3591; Fax: 416-862-2321; e-mail: jennifer.ratcliff@cgi.com
Web Site: www.cgi.com
Clients of CGI gain the advantage of knowledgeable, dedicated partners working to develop and implement IT-oriented solutions for business and technology challenges. CGI couples industry sector expertise with a full range of IT services including management and IT consulting, systems integration, and management of IT and business functions (outsourcing). CGI is one of the largest independent IT services provider in North America, based on its 25,000 professionals. In addition to their expertise in working with leading technologies and software applications, CGI provides custom application development services that leverage their ISO 9001 and CMM certified methodologies and the option of economies from offshore development.

CheckPoint HR

Contact: Tim Padva
Phone: 800-385-0331 or 732-287-8270; Fax: 732-287-2297;
e-mail: david.flook@checkpointhr.com
Web Site: www.checkpointhr.com
This New Jersey-based company provides HR and payroll outsourcing through both Web-based HRMS and personalized customer service. Targeting small and mid-sized companies (50 to 2,000 employees) it currently services more than 175 clients nationwide.

CIC Enterprises

Contact: Derrick Wilson
Phone: 317-844-4242; Fax: 317-844-4577; e-mail: derrickw@cicenterprises.com
Web Site: www.cicenterprises.com
Since 1980, CIC Enterprises has been providing third-party federal and state tax credit services to over 350 of the largest employers in the nation. These programs offer employers significant federal and state income tax and wage credits for hiring individuals from targeted groups. Services include: Work Opportunity Tax Credit (WOTC), Welfare to Work tax credits, state incentives, workforce development, sales and use tax consulting, transportation consulting, and W2/1099 original printing and reprinting.

CISCO

Contact: Doug Dennerline
Phone: 408-526-4000 or Toll Free 800-553-6387
Web Site: www.cisco.com/en/U.S./hmpgs
Cisco Powered Network Managed Security Services Designation: The popular Cisco Powered Network program, which has about 500 members in 52 countries, has been extended to recognize key infrastructure partners who offer managed security services based on Cisco's industry leading firewall and intrusion detection products. This new service category complements the existing and well-established VPN services category. Cisco AVVID Partner Program, Security and VPN Solution Set: The Security and VPN Solutions category of the Cisco AVVID Partner Program (an interoperability testing and co-marketing program based on Cisco AVVID—the Cisco Architecture for Voice, Video and Integrated Data) includes a new Outsourced Management and Monitoring section for qualified vendors. This is of particular interest to aggressive new providers who are specifically building their businesses for the delivery of managed security and VPN services.

ClientLogic
Contact: Julie M. Casteel
Phone: 615-301-7100; Fax: 615-301-7150; e-mail: pr@clientlogic.com
Web Site: www.clientlogic.com
ClientLogic provides customer service, sales and technical support to its clients' customers on a 24/7/365 basis through e-mail, online chat, fax, phone, self-help, and mail.

CoEfficient Back Office Solutions
Contact: Ron Bays
Phone: 310-850-9630; e-mail: HR@CoEfficientSolutions.com
Web Site: www.coefficientsolutions.com
CoEfficient is the leading *Client-Centric* BPO company, specializing in Finance & Accounting processes. CoEfficient offers accounts payable outsourcing, accounts receivable outsourcing, and complete accounting outsourcing solutions to a variety of industries.

Cognizant Technology Solutions
Contact: Jennifer Schelling
Phone: 201-678-2794; Fax: 201-801-0243; e-mail: jschelli@cognizant.com or
Contact: Chandra Sekaran
Phone: 201-801-0233 Toll Free: 888-937-3277; e-mail: csekaran@cognizant.com
Web Site: www.cognizant.com
Recently named number-one small business in America by *Forbes* magazine, Cognizant Technology Solutions delivers high-quality, cost-effective, full life-cycle solutions to complex software development and maintenance problems. The company provides the following services: application development, application maintenance, e-business, data warehousing, decimalization, Euro-currency compliance, testing and quality assurance, and re-hosting and reengineering.

Compass Technology Management
Contact: Erin Hartless
Phone: 757-233-7308; Toll Free Phone: 888-239-8515; e-mail: erin.hartless@compass.net
Web Site: www.compass.net
Compass Technology Management delivers IT solutions that promote operational efficiency, reduce operating costs, and manage critical business information. Solutions include business and financial software, Web content and commerce management, CRM, call center solutions, constituent relationship management, business intelligence, and managed IT services. The company is a Microsoft Gold Certified Partner headquartered in Chesapeake, Virginia, with data centers in Virginia Beach, Virginia, and Nashville, Tennessee.

Complete HR
Contact: Steven Singer
Phone: 617-875-5703; e-mail: sas@complete-hr.com
Web Site: www.complete-hr.com
Complete HR delivers Fortune 100 quality human resources management and administration services tailored to small to medium-sized companies. Its HR support ranges from tactical assistance to strategic HR leadership. With its Web-based HRIS/HRMS technology, you can have fully integrated seamless HR, payroll and benefits administration. Its unique approach to HR outsourcing makes human resources management simple, flexible, and affordable.

CompuCom
Contact: Marla McManus
Phone: 972-856-3600; e-mail: mmcmanus@compucom.com
Web Site: www.compucom.com

Founded in 1987 and profitable for all 17 years of operation, CompuCom has infrastructure experience, financial strength, industry talent, and proven methodologies to help clients minimize risks, reduce costs, and increase profit potential. As one of the largest multivendor support providers in the nation, CompuCom is well positioned and trusted by some of the most recognized names in the country, including Fortune 1000 enterprises, high-growth companies, vertical market leaders, major technology equipment manufacturers, leading-edge system integrators, and wireless technology providers. These companies rely on CompuCom for superior, unbiased IT services and systems integration.

Computer Enterprises Inc.
Contact: Pete Barrouk
Phone: 800-354-9155; Fax: 818-752-9195; e-mail: alliances@ceiamerica.com
Web Site: http://www.ceiamerica.com
CEI offers the following services: Consulting, Project Management and End-User Training. In these environments: Internet, Client/Server, ERP (Oracle, Peoplesoft) and Mainframe. CEI also has expertise in the following tools and technologies: Hardware, Operating Systems, Object Oriented Methodology, ERP, Communications/Networks, GUI Tools, Case Tools, Computer Languages, Databases and 4 GL's, Windowing Systems, Testing Tools and E-Commerce/Web Technologies.

Convergys Corporation
Contact: Teresa Williams
Phone: 800-344-3000; Fax: 513-458-1315; e-mail: marketing@convergys.com
Web Site: www.convergys.com
Convergys Corporation, a member of the S&P 500 and the Forbes' Platinum 400, is the global leader in employee care and customer care services. Convergys serves top companies in telecommunications, Internet, cable and broadband, technology, financial services, and other industries in nearly 60 countries. By bringing together world-class resources, software, and expertise, Convergys helps create valuable relationships between our clients and their customers and employees. This commitment is validated by the more than 1.7 million customer and employee contacts they manage each day.

Convergys Employee Care
Contact: Karen R. Bowman
Phone: 800-344-3000; Fax: 513-458-1315; e-mail: HRPartner@convergys.com or marketing@convergys.com
Web Site: www.convergys.com/emcare.htm
Through Convergys Employee Care solutions, HR departments worldwide are rapidly becoming the agile, highly efficient workforce management centers that support global decision making with critical business intelligence. They are regaining the time and resources to drive bottom-line savings through transformed management practices, streamlined business processing, and continuous improvement. Building on a nearly 20-year legacy of outsourcing leadership, Convergys offers comprehensive Employee Care HR management solutions across the entire employment life cycle.

CoreBriX
Contact: Mohit Sharma
Phone: 704-632-7701, Ext. 102; e-mail: msharma@corebrix.com
Web Site: www.corebrix.com
CoreBriX is a commercial real estate f inancial services outsourcing company. With its team of real estate professionals in the United States and India, and an integrated technology platform, Corebrix helps you identify and implement cost-saving opportunities in operations, analysis, and

technology needs across your company. Its staff understands the capital markets, banking products, CMBS-agency-construction servicing and risk management needs for the commercial real estate industry.

Covansys

Contact: Rajendra B. Vattikuti
Phone: 248-488-2088 or 800-688-2088; Fax: 248-488-2089; e-mail: info@covansys.com
Web Site: http://www.covansys.com
Enterprises turn to Covansys Corporation (Nasdaq: CVNS) for application maintenance and development, public sector solutions and offshore outsourcing. Flexible delivery capability helps them achieve rapid deployment, world-class quality, and reduced costs. Since its inception in 1985, Covansys has rooted itself in high-quality software engineering principles and an unwavering commitment to delivery. These twin strengths enable them to smoothly adapt to the rapid evolution of technology while maintaining constant focus on the changing business needs of their clients.

CSC (Computer Sciences Corp.) Credit Services

Contact: Mike Dickerson
Phone: 800-753-1312; e-mail: Cac@csc.com or mdickers@csc.com
Web Site: www.csc.com/solutions/creditservices
CSC Credit Services provides a wide range of consumer credit reporting, mortgage reporting, and portfolio and communications solutions to more than 52,000 credit grantors nationwide. Through its affiliation with Equifax, the largest provider of consumer information in the United States, Credit Services gives credit grantors access to more than 200 million consumer credit files nationwide. CSC Credit Services facilitates the transaction process for its clients by providing services and systems that help grant all types of consumer and mortgage credit, manage receivables, acquire new accounts, market new products, and manage risk. Credit Services' direct-to-consumer services include providing consumers with the option to order their credit reports online.

CSC (Computer Sciences Corp.) Financial

Contact: Kathy Sadden
Phone: 214-523-5535; e-mail: ksadden@csc.com
Phone: 800-345-7672; Fax: 803-333-6980; e-mail: info@csc-fs.com
Web Site: www.csc-fs.com
CSC combines insurance, banking, healthcare, and securities expertise with proven application systems to deliver tailored solutions. IT outsourcing spans applications management, desktop/distributed systems management, help desk, and network/data center operations. BPO involves processing selected business functions, including supporting staff and systems. No other outsourcing provider has CSC's experience in providing comprehensive outsourcing services to the financial services industry. CSC combines insurance, banking, healthcare, and securities expertise with proven application systems to deliver tailored solutions. IT outsourcing spans applications management, desktop/distributed systems management, help desk, and network/data center operations. BPO involves processing selected business functions, including supporting staff and systems.

CTG

Contact: Curtiss Montgomery
Phone: 800-992-5350, Ext. 3631; Fax: 716-888-4129; e-mail: curt.montgomery@ctg.com
Web Site: www.ctg.com
CTG has earned international recognition as a top provider of application outsourcing services. CTG's capabilities range from the support of single or multiple applications, facilities management, and help desk through a full suite of maintenance, enhancement, and systems development and integration solutions.

Customer First Call Centers
Contact: Michael Roby
Phone: 888-205-8025; Fax: 603-394-0509; e-mail: mike.roby@customerfirst.com
Web Site: www.customerfirst.com
Customer First Call Centers is a full-service call center outsourcing company specializing in food and consumer goods. Its services include toll-free number consumer product information, complaint handling, e-mail, white mail, and complete fulfillment and warehouse services.

D&B Receivable Management Services
Contact: David Caruba
Phone: 484-242-6821 or Toll-Free: 866-205-9947; e-mail: CarubaD@dnb.com
Web Site: www.dnbcollections.com
D&B Receivable Management Services, headquartered in Bethlehem, Pennsylvania, with operations in the United States, Canada, Hong Kong, Mexico, and Europe (through a strategic alliance with Intrum Justitia), is a leading global supplier of receivable management services. D&B RMS provides customers a continuum of services from electronic bill presentment, receivable outsourcing, traditional collections, bankruptcy services, deductions management, and much more.

Daksh (IBM)
Contact: Martin Prescott (UK/Europe)
Headquarters Phone 91-124-2439816-25 Fax: 91-124-2439845
e-mail: sareensh@daksh.com or info@daksh.com
Web Site: www.daksh.com
Daksh eServices is the fastest growing Business Process Outsourcing (BPO) services provider in India. They manage customer care services and back office processes for leading global organizations in the domains of banking, insurance, financial services, travel, technology, telecom and retail. Their services include customer care, technical support, data conversion, collections, telesales, transaction processing and other value additions. Daksh ensures exceptional client experience through world-class talent, strong management focus, dedicated business units and a strong financial platform. Their clientele comprises a formidable list of Fortune 500 companies who are market leaders in their domains. They have an experienced team at the helm with a cumulative experience of over 350 years in leading global organizations. In addition to this, a robust infrastructure spread over five facilities in India of which four are in Gurgaon (New Delhi, NCR), one in Mumbai.

Data Infosys Ltd.
Contact: Manoj K. Chandna
Phone: 91-141-367800; Fax: 91-141-367738; e-mail: manoj@dil.in
U.S. e-mail: support@datainfosys.com
U.K. e-mail: sales@myxgen.co.uk
Web Site: www.datainfosys.com
Data Infosys Ltd.'s service offering includes: web site designing/hosting and database development, integration, software development, one-stop intranet and Internet solutions, programming in any language, using any platform; complete Internet service provider (ISP setup), LAN, MAN, WAN, mail service solutions. Other services are: application development, application customization, maintenance, reengineering, high-quality approach, and strong integrity for a comprehensive solution for your enterprise.

Datamatics
Contact: Vijay Singh
Phone: +91-22-2837-5519; Fax: 91-22-2835-0217
U.S. Contact: Arvind Sirrah
Phone: 888-772-5532
Web Site: www.datamaticsoutsourcing.com
Datamatics is one of India's premier providers of IT and outsourcing solutions including software development, knowledge management, and business process outsourcing. It has over 27 years of experience of delivering quality solutions to 1,100 global clients across 58 countries. Its offerings include: investor record keeping, payroll, accounting and bookkeeping services, forms processing and data digitization, financial transaction processing, and contact centers. With over two decades of experience in large volume transaction processing, Datamatics is India's premier Transaction Processing and Back-office Outsourcing Solutions Company. As India's leading Registrar & Transfer Agent, they have successfully processed over 100 million transactions worth over US$ 10 billion, serviced over 27 million investors and currently warehouse in excess of 40 million documents.

Data Return
Contact: Adam Drutz
Phone: 800-767-1514; Fax: 972-869-0150; e-mail: adam.drutz@datareturn.com
Web Site: www.datareturn.com
Data Return is a profitable company that delivers highly managed services to Global 2000 companies. It has a proven track record in supporting business-critical applications running on the Microsoft, Sun, and Linux platforms. These applications are typically customer-facing, revenue-generating, transaction-intensive, and/or brand-focused, and include e-Commerce, Back-Office, ERP, and/or Supply Chain systems.

DecisionOne Corporation
Contact: Ron Cerniglio
Phone: 813-249-6649; Fax: 813-880-8419; e-mail: info@decisionone.com
Web Site: www.decisionone.com
DecisionOne Corp. is the largest independent multi-vendor technology support provider in North America, enabling clients to enhance levels of technical service, optimize the value of service expenditures, improve cash f low, and free resources to focus on core competencies. Its broad range of services, offered across wide geographic areas through a single point of contact, include planning and consulting, deployment and support (data center to desktop), call center/help desk, network, and logistic services.

Deloitte
Contact: Sandra Little
Phone: 216-589-1380; Fax: 216-774-5265; e-mail: salittle@deloitte.com
Web Site: www.deloitte.com/us/outsourcing
Through their finance and accounting (F&A) BPO services, Deloitte takes over a client's back office F&A and related procurement business processes and manage them on an ongoing basis. They offer a full suite of Sarbanes-Oxley and GAAP-compliant services and solutions, including transaction processing; financial accounting and reporting; statutory/regulatory accounting and reporting; and, transaction processing. Their transaction processing services cover payables, disbursements and expenses; receivables, receipts, and revenues; general ledger; and payroll.

Digica Ltd.
Contact: Amanda Dring
Phone: 44-15-977-1177; Fax: 44-15-977-7043; e-mail: amanda.dring@digica.com
Web Site: www.digica.com
Digica provides full operations and technical support, including complete management and support of your support center, applications support, change management, enhancements, software version control, system administration, and more. Digica gives customers access to applications over a secure virtual private network or a dedicated network on a price per user rental basis.

Direction Inc.
Contact: Chirs Lasso Phone: 519-894-6514; Fax: 519-894-6515;
e-mail: info@directionsolutions.com
Web Site: www.directionsolutions.com
Direction Inc.'s in-house designers, developers, and programmers work effectively together to provide the following Web services: web site and solution hosting, secure commerce transaction processing, web site and e-business solution maintenance, corporate e-mail services, database development, custom programming, interface design, information architecture, search engine positioning, Web marketing and promotion, computer networking consulting, and training.

Diversified Information Technologies
Contact: William E. Yeomans
Phone: 570-343-2300, Ext. 1820; Fax: 570-342-5291; e-mail: byeomans@divintech.com
Web Site: www.divintech.com
Divisified's service offering covers these areas: document capture and conversion, automated forms processing, mailroom processing, fulfillment, database development, "NetView" secure electronic storage and retrieval via Internet, "CIRM" automated records tracking system, active archival records management with Scan-on-Demand, claims processing, billing and eligibility enrollment, policyholder contracts, policy holder relations, administrative A/R and A/P, contracts, corporate/legal, f ile room, HR/personnel, mail, purchasing, medical record storage (HIPPA-compliant), medical transcription services, personal and corporate record storage.

DOW Networks
Contact: James Wilson
Phone: 770-937-9519; Fax: 770-037-9720; e-mail: James@downetworks.com
Web Site: www.downetworks.com
DOW Networks is a next-generation telecommunications service provider focused on serving Call Centers, Business Processing Outsource Centers (BPOs) and other international businesses. DOW Networks is a leader in providing Voice Over IP (VoIP) solutions which have call centers, BPOs and other international businesses up to 70 percent on their international calls.

EADS (European Aeronautic Defense and Space Company)
Contact: Andrew Jeacock
Phone (U.K.): +44-20-7845 8419 or
Contact: Diane Murphy
Web Site: www.eads.net
EADS, a global leader in aerospace, defense, and related services, surprised the HRO world in 2004 when it announced a joint venture with IBM to provide HR services. The venture, called HR Technologies and Management, or HRTM, launched with 100 employees and 35 business customers, including Airbus. EADS was created in 2000 from a union between some of the biggest European aeronautics businesses in France, Spain, and Germany.

Earnest John Technologies (EJTL)

Contact: Kailash Ramrakhiyani
Phone: +91-22-22832017; e-mail: kailash@earnestjohn.net
Web Site: http://earnestjohn.net
Earnest John Technologies Ltd. (EJTL) is a BPO company having proven capability in back-office operations for financial services. They understand the critical success factors of an outsourced process and the significance of working as an extended enterprise for their global clients. EJTL is a wholly owned subsidiary of multimillion dollar Earnest John Group. The group, since inception in 1925, has grown and diversified in Real Estate and Property Development, Shipping, Pharmaceuticals, and Finance. The group has cultivated a niche in all of its businesses. At the core of the organization is a team of professionals who persevere to execute a well-defined business strategy.

Eastco Building Services

Contact: Rose Mattos
Phone: 516-924-9553; Fax: 631-243-5772; e-mail: mattosr@eastcobuildingservices.com
Web Site: www.eastcobuildingservices.com
Eastco provides a vast array of services, such as complete facility management, HVAC operations and mechanical maintenance, janitorial and support services, repairs and alterations, window washing, relamping, mold testing and remediation, indoor air quality and power washing. Its programs eliminate the need to hire and manage multiple subcontractors, and its professional management team is available 24/7 across the United States.

eBenX, Inc.

Contact: Scott Halstead
Phone: 763-614-2000; Fax: 763-614-6000; e-mail: info@ebenx.com
Web Site: www.ebenx.com
eBenX is the leading health welfare supply chain management specialist. By improving the purchase, administration, and payment of group health welfare benefits, it dramatically reduces costs while significantly improving the quality of services to employees. Services include strategic consulting, procurement, Web/IVR self-service enrollment, billing payment, customer service, carrier management, FSA, COBRA/HIPAA, direct billing, and retiree program management.

Ebix Inc.

Contact: Kallol Paul
Phone: 678-528-3098, Ext. 163; e-mail: kpaul@ebix.com
Web Site: www.ebix.com/india
Ebix Inc. provides services in: custom software development solutions for insurance carriers, reinsurance companies, financial institutions, mortgage companies, agencies, brokers, hospitals, and other institutions. It also provides contact center facilities to insurance, reinsurance, mortgage companies, financial institutions, and other industries.

EchoData West

Contact: Jim Chick
Phone: 800-635-2679, Ext. 113; e-mail: jchick@echodata.com
Web Site: www.echodata.com
EchoData West offers integrated outsourced solutions. Platforms include a comprehensive offering of: supply chain management (order processing, e-commerce fulfillment, assembly/packaging, inventory management, returns, distribution) end-to-end e-commerce and Internet support (web site hosting, order management, e-fulfillment, order processing).

Eclipsys

Contacts: Pete Mounts or Gary Trickett
Phone: 404-847-5410; Fax: 404-847-5086; e-mail: gary.trickett@eclipsys.com
Web Site: www.eclipsys.com/outsourcing
The Eclipsys Outsourcing Solutions Group provides strategic services to help healthcare organizations maximize the power of IT. To best serve their customers, the Eclipsys Outsourcing Solutions Group offers a variety of service levels from long-term, total-solutions outsourcing to short-term, project-specific outsourcing. These customizable options make it possible for you to choose a service level that meets your specific needs. Eclipsys, IT outsourcing services include Total-Solution Outsourcing, Transformational Outsourcing, Transition Management and Operational Outsourcing.

eDATA Infotechp Ltd.

Contact: Ramani Natarajan
Phone: 91+44+52121451; Fax: 91+44+28206655; e-mail: nramani@vsnl.com
Web Site: www.edatainfotech.com
eData is an Indian company specializing in Reconciliations, Data conversions, Loan Processing, Back office for Finance and Accounting functions which include Payroll processing, preparation of Tax Returns, Financial Transaction Processing. EDATA's profile of services offered span from simple data conversions to complex tasks involving knowledge management solutions. EDATA's core strength as an execution partner lies in their quick assimilation and adoption of the established systems, which serves to customize services.

Edcor

Contact: John McBride
Phone: 248-836-1323; Fax: 248-836-1402; e-mail: jmcbride@edcor.com
Web Site: www.edcor.com
Edcor, an ISO 9002-certif ied organization, lowers the total cost of ownership associated with administrative processes in human resources and learning management organizations through the use of managed, technology-enabled solutions and services. Areas of focus include learning management solutions, learning portals, compliance management and reporting, and tuition assistance administration programs. Edcor's services are delivered through Internet, IVR, and call center technologies.

EDS

Contact: Renee Montcalm
Phone: 972-605-2360; Fax: 972-605-8316; e-mail: renee.montcalm@eds.com
Web Site: www.eds.com
EDS, the premier global outsourcing services company, delivers superior returns to clients through its cost-effective, high-value services model. EDS' core portfolio comprises information technology and business process outsourcing services, as well as information technology transformation services. EDS offers a broad portfolio of business and technology solutions to clients worldwide. With more than 130,000 employees, EDS supports companies and governments in 60 countries with IT, applications, and business process services; IT transformation; and management consulting. Its Enterprise Support Services unit manages key enterprise functions, such as HR relocation, and finance and accounting.

eFunds Corporation

Contact: Jim Wood
Phone: 973-615-4202; Fax: 480-629-7675; e-mail: james_wood@efunds.com
Web Site: www.efunds.com
Based in the United States, eFunds Corporation is the third largest BPO provider in India providing end-to-end account management for financial services, retail, and telecommunications

companies. Areas of expertise include transaction account acquisition, servicing, retention and collections related to mortgage services, card operations, demand deposit accounts, and ATM operations.

emr Technology Ventures

Contact: Atul Grover

Phone: 703-652-2506; Corporate Phone (India): +91-124-239 8392-93;

Fax: + 91-124-500 1901; e-mail: atul.grover@emrtechventures.com

Web Site: www.emrtechventures.com

emr Technology Ventures is a leading provider of world-class business process outsourcing (BPO) services to global customers, with specific focus in the insurance, financial services, and health-care segments. emr is certified by BSI as BS7799-2:2002-compliant for information security. Its processes include: healthcare claims processing, retail loans and credit cards underwriting, claims adjudication, subrogation claims processing, commercial mortgage processing, collections, and customer service.

eonBusiness

Contact: Becky Delhotal

Phone: 303-850-9300; Fax: 303-850-9383; e-mail: info@eonbusiness.com

Web Site: www.eonbusiness.com

eonBusiness is an e-commerce ASP, specializing in development, integration, and hosting of e-business solutions for clients that require rapid growth and fast time-to-market. eonBusiness works with the client to develop a strategy, and then offers the following services: web site design, legacy and database integration, e-mail management, e-commerce, ASP, logistics, web site hosting, Internet marketing, intranet/extranet, customer service, and security management.

Epicenter

Contact: Raja Chaudhuri

Phone: 866-883-7702, Ext. 2 or Ext. 93940; India Direct: 91-22-5694-8843 or 91-22-5694-8940; e-mail: RajaC@Epicentertechnology.com

Web Site: www.epicentertechnology.com

Epicenter is the market leader in providing offshore collection services, with over 800 skilled collectors. Its Fortune 300 companies use the services of Epicenter's collectors and rank them among the best in the world.

Equitant

Contact: Chris Jenkins

Ireland Phone: +353 1 406 0600 Ireland Fax: 353 1 496 9377

U.S. Phone: 203 359 5643; Fax: 203 359 5843; e-mail: partners@equitant.com

Web Site: www.equitant.com

Launched in 1987 to provide working capital management to large enterprises, Equitant quickly evolved to address a more pressing customer need: the management and optimization of the entire Order-to-Cash (O2C™) cycle. Built on a strong foundation of knowledge management, which integrates the strategic use of information into key decision-making processes, and recognizing the role of the customer in driving the financial outsourcing process, Equitant created a unique solution capability around O2C™ outsourcing. Their solutions are specifically designed to help their clients get closer to their customers, building stronger relationships with them in order to enable financial value transformation across the organization. Today, Equitant manages billions of dollars of revenue for leading global companies such as Cisco, Hewlett-Packard, Lucent, Microsoft, Visteon and others. They have also achieved nearly $1 billion in financial improvements to their clients' P/L, balance sheets and overall customer relationships.

Ernst & Young LLP
U.S. Contact: Charlie Perkins; Phone: 212-773-2418; e-mail: charlie.perkins@ey.com
U.K. Global Contact: Ian Sadler; Phone: 020-7951-8127; Fax: 020-7951-1345;
e-mail: isadler@uk.ey.com
Web Site: www.ey.com/uk/gto
At Ernst & Young, the GTO team will work with multinational corporations to provide a range of outsourced services such as tax, accounting, and company secretarial, over long-term co-developed contracts. They do this by harnessing the ability of their network of offices to deliver and drive through a globally consistent approach. They then give their clients total visibility of the services through a leading edge coordination and management model, especially vital in the new corporate governance environment.

ERP Outsourcing Asia Pte Ltd.
Contact: Garapati Chakri
Phone: 65-6832-5066; Fax: 65-6838-5296; e-mail: chakri@erpoutsourcing.net
Web Site: www.erpoutsourcing.net
ERP Outsourcing Asia Pte Ltd. is a specialist Singapore-based IT company. As a part of its SAP practice ERP Outsourcing Asia provides industry expertise in several segments including: banking, CPG, sales and distribution, finance, manufacturing, retail and telecomm industries.

Espire Infolabs Inc.
Contact: Rajiv Tarafdar
Phone: +91 (11) 5152-0000, Ext. 529; Fax: +91 (11) 5167-8790;
e-mail: rrtarafdar@espireinfo.com
Web Site: www.espireinfo.com
Espire is a leading Software and Business Process Outsourcing company, providing solutions to organizations across the globe. Espire Offshore Services feature a continuum of superior, blended solutions including a portfolio of operations (onshore/near-shore/offshore), services (contact center, back-office BPO), and capabilities (people, processes, and technologies). These solutions help to optimize customer interactions at competitive, guaranteed prices and with risk-free implementation.

Estco Medical
Contact: John Estafanous
Phone: 301-657-9332; Fax: 301-657-9435; e-mail: johne@estcomedical.com
Web Site: www.estcomedical.com
The Medigent software suite aids pharmaceutical, medical device, biotech, and other life science companies in launching and managing online marketing initiatives. The Web-based Medigent software suite includes components for content management, media and investor relations, product and clinical education, community development, and outcomes and market research studies.

eTelecare
Contact: Natalie Fischer
Phone: 626-256-7584; Fax: 626-256-7565; e-mail: natalie.fischer@etelecare.com
Web Site: www.etelecare.com
eTelecare International, a leader in outsourced contact center services, provides superior value to its clients by delivering the highest-quality customer care. With more than 3,000 employees, eTelecare has one of the largest call center presences in the Philippines.

Eurobase Limited
Contact: Julie Colclough
Phone: 00-353-51-379755; Fax: 00-353-51-379772; e-mail: info@euro-base.com
Web Site: www.euro-base.com

Eurobase Limited services include: full e-commerce European logistics support; full range of supply chain services; variable cost global distribution and freight management inventory management. Its clients include many blue-chip multinationals, such as Waterford Crystal, Hasbro, Allied Signal, Wyeth Medica, Huffy Sports. Its international experienced, dynamic, and forward-looking innovators will help you achieve more effective solutions to your supply chain requirements.

EXL Service
Contact: Shiv Kumar; e-mail: shiv.kumar@exlservice.com; or
Contact: Nandita Khanna
Phone: 212-277-7100; Fax: 212-277-7111; e-mail: nandita.khanna@exlservice.com; Phone: +44-207-484-5026
Web Site: www.exlservice.com
EXL provides integrated business process outsourcing solutions, encompassing back-office processes, contact center operations, and Web-based customer care to global corporations from its operations centers in India. EXL's outsourcing solutions emanate from deep domain knowledge, and assure successful first-time implementation, process reengineering for considerable improvements in efficiency and quality and significant additional cost savings. EXL thereby results in enhancing the competitive advantage and increasing the shareholder value of progressive corporations.

Exult, Inc. (see Hewitt)
Contact: Trey Campbell
Phone: 949-856-8840; Fax: 949-856-8806; e-mail: trey.campbell@exult.net
Web Site: www.exult.net
Exult's HR BPO is the integration and seamless delivery of discrete human resources processes including: payroll, benefits administration, recruiting and staffing, relocation and expatriate support, learning (training), employee contact (call) center, HR technology (integrated software), and employee self-service ("ESS") Internet tools. Acquired by Hewitt in 2004.

FBD Consulting, Inc.
Contact: Jay Gould
Phone: 913-319-8806; e-mail: jgould@fbdconsult.com
Web Site: www.fbdconsult.com
Established in 1967, FBD is a benefits consulting firm specializing in defined contribution and benefit administration, flexible spending account administration, health and welfare consulting, benefits communications, human resources services, and investments. Client base ranges from 100 employees to Fortune 100 companies.

First Outsourcing
Contacts: Douglas Brown or Scott Wilson
Phone: 727-784-5461; Fax: 727-784-6689; e-mail: outsourcingmanagement@earthlink.net
Web Site: www.firstoutsourcing.com
The leadership and consulting staff of First Outsourcing delivers renowned results and practical insourcing, intersourcing, and outsourcing consultative services to: corporations and multinationals, state and local governments, and venture capitalists and start-ups. First Consulting's most prominent deliverables have included the impact of insourcing and/or outsourcing on the client's operations or constituency, opportunities for reinvestment via insourcing, and cross-investment to re-prosper and reengineer companies/communities affected by job losses. First Outsourcing is a highly sought and respected advisor to post-outsourcing clients of all sizes. First Outsourcing also offers expert public relations direction, as well as outsourcing/insourcing strategic assessments and planning for best return on outsourcing (ROO), including continued pro itability and revitalization of labor markets domestically.

Forms Processing, Inc. (FPI)
Contact: Barry Matz
Phone: 305-702-7374; Fax: 305-702-7329; e-mail: Sales@FormsProcessing.com
Web Site: www.formsprocessing.com
Forms Processing is a professional service bureau specializing in forms, document processing, and information management. FPI facilitates the capture and utilization of information. It services customers in the insurance, government, and retail sectors with a broad range of information management solutions. FPI provides outsourced data entry, imaging, and warehouse retrieval services; and processes from paper, fax, or Internet, turns the document into data, and quickly transmits the formatted data to the client.

FOCUS AMC
Contact: Karla Williams
Phone: 703-299-6629; Fax: 703-299-6528; e-mail: Karla@focusamc.com
Web Site: www.focusamc.com
FOCUS offers professional outsource partnerships, specializing in administrative and back-office solutions to support your core business areas. Current management engagements include: mail facility, warehousing, distribution, supply, parking facility, health care logistics support, courier services, management consulting, and training.

Fortune Infotech
Phone: +91-22-5599 7970, 2594 7278; Fax: +91-22-2594 8141; U.S. Phone: 909-972-5214;
e-mail: us@fortuneinfotech.com
Web Site: www.fortuneinfotech.com
Founded in 1998, Fortune Infotech is a leading provider of software and web based services and mobile infrastructure software and services. Fortune Infotech's Expertise includes: Client Server Software Web based Applications Wireless Applications—for Mobile Phones and Handheld Devices Multimedia and Graphical Presentation. Communication Channels: Sectors: Engineering (Automotive, Heavy Engineering and Trading) Insurance (Life and Non Life, Claims Settlement) Healthcare (Hospital and Laboratory Management) Finance (Advisory, Stocks, M&F) IT (BPO, Marketing, E-Learning).

Gateway TechnoLabs
Contact: Niraj Gemawat
Phone: 91-79-2685 2554, 55, 56; Fax: 91-79-2685-8591;
e-mail: ngemawat@gatewaytechnolabs.com
Web Site: www.gatewaytechnolabs.com
Gateway TechnoLabs specializes in offshore software development, outsourcing and on-site development work for clients across the globe. It provides services in the field of .net application development, application development, application management, strategic offshore software product development, legacy software migration services, UI improvement using Internet technologies, multimedia creations, and wireless/mobile solutions.

GE Capital International Services
Contact: Ashok Tyagi or Michael Corning Phone: 203-373-2211; e-mail: gecis.hr@ge.com
Web Site www.gecapitalindia.com/gecapital/gecis_india.htm
Contact: Iqbal Singh
Phone: 91 22 444 5267; Fax: 91 22 444 8571
GE Capital International Services (GECIS) is a world-class remote processing operation that services its clients from around the world through its IT-enabled services. It was set up in 1997 to carry out back office operations for a number of the Capital businesses in order to leverage the English speaking, highly educated, intellectual capital of India to deliver processes that do not

require face-to-face contact with the customer. GECIS operates on a high technology platform to offer diverse IT enabled services with a quality, service and cost advantage to its customers worldwide. These services include ERP and Oracle database consulting, IT help desks, knowledge services, software solutions, analytics, data mining and modeling, remote network monitoring, e-learning and customer contact centers. GECIS is always strategizing to find new locations, spread its processes across the map of this country and get new talent. GECIS is the largest shared Services environment in India. It employs more than 11,500 people delivering over 450 processes to 30 different businesses in the U.S., Europe, Japan and Australia. Starting with simple data processing, GECIS has constantly moved up the value chain over the last five years migrating more and more complex processes from diverse businesses across GE.

Gelco Information Network
Contact: Linda Orwoll
Phone: 800-444-6588 or 952-947-1500; Fax: 952-947-8383; e-mail: info@gelco.com
Web Site: www.gelco.com
Gelco is the largest and most experienced provider of e-commerce software and services for employee optimization, specializing in business expense management and reimbursement and electronic business solutions to the consumer goods industry. Today, Gelco manages over $10 billion in business expenses for over 1.3 million users.

Geller & Company
Contact: Laurie Caplane
Phone: 212-583-6120; Fax: 212-583-6243; e-mail: info@gellerco.com
Web Site: www.gellerco.com
Geller & Company provides finance, accounting, procurement, and tax outsourcing services to middle-market companies, small businesses, entrepreneurs, investment partnerships, and high net-worth individuals. For more than 18 years, it has been providing CEOs and CFOs with the information they need to manage and grow their business.

GENCO
Contact: Debbie Beck
Phone: 412-820-2289; Fax: 412-820-2285; e-mail: beckd@genco.com
Web Site: www.genco.com
GENCO is a recognized leader in supply chain management. As a nonasset-based company, it provides unbiased logistics solutions through disciplines of technology, execution excellence, and indepth analysis. GENCO delivers proven results through: distribution and return center operations; transportation management, fulfillment, postponement, asset recovery; unsaleables management, and analysis tools. GENCO creates seamless, profitable solutions for the entire supply chain.

Getronics
Contact: Cathleen Blair
Phone: 978-858-6147; e-mail: cathleen.blair@getronics.com
Web Site: www.Getronics.com/us
With 23,000 employees in over 30 countries and revenue of $3 billion, Getronics is a leading provider of vendor-independent information and communication technology (ICT) solutions and services. Getronics combines the service capabilities of the original Dutch company with those of Wang Global, acquired in 1999, and of the Olivetti systems and services division. It is ranked second worldwide in network and desktop outsourcing, and fifth in network consulting and integration. Services include: network and desktop, help desk, server management, remote and mobile worker support, network management, applications management, multi-vendor support and maintenance, asset management, desktop and network technologies deployment and migration, server consolidation, security, and IP telephony implementation and management.

Gevity HR
Contact: Sal Uglietta
Phone: 800-243-8489, Fax: 941-744-8784; e-mail: sal.uglietta@gevityhr.com
Web Site: www.gevityhr.com
Gevity is one of the largest, most experienced providers of human capital management solutions in the nation. Our services provide specif ic offerings, such as recruiting assistance, training, benefits administration, payroll processing and related paperwork management, and legal compliance. Our solutions are delivered through expert personal consultation and leading-edge technology, embodied in Gevity Central, an online payroll and HR community designed for business owners, managers and employees.

Global Business Services
Contact: Lew Pulvino
Phone: 585-292-6073; Fax: 585-424-4808; e-mail: lpulvino@egbs.net
Web Site: www.global-business-services.net
Global Business Services (GBS) offers: business process outsourcing, including CRM/call centers, application outsourcing of all enterprise business operations, management consulting, and process redesign, e-procurement; IT services, including ERP implementation/integration, application design, development and maintenance/remote monitoring, solutions framework, security services, infrastructure services; and document management, including scanning services and image systems management.

Global Outsourcing Partnership
Contacts: Doug Brown and Scott Wilson
Phone: 727-784-5461; e-mail: dbrown@chiefresourceofficer.com[†], or
swilson@chiefresourceofficer.com[†]
Web Site: www.outsourcingpartership.com[†]
Global Outsourcing Partnership is an objective and independent buyer/vendor matching firm offering full RFP and vendor selection services. It is one of the world's foremost providers of outsourcing consulting in the world, renowned for best practices, readiness assessment services, governance building, vendor selection, and transition strategies. Outsourcing's collaborative approach is designed to help its clients achieve better, faster, more sustainable results through seamless access to its network of world-leading vendors, buyers, consultants, service providers, and other partners. Through commitment to mutual success and the achievement of tangible value, it helps businesses implement growth strategies, leverage technology, and thrive through the power of collaboration. The GOP conducts the widely popular and trademarked "reverse auctions" exclusively for global outsourcing.

GTL Limited
Contacts: Pradeep Phadke or Shariq Vahanvaty
Phone: 212-812-5088; Fax: 212-931-8350; e-mail: shariqv@gtllimited.com
Web Site: www.globalecms.com
Contact: Richard Wheeler
Phone: +44-1483-730-712; Fax: +44-1483-730-712; e-mail: richardw@gtllimited.com
GTL is a leading contact center and business process outsourcing services company for global corporations. It is one of the largest third-party outsourced contact center services providers in India. As part of GTL Limited, India's leading Network Engineering and IT Services Company, GTL has endeavored to stand for excellence in customer management through world-class service delivery. GTL has strong capabilities in the back-office processing in the verticals like financial services, banking, insurance, and telecom. Its back-office processing service capabilities and facilities are highly scalable and have attained a very high degree of maturity. GTL has gained strong ex-

pertise in offshore legal services with a team trained in American jurisdiction structure, legal and insurance terminology, citations, and abbreviations.

HCL BPO

Contact: Saurav Adhikari
Phone: 203-482-6498; (India) Phone: 91-120-253 8958; Fax: 203-326-3368;
e-mail: sadhikari@corp.hcltech.com
Web Site: www.hclbpo.com
Contact: Pawan Sharma
Phone: 91-120-4588972 or 44-7736497235; Fax: 91-120-4589688;
e-mail: pawan.sharma@hclbpo.com
HCL Technologies BPO Services Ltd is one of the most respected BPO and contact management services company in the world. With eight centers in India, the United Kingdom, Malaysia, and the United States, HCL is known to deliver an integrated solution to customers' business that builds around IT and IT enables services. HCL-T's global relationship base consists of approximately 454 clients, including 61 Fortune 500 organizations, in such high propensity to and potential of outsourcing Sectors as IT/I.S/Insurance/Financial Services/Retail.

Heritage Environmental Services

Contact: Holly Gamage
Phone: 877-436-8778
Web Site: www.heritage-enviro.com/index.html
Heritage Environmental Services is the largest privately held environmental management company in North America. Heritage has been a leader in providing responsible methods of managing secondary materials for over 30 years.

Hewitt Associates

Contact: Kelly Zitlow
Phone: 847-442-7662; Fax: 847-883-9019; e-mail: kelly.zitlow@hewitt.com
Web Site: http://was4.hewitt.com/hewitt
With more than 60 years of human resources experience and more than 20 outsourcing experience, Hewitt Associates is the world's foremost provider of HR outsourcing and consulting services to large organizations. Hewitt is the only provider of HR BPO services that has HR as its core business, offering total HR outsourcing services—benefits, payroll and workforce management—with HR consulting expertise including talent, health care, and retirement. The firm consults with more than 2,300 companies and administers human resources, health care, payroll and retirement programs on behalf of more than 300 companies to millions of employees and retirees worldwide.

Hewlett-Packard (HP)

Contact: Jim Wardrup
Phone: 972-497-3839; Fax: 972-437-1208; e-mail: jim.wardrup@hp.com
Web Site: www.hp.com/hps/process/bp_finance.html
As your company sets and enforces stringent accounting policies to comply with Sarbanes-Oxley 404, increased transparency into your company's financials—along with more timely and accurate financial information—are now executive imperatives. The ability to leverage rapidly evolving new technologies while lowering cost of transaction at the same time has become more difficult in today's economic market. For companies looking to focus management attention on strategic issues rather than low value-add transactional activities, HP finance and accounting services can help you reduce operating costs by managing outsourced transactional activities including: accounts payable, accounts receivable, time and expense administration, fixed asset

management, general ledger, project accounting, and reporting. Protect your vital business processes against crippling service interruptions. Today any amount of IT downtime can mean lost productivity, lost revenue, lost customers, and lost opportunities. HP provides proven strategies, services, and technologies to reduce your exposure and vulnerability, help protect your mission-critical operations against diverse downtime threats, and ease your recovery if an unforeseeable catastrophe strikes. Take advantage of special strengths that set HP apart: Global reach via over 50 recovery facilities, A track record of helping clients recover from more than 5,000 disasters, and One-stop shopping for solutions from planning to prevention to recovery.

Hexacta
Contact: Juan Navarro
Phone: 54-11-4779-6400; e-mail: juan@hexacta.com
Web Site: www.hexacta.com
Hexacta is an offshore development company based in Latin America. Its Brazil-, Argentina-, and Mexico-based offices provide excellent quality development services at very attractive prices and no time difference with the United States. Its clients include large multinational firms in Latin America, the United States, and Europe.

Hinduja TMT Ltd.
Contact: A. P. Hinduja
Phone: 91-80-5732620/50; Fax: 91-80-5731592; e-mail: marketing@htmt.soft.net
Web Site: www.hindujatmt.com
HTMT is a one stop Outsourcing company that can provide IT Services and BPO/Contact Center Services to customers all under one roof. HTMT's IT Services provides Application Development and Maintenance, Legacy Migration Services, Engineering Design Services and SAP Implementation Services. These services are complemented by HTMTs BPO services in the area of Back office Processing—Claims Processing, Technical Help Desk Support, Contact Center Services, Payroll Processing, Accounts Receivable and Accounts Payable services.

HRCentral
Contact: Kevin Osborne
Phone: 425-462-6286; Fax: 425-455-5995; e-mail: brudkin@hrcentral.com
Web Site: www.hrcentral.com
HRCentral is a fully staffed human resources company that provides customized, comprehensive outsourced HR services. Its service allows organizations to have effective human resources systems and support without the ongoing overhead tied to a traditional human resources department.

HR XCEL
Contact: Jeff Mortland
Phone: 704-357-6008; Fax: 704-357-1688; e-mail: jmortland@hrxcel.com
Web Site: www.hrxcel.com
HR XCEL is an exceptionally experienced provider of human resource and benefits administration services. Companies who understand the advantage of outsourcing these critical HR functions will benefit greatly from our experience in all of the following areas: Human Resource Management, Benefits Administration, Compliance Services including COBRA administration and FMLA tracking, Payroll and Time and attendance solutions and Web-native Human Resource Information Systems.

Hudson Resourcing
Contacts: Thomas Moran or Christine Raynaud
Phone (U.S.): 212-351-7300; Fax: 646-658-0544;
Phone (U.K.): +44-20-7187-6000; Fax: +44-20-7187-6001
Web Site: www.hudson.com

Hudson's service scope is comprehensive. Recruitment: Hudson provides both contract and permanent services; it sources, screens, and selects midlevel professional, technical, and managerial talent. Outsourcing: Provides managed recruitment solutions, including complete talent acquisition outsourcing, vendor management, and on-site representation as appropriate. Human Resource Consulting: Offers human resources consulting to assess competencies for selection and development, manage careers, and support retention efforts. Performance and Training Solutions: Creates customized, competency-based training, performance support, and employee development solutions.

Hughes BPO Services
Contact: Amalendu Das
Phone: 91-124-509-5555, Ext. 5546; e-mail: amdas@hss.hns.com
Web Site: www.hughesbpo.com
Hughes BPO offers a unique offshore service delivery model and is rated among the best employers to work for in India, has proven ability to scale, and world class infrastructure. It provides various call center and back-office services, cost-effective solutions and well-defined processes for higher productivity and quality. Hughes BPO is a division of corporate HSS. They are used interchangeably. Hughes BPO is recognized in the offshore BPO marketplace as an integrated technology and telecom outsourcer. Leveraging mature outsourcing expertise, long association with OEMs and service providers, and experience in providing Technical helpdesk, call center, software development and systems integration services, Hughes BPO is uniquely positioned to offer highly customized and best-of-the-breed BPO solutions. Providing Technical helpdesk and support services to a leading North American Broadband ISPs, making it a leading offshore provider of ISP helpdesk services. Services include: Internet Service Providers, fixed line, wireless, data services, cable and satellite services provider, Integrated Communications Providers—ICPs.

Hyrian
Contact: Daniel Solomons
Phone: 877-448-6837 or Toll-Free: 323-525-3400; e-mail: sales@hyrian.com
Web Site: www.hyrian.com
Hyrian provides nationwide, end-to-end RPO to Fortune 500 and Global 1000 companies. Its programs cover the entire recruitment process from job design to requisition management to sourcing to applicant screening to background checking and onboarding, and even to posthire employee retention. Hyrian's distributed recruiting model combines supply chain, capacity planning, assembly line, and quality-control practices adapted from the manufacturing industry, for a scientific and proactive approach to large-scale, complex recruitment.

IBM Business Consulting Services
Contact: Catherine Roberts
Phone: 818-539-3091; e-mail: catherine.a.roberts@us.ibm.com
Corporate Contact: 800-IBM-7080, Ext. ONDEMAND
Web Sites: http://www-1.ibm.com/services/us/index.wss/it/so/a1000414 and
http://www-306.ibm.com/e-business/ondemand/us/operations/outsourcing.shtml
IBM Business Transformation Outsourcing is an IBM Business Consulting Services program that provides business value by combining process, people, and technology transformation with an outsourced delivery model. IBM Strategic Outsourcing Services is the management of a companies' applications and information technology (IT) systems. Customers strategically partner with IBM to manage and operate their applications and IT systems, generally under a mutually beneficial agreement. The outsourcing agreement may include the transfer of IT employees and IT assets to IBM. IBM provides service level assurances to ensure quality of service is attained and measured.

ICG Commerce

Contact: Jason Gilroy
Phone: 312-558-4590; Fax: 877-424-2339; e-mail: jgilroy@icgcommerce.com
Web Site: www.icgcommerce.com
ICG Commerce provides comprehensive spend management services (sourcing, purchase to pay transaction management, hosted technology, and ongoing category management). It is driving significant savings through outsourcing for over 50 companies utilizing its proven implementation and transition methodologies applied to over 800 buying sites, detailed category operating procedures or "playbooks," and sourcing and category experts that bring best practices and deep market and category knowledge.

ICICI OneSource

Contact: Bhupender Singh
Phone: +91-6531414, Ext. 7524; Fax: +91-6531414; e-mail:
bhupender.singh@icicionesource.com
Web Site: http://ICICIOneSource.com
ICICI OneSource (I-OneSource) provides transaction processing services for five verticals in the financial services domain: retail banking, credit cards, insurance, mortgage and asset management. In addition it provides contact center services across multiple industries. I-OneSource has demonstrated expertise in these processes having handled more than 8 million customer interactions and back-office processes for clients who include Fortune 500 companies and FTSE 100 companies.

i-flex Solutions

Contact (United States): Sajal Mukherjee
Phone: 646-619-5300; Fax: 212-430-1918 or 212-430-5808;
e-mail: sajal.mukherjee@if lexsolutions.com or
Contact: Dennis Roman Phone: +44-207-531-4400; Fax: +44-207-531-4401; e-mail:
v.senthilkumar@if lexsolutions.com
Contact (India): Rakesh Khanna Phone: +91-22-2839-1909; Fax: +91-22-2823-5231; e-mail:
rakesh.khanna@ilexsolutions.com
Web Site: www.iflexsolutions.com
PrimeSourcing is a comprehensive range of service providing value-added IT solutions to commercial banks, retail banks, asset management firms, central banks, private and investment banks, capital markets, and insurance companies. i-flex Solutions is a world leader in providing IT solutions to the financial services industry. It has serviced over 500 customers in more than 105 countries. The i-flex range of products and customized services enable financial institutions to cut costs, respond rapidly to market needs, enhance customer service levels, and mitigate risk. The i-flex portfolio of offerings comprise FLEXCUBE, a complete product suite for retail, consumer, corporate, investment, and Internet banking, asset management, and investor servicing. Since its launch in 1997, more than 200 financial institutions in over 90 countries have chosen FLEXCUBE has been ranked the world's number-one-selling banking solution for two consecutive years, 2002 and 2003, by the U.K.-based International Banking Systems (IBS). FLEXCUBE was also named the Core Banking Solution of the Year and Application of the Year (2003) by the *Banker* (published by the Financial Times Group, London).

IKON

Contacts: David Mills and Cathy Lewis
Phone: 888-275-4566; Corporate Offices: 610-296-8000; e-mail: sales@ikon.com
Web Site: www.ikon.com
Partnering with customers to assess needs, costs, processes and future expectations is a critical part of developing an effective document strategy. IKON's document management services

offerings include: professional services, on-site management services, off-site print production, legal document services, digital imaging and conversion, e-services, and financing.

iGATE
Contact: Aprajita Rathore
Phone: 412-257-4277; e-mail: aprajitar@advisore.com
Contact: Vivien Jones
Phone: +91-80-51040000; e-mail: viv.jones@igate.com; Fax: +91-80-51259090;
U.S. Toll Free: 877-924-4283
Web Site: http://www.igate.com
iGATE is a NASDAQ listed, global IT & Process Outsourcing company with 4000+ resources across 27 countries and 8 Offshore Delivery centers in India, China, Singapore, Japan, and Canada. iGATE's outsourcing services portfolio includes Application Maintenance Outsourcing, Data Management, Software Development, Contact Center Management Help desk/Technical Support, and back-office processing. With a 10-year offshore track record, iGATE has delivered 40 to 60 percent cost savings to several Fortune 500 customers.

India Life Capital
Contact: Kavitha Reddy
Phone: 91 080 238 4801, Ext. 837; Fax: 91 080 238 4802; e-mail: kavitha@india-life.com
Web Site: www.india-life.com
India Life is India's largest HR BPO, they provide strategic HR BPO solutions to achieve world-class standards. Core business comprises Outsourcing services for Payroll and Benefits, Benefits consulting and Pension Fund Management that are powered by a self-service suite providing an Anytime Anywhere Benefits Payroll Office TM for Employer & Employee. They service over 250 companies and over 250,000 employee records.

Infocrossing
Contact: Michael Bendit
Phone: 866-392-4369; Fax: 201-840-7250; e-mail:marketing@infocrossing.com
Web Site: www.infocrossing.com
Infocrossing, Inc. is a premier provider of IT outsourcing services, including: mainframe outsourcing, AS/400 and iSeries management, open systems management, business continuity services, and IT infrastructure consulting services.

Intelligroup
Contact: Douglas Berto
Phone: 800-535-0156 or 732-590-1600 or
Contact: Bosco Malapatti
India Phone: 91-40-2329 7487/88; Fax: 91-40-2323 4978;
e-mail: marketing@intelligroup.com
Web Site: www.intelligroup.com
Intelligroup is a strategic outsourcing partner to the world's largest companies. Its proven on-site/offshore delivery model has enabled hundreds of customers to accelerate results and reduce costs. With deep expertise in industry-specific enterprise solutions, Intelligroup has earned a reputation for consistently exceeding client expectations. Intelligroup's strategic outsourcing services address the implementation, upgrade, application management, and development needs of business executives. Its proven methodologies and innovative tools allow customers to reduce costs by accelerating implementations, upgrades, and support services.

International Network Administration

Contact: Setup Shah

Phone: 718-460-2118; Fax: 718-460-2118; e-mail: sshah@netadmin.net

Web Site: www.netadmin.net

International Network Administration provides services in several areas: Consulting/placement services in all IT/MIS and telecommunications-related fields—for example, systems administration in Unix (all flavors), NT, and other networking/operating systems; networking hardware: routers, switches, and hubs made by vendors like Cisco, Bay Networks, Nortel Networks, and others; programming languages: C, C, Visual Basic, and other languages; Internet: Web servers (all flavors), Java, CGI scripting, JavaScript's, Purl scripts, firewall, corporate intranets, and custom applications; databases: SQL, Oracle, Sybase, PeopleSoft, MS Access.

Information Management Systems, Inc.

Contact: Roosevelt Giles

Phone: 404-329-6260; Fax: 404-329-6365; e-mail: cservice@imsinc.com

Web Site: www.imsinc.com

Offers the following services: Networking and Certification, Help Desk, Prototyping and Proof of Concept Testing, Network Baselining and Modeling, Implementation Services, Router Installation and Training, Network and Systems Management Implementation and Certified Cisco, Checkpoint, ISS Security, Microsoft WatchGuard, and Nortel Networks.

Infosys Technologies Limited

Contact: Sunder Sarangan

Phone: 510-742-3038; Fax: 510-742-3090; e-mail: Infosys@infy.com

Web Site: www.infy.com

Infosys Technologies Ltd. provides consulting and IT services to clients globally, as partners, to conceptualize and realize technology-driven business transformation initiatives.

Infosys—Progeon BPO Division

Contact: Subrat Mohanty

Phone: +91-80-5117-5142 (Direct); Corporate Phone: +91-80-2852-2405;
Fax: +91-80-2852-2411

U.S. Contact: Gautam Thakkar Phone: 972-770-0456; Fax: 972-770-0490;
e-mail: gautam_thakkar@progeon.com

U.K. Contact: Ramkumar Akella

Phone: +44 208 774 3388 (Direct); Fax: +44 208 686 6631;
e-mail: ramkumar_akella@progeon.com

Web Site: www.infosys.com

Infosys, a world leader in consulting and information technology services, partners with Global 2000 companies to provide business consulting, systems integration, application development, and product engineering services. Through these services, Infosys enables clients to fully exploit technology for business transformation. Clients leverage the Infosys Global Delivery Model to achieve higher-quality, rapid time-to-market and cost-effective solutions. Infosys has 20,000 employees in over 30 offices worldwide.

Insurance Data Services

Contact: Lee Roth

Phone: 949-661-2046; Fax: 949-661-2749; e-mail: Lee.Roth@certsonline.com

Web Site: www.certsonline.com

Insurance Data Services is the country's leading provider of insurance certificate tracking and outsourcing services. This service appeals to organizations looking to put a cost-effective, professionally managed approach in place to collect certificates of insurance and monitor compliance with contractual insurance obligations. Its clients include many Fortune 500 companies as well as smaller, regional organizations. Service is offered throughout the United States and Canada.

International Smart Sourcing (ISS)
Contact: Brian Strebel
Phone: 631-293-4796; Fax: 631-752-6907; e-mail: brains@smart-sourcing.com
Web Site: www.smart-sourcing.com
Through its headquarters in the United States and branch office in China, ISS has established a full-range infrastructure to simplify the transition and facilitate the outsourcing of manufactured products to China. Key service elements are: project management, source selection, engineering coordination, quality assurance, and logistical management. Cost reduction and product specialization includes: tooling, injection molding, die-castings, metal stampings, mechanical assemblies, and electromechanical assemblies.

Interpro Global
Contact: Nandan Setlur
Phone: 866-367-2100; Fax: 240-238-2101; e-mail: nandan.setlur@interprobps.com
Web Site: www.interprobps.com
Interpro Global, with a turnover of over $500 million, provides a range of business process outsourcing services. Headquartered in the United States, it has established itself as a leading service provider, with a range of back office, IT processing, and consulting services to suit different verticals. InterPro also delivers transcription services, contact center solutions, document management, enterprise portal development, employer services, medical revenue life cycle support, and technology development and support.

Intetics Co. / Web Space Station
Contact: Svetlana Savitskaya
Phone: 877-SOFTDEV; Fax: 847-256-3190; e-mail: svs@intetics.com
Web Site: www.WebSpaceStation.com or www.intetics.com
Intetics is an Illinois-based IT company focused on all areas of custom software and Web development. The company has development offices in Eastern Europe and leverages the expertise of an international team of 80 full-time IT professionals. Since 1995 it has completed about 400 projects for over 130 customers in 31 countries.

Investment Administration Sciences Inc.
Contact: Chris Jackson
Phone: 416-360-8966, Ext. 241; Fax: 416-360-8970; e-mail: cjackson@iasciences.com
Web Site: www.iasciences.com
IA Sciences provides premium BPO of front-, mid-, and back-office administrative services for investment management f irms and investment dealers. A specialty is the creation of turnkey separately managed account programs. IAS's core business activities include consulting and development of IMA programs for sponsor organizations, out-sourced individually managed account administration programs.

iSeva
Contact: Sridhar Turaga
Phone: 866-828-2281 or 408-764-5100; Fax: 408-982-5401; e-mail: sales@iseva.com or marketing@india.iseva.com
iSEVA is headquartered in Santa Clara, California, with sales and marketing offices in New Jersey, Texas, and California. It has two delivery centers located in Bangalore, India, offering end-to-end mortgage BPO solutions. Players in the mortgage industry have a distinct environment of

regulation, competition, technology, and risk. Whether you are a lender (midtier or large), broker, realtor, vendor, new entrant, credit union and/or a service, iSEVA can help you increase the effectiveness and efficiency of your business through its outsourcing services. With over $13 billion in loan originations for its clients in the last 24 months, and over 600 hours of telesales per day, its experience in offshore mortgage origination services is unmatched.

(i)Structure, Inc.

Contact: Jeff Washburn
Phone: 888-757-7501; Fax: 480-775-5398; e-mail: info@i-structure.com
Web Site: www.i-structure.com
(i)Structure assumes responsibility for your computing operations 24 hours a day, 7 days a week. Services include: AS400 consulting services, capacity planning, database services, monitoring, network services, performance tuning, remote high availability, remote monitoring and management, service desk, storage solutions, system administration and management.

i-Vantage Inc.

Contact: Mahendra Penumathsa
Phone: 617-393-2338, Ext. 1306; Fax: 253-679-2959; e-mail: mahendrap@i-vantage.com
Web Site: www.i-vantage.com
i-Vantage's expertise includes software development, systems integration, application maintenance, remote admin and technical support. They can also augment their technology services with a whole range of Business Process Outsourcing services such as back office processes and customer service.

Jacobson Companies

Contact: John Rolf
Phone: 515-265-6171; Fax: 515-265-8927; e-mail: marketing@jacobsonco.com
Web Site: www.jacobsonco.com
Jacobson Companies is a full-service logistics group compromised of six individual companies: Jacobson Warehouse, Jacobson Transportation, Jacobson Packaging, Jacobson Logistics, and Jacobson Industrial Services.

Johnson Controls-Facilities Management

Contact: Denise M. Zutz
Phone: 414-524-1200; Fax: 414-524-2077; e-mail: Denise.M.Lutz@jci.com
Web Site: www.johnsoncontrols.com/cg-services/Default.htm
Johnson Controls is the leading global facilities management solutions provider. With over 50 years in the facilities management business, Johnson Controls has the expertise to deliver comprehensive workplace strategies that support your global facility portfolio and keep your facilities, and organization moving in the right direction. Johnson Controls can work with you to create a service plan that delivers measurable benefits: lower or more predictable costs, optimized environments, and guaranteed results.

JPMorgan

Contact: Doug Criscitello
Phone: 202-533-2128; e-mail: douglas.a.criscitello@jpmorgan.com
Web Site: www.jpmorgan.com/cm/cs?pagename=Chase/Href&urlname=jpmorgan
/trust/government
JPMorgan Government Outsourcing Services delivers comprehensive solutions to U.S. federal, state, and international government entities. Our solutions include payment services, loan accounting services, trustee and escrow services, investment and portfolio management, records organization, maintenance and preservation, facilitation of government contract procedures, and MIS.

Kanbay International.
Contact: Debra Johnson
Phone: 847 384 6100 Fax: 847 384 0500; e-mail: solutions@kanbay.com
Web Site: www.kanbay.com
The combination of business focus and technology expertise makes Kanbay a unique player in the technology consulting arena—and the right choice for some of the most distinguished names in the financial services industry. Kanbay's four industry practices include: Credit Services, including credit cards, debit cards, smart cards and all the systems that make them work. Banking, serving retail and private banking, business and consumer lending, and general financial services. Insurance, including health, life, and property and casualty lines and functions from membership and rate changes to billing and claims processing. Capital Markets, encompassing trading, brokerage, and investment banking. Kanbay focuses where it has the most expertise, the most industry veterans, and the most significant problem-solving experience—financial services.

Kawin Interactive Inc.
Contact: Kaushal Chokshi
Phone: 630-355-9377; e-mail: info@kawin.net
Web Site: www.backupoffice.net
Kawin offers outsourcing solutions for Web development, e-store development, vertical portal (vortal) development, application development engineering, Web management, Web marketing, Web maintenance, and portal management. It uses various software packages, languages, tools, and database products to provide turnkey projects or elements of project. It can handle seamless project management through its U.S. office.

Kaye-Smith
Contact: Vicki LaBarge
Phone: 425-228-8600 or 800-822-9987 or 925-294-5300, Ext. 217;
Fax: 425-226-4312 or 925-294-5301; e-mail: vicki.labarge@kayesmith.com
Web Site: www.kayesmith.com
Kaye-Smith is a premier document management company offering solutions in the area of statement and bill processing, one-to-one direct marketing, database programming, database management, data repurposing, and print/forms management. Kaye-Smith offers state-of-the-art technologies and value-added services focusing on custom programs specific to your business. It provides a variety of manufacturing methods and full-service fulfillment, warehousing, and distribution programs. Its expertise is designing supply chain processes for the document-related functions of your organization. It offers a complete end-to-end management solution, providing an outsource alternative to replace costly internal operations and software.

Keane, Inc.
Contact: Gary Rader
Phone: 617-241-9200; 800-73-KEANE, 617-241-9507; e-mail: Gary.D.Rader@keane.com
Web Site: www.keane.com
Corporate Contact: U.S. and Canada: 312-787-6777; U.K.: Sharron Lloyd, 0870 191 6243;
e-mail: bpo@keane.com
Keane, Inc. (NYSE: KEA), helps clients to improve their business operations and IT effectiveness by delivering a broad range of business consulting and outsourcing services designed to achieve near-term and sustainable business benefit. Specifically, Keane focuses on highly synergistic service offerings, including: Application Development & Integration, Application Outsourcing, and Business Process Outsourcing. Keane believes that business and IT improvements are best realized by streamlining and optimizing business and IT processes, implementing rigorous management disciplines, and fostering a culture of accountability through meaningful performance metrics. Keane

delivers its services through an integrated network of branch offices in North America and the United Kingdom, and via SEI CMMI Level 5 evaluated Advanced Development Centers (ADCs) in Canada and India.

Keane Worldzen

Contact: Kate Duggan
Phone: 925-398-8810; Fax: 925-398-8810; e-mail: Kate_Duggan@keane.com
Web Site: www.keaneworldzen.com
Keane Worldzen is a business process outsourcing and operations consulting firm that helps clients optimize their business through a unique transition model that combines process redesign, technology improvements, and outsourcing. For more than 25 years, Keane Worldzen has implemented complex operations changes for Fortune 500 companies, focusing on the healthcare, insurance, financial services, and debt management industries. Keane Worldzen is the business process outsourcing arm of Keane, Inc.

Kenexa

Contact: Donald F. Volk or Sora Teten
Phone (U.S.): 610-971-9171; Fax: 610-971-9181; e-mail: Don.Volk@kenexa.com or sora.teten@kenexa.com
Web Site: www.kenexa.com
Phone (U.K.): +44 (0) 207-851-8120; Fax: +44 (0) 207-851-8121;
e-mail: europeaninfo@kenexa.com
Kenexa manages portions of the employment process or the entire staffing operation for Fortune 500 and midsized companies. Since the mid-1990s, Kenexa has provided single-source accountability and performance-based service-level agreements and fee structures to fully optimize the speed, cost, and quality of staffing operations worldwide. Kenexa's primary focus is on RPO and talent management, rather than being a small percentage of the company's overall revenues.

KPMG LLP

Contact: Ted Senko
Phone: 303-295-8828; Fax: 303-382-7439; e-mail: tsenko@kpmg.com
Web Site: www.us.kpmg.com
KPMG is a leader in providing internal audit services to organizations worldwide. KPMG Management Assurance Services professionals can help manage your financial and operational risks and transform your internal audit function into one that delivers strategic business information and value.

Larsen & Toubro (L&T) Infotech

Contact: Anand Vyas
Phone: 770-956-4019 or 770-329-6585; Fax: 770-980-2050; e-mail: avyas@lntinfotech.com
Web Site: www.lntinfotech.com
L&T Infotech is a premier IT services company providing end-to-end offshore/on-site services. Its expertise is in application development, maintenance and support, packaged implementation and upgrade, and EAI around ERP, SCM, CRM, mobile, and client/server technologies. L&T is a CMM Level 5 and ISO 9001-certified company with seven centers in India and two centers in the United States. It is part of the $2 billion, L&T Group, one of India's most admired organizations with interests in engineering, construction, MFG, and telecom.

LASON

Contact: Jeni Grasman
Phone: 847-995-7012; Fax: 786-524-7655; e-mail: jgrasman@lason.com
Web Site: www.lason.com

LASON is a leading provider of integrated information outsourcing solutions through over 60 locations and facilities management sites in 26 states, India, China, Mexico, the Caribbean, and Canada. LASON's core competency resides in its ability to enhance the performance of its customers' business by outsourcing their noncore business processes. LASON's primary services are data, document, and image capture; web-based document repository services via their Document DNA solution; analog services; print and mail services; database management, and other professional services. Healthcare: By working with a leading Healthcare BPO and outsourcing your healthcare claims processing, your company will be able to process claims faster and more cost effectively than performing the work in-house. LASON is able to convert over 17 different claim types in less than 48 hours with a 99.5 percent or higher rate of accuracy. LASON also prides itself in being one of the only industry providers to process Explanation of Benefits, Explanation of Payments, enrollment and referral documents. And with the capability to reduce your adjudication costs by up to 35 percent LASON has established itself as the leader of Business Process Outsourcing in the healthcare industry. Loan Processing: LASON transforms manual and paper intensive mortgage servicing operations into a fully automated efficient process utilizing state-of-the-art document imaging services and solutions. In addition to offering a total document imaging and data entry solution to mortgage companies or departments, LASON can also distinguish itself from its competitors by offering the following incremental opportunities: Compress Process Cycle Time, Decrease Processing Costs, Reduce Processing Complexity and improved Document identification and index data accuracy.

Lead Dog Design & Development
Contact: Sales Department
Phone: 212-564-5070; Fax: 212-564-6886; e-mail: sales@idd.com
Web Site: www.ldd.com
Lead Dog Design & Development is a full-service e-solutions provider and market strategy consultant. It is a world-class provider of Internet design and development, with a client list representing the best in industry companies.

Liberata
Contact: Patrick McGuirk
Phone: 07974 321 491 or 01494 731700; Fax: 01494 731600;
e-mail: patrickmcguirk@liberata.com
Web Site: www.liberata.com
Liberata offers BPO services in these areas: actuarial and compliance, claim handling, customer relationship management, finance and accounting, human resources, information and communication technology, policy administration and management, procurement, revenue collection, transaction and administration. Liberata is one of the United Kingdom's leading specialists in business process outsourcing services.

LiveBridge
Contact: John Bartholomew
Phone: 800-783-6000 or 503-652-6000; Fax: 503-653-3994;
e-mail: cdelambo@livebridge.com
Web Site: www.livebridge.com
LiveBridge offers expertise in call center development, management and operations. It also builds and maintains contact center infrastructures.

Logisteon Supply Chain Solutions
Contact: Thomas Marlow
Phone: 630-400-7570; Fax: 630-563-1973; e-mail: info@logisteon.com
Web Site: www.logisteon.com

Logisteon Supply Chain Solutions assists companies in developing smart business and branding strategies through innovative supply chain solutions, including consulting, design, reengineering, and domestic and global supply chain operations management.

MachroTech, LLC
Contact: Manish Chowdhary
Phone: 203-336-2284, Ext. 202; Fax: 203-384-6327; e-mail: sales@machrotech.com
Web Site: www.machrotech.com
MachroTech is a leading Offshore software development and e-commerce consulting company with state-of-the-art development center in Connecticut, United States, and offshore development center in Pune, India. Its offshore outsourcing services includes offshore programming for custom applications; e-commerce solutions; application integration; SCM; CRM; BPO services, which include data processing, payroll, accounting and HR; inbound and outbound call centers; quality assurance and testing; tech support, and online marketing and research.

Mahindra-British Telecom (MBT)
Contact: Jagdish Mitra
Phone: +91 22 5679 2000; Fax: +91 22 2852 8959; e-mail: jagdish.mitra@mahindrabt.com
Web Site: www.mahindrabt.com
MBT is a leading software services provider for the telecom sector, including operators, equipment suppliers, software vendors, and integrators. MBT is a proven leader in application outsourcing and offshoring of large-scale mission-critical telecom applications. Services are in the areas of application outsourcing, application management and maintenance, accelerated value management, package integration and implementation, coupled with extensive domain knowledge of the telecom industry.

Manpower
Contacts: Tammy Johns and Margaret Gerstenkorn
Phone: 414-906-6336; Fax: 414-906-7822; e-mail: mgersten@na.manpower.com;
e-mail: tammy.johns@na.manpower.com or
Contact: Tracy Shilobrit
Phone: 414-906-6088; Fax: 414-961-8780; e-mail: tracy.shilobrit@na.manpower.com
Web Site: www.manpower.com
With more than 4,300 offices in 67 countries, Manpower is a leader in employment services—serving customers in small, medium-sized, and large multinational corporations. Specializing in permanent, temporary, and contract recruitment; employee assessment; training; career transition and organizational consulting services; as well as BPO; the company operates under additional brand names of Right Management Consultants, Jefferson Wells, Elan, Brook Street, and Empower.

Marlborough Stirling
Phone: +44(0)1242 547000; Fax: +44(0)1242 547100; e-mail: info@marlborough-stirling.com
Web Site: www.marlborough-stirling.com/channels/uk/default.htm
Marlborough Stirling Mortgage Services (MSMS) offers the flexibility and expertise to support multiple distribution channels, for a wide range of products, with e-enabled end-to-end processes. Using advanced technologies available from within the Marlborough Stirling Group, MSMS delivers flexible, service driven solutions to satisfy the business needs of a constantly changing mortgage market.

Mastek
Contact: Sanjay Mudnaney
Phone: 91-22-829-0182, Ext. 1155; Fax: 91-22-829-0557; e-mail: marketing@mastek.com
Web Site: www.mastek.com

Mastek Ltd. is an ISO 9001-accredited global IT services company, with subsidiaries in the United States, the United Kingdom, Germany, Singapore, and Malaysia. It has five state-of-the-art technologically equipped offshore software development centers in Mumbai (INDIA), spanning an area of 150,000 square feet. With 800-plus skilled IT staff, Mastek provides the following offshore outsourcing services: application development, application migration and support, product development and support, and Web-based applications.

MBS
Contact: Gabriel Romero
Phone: 678-795-5700; Fax: 678-795-5747; e-mail: gromero@theMBSsolution.com
Web Site: www.theMBSsolution.com
MBS, an H&R Block company, provides integrated payroll processing, benefits brokerage, and benefits administration services through SingleSource Technology to help employers take the best care of their employees. MBS is unique among payroll companies in that it is also a licensed, full service broker providing core benefits, cafeteria plans, 401(k), workers comp, and other insurance and financial services.

Mellon HR Solutions
Contact: James Calver
Phone: 86mellonhris; e-mail: calver.j@mellon.com
Web Site: http://mellon.com/hris
Leveraging the expertise of the entire Mellon organization, HR&IS fuses finance and human capital experience to help clients design, build, and operate integrated HR and investor services for their business: HR admin, compensation, training and development, retirement consulting, BPO, communication strategies and corporate restructuring. Human Resources & Investor Solutions provides services to clients in 56 countries.

Mercer
Contact: Barbara Perlmutter
Phone: 212-345-5585 or 866-879-3384; e-mail: Barbara.perlmutter@mercer.com
Web Site: www.mercer.com
Building on 60-plus years of employee benefits experience, this consulting arm of Marsh & McLennan employs more than 15,000 individuals in 40 countries. Working with a broad array of clients on both domestic and global HR issues, it specializes in compensation, benefits, communication, and human capital strategy. Services include: benefits admin, compensation, HRIT, communications, workforce development.

Meridian
Contact: Clemens Wolbers
Phone: +49 171 460 2025; Fax: +49 611 205 9068; e-mail: clemens.wolbers@meridianp2p.com
Web Site: www.meridianp2p.com
Meridian provides total solutions for the T&E and Accounts Payable back-office functions for the Fortune 500. Our global processing center in Dublin, Ireland supports all your needs from data entry (OCR technologies), document reconciliation, compliance checking, VAT reclaim, interactive data portals and e-archiving, and VAT consultancy Meridian is the global leader in VAT reclaim processing with offices in almost 40 countries. Our customers are blue chip clients around the world.

Motif, Inc.
Contact: Samir Parekh or Parul Mehta
Phone: +91-79-2656-9828; Fax: +91-79-2656-3825; e-mail: samir.parekh@motif inc.com
Web Site: www.motif inc.com
Motif's services include: e-mail management/support, back-office transaction processing, financial services, human resources services, benefits administration, loan repayment, reconciliation of 401k plans, technical support, voice support, inbound and outbound teleservices.

Morneau Sobeco
Contact: David Osterhaus
Phone: 412-802-4801; Fax: 412-622-5665; e-mail: dosterhaus@morneausobeco.com
Web Site: www.morneausobeco.com
Morneau Sobeco is one of North America's largest administrators of DB pension and health and welfare benefit plans.

MphasiS
Contact: Anita Singh
Phone: 91-80-2556-7500, Ext. 1720; Fax: 91-80-2552-2719;
e-mail: Shreya.Ukil@mphasis.com
Web Site: www.mphasis.com
MphasiS has organized skill sets and experience across industries and technologies into the MphasiS Competency Centers. Each of these centers has grown in response to the evolving needs of the market, under the aegis of the MphasiS Architects Community (MAC). MphasiS—a global IT and BPO service provider to G2000 companies around the globe, assists its clients in innovating and streamlining their business processes by offering custom solutions for technology and operations outsourcing. The Company's expertise is focused on financial services, logistics and technology verticals and spans across architecture, application development and integration, application management and business process outsourcing, including the operation of large-scale customer contact centers. MphasiS specializes in multi-channel solutions, which optimize sales and service processes from a cost and quality perspective. Besides an onsite presence at key locations, the Company has an extensive offshore infrastructure for IT Development and Business Process Outsourcing with centers in India, China and Mexico. MphasiS has a strong quality culture, reflected in ISO 9000 and BS 7799 certifications, CMMi Level 5 rating and Six Sigma quality initiatives. The company currently employs over 6500 professionals.

MSS★Group, Inc.
Contact: Shannon Murphy
Phone: 510-645-1982; e-mail: Shannon.Murphy@mssgroup.com
Web Site: www.mssgroup.com
MSS★Group is the largest and most successful provider of telecom expense management (TEM) services in the industry. In 2003, it recovered $950 million in refunds and processed 3.5 million invoices and 1.5 billion call records.

NEC
Contact: Beth Makosey
Phone: 408-844-1320 Corporate Headquarters: 916-463-7000;
e-mail: beth.makosey@necsam.com
Web Site: www.necsam.com
NEC helps financial services firms optimize their IT investments by aligning IT with core business processes and strategic goals. NEC leverages its world-class expertise to develop specialized solutions that shift the focus from managing technologies to managing your core business. NEC Solutions America is a premier provider of integrated solutions for the Connected Enterprise.

NEC Solutions America strategic and practical consulting services are borne from the experiences of a global solutions company that has grown for more than 100 years. From business services management, biometric security solutions, business intelligence, visual display systems, and high availability servers and services, all NEC Solutions America's clients gain the personal attention needed to create and manage a Connected Enterprise.

NCO Group
Contact: Chuck Burns
Phone: 215-441-2335; Fax: 215-441-3908; e-mail: chuck.burns@ncogroup.com
Phone (U.S.): 215-441-3000; Fax: 215-441-3929; 800-220-2274;
Phone (U.K.): 020-8565-4700
Web Site: www.ncogroup.com
NCO, the world's largest provider of revenue cycle management solutions, offers a broad range of flexible solutions designed to improve customer efficiency and effectiveness. NCO improves cash f low and customer relationships at each stage of the revenue cycle. Its integrated contact solutions help customers provide effective service to their at-risk customers. Its precollection solutions provide the resources needed to motivate customers to pay recently delinquent accounts. Its bad debt recovery solutions help customers salvage revenue by collecting accounts as a third party after all other recovery efforts have been exhausted.

NIIT SmartServe Ltd.
Contact: D. Ayappane
Phone: 91-124-8902702; Fax: 91-124-8902701; e-mail: ayappane@niitsmartserve.com
Web Site: www.niitsmartserve.com
Back-office operations—Finance, Insurance, Banking, Telecom, Retail Contact Center operations—Inbound and outbound; education and training, and tech help desk outsourcing.

NIIT Technologies
Contact: Lee Anne Wimberly
Phone: 770-55-9494; 888-454-NIIT; Fax: 770-551 9229; e-mail: lawimberly@niit.com
Web Site: www.niit.com/tech
NIIT Technologies applies advanced software-development processes and innovative thinking to help customers across the globe outsource critical business functions with confidence. Its services include knowledge solutions: custom learning content development, on-site training delivery, custom learning technology solutions, and enterprise knowledge solutions; and software solutions: custom software development and maintenance, legacy maintenance and modernization, and enterprise application integration.

Northrop Grumann
Contact: Juli Ballesteros
Phone: 703-713-4675; e-mail: juli.ballesteros@ngc.com; e-mail: sales@ngc.com
Web Site: www.northropgrumman.com
Northrop Grumman provides outsourcing solutions for federal, state, local, and commercial clients that leverage its expertise in IT infrastructure and systems integration. Northrop helps clients meet today's complex outsourcing challenges, from designing, building, and managing enterprise-wide environments to providing cybersecurity, infrastructure support, and customized solutions for the most demanding applications. Northrop Grumman is the trusted partner in achieving your business-critical objectives.

Office Tiger
Contact: M. Breault or Anupam Ahuja; e-mail: aahuja@officetiger.com
Phone: 212-629-9275; Fax 212-629-9276; e-mail: mbreault@officetiger.com
Web Site: www.officetiger.com

Since 1999, Office Tiger has worked with domestic outsourcers and third-party administrators, improving their performance and maximizing their revenue. They are pioneers in judgment-based, industry-focused outsourcing services on a global scale. The market demand for better, faster, cheaper services and the underlying costs for supplying them have impacted the pace of growth for the business services industry. Office Tiger structures documents for intelligent information retrieval. They manage the life cycle of documents from paper to coded/indexed databases rapidly and error free. Through this process they apply specialized software for OCR conversion, data extraction and content standardization. They have developed dedicated applications for litigation support services and corporate information management.

OKS Group
Contact: Brian Johnson
Phone: 772-229-8625; Fax: 772-229-5778; e-mail: bjohnson@oksgroup.com
Web Site: www.oksgroup.com
OKS Group is a global provider of offshore and domestic BPO, ITO, and Call Center Services. Services include Inbound & Outbound Calling; Data Capture & Enhancement; Transaction Processing; back-office clerical processing; Web-mining; Voice Transcription; Business Process Consulting; Direct Mail & Direct Marketing Services; and a full suite of other BPO, ITO, Call Center, and CRM Services. OKS has consulting offices in the United States, United Kingdom, Canada, and Germany, and production centers in the United States, India, and Manila.

Olive Optimized e-Business Solutions
Contact: Dipin Kapur
Phone: 91-11-2699-1100; Fax: 91-11-2699-1110; e-mail: enquiry@oliveglobal.com
Web Site: www.oliveglobal.com
Olive e-Business is a top-level global Web solutions and software outsourcing company with an offshore development center in India. It offers offshore outsourcing solutions to enterprises worldwide. With proven expertise in technology, Olive provides an array of outsourcing services that include customized applications development, web site design and development, Web hosting, search engine ranking, business process automation solutions, portal development, b2B site development, CRM solutions, content development, content management systems, document management solutions, product catalogue development, e-commerce solutions, and Internet and extranet solutions.

Oracle On Demand
Contacts: Timothy Chou or Glenn P. Lim
Phone: 800-833-3536; California HQ: 650-506-7000; Reston, VA: 703-478-9000;
Main Fax: 703-318-6340; e-mail: Glenn.Lim@Oracle.com
Web Site: www.oracle.com
Oracle On Demand helps you reduce your IT costs to a predictable monthly fee by hosting your enterprise technology in Oracle's state-of-the-art data center. Allow Oracle's expert technicians to run your enterprise database, applications, and training and focus your IT staff and tools on strategic technology projects that impact your bottom line. Oracle On Demand helps your enterprise: improve the reliability, availability, scalability, and security of your information infrastructure by hosting your enterprise technology in Oracle's state-of-the-art data center. Access product and technology experts dedicated to Oracle products.

Outsource Management Group
Contact: Celeste Smith-Parkerson
Phone: 502-515-7656; e-mail: celestes@omgservices.com
Web Site: www.omgservices.com

Outsource Management Group provides outsourcing solutions for: mailroom facilities management, copy center imaging, switchboard disaster recovery plans, shipping/receiving, and warehouse operations equipment evaluation consulting.

Outsource Partners International, Inc.
Contact: Kishore H. Mirchandani; e-mail: kmirchandani@opiglobal.com or
Contact: James H. Liggett
Phone: 212-768-9393; Fax: 212-768-9414; e-mail: jliggett@opiglobal.com
Web Site: www.opiglobal.com
Outsource Partners International, Inc. (OPI) is a leading business process outsourcing firm. Specializing in finance and accounting services, they provide innovative business solutions that empower clients with a competitive advantage, enabling them to focus on their core activities. They deliver high-quality products and services with highly motivated and qualified teams who are focused on exceeding client expectations. OPI offers clients a flexible service offering with a good product mix of high volume low risk transaction processing. In a typical organization, running a transaction processing department is typically the most laborious, time-consuming, and prone to errors. Utilizing a best practice service center approach they provide quick turn around data entry and exception handling. Further, through a combination of both manual and programmed procedures, they monitor transaction processing and reporting to ensure completeness, accuracy and validity of all data. Some of the services provided by OPI are: Accounts payable, Accounts receivable, Cash disbursements, Credit and collection, Cash application, Billings, Bank, and other reconciliation, Ancillary transaction processing, T&E report processing and Pension accounting and reporting.

Outsourced Venture Capital Solutions
Contact: Scott Wilson
Phone: 727-784-5461; Fax: 727-784-6689; e-mail: swilson@chiefresourceofficer.com
Web Site: www.outsourcedvcsolutions.com
Outsourced VC Solutions assesses for start-ups the outsourcing potential and impact on profitability through outsourcing objectively for VCs. It recommends outsourcing solutions, where appropriate, in phase-in/phase-out approaches to achieve immediate return and swifter profits. VCs can find comprehensive resources on impact of outsourcing on profitability, need for outsourcing on return on investment, and due diligence at Outsourced VC Solutions.com. Assessments and consultation services provide VCs with the information they need to make knowledgeable decisions on all types of new businesses, to include outsourced services.

Outsourcing Solutions, Inc. (OSI)
Contact: Timothy J. Bauer
Phone: 800-487-2005
Web Site: www.osioutsourcing.com
Outsourcing Solutions Inc. (OSI) is the nation's leading provider of business process outsourcing (BPO) services designed to boost client profitability through strategic receivables management. Best-in-class people practices and business practices, deep industry knowledge, and more than 50 years experience power a proven receivables outsourcing approach that consistently delivers maximum netback for clients. OSI has more than 65 offices in 25 states, plus Canada, Mexico, and Puerto Rico, as well as associates based on-site at client locations.

PacificNet Communications
Contact: Victor Tong
Phone: 605-229-6678; Fax: 605-229-0394; e-mail: usoffice@pacificnet.com
Web Site: www.pacificnet.com
PacificNet is the largest outsourced call center, data entry center in China. Its outsourcing team has 5,000 seats and 2,000 staff. PacificNet Communications Limited is a subsidiary of Pacific-Net

Inc. (Nasdaq: PACT) and a leading provider of value-added telecom services including call center, CRM, telemarketing, and data-mining services, and mobile data services such as SMS, MMS, UMS, LBS, mobile commerce, roaming, paging, wireless Internet, VPN and VoIP services in the Greater China Region.

PAR Computer Sciences (Int.) Ltd.

Contact: Dipa Kapadia
Phone: 91-22-2497-1450; Fax: 91-22-2497-1460; e-mail: par@parcomputers.com
Web Site: www.parcomputers.com
PAR's core areas of focus involve web based software solutions, web designing, multimedia solutions and back office-processing services. Their back office services include bill processing, financial data analysis, forms processing, e-book conversion, web content development, document migration and digitizing product catalogues.

Patni Computer Systems Limited

Contact: Ravi Ramabuja
Phone: 91-22-5693-0500; Fax: 91-22-2832-4856; e-mail: mktg@patni.com
Web Site: www.patni.com
Patni Computer Systems Limited is a global IT services provider servicing Global 2000 clients in the manufacturing, insurance, banking and financial services, retail, and energy and utilities industries. With a skilled employee strength of over 8,000, multiple offshore development facilities across seven cities, and 22 international offices across the Americas, Europe, and Asia-Pacific, Patni registered revenues in excess of U.S. $250 million for the year 2003. Patni's technology focus spans e-business solutions, enterprise applications, embedded technology solutions, and enterprise systems management. Its service offerings include application development and reengineering, application management, and business process outsourcing. Committed to quality, Patni adds value to its clients' businesses through well-established and structured methodologies, tools, and techniques.

Perimeter Technology

Contact: Howard Smedley
Phone: 603-645-1616, Ext. 1211; Fax: 603-329-5464; e-mail: sales@perimetertechnology.com
Web Site: www.perimetertechnology.com
Perimeter Technology is the leading provider of call center, Centrex and ACD solutions, including the VU-ACD/100 Management Information System with real-time display. Additional solutions include: NET-VU Internet ACD to Web-enable call centers; CALLER-VU agent desktop CTI; and CUSTOMER-VU PC-based Centrex consoles.

Perot Systems Corporation

Contact: Georgia Engle
Phone: 972-577-6012; Fax: 972-577-5142; e-mail: georgia.engle@ps.net
Web Site: www.perotsystems.com
Perot Systems is a worldwide provider of information technology services and business solutions. Through its flexible and collaborative approach, Perot Systems integrates expertise from across the company to deliver custom solutions that enable clients to accelerate growth, streamline operations, and create new levels of customer value. Headquartered in Plano, Texas, Perot Systems has more than 10,000 associates located in North America, Europe, and Asia.

Perot Systems TSI India, Limited

Contact: Anurag Sharma
Phone: +91 120 2432750; Fax: +91 120 2430545; e-mail: anurag.sharma@pstsi.com
Web Site: www.psti.com

Application Development range of services comprises developing new applications, features and extensions and enhancements, interfaces and upgrades for existing and emerging business operations. Onsite/offshore approach provides Clients with a framework for application development outsourcing and ensures that the solution is "to customer specification, on time and within budget." Teams have expertise in a variety of technologies from mainframe platforms to web and PC-based applications, and can develop host as well as distributed applications. They use state-of-the-art tools for our development efforts.

PFSweb, Inc.
Contacts: Laura Osborne or Miriam Kertzman
Phone: 972-881-2900, Ext. 3574; 888-600-6661, Ext. 18; Fax: 972-509-7813;
e-mail: losborne@pfsweb.com
Web Site: www.PFSweb.com
PFSweb, Inc. is an international business process outsourcing provider, supporting global leaders like IBM, Lancôme, HP, The Smithsonian Catalogue, DuPont, and Nokia. Customized solutions include fulfillment and distribution, Web-enabled customer care, Web design and hosting, returns management, e-commerce software, and payment processing services.

Pilgrim
Contact: Linda Gillen
Phone: 800-526-4616; Fax: 617-956-6448; e-mail: Linda@discoverpilgrim.net
Web Site: www.discoverpilgrim.net
Pilgrim provides complete insurance processing and turnkey business process outsourcing (BPO) services for the private passenger and commercial automobile insurance industry, which can be bundled or purchased individually.

Pitney Bowes, Inc.
Contact: Natalie Forrest
Phone: 212-808-3867
Web Site: www.pb.com
International Contact: Catherine Verrall
Phone: +44 1442 416000
Pitney Bowes Management Services (PBMS) is a premier global outsourcing solutions provider with over 1,300 client locations across twelve countries. PBMS provides customized integrated mail services, document management, and imaging solutions for their customers. Core competencies include mail and message management, creative services, return mail service, digital mail, asset recovery and management, digital print, print on demand, variable data print, records archive and retrieval and business recovery services. Key vertical markets served include Litigation Support Services, Government, Finance, Insurance, and Pharmaceutical. PBMS provides business process improvements utilizing six sigma methodologies.

PlanTech, Inc
Contact: Jim Bongiorno
Phone: 248-737-2100, Ext. 223; Fax: 914-273-2631; e-mail: mrzeznik@gagebabcock.com
Web Site: www.gagebabcock.com
GBA Consulting Engineers, LLC is a specialty firm of professional f ire protection, life safety, and security engineers, offers life safety surveys, code consulting, "due diligence" surveys, loss control engineering, JCAHO Statements of Conditions, litigation support, and design of fire detection, alarm and suppression systems, CCTV, access control, and intrusion detection systems.

PlatformOne

Contact: Dusty Rhodes

Phone: 800-444-6211 or 770-623-9143; Fax: 770-623-5710; e-mail: sales@platformone.com

Web Site: www.Platformone.com

Part of SCI Companies, PlatformOne has evolved over 18 years to deliver HR BPO solutions to more than 450 clients and is one of the fastest-growing HR BPO providers to the midmarket. The company offers two HR BPO solutions: the f irst is aimed at mid-market companies and includes HR technology infrastructure, HR administrative services, and HR professional support; the second is an industry-specific, turnkey technology solution for PEOs.

Polaris Software Lab Limited

Contact: K. Srinivasan

Phone: 732-590-8102; Fax: 732-404-1188; e-mail: info@polaris.co.in

Web Site: www.polaris.co.in

Polaris offers services in these areas: application migration, new application development, component and Web-based development, maintenance of applications, testing and validation, with a focus on the FSI segment, end-to-end banking, credit cards, risk management, treasury and forex, commodities and futures, implementation of CRM solutions, and ERP.

Power Logistics

Contact: Carman Imrisek

Phone: 630-377-3838; Fax: 630-377-8322; e-mail: info@powergroup.com

Web Site: www.powergroup.com

Power Logistics is an operating unit of The Power Group, a world-class manufacturing and logistics provider with over 20 facilities in four countries and on two continents. Based near Chicago and privately held, The Power Group specializes in providing customer logistics and manufacturing services for a diverse Fortune 500 customer base. The Power Group's 3,100-plus employees and three decades of outsourcing experience combine to produce lasting value for our customers.

PricewaterhouseCoopers (PwC)

Contact: Joseph Postighone

Phone: 646-394-9319; e-mail: joseph.postighone@us.pwc.com

Web Site: www.pwc.com

Tax compliance can be challenging for companies, burdening in-house tax staff with specialized compliance demands that take the focus off of value-added tax department activities. PricewaterhouseCoopers offers a scaleable solution to address the compliance needs of corporations and other business entities. Its services can be tailored to leverage PwC's specialized tax professionals and technology resources to maximize your tax department's strengths and minimize the impact on company resources.

PrintGPO, Inc.

Contact: S. Wilson

Phone: 727-784-6689; e-mail: info@PrintGPO.com

Web Site: www.PrintGPO.com

PrintGPO is the fastest-growing group purchasing and outsourcing buyer/vendor matching company globally. Through the Group Purchasing Program, PrintGPO has negotiated substantial discounts on products and services with numerous, well-respected print industry suppliers.

ProcessMind, Inc.
Contact: Nimish Soni
Phone: 91-80-5110-5000, Ext. 1001; Fax: 91-80-5110-5200; e-mail: nsoni@processmind.com
Web Site: www.processmind.com
ProcessMind Inc provides business process management solutions in the healthcare, insurance, and financial services sectors, along with specialized services in process consulting and project management. The core strength of ProcessMind lies in leveraging the specialist skills in process management and translating business process outsourcing solutions into highly effective client relationships.

Prosero
Contact: David Wire
Phone: 678-731-8500 Fax: 678-731-8700; e-mail: sales@prosero.net
Web Site: www.prosero.com
Prosero brings passion to procurement. As a pioneer in collaborative Procurement Co-Sourcing, Prosero developed the Procurement Center of Excellence model to deliver Strategic Sourcing, Contract Deployment, Compliance Management and Supplier Management services to fit customer needs. Their Co-Sourcing approach differs from typical outsourcing because they typically augment rather than replace your resources. Prosero brings additional resources to help you address unmanaged expenditure categories and free your resources to focus on core business activities. For manufacturing customers, Prosero also delivers Material Logistics & Planning services to streamline processes and optimize inventory investments.

Raytheon Professional Services (RPS)
Contact: Jeffrey Lucas
Phone: 972-344-1092; e-mail: jslucas@raytheon.com
Web Site: www.rps.com
A business within Raytheon Company, Raytheon Professional Services (RPS) is a global provider of outsourced learning services. Headquartered in Plano, Texas, and with offices throughout Asia, Australia, Europe, and the United States, RPS provides outsourced learning services to companies in the automotive, defense, financial services, and high-tech industries.

Redix Web Solutions
Contact: Dharmesh Acharya
Phone: 91-79-6400685; Fax: 91-79-6566681; e-mail: se@web-design-india.com
Web Site: web-design-india.com
This India-based firm provides customized Web page designing, Web application development, ecommerce development, and data processing solutions to businesses and acts as an offshore development center for overseas development firms. Core strength is PHP, PERL, ASP, C, MySQL, MS SQL, PostGres. Redix also has extensive Web design skills in HTML, Photoshop, and Macromedia Flash.

Reliable Integration Services
Contact: Gary Markin
Phone: 703-205-0930; Fax: 703-205-0920; e-mail: info@risi.com
Web Site: www.risi.com
Since 1988, Reliable, based in Tyson's Corner, Virginia, has provided premium service to commercial enterprises and government IT organizations of up to 500,000 users. Reliable designs, implements, manages, and maintains networks of multivendor software and systems carrying mission-critical, multimedia traffic. With a unique, metrics-based methodology, Reliable

ensures that every network function and attribute traces directly to a business requirement and that the network is poised to accommodate growth in users and application complexity.

ReSourcePhoenix.com

Contact: Cynthia Randall

Phone: 415-485-4712; Fax: 415-485-4823; e-mail: crandall@resourcephoenix.com

Web Site: www.resourcephoenix.com

ReSourcePhoenix provides services in accounting, enterprise resource planning (ERP), customer relationship management (CRM), and business information processing. It offers a comprehensive suite of best-in-class accounting and ERP applications, delivered over secure Internet connections and managed by highly trained accounting and information technology professionals.

RightNow Technologies

Contact: Dean Brown

Phone: 972-232-3928; e-mail: dbrown@rightnow.com

Web Site: www.rightnow.com

RightNow Technologies is the leading on demand CRM company focused on customer service. RightNow has delivered these benefits to more than 1,000 customers worldwide. Founded in 1997, RightNow has offices in Bozeman, Dallas, San Mateo, New Jersey, London, Sydney and Tokyo. RightNow's products are available in 13 languages worldwide.

RSM McGladrey Employer Services

Contact: Louise Sharer

Phone: 800-274-3978; e-mail: louise.sharer@rsmi.com

Web Site: www.rsmmcgladrey.com

When the consulting firm RSM McGladrey acquired MyBenefitSource in 2004, it added end-to-end HRO to its existing HR service portfolio of payroll and benefits administration. Serving hundreds of clients nationwide, small and large, RSM offers integrated payroll and benefits systems, in addition to benefits brokerage.

SAIC

Contact: Joseph P. Walkush

Phone: 800-430-7629 or 44 (0) 845-366-7242 in Europe or

Contact: Zuraidah Hashim

Phone: 703-676-2541; e-mail: hashimz@saic.com

Web Site: www.saic.com/outsourcing/business-process.html

SAIC recognizes that the next level of business process outsourcing means going far beyond the skills and capabilities of a conventional IT outsourcer. It requires engineering, scientific, and technology expertise in your vertical market. Trust is critical because you are allowing someone else to manage and execute your "core" engineering processes. And the partnership model must be based on a high level of strategic involvement. These are the core capabilities necessary to capitalize on SAIC's scientific, engineering, and technology assets to fully leverage your business core. SAIC provides these capabilities in an array of industries: utilities and power—asset optimization (turbines, power lines, nuclear power plants); oil and gas—the oilfield and the science and technology to drive exploration and production; life sciences—research and drug discovery; telecommunications—telecom expense management, wireless plan optimization, provisioning, billing, invoice validation, inventory management; government—end-to-end supply chain (inventory and asset management); automotive; textile; high-tech—design, component manufacturing.

Sand Martin

Contact: Shiveti Ahuja
Phone: 91-11-5166-3000; Fax: 91-11-5166-2000
Contact: Sunil Goel
Phone: +91-11-51663000; Fax: +91-11-51662000; e-mail: sgoel@sandmartin.com
Web Site: www.sandmartin.com
Sand Martin Consultants has been one of the pioneers in providing IT-enabled outsourcing services from India. The company serves clientele worldwide in the areas of finance and accounting, human resources, taxation, 401(k) retirement plan benefit accounting and administration, as well as health, accident, and royalty claims processing.

SARCOM

Contact: Rick Allen
Phone: 614-854-1520; Fax: 614-854-1508; e-mail: inquiry@sarcom.com
Web Site: www.sarcom.com
SARCOM offers IT services, including: help desk, desktop support, server administration, data center, IT projects, network maintenance and monitoring, and IT procurement. SARCOM provides IT outsourcing services on a selective and full outsource basis.

Satyam

Contact: Priyank Tripathi
Phone: 908-922-7652; e-mail: priyank_tripathi@satyam.com
Web Site: www.satyam.com
The Engineering Solutions Group at Satyam has a multifaceted team of skilled engineers who apply their experience in design, automation, engineering analysis, and product development to the needs of customers in a variety of industries. Based on a combination of engineering knowledge, software skills, and industrial experience, the group offers a spectrum of engineering services in CAD, CAM, CAE, PDM, and customization. The group also partners with organizations to set up state-of-the-art India Development Centers (IDCs), which function as virtual extensions of the customers' engineering teams. Services include: CAD solutions, CAM solutions, CAE solutions, product data management, CAD customization/automation, and technical publications. Satyam Computer Services Ltd. is a leading global consulting and IT services company that offers a wide array of solutions for a range of key verticals and horizontals. Starting from the strategy consulting right through to implementing IT solutions for clients, Satyam straddles this entire space. It has excellent domain competencies in verticals such as automotive, banking and financial service, insurance and healthcare, manufacturing, telecom-infrastructure-media-entertainment-semiconductors. Satyam's storage offers the following services: storage software development, testing (QA, interoperability) and maintenance services, both on-site and offshore; system integration/administration for enterprise storage area networks; ODC (offshore development center) and TAC (technical assistance center) setup in India for major companies in the storage domain.

Scholarship Management Services

Contact: Dorothy Hamilton
Phone: 507-931-0416; Fax: 507-931-8034; e-mail: dhamilton@scholarshipamerica.org
Web Site: www.scholarshipamerica.org
ScholarShop is a curriculum and multimedia resource center to motivate and prepare young people to achieve their full potential as students and as productive members of society. ScholarShop is a fresh way of approaching career and postsecondary exploration. ScholarShop makes learning about yourself, careers, colleges, and other postsecondary schools fun. For schools, colleges, and youth-serving agencies with existing programs for career and college exploration, ScholarShop is

a tool to make the job easier. For organizations that do not currently have a career and college exploration program, ScholarShop pulls together all the pieces needed for a comprehensive program that includes activities for parent involvement.

SEEC Software

Contact: Dave Dalton

Phone: 412-893-0300 or 800-682-SEEC or 800-940-3336 (Sales);

Fax: 412-893-0417; e-mail: ddalton@SEEC.com

Web Site: www.seec.com

At the core of SEEC's legacy modernization capabilities is a powerful suite of products that provide sophisticated application portfolio understanding, and enable companies to reduce legacy application complexity, eliminate redundancy, restructure applications, and rapidly identify and define optimal points for integration with other systems. In addition, SEEC's products include powerful business rule mining capabilities and predefined process components that enable the rapid deployment of new applications to meet today's challenging business requirements.

Siemens Building Technologies, Inc.

Contact: Brad Haeberle

Phone: 800-877-7545, Ext. 5744; Fax: 847-229-3721; e-mail: info.sbt@siemens.com

Web Site: www.sbt.siemens.com

Siemens Facility Management Services business unit is responsible for the on-site management of facility departments and related functions. It specializes in operations and maintenance of the facility, which consist of: professional management, on-site technical staff, subcontract management, energy programs.

Siemens Business Services, Inc.

Contact: James Faletra

Phone: 781-830-2274; e-mail: james.faletra@siemens.com or Jürgen Frischmuth

Phone: 203-642-2300; Fax: 203-642-2399; e-mail: Sales@sbs.siemens.com

Web Site: www.usa.siemens.com/sbs

Corporate Contacts: +49 0800-225 53 36; Fax. +49 0800-736 33 36

Siemens Business Services is one of the world's leading IT service providers. With its comprehensive know-how and specific sector knowledge, this division of Siemens offers solutions and services from a single source, from consulting through system integration and management of IT infrastructures to IT outsourcing. In fiscal year 2002 (09/30/02), Siemens Business Services achieved sales of $5.8 billion, from which more than 70 percent came from outside Siemens. The company has more than 34,000 employees in 44 countries. Siemens Business Services delivers its capabilities through its managed service offerings, which provide fixed-cost, service-level based solutions for specific IT management challenges in the following areas. Depot operations center (DOC): Emergency exchange and problem diagnosis/resolution services tailored to the needs to mobile computing users. Deskside support: Problem diagnosis and resolution for desktop computers. Enterprise Help desk: Distributed computing problem resolution, with single-point-of-contact (SPOC) capabilities. Enterprise support services (ESS): Proactive problem diagnosis and resolution for servers and network components. Install, move, add, delete/disposal (IMAC/D): Complete life-cycle management of the distributed computing environment. Remote network services (RNS): Remote monitoring and administration of multi-vendor networking infrastructures.

Siri Technologies Pvt. Ltd.

Contact: Sujatha Kapoor

Phone: 91-80-2-6340050, Ext. 1009; Fax: +91-80-2634-0066; eFax: 208-545-5055; e-mail: sujatha.kapoor@siritech.com

Web Site: www.siritech.com

Siri Technologies is an ISO9001:2000 and SEI-CMM Level 4 certified company providing software development and quality assurance services to clients globally. Executed projects involve custom application development, application/platform migration and pr-production testing of applications, working on diverse platforms and technologies, including client/server, Internet, wireless, COBOL, Delphi .Net, J2EE, EDI, XML.

SmartSource Corporation
Contact: Amanda DeBurro
Phone: 781-785-3331; e-mail: adeburro@smartsourceonline.com
Web Site: www.smartsourceonline.com
SmartSource provides outsourced services for e-mail and Fax message delivery. They handle broadcast jobs and build tailored products for e-mail/fax-on-demand solutions. All applications include client access to customized web-based reporting. For financial institutions, SmartSource has recently launched several applications for Cash Management and other transactional communication requirements.

Softtek
Contact: Alejandra Maria Ancira Cardenas or John Beischer
Phone: 703-288-5800; Fax: 703-288-5833; e-mail: alejandra.ancira@softtek.com
Web Site: www.softtek.com
Softtek offers a wide range of IT solutions to meet today's complex business challenges. Whether you are in a service or manufacturing industry, Softtek's solution offering addresses the technology needs of your company. It develops, implements, and supports advanced software applications and platforms to help multinational companies do business better. Whether the task is improving existing systems or creating something new, Softtek can provide a solution, on time and on budget. Softek provides companies the power to see, manage and protect their information. Since 1996, Softek solutions have helped enterprise customers improve data and application availability while reducing the risk, cost and complexity associated with optimizing multi-vendor storage infrastructures. Softek offers the industry leading ESRM solution, enabling active management of multi-vendor storage environments. With Softek, enterprises gain a unified view of heterogeneous storage, profile and analyze data across the enterprise, and take direct actions that result in the reclamation of wasted space, optimized use of differentiated classes or tiers of storage and the retirement of data no longer needed—in short, they provide the foundation of an enterprise ILM strategy.

SourceNet Solutions
Contact: Dan Reiff
Phone: 979-691-7700; Fax: 979-691-7766; e-mail:
business.development@sourcenetsolutions.com
Web Site: www.sourcenetsolutions.com
For most companies, energy costs and the related expenses of their management are a multimillion dollar consideration. Between tracking data, monitoring market changes, validation of rates, detection and resolution of billing errors, and development and analysis of cost and usage exception reports, companies can spend a significant amount of precious resources: Time and Money. SourceNet's Energy Information Group is your source for outsourcing all of those activities and more, and provides a comprehensive web-based bill management solution. That translates to less overhead, a more accurate picture of your energy usage and costs, and in the end, a healthier bottom line.

Spherion
Contacts: Robert W. Morgan, Lisa Lovas, or Kip Havel
Phone: 800-422-3819 or 678-867-3000; e-mail: Kiphavel@spherion.com
Web Site: www.spherion.com

Spherion's broad-based experience in recruiting is founded on an in-depth understanding of the workforce and the issues that drive performance. It has extended this expertise into high-value workforce management solutions that incorporate specialized knowledge of many workplace processes and technologies. It is these core competencies that Spherion offers to clients who want to more effectively plan, acquire, and optimize talent to improve their bottom line. Planning: Workforce planning and design—Benchmarking and analyzing enterprise-wide workforce practices and operation. Acquisition: recruitment, assessment and screening. Optimization: on-boarding and training, development, and outplacement.

SSI Inc.

Contact: Raj Agarwal
Phone: 508-410-8930; Toll Free Phone: 866-202-119; Fax: 508-256-6553; e-mail: dhiraj@ssi-incusa.com
Web Site: www.ssiincusa.com
SSI Inc., a U.S.-based organization, specializes in contact center and back-office processes outsourcing, with a state-of-art, 24/7 call center in Pune, India, and a wide network of call centers in the United States, Costa Rica, Latin America, and the Philippines.

STA International

Contact: Robert Williams
Phone: 516-997-2400; Fax: 516-997-2632; e-mail: bwilliams@stacollect.com,
or ny@stacollect.com
Web Site: www.stacollect.com
STA International is the world's largest independent commercial credit management company, with branches across the United States, Europe, the Far East, Mexico, and affiliates around the globe. With over 50 years experience in debt collection and receivables outsourcing, it has grown to offer a portfolio of credit management services including credit insurance and credit management training.

StarTek, Inc.

Contact: Ruth Jenkins
Phone: 970-352-6800; Fax: 970-353-7652; e-mail: sales@startek.com
Web Site: www.startek.com
StarTek identifies each partner's specific needs from support for e-commerce and Internet ventures to technical support, inventory management, fulfillment, and order processing to distribution and supply chain management, then provides a tailored solution. Global service platforms include a comprehensive offering.

Staubach Management Services (SMS)

Contact: Louis G. Erskine
Phone: 972-361-5000; Fax: 972-361-5908; e-mail: info@staubach.com
Web Site: www.staubach.com
Staubach Management Services (SMS) provides strategic property facility management services including: building management, operations maintenance, vendor management, project design, move management and 24-hour call center services.

Strategic Alliances LLC

Contact: Marty Bodelson
Phone: 770-205-7042; Fax: 770-476-7222; e-mail: mbodelson@strategicalliancesllc.com
Web Site: www.strategicalliancesllc.com
Strategic Alliances is a leading professional Sales Outsourcing Company for direct/indirect channels. They are a company that can be your sales team or augment your existing resources. They

provide professional sales and business support on a contract basis for the Call Center/CRM industry.

StratSource
Contact: Kevin Leonard
Phone: 972-437-2220, Ext. 357; e-mail: kevin.leonard@straightsource.com
Web Site: www.stratsource.com
StratSource, a specialist in RPO, uses its rigorous tools and support services to manage the complete recruitment process—from resource planning to retained hire—fortifying the HR function with increased value, reduced costs, improved hires, and more control.

Sundaram Finance Group
Contact: Sri S. Venkatesan
Phone: +91-44-2852-6353; Fax: +91-44-2858-7054; e-mail: info@sundarambpo.com
Web Site: www.sundarambpo.com
Sundaram Business Services (SBS) is the Business Process Outsourcing (BPO) division of Sundaram Finance Limited (SFL). SFL is one of India's largest Non-Banking Financial Companies with a 50-year history. The business activities of the SF Group include auto finance, general insurance, asset management, logistics, information technology and business process outsourcing. SF enjoys successful associations with multinational companies such as Royal and Sun Alliance (U.K.), International Finance Corporation (IFC-Washington, United States) and FMO (Netherlands).

Supply Chain Dynamics Inc.
Contact: Bill Cantrell
Phone: 360-833-8883; Fax: 360-833-8810; e-mail: bill.cantrell@scdconsulting.com
Web Site: www.scdconsulting.com
Supply Chain Dynamics is a specialized supply chain management consulting organization that is focused on assisting corporations penetrate global markets. It works with clients in areas from product development, sourcing, manufacturing, business development, to domestic and international transportation. Its clients realize improvements in service, efficiency, and profitability. It helps organizations create winning world-class supply chains that support mission, strategy, and operations objectives.

Sutherland Global Services
Contact: Dan Lang
Phone: 800-388-4557, Ext. 6111; Fax: 585-784-2200; e-mail: Dan_Lang@suth.com
Web Site: www.suth.com
Sutherland Global Services, Inc. is a premier customer management company with 17 years of practitioner heritage in Business Process Outsourcing. Sutherland Global Services helps Fortune 1000 clients design and build front-office and back-office operations, offering Process Consulting, Technology Support and Help Desk services, Customer Care and Account Management. Because of their expertise and industry leadership, Sutherland Global Services have built operations for over 100 clients in 17 years.

Syntel, Inc.
Contact: Jonathan James
Phone: 919-233-6200; Fax: 919-233-6210; e-mail: jonathan_james@syntelinc.com
Web Site: www.syntelinc.com
IT Applications Management: Development, Integration, Maintenance; Electronic Commerce: Business to Business, Business to Consumer; Enterprise Applications: Data Warehousing, Front Office, Package Implementation. Application Management/Production Support, Application Enhancements, On-Call Support, including Emergency Response, Production Support, User Support,

and Customer Inquiries and 24/7 Application Support. Syntel offers services in IT applications management: development, integration, maintenance; electronic commerce: business to business, business to consumer; enterprise applications: data warehousing, front office, package implementation.

TalentFusion
Contact: David Pollard
Phone: 413-584-2552; e-mail: info@talentfusion.com
Web Site: www.talentfusion.com
TalentFusion is a full-service RPO that applies leading technology, processes, and people to improve the performance of its clients' talent acquisition operations while driving down costs. Its proprietary methodology, TalentPath, combined with its eCommerce platform, TalentView, creates a recruitment solution that enables clients to achieve high productivity levels.

TATA Consultancy Services (TCS)
Contact: Frank Lewis
Phone: 972-484-6465; Fax: 972-484-0450; e-mail: f.lewis@usa-tcs.com
Web Site: www.tcs.com or
Contact: Arup Gupta
Phone: 212-557-8038; Fax: 212867-8652; e-mail: a.gupta@usa-tcs.com
TATA Consultancy Services (TCS) is the world's leading information technology consulting, services, and business process outsourcing organization. It envisioned and pioneered the adoption of the flexible global business practices that today enable companies to operate more efficiently and produce more value. With a presence in 32 countries across 5 continents, and a comprehensive range of services across diverse industries, TCS is one of the world's leading Information Technology companies. Six of the Fortune Top 10 companies are among their valued customers. TCS is part of one of Asia's largest conglomerates—the TATA Group—which, with its interests in Energy, Telecommunications, Financial Services, Chemicals, Engineering and Materials, provides them with a grounded understanding of specific business challenges facing global companies.

TATA Infotech Ltd.
Contact: Rahul Thapan
Phone (U.S.): 847-240-1122; Fax: 847-517-7240;
Phone (U.K.): +44-207-838-8910/11/12/13/14; Fax: +44-207-838-8929;
Phone (India HQ): +91-22-5666-4300;
Fax: +91-22-5666-4333; e-mail: marketing@tatainfotech.com
Web Site: www.tatainfotech.com
TATA Infotech provides multilevel learning solutions across the entire spectrum of the enterprise through a customer-driven approach. For learning solutions, organizations need partners, not vendors. TATA Infotech provides complete end-to-end solutions and effective implementation as your learning solutions partner. TATA Infotech's solutions are a unique combination of learning and human resource development tools to provide skill gap identification, creation of customized solutions, and implementation within a predecided time frame. This makes the whole process cost-effective and ensures maximum returns on the training investments. Offerings: competency management (defining of roles in the organization and competencies required for each role); skill enhancement training and development (to bridge the gaps identified by the competency suite to equip employees with actionable knowledge, and work effectively toward getting the right learning to the right people at the right time); training content customization (state-of-the-art simulation models to enable people to gain additional skill sets). These include a wide range of essential business areas like product and process training, end-user training on enterprise software applications.

TechBooks
Contact: Michael O'Brien
Phone: 703-352-0001; Fax: 703-352-8862; or
Contact: Gurvinder Batra
Phone: 703-352-0001, Ext. 119; Fax: 703-352-0005; e-mail: gbatra@techbooks.com
TechBooks is a fast-growing global company that provides composition and data conversion services and solutions to content-rich business verticals. Its clients include publishers, information aggregators, professional societies, government agencies, universities, and major corporations. Its Educational Publishing Group, TechBooks/GTS, provides composition, prepress, design, and editorial development services to publishers of elementary-high school (el-hi) and college textbooks, as well as digital content services for Web, wireless, and e-book versions of their textbooks. Its Professional Publishing Group, TechBooks PPG, provides composition and data conversion solutions to scientific, technical, and medical publishers. Its Information Publishing Group, Tech-Books IPG, provides data conversion services and solutions to information aggregators, universities, libraries, major corporations, and financial institutions. Its Financial Publishing Group, TechBooks Financial, provides data conversion, composition, and graphic arts services to financial printers.

Tecnovate eSolutions
Contact: Shashank Joshi
Phone: 91-11-263-32751-59; Fax: 91-11-2633-2760; e-mail: information@tecnovate.co.in
Web Site: www.tecnovate.co.in
Tecnovate eSolutions, established in India in July 2001 by eBookers, Europe's No.1 Online Travel Business, is a pioneer in Multilingual Offshore Business Process Outsourcing in India. Tecnovate is a high growth Center of Excellence, providing an offshore hub for a full spectrum of Contact Center Services, BPO Services and IT Services.

Telelink, The Call Center, Inc.
Contact: Sydney Ryan
Phone: 888-693-2255; Fax: 709-722-5220; e-mail: sydney@thecallcentreinc.com
Web Site: www.thecallcentreinc.com
This award-winning, Web-enabled call center has over 35 years of experience providing inbound virtual reception, direct response, order entry, and product support. Telelink offers e-mail management and live Web assistance through Live-e-Support, outbound market research, and customer satisfactions surveys. It can provide short-term campaigns or long-term outsourcing partnerships.

Terra Solutions
Contact: Susan Sanner
Phone: 949-481-7217; Fax: 949-481-7217; e-mail: ssanner@terrasolutionsonline.com
Web Site: www.terrasolutionsonline.com
Terra Solutions provides the full range of ERP and GIS services, including outsourcing, application development, and consulting. Its goal is to assist and lead in the development, implementation, and maintenance of most ERP and GIS applications. Terra Solutions has access to a state-of-the-art secure data center for those projects that require a full project approach, to meet the security standards you require. Terra Solutions is positioned to plan, build and operate your ERP and GIS mission-critical applications.

TGA Sciences, Inc.
Contact: Michael Settles
Phone: 781-393-6910, Ext. 203; Fax: 781-393-6894; e-mail: msettles@tgasciences.com
Web Site: www.tgasciences.com

TGA Sciences, Inc. is a contract research laboratory offering the pharmaceutical, biotechnology and research communities a comprehensive range of services from antibody and immunoassay development to clinical monitoring and data management. TGA Sciences, Inc. specializes in customized immunoassay systems for the detection of target molecules, antibody responses, and quantification, all in total compliance with QA and GMP standards, in support of your clinical studies.

Thinksoft Global Services
Contact: A V Asvini Kumar
Phone: 91-44-28525966; Fax: 91-44-28412999; e-mail: asvini.kumar@thinksoftglobal.com
Web Site: www.thinksoftglobal.com
Thinksoft Global is India's largest independent software testing company focused on Banking, Finance and Insurance. Thinksoft helps Global 500 Banking, Financial, Insurance organizations to—Benefit from the objectivity and rigor of Independent Outsourced software testing—Unearth critical software defects early on using a domain focused methodology—Compress time-to-market by outsourcing parallel activities in the product life cycle, and Extract costs by deploying a cost-effective onsite–offshore delivery model.

Tim Kirker Creative
Contact: Tim Kirker
Phone: 914-232-3564; e-mail: info@timkirkercreative.com
Web Site: www.timkirkercreative.com
New York City-based independent design studios specializing in all aspects of outsourced digital media, including Web design and application development, site hosting, interactive media, including audio and video production, digital imaging, and print design and fulfillment.

TMA Resources
Contact: Jim Roche
Phone: 888-878-TMAR, Ext. 2872; Fax: 703-847-2899;
e-mail: roche_james@tmaresources.com
Web Site: www.tmaresources.com
TMA Resources is the leading force in the development of advanced software for the management of member-centric organizations, impressing the industry year after year with its technology developments, commitment to service, and solid growth. TMA Resources renown single source provider system (TIMSS) is a fully integrated member relationship management solution for all your information management, e-commerce, community building, and business reporting needs. TIMSS is available through an application hosting service, which enables small to medium-sized organizations to utilize its rich functionality for a low monthly subscriber fee, without the costly up-front capital expenditures or database and systems administration frustrations.

TopSource Global
Contact: Richard Lynch
Phone: 44 (0) 845-129-4993; Fax: 44 (0) 207-900-1989; e-mail: sales@topsource.co.uk
Web Site: www.topsource.co.uk
TopSource Global offers support in these areas: recruitment services, legal services, direct marketing support, AR/AP, payroll, financial support, and data management. From simple processing to complex multi-step operations, TopSource can outsource almost any type of administrative activity.

Totality Corporation
Contact: Dale Brown
Phone: 415-402-2880; e-mail: dbrown@totality.com
Web Site: www.totality.com

Totality provides a complete, remote outsourced solution for Application and Infrastructure Management (AIM), taking accountability for the entire infrastructure and 24/7 operations to maximize performance, scaleability, and reliability. Through breakthroughs in standardization and automation, Totality provides an unparalleled solution for infrastructure implementation, system deployment, and ongoing management. Totality primarily services Fortune 2000 companies.

Trammell Crow Company
Contact: John Maher
Phone: 203-359-2222; Fax: 203-353-1139; e-mail: info@trammellcrow.com
Web Site: www.trammellcrow.com
Trammell Crow Company Outsourcing Services utilizes proven best practices, industry benchmarks, and state-of-the-art technology to tailor its services to meet the core business requirements of each client. It provides the following real estate outsourcing services: facilities management, project management, transaction services, office services, corporate advisory services, portfolio administration management, and development services.

TriActive, Inc.
Contact: Alison Raffalovich
Phone: 512-330-0337, Ext. 113; Fax: 512-328-2504; e-mail: info@triactive.com
Web Site: www.triactive.com
TriActive, Inc. is a management service provider that delivers simplified enterprise systems management for midsized IT organizations (those supporting 200 to 5,000 devices). TriActive's full MSP approach includes monitoring and management of PCs, servers, networks and Web servers, including a robust range of systems management capabilities.

Trinity Partners
Contact: Amit Goyal
Phone: 91124-501-8670/71/72; Fax: 91124-245-0139; e-mail:
amit.goyal@india.trinitybpm.com
Web Site: www.trinitybpm.com
Trinity Partners, Inc. is a leading business process management solutions provider to global financial institutions. Trinity Partners deliver technology-enabled, world-class services that span business process optimization, transformation, and outsourcing, delivered through a global, distributed, and seamless offshore model. A U.S.-based company with headquarters in Tucson, Arizona, Trinity Partners delivers its offshore services from its state-of-the-art facilities located in New Delhi, India.

Trowbridge Group
Contact: Ben Trowbridge
Phone: 214-696-6410, Fax: 214-239-0698, Email: info@trowbridgegroup.net
Web Site: www.trowbridgegroup.net
Outsourcing or Shared Services, Traditional Contract or Joint Venture, these are specific questions that are uniquely answered by the Trowbridge Group every day. As independent advisors, our consultants provide unbiased knowledge and extensive strategic planning that draws on experience from some of the largest BPO, ITO, and HRO contracts in Asia, Europe, and the Americas with a total contract value of over $40 billion. The Trowbridge Group uses FastSource, a unique comprehensive sourcing methodology, to deliver innovative deal structures involving outsourcing and shared services as components of a total sourcing solution.

TSi Logistics
Contact: John Stinnette
Phone: 770-474-1555; Fax: 770-474-5095; e-mail: TSisales@TSiLogistics.com
Web Site: www.tsilogistics.com

TSi Logistics offers services for the logistics community. Services include freight bill audit and payment, loss and damage claims, vendor compliance monitoring, shipment optimization, and transportation management. TSi utilizes the iVelocity Logistics Management Suite designed to provide superior functionality with special reporting and analysis tools.

UNICCO
Contact: Michael F. Dunn
Phone: 617-527-5222 or 800-283-9222; Fax: 617-969-2210; e-mail: Mdunn@Unicco.com
Web Site: www.unicco.com
UNICCO Service Company is one of North America's largest facilities outsourcing companies, with over $690 million in annual sales, 1,000 customers and 20,000 employees. With over 55 years experience, UNICCO offers the industry's most comprehensive suite of facilities services, from maintenance, engineering, and janitorial to production support, lighting, and administrative/office services. UNICCO also has an industry-leading 95 percent customer retention rate.

Unisys Corporation
Contact: Alan Aptheker
Phone: 904-332-9454; Fax: 904-733-2951; e-mail: alan.aptheker@unisys.com
Web Site www.unisys.com/outsourcing
Unisys has decades of hands-on experience in government operations such as administration and finance, justice and public safety, human services, defense, education, and healthcare payer and provider administration. Unisys draws on their domain expertise to perform specific business functions more efficiently than their clients could in-house, because they don't just off load the transactions from their plate. As their strategic partner in business process outsourcing (BPO), Unisys has the credentials to reengineer, build and run new technology-enabled processes that translate government strategies into real-world successes.

Unisys Managed Application Services
Contact: Susan Beck
Phone: 215-986-6036; e-mail: susan.beck@unisys.com; Support Sales General Information on Products and Services: 800-874-8647, Ext. 731 or 585-742-6865
Web Site: www.unisys.com
Unisys Managed Application Services provide high-end business applications and minimize capital investments. Companies today want to avoid the expense of buying and managing high-end business applications. With Unisys Managed Application Services, you can lease leading-edge applications—leveraging skilled staff and the latest technology—to solve critical business needs. The Unisys model, unlike that offered by application service providers, delivers these services on a one-to-one basis. Unisys is a high-end application provider that understands high-volume, complex business applications. It has implemented comprehensive applications at 2,000-plus financial institutions, 1,500 government agencies, 90 communications companies, 18 of the world's top 25 airlines, and 200 newspapers. Clients worldwide benefit from its outsourcing expertise. Unisys manages applications at any of 60 global data centers worldwide.

United Customer Management Solutions (UCMS Inc.)
Contact: Cynthia McMillin
Phone: 650-610-7890; Fax: 650-610-7889; e-mail: info@ucms.net
Web Site: www.ucms.net
UCMS is a leading provider of complete end-to-end eCRM solutions. Its solutions span the full customer life cycle, from acquisition through retention. Its solution process includes: design (a customized CRM solution using proprietary methodology, CMDesign, whereby a detailed analysis is performed to document your detailed requirements); build (based on your specific requirements, UCMS implements a solution by bringing together best-of-breed technologies using its

framework architecture, CMFramework and a leading middleware solution. This solution is integrated to your enterprise applications to provide one common customer information platform); and operate (providing a state-of-the-art operations center to manage your customized solution on an ongoing basis). Whether it's customer service representatives (CSRs) or domain experts providing back-office expertise, your customers are provided a superior service. Formed in 1995 and beginning operations in early 1996, UCMS is an Australian-based company with a proud heritage of a service-driven approach.

United Systems Integrators Corporation (USI)

Contact: Rick Bertasi

Phone: 203-327-7272; Fax: 203-327-7264; e-mail: rbertasi@usirealestate.com

Web Site: www.usirealestate.com

United Systems Integrators Corporation (USI) was founded in 1991 to provide corporations with fully integrated real estate solutions through mutually beneficial long-term Strategic Alliance relationships. The Strategic Alliance model is simple and effective: by fully integrating all of the services a corporate real estate department would historically buy from multiple vendors, USI is able to create process efficiencies and drive substantial cost savings through increased project effectiveness.

U.S. Bank

Contact: Steve Dale

Phone: 612-303-0784; Fax: 612-303-0735; e-mail: steve.dale@usbank.com

Web Site: www.usbank.com

U.S. Bancorp (NYSE: USB), with $193 billion in assets, is the 6th largest financial services holding company in the United States. The company operates 2,346 banking offices and 4,621 ATMs in 24 states, and provides a comprehensive line of banking, brokerage, insurance, investment, mortgage, trust and payment services products to consumers, businesses and institutions. U.S. Bancorp is home of the Five Star Service Guarantee in which the company pays customers if certain key banking benefits and services are not met. U.S. Bancorp is the parent company of U.S. Bank.

USA-BPO

Contact: Peter F. Hessney

Phone: 585-586-5855, Ext. 2203; Fax: 585-586-1512; e-mail: phessney@usa-bpo.com

Web Site: www.usa-bpo.com

Unique Sourcing Alternatives (USA-BPO) specializes in the acquisition of engineering support functions for original equipment manufacturers. It is a technical service and consulting firm specializing in the acquisition of engineering support services while providing business assessments, valuation, financial services, acquisitions, and organizational development services to original equipment manufacturers. Its management team has more than 20 years experience in the engineering services industry.

U.S. Personnel, Inc.

Contact: Neal England

Phone: 972-871-0400; e-mail: Neale@uspersonnel.com

Web Site: www.uspersonnel.com

U.S. Personnel provides human resources, payroll, insurance, and benefits administration outsourcing services to a nationwide customer base.

vCustomer

Contact: Chris Massot

Phone: 206-802-0200; Fax: 206-802-0201; e-mail: massot@vcustomer.com

Web Site: www.vcustomer.com

vCustomer is a leading U.S.-based global provider of process-driven, quality-centric BPO, contact center and technology support services from its multi-city, state-of-the-art processing centers in India, equipped with the most reliable computing and communications solutions. vCustomer delivers the only truly customized contact center solution starting from customized agent desktops, CTI integration, and real-time web based monitoring and reporting capabilities.

Vedior
Contact: Justine Eggers
Phone: 31-20-573-5600; Fax: 31-20-573-5601; e-mail: j.eggers@vedior.co.uk
Web Site: www.vedior.com
Vedior is one of the world's leading staffing services companies, providing flexible labor to a wide range of needs in 36 countries. More than 15,000 employees in over 2,300 offices deliver their services to a growing number of satisfied customers. On an annual basis Vedior offers long- or short-term work to approximately 1,000,000 people.

Veritude
Contacts: Peter Dennis or Kate Donovan
Phone: 617-563-4915; Fax: 617-476-4264; e-mail: inquire@veritude.com
Web Site: www.veritude.com
Veritude partners with you to identify ways to increase quality, flexibility, and productivity; mitigate business risk; reduce administrative burden; and lower costs. Since its inception, Veritude has been a pioneer in working with clients to help them optimize the effectiveness of their workforce. Veritude offers a variety of workforce solutions to meet your unique business goals: managed services: total program management with unparalleled flexibility and control; staffing services: the right talent at the right time; workforce consulting: delivering organizational value through advanced workforce planning techniques; outsourced recruiting: improve service while reducing fixed expenses; technology and software: tools that power your recruiting and staffing management capabilities.

VMC
Contact: Kevin Chelius
Phone: 425-558-7700; Toll Free: 877-393-8622; Fax: 425-558-7703; e-mail: info@vmc.com
Web Site: www.vmc.com
VMC is a global provider of employee and customer contact solutions to some of the world's most prestigious companies. Services include help desk, outbound telesales, and inbound customer support, and VMC can tailor any solution to any specific client need. VMC's ties to its parent, staffing giant Volt (NYSE: VOL), ensure that your operations are quickly, flexibly, and cost-effectively staffed by expertly trained employees.

Wipro Spectramind
Contact: David Lewis
Phone: 480-515-1009; Fax: 480-502-5378; e-mail: David.Lewis@spectramind.com
Web Site: www.wipro.com
Wipro Spectramind, is the largest third-party offshore BPO (Business process outsourcing) provider in India, partner with clients to provide a full spectrum of BPO services covering all five levels: Data entry, Rules-set processing, Decision making, Direct customer interface, and Expert knowledge services.

Wipro Technologies
Contact: Arjun Viswanathan
Phone: +91-80-28440251; e-mail: arjun.viswanathan@wipro.com
Web Site: www:wipro.com

Wipro offers three major service lines: BPO services—customer interaction services, finance and accounting, payments, HR processing, supply chain, knowledge services, claims, and mortgage processing.

WNS Global Services

Contact: Eric Selvadurai

Phone: +91-22-5597-6100; Fax: +91-22-2518-8350 or

(U.S.) 212-599-6960; Fax: 212-599-6962; Phone (U.K.): +44 (0) 1784-224216;

Fax: +44 (0) 1784-224256

WNS is a leading provider of business process outsourcing services. It provides a wide variety of customer service and data management services in addition to industry-specific back-office administration services for the airline, travel and transportation, insurance, and telecom sectors. WNS's horizontal service offerings include data input, rules-based transaction processing, and action initiation in the areas of accounting and finance, core business administration, marketing program support, HR administration and benefits management and knowledge services, in addition to client interaction management. A former subsidiary of British Airways, WNS is now owned by leading global private equity investor Warburg Pincus, British Airways and management.

Workscape, Inc.

Contact: Karen Shernan

Phone: 877-975-7227; Fax: 508-861-6200; e-mail: info@workscape.com

Web Site: www.workscape.com

Designed for the workforce, Workscape's benefits administration and workforce management solutions transform the delivery and adoption of HR services across the enterprise to enable a higher-performing organization. Workscape's award-winning applications have been embraced by millions of employees at more than 180 major corporations worldwide.

Xansa

Contact: Alistair Cox

Phone: +44 (0) 8702 416181; Fax: +44 (0) 8702 426282; e-mail: sales@xansa.com

Web Site: www.xansa.com

Xansa is an international business process and IT services company. They create and deliver process and technology solutions that significantly improve our clients' bness performance. Through strong relationships, commercial innovation and their integrated Indian delivery capability, they drive real and long-term cost reductions, performance improvements and new ways of working tailored to each client. The services Xansa provides are Business and Technology Consulting, IT Implementation, IT Outsourcing and Business Process Outsourcing. Xansa is listed in the London Stock Exchange under the code XAN.L.

Xchanging

Contact: David Andrews

Phone (U.K.): +44 (0) 20-7780-6999; Fax: +44 (0) 20-7780-6998;

Phone (U.S.): 201-223-2900; Fax: 201-223-2744; e-mail: alistair.lamb@xchanging. com

Web Site: www.xchanging.com

Founded in 1998, this U.K. company offers BPO, FAO, ITO, as well as HRO to clients as renowned as the London Stock Exchange, Lloyds, and BAE systems. Its acquisition of RebusIS in 2004 expanded its capabilities in IT and HR and its reach in the United States and Asia.

Xerox

Contact: Mike Morales

Phone: 713-888-6310 or 800-ASK-XEROX; Fax: 585-383-9452;

e-mail: michael.morales@usa.xerox.com

Web Site: www.xerox.com

As the market leader in document outsourcing and facilities management, Xerox Global Services offers a comprehensive range of outsourcing solutions. Xerox Office Services: Xerox can implement the solution, even managing your entire office document production. Mailroom: Xerox Mailroom Services is a managed service designed to ensure optimum operating efficiency across all aspects of the modern mailroom. Imaging and Archive Services: A core managed service that enables customers to capture documents electronically, convert them, and manage them within a business-critical process, including image capture, hosting and presentment, document conversion, and data capture and processing.

Zenta Technologies
Contact: Ashish Khandelwal
Phone: 91 22 576 2524, Ext. 2509; Corporate: U.S. Phone: 610-230-2328;
Fax: 610-230-2329; e-mail: info@zentagroup.com
India: Phone: 877-936-8283; Fax: +91 22 2576 2540
Zenta provides end-to-end processing for all aspects of the business you outsource so you can interact with a single vendor. This deep level of integration ensures a seamless customer experience and allows your company to remain focused on your core business to increase profitability and maintain a competitive edge in today's marketplace.

CHAPTER 11

AVOIDING COMMON OUTSOURCING MISTAKES

When outsourcing relationships fall short, most often it is due to a disconnect between the buyer organization's expectations and the professed results. Whether the cause is too-high expectations or too-low, performance can only be determined on a case-by-case basis. What can be said with certainty is that clients need to do a better job of communicating expectations at the start of the relationship, and suppliers need to do a better job of executing and measuring outcomes against those expectations. Outsourcing ventures may also fail because of misguided motives or a lack of preparation. The cure for those *deal breakers* is to be properly motivated and sufficiently prepared. That's the purpose of this chapter: to serve as "preventive maintenance" for your outsourcing initiative.

KNOWING WHEN TO SAY NO TO OUTSOURCING

We cautioned earlier that it's just as important to know when not to outsource as it is to know when to do so. In this section, we want to delve more deeply into this important guideline because knowing when to say no is the best way to prevent all other mistakes.

Knowing Thyself

To know when to say no to outsourcing you first have to be honest with yourself about your motivations for considering this powerful business tool. For example:

- If you only want to escape dealing with normal operational dilemmas, outsourcing is not the answer. Solve your problems in-house; don't move them offshore.

- If you are not prepared to "get down and dirty" with the details, you're in no position to outsource. Outsourcing is a complicated task, which involves a great deal of planning and preparation.
- If you want to turn over a project you have been managing poorly, in the hope that your "hired hands" will be better able to handle it, think again. If you don't have a thorough understanding of the project you are outsourcing, chances are you won't be able to communicate properly with the vendor you choose, who will then prove unable to meet your expectations.
- If you are not ready to follow through on your outsourcing project step-by-step, step away. The success of a project depends on a smooth working relationship between you and your consultants, from day one to delivery date.

Knowing Thy Business

As a general rule of thumb (though, of course, every situation is different), we advise you not to outsource:

- *Core business competencies.* If it sounds like we harp on this point, it's because it's that important. Never delegate, transfer, or compromise your core business competencies. Never.
- *Legal right to make business judgments.* Outsourcing is entirely inappropriate for functions where the vendor will have the legal right to exercise discretionary business judgment that cannot lawfully be delegated.
- *Knowledge-based functions dependent on proprietary company information.* These include business functions that are highly volatile or unpredictable in scope or risk structure, such as financial projections, growth forecasts, and market performance. The key to deriving business benefits of outsourced services lies in the provider's capacity to deliver predictable service.
- *Interdepartmental or multidisciplinary functionality.* Throughout this book, we've stressed the importance of retaining responsibility for managing your service provider's performance. If the outsourced services cover a range of disciplines and departments, the enterprise will need a multidisciplinary team to manage the outsourced services.
- *Critical business functions subject to unacceptable levels of political risk.* Even domestic outsourcing operations may involve foreign subcontractors whose right to deliver services, or right to receive payment, could be severely impaired for political reasons. Embargoes, quotas,

political restraints, inconvertibility, nationalization, expropriation, and similar factors may suggest that special measures be adopted to mitigate any political risks that are dependent on the legal limitations and regulations of the locations you outsource to. We suggest employing legal assistance directly in the geography in question.

- *During the period prior to a shift in senior management.* Do not initiate an outsourcing project when management, in particular the CRO, will not be on hand to ensure satisfactory implementation. Proper outsourcing strategies require substantial amounts of time and money for planning and implementation. Every member of the board of directors and every senior officer have a fiduciary duty to manage the company assets. A new CRO's hands will be tied by previously made long-term commitments in an outsourcing agreement. Even contracts that permit a company to terminate for convenience may cost it, not only in payment of termination charges, but also in lost momentum and distractions arising from the transitioning to a new vendor or to return to an in-house sourcing strategy.

- *During a major restructuring without an outsourcing orientation.* In a weak economy, enterprises may restructure internal operations to reduce costs, eliminate hierarchies, reshuffle teams, divest unprofitable operations, refinance with complex or operationally restrictive covenants, consolidate, recapitalize, transfer to new locations, or otherwise undertake other strategic initiatives. In a strong economy, enterprises may launch new initiatives for growth with similar short-term destabilizing effects on "business as usual." Where such restructurings are in progress without an outsourcing orientation, the stability needed for analysis, structuring, negotiation, and transition to outsourcing will be absent. Under such conditions, any major outsourcing transaction could pose high risks by causing complications and distractions to senior executives and the project team.

COVERING YOUR BUSINESS BACK

Assuming you've decided to collect on the many potential business benefits outsourcing has to offer, we suggest a few guidelines for smoothing your way.

Uncover Hidden Costs

Whether in personal or professional relationships, the most common cause of disagreements is money. In outsourcing relationships, specifically, this centers most often on the expectations of the buyer organization as to how

---

Safeguarding Success

Based on our experience, we've identified what we call the top 10 major sins of outsourcing, destined to sideline success of these initiatives:

1. Failure to obtain commitment from executive management.
2. Failure to develop an outsourcing communications plan.
3. Failure to learn about outsourcing methodologies.
4. Failure to recognize outsourcing business risks.
5. Failure to consult outsourcing professionals when internal knowledge in this area is lacking.
6. Failure to dedicate the best and brightest internal resources.
7. Failure to proceed carefully through each of the outsourcing phases.
8. Failure to recognize the impact of cultural differences.
9. Failure to acknowledge what it will take to ensure vendor productivity.
10. Failure to put in place a formal outsourcing governance program.

---

much it will save by outsourcing. Many executives assume that they can make person-to-person comparisons (e.g., a full-time equivalent of an in-house staff member in India will cost 40 percent less). They fail to factor in the hidden costs and differences in operating models. In practice, most organizations save between 15 and 25 percent during the first year of an outsourcing venture; by the third year, cost savings often reach 35 to 40 percent as companies progress up the learning curve and modify operations to align to an offshore model.

Verify Data Security/Protection Measures

No matter what kind of outsourcing you're considering, always investigate your vendor's security practices, to ensure they're as robust as you require. Though most organizations find offshore vendor security practices impressive (often exceeding those internally), you can never be too cautious when it comes to protecting intellectual property or proprietary information, especially when working in an international arena. Address privacy concerns up front and manage them all along the way. Document your requirements and define in detail the methods and integration with your vendors.

Evaluate Company Expertise

Most companies and governmental agencies have business knowledge that resides within the developers of applications. In some cases, this expertise may be a proprietary or competitive advantage. Carefully assess this business knowledge to determine whether moving it outside the company or to an offshore location will compromise company practices.

Plan for Contingencies

What happens if the vendor, in spite of carefully developed plans and a professionally drafted contract, fails, for one reason or another, to deliver? Although such failures are exceptions, they do occur, even with the superb quality methodologies of most offshore vendors. Assess the implications of vendor failure: What are the business performance implications? High risk or exposure might deter the organization from outsourcing; it might shift the outsourcing strategy (e.g., from a single vendor to multiple vendors); or it might drive the company toward outsourcing (if the vendor has specific skills to reduce risks). We've said it before, risk analysis is critical.

Monitor Scope Creep

There is no such thing as a fixed-price outsourcing contract. All outsourcing contracts contain baselines and assumptions. If the actual work varies from estimates, the client will pay the difference. This simple fact has become a major obstacle for organizations that are surprised that the price was variable or that the vendor expects to be paid for incremental scope creep. Don't be caught unawares: Expect that most projects change by 10 to 15 percent during the development cycle.

Comply with Government Regulations

Utilities, financial services institutions, and healthcare organizations, among others, face various degrees of government oversight. These organizations must ensure that their offshore vendors are sensitive to industry-specific requirements; specifically, that the vendor has the capability to: (1) comply with government regulations, and (2) can demonstrate it does comply and is thus accountable during audits.

Care about Cultural Differences

Corporate cultures are unique to each company, even those in the same industry. Cross-industry differences are more marked; add in an entirely different culture of an offshore vendor, and the potential for cultural clashes rises exponentially. Never underestimate what it will take to address these differences and do what you must to avoid misunderstandings, whether that means putting outsource call center employees through accent training or educating in-house staff about the religion, mode of dress, and social practices in the country where the outsourcer is headquartered.

Track Key Personnel

Rapid growth among outsourcing vendors has created a dynamic labor market, particularly in such overseas meccas for low-cost employees as Bangalore, India. Key personnel are in demand for new, high-profile projects, thus, may be recruited by other offshore vendors. Offshore vendors will often quote overall turnover statistics that appear relatively low; what you need to track is the *turnover rate of key personnel on your account*. According to an annual report released by the META Group, common turnover levels are in the 15 to 20 percent range and drafting contractual terms around those levels is a reasonable request.[1]

Account for Knowledge Transfer Costs

The time and effort to transfer knowledge to the vendor is a cost often overlooked by buyer companies. Indeed, we observe that most organizations experience a 20 percent decline in productivity during the first year of an outsourcing agreement, largely due to time spent transferring both technical and business knowledge to the vendor. Many vendors are deploying videoconferencing (to minimize travel expenses) and classroom settings (creating one-to-many transfer) to improve the efficacy of knowledge transfer. In addition, employee turnover often places a burden on the buyer organization to continually provide additional information for new team members.

CONCLUSION

In closing, we offer these reminders for bypassing the pitfalls associated with outsourcing. Approach the relationship as a strategic investment, not as a purchasing decision. Invest however much time it takes to truly understand, and align, the interests of both parties. Establish an objectives scorecard in advance and use it as a foundation of the governance process. Define the process for addressing problems and negotiating changes, and make it part of the relationship management process. Finally, put qualified people in place to manage the relationship—people who have outsourcing certification and the personal and professional skills to make it work.

NOTE

1. META Group IT Staffing and Compensation Guide, 2004; available online at www.metagroup.com/us/commerce/catalog.do.

PART TWO

THE INDISPENSABLE GUIDE TO FINDING AN OUTSOURCING CAREER

CHAPTER 12

STRATEGIZING FOR SUCCESS IN THE NEW GLOBAL ECONOMY

Outsourcing is a good thing in the long run, but, in the short term, it does cause a lot of pain for people who find themselves out of a job. Jobs have been going overseas for quite some time, and history shows that for every job lost, many more are created in ways that may at present seem unfathomable.

—James W. Michaels, editor emeritus of *Forbes* magazine[1]

Throughout this book we've made no secret of the fact that outsourcing is causing tremendous upheaval in the way America works, and that this is prompting vehement debates over whether this change bodes well for this country's long-term economic health. We've also made it clear on which side of this debate we stand: Yes, outsourcing is eliminating jobs, but we believe that those who keep themselves prepared and informed will find many new career opportunities.

LEARNING TO STRATEGIZE

Never in the history of modern-day business have you, a working adult, had so many different career options. Despite the uncertainty of financial markets, the recent poor performance of the technology sector, and other depressing economic news, the opportunities for employment do exist today and will in the future—though finding them might take a bit more effort and creativity than in years past. In this chapter, we share nine strategies to help you succeed in this new global economy.

Strategy 1: Focus on the Possibilities

Reshaping a career is, unquestionably, a daunting prospect for anyone. The best way to begin is by focusing on all the possibilities, as opposed to the challenges. When your point of view changes, you improve your understanding of your prospects, thus, raise your competency in your job search.

TIP Think of outsourcing as the beginning of a new career path, not the end of the road.

Before you actually start looking for a job, take time to reevaluate your goals and, if necessary, set new ones. It's all about you right now, for when all is said and done, you're the one who must live with your choices. Thus, the career path you choose must be informed by your interests, your skills, your values, and your goals. Regardless how the advent of outsourcing has altered—perhaps even entirely dismantled—your former plans, keep in mind that you are still free to make new choices, which should include outsourcing employment options.

That said, don't make the mistake that many people do of not spending enough time considering your career. There are so many interesting and exciting outsourcing jobs out there, you might be tempted to go from job to job, instead of drawing a clear map of your new career in outsourcing. Closely examine organizations that work will with you and help you move in directions that develop your new career path.

Strategy 2: Face the Realities of Outsourcing and the New Global Economy

The growth in outsourcing marks the culmination of a long-term trend toward labor globalization. It's not reversible, so you must be prepared to climb onboard this new "ship" of success or be left standing on the shore, going nowhere.

TIP Follow the winds of change.

As soon as you see that an entire class of jobs is setting sail for foreign shores, so to speak, note which way the wind is blowing in terms of your own current position. Say you're a computer programmer who isn't yet qualified to climb the corporate ladder to an offshore-resistant position like systems architect; instead, why not consider a technical marketing position, one that requires face-to-face contact with customers and a deep knowledge of American corporate culture?

How high up the hierarchy jobs will be sent offshore depends of course on company culture and the specific industry. Those employers that want to maintain the long-term value of their top employees will help them transition out of vulnerable positions. Some large companies, for example, are devising ways to retrain their people whose jobs are sent offshore. One possibility is offering certification coursework in outsourcing management.

What about workers whose employers are not so forward-thinking? Take the responsibility yourself to stay competitive in the job market by keeping your technical and business skills updated.

TIP Be ready to change by keeping your skill base current.

In short, if you can't beat the outsourcing trend, join it. That's the advice of experts who see excellent career opportunities in transitioning to and managing offshore operations. Problem-solving skills are the glue that holds these operations together across borders. Employers will select professionals who can continue, and even prosper, in their current line of work by taking on the many difficult challenges of structuring and implementing offshore deals.

Strategy 3: Become a Global Player

To be competitive in the new global economy, new outsourcing leaders must be capable of strategizing locally and internationally. This requires "phasing"; that is, the process must be deliberate and planned, not rushed. Profitable outsourcing industry development still happens the traditional way: through selective, ground-up investments to make the most of specific outsourcing business opportunities.

TIP Phase in global business strategies.

Strategy 4: Follow All Leads

The competition for outsourcing jobs will be intense and you will need to implement a job search strategy to succeed. No one but you can find your next job. You must be a job *hunter,* following all leads. You may discover you have to "circle" around an industry segment or a technology for a while before you "pick up the trail" of a company that may not need you yet, but might soon. We can tell you how and where to start, but it's up to you to track down each lead and "snare your prey."

TIP Learn to think outside the traditional employer/employee career box.

You must also learn to think big, bigger. For example, is there a way to turn your passion, your former career successes, or your vision into a small outsourcing business? You can often start something for very little capital. And if it doesn't succeed, it will nonetheless demonstrate to a future employer that you are willing to take risks and have strong initiative, as well as outsourcing expertise.

TIP Learn to use cutting-edge, job-hunting tools.

Wherever your future career path takes you, you will have to know how to:

- Craft a personal mission statement that embraces outsourcing careers.
- Identify skills that are transferable to outsourcing.
- Research companies in outsourcing buyer and vendor industries.
- Network in outsourcing arenas and conduct informational interviews.
- Convert your paper resume to a digital, scannable version, for transmission via e-mail and publication of your personal web page.
- Maximize your international Internet job-hunting experiences.
- Improve your interview skills to include foreign employers.

TIP Become an expert at online job search due diligence.

As you no doubt noted from the preceding list, developing proficiency in using the Internet to job hunt is an imperative today if you intend to be a member of the global workforce.

Likewise, you must be disciplined about conducting due diligence on the companies you're interested in. Fortunately, it's now easy to find out a great deal about public companies. Online, you can access, for example: 10-Qs, 10-Ks, and other filings required by the SEC; press releases and media coverage; reports from industry and technology analysts; and other financial, organizational, and market-related information. However, one piece of information you might have more difficulty finding is whether a given company is involved in an outsourcing initiative. This may be well hidden to avoid negative PR situations. That means you'll have to learn to be a good detective. You're going have to do extensive due diligence:

- Read corporate press releases for explanations.
- Review Internet outsourcing BLOGS.
- Use the search engines of other countries (beyond Google, AOL, and Yahoo).
- Investigate the claims of anti-outsourcing web sites and pundits for truths among the hype.

Strategy 5: Offshore-Proof Your Career

Morgan Stanley estimates that as many as two million white-collar jobs in the United States will shift to low-cost centers within 10 years.[2] And another report concluded that offshoring could leave as many as 14 million service jobs in the United States vulnerable.[3] But what if you don't want to jump on the outsourcing bandwagon? What are your options? Here are seven suggestions for offshore-proofing your career:

- *Work for the government.* This is another safety net employment strategy. Most state governments are pursuing legislation to keep from outsourcing state agency related jobs or work outside the United States, or even the state itself. As a result, governmental jobs tend to stay in the country. Moreover, the government is hiring. Through 2003 and 2004, more than 30,000 federal and state government job openings were listed on the agency web sites.
- *Work for a government contractor.* Government agencies hire contractors to do everything from providing desks for the Army to evaluating ways to improve education in inner cities.

- *Move into a nonexportable career.* Explore face-to-face, hands-on, service, entertainment, and production-related career paths that are more export-proof, a number of which are listed next:

Actors
Aircraft cargo handlers
Ambulance drivers
Amusement park attendants
Anesthesiologists
Auto mechanics
Bakers
Bartenders
Bus drivers
Carpenters
Cashiers
Casino and gaming workers
Chefs
Child care workers
Chiropractors
Clergy
Coaches
Construction labors
Cosmetologists
Criminal investigators
Dentists and dental assistants
Dieticians
Electricians
Elevator installers and repairmen
Equipment repairers
Family and general practice physicians
Farmers and ranchers
Firefighters
Fitness instructors
Flight attendants
Floral designers
Food preparers
Food servers/waiters
Foresters
Hairdressers
Hazardous materials workers
Heating and air conditioning repairers
Heavy equipment operators
Home health aides
Hostesses
Hotel workers
Housekeepers/janitors
Immigration and customs workers
Interior designers
Lab technologists
Labor supervisors
Landscapers and supervisors
Launderers and dry cleaners
Machinists
Maintenance workers
Manicurists
Massage therapists
Medical assistants and secretaries
Mental health workers
Movers
Musicians and singers
Nuclear medicine techs
OB/GYN physicians
Occupational therapists
Optometrists
Painters
Paperhangers
Parking lot attendants
Pediatricians
Pest control workers
Photographers
Physical therapists
Plumbers
Police
Postal mail workers
Probation officers
Property managers
Psychiatrists
Real estate sales
Receptionists
Recreation workers
Refuge and garbage collectors
Registered nurses
Respiratory therapists
Retail sales
Retail sales and supervisors
Roofers
RV service techs
Security and alarm installers
Security and prison guards
Social workers
Soldiers/military personnel
Speech therapists
Stage, TV, motion picture directors
Stevedores
Substance abuse counselors
Surgeons
Teachers
Trade helpers
Tree trimmers
Veterinarians
Water and liquid waste techs
Welders

- *Train offshore workers.* Offshore workers typically need training in how to work effectively with American colleagues. If you have good technical and people skills, consider working for a company that provides American firms with offshore workers.
- *Become an outsourcing consultant.* Five years ago, there were few outsourcing industry consultants. The ones that existed most often worked for large, well-established consulting firms and did not spend much of their time in the outsourcing business sectors. Today, in contrast, outsourcing consulting is a quickly growing profession, advantageous for both the consultants and the companies that engage them. Once you establish yourself as an outsourcing consultant and build a solid reputation, you will be free to pick and choose your assignments, concentrating on areas you find interesting and challenging. Furthermore, outsourcing consultants are often paid well for their expertise. There are, for example, outsourcing consultants who specialize in strategic planning, sales, marketing, IT, HR, productivity and efficiency improvement, corporate and investment finance, mergers and acquisitions, operations, and virtually every other profession.
- *Become an outsourcing entrepreneur.* Entrepreneurs are hardworking individuals who have chosen self-motivated career paths for a diversity of personal and professional reasons. These individuals are often referred to as *outventurists* (a combination of outsourcing and venture). We talk more about outventurists in Chapter 17.
- *Achieve career differentiation through professional outsourcing certifications.* We talked about this in Chapter 9 and will again in Chapter 13. By following the certification tracks in outsourcing management either for vendor organizations (Certified Outsourcing Administrators) and outsourcing buyer companies (Certified Chief Resource Officers and Certified Outsourcing Procurement Professionals), you'll distinguish yourself from your competition when being evaluated by companies interested in outsourcing initiatives. Eight of every ten outsourcing recruiters now require these certifications for their middle to top outsourcing managers. Similarly, outsourcing vendors are seeking candidates with credentials as Certified Outsourcing Administrators.

Strategy 6: Be Flexible and Open to Change

Turmoil, stops and starts, twists and turns—all will almost certainly characterize your new career path. Recognize that probably you won't do anything for "the rest of your life." So instead of adding "be-all/end-all" decision-making pressure to your job hunt, think in terms of what to do first or next, as opposed to forever.

TIP Recognize that your outsourcing career path will be winding, not straight.

Be ready every day to divert your path and your plans to accommodate shifts in the global economy. Keep your eyes and ears open; become aware of the trends, the regulations, and the politics that may induce further changes in the outsourcing career marketplace. By being flexible, you put yourself in a position of proactive maneuverability, ready to move at any time into a challenging, enjoyable career opportunity.

TIP Be ready to rewrite your career program at any time.

Ultimately, the job seeker who can demonstrate the greatest adaptability will be the most marketable as the global economy continues to evolve.

Strategy 7: Learn to Navigate Electronic Job Listings

We touched on the importance of becoming proficient in using the Internet to conduct job searches in Strategy 4. Here, we expand on that, in terms of using employment web sites to identify your outsourcing niche and market. Untargeted personal career marketing is a waste of your time and money.

TIP Learn how to harness the global reach of the Internet.

First and foremost, learn how electronic job sites work. On most, you can search for employment by job title, job keywords, and location. Once you find a job of interest, you are typically directed to e-mail your resume to the company (although it may pay to also send a hard copy). This service is free; the companies pay to post their job openings. On many of these sites, you can also post your resume (some charge for this service, others do not).

TIP Many companies no longer list jobs on their corporate sites, instead preferring to do so on professional employment firm sites. Many employment agencies, search firms, and consulting companies also use these sites to list jobs for their client firms.

International job sites are also potential sources, in particular for finding companies that are looking for qualified professionals with outsourcing skills. They should not be your only means of finding a job, but they can be especially useful if you are looking to relocate.

TIP Get into a sales mind-set no matter what your career path.

No matter what field you're in, when you get ready to respond to any job listing, think of yourself as a salesperson, and act like one: You're selling yourself, specifically to those in the new outsourcing industries. Buy a book on selling and learn how to create a thirty-second personal job sales pitch and how to handle rejections. Learn how to spin what you've done toward the job opportunities in outsourcing.

Strategy 8: Build Quality Relationships

You've heard the saying, "It's not what you know, it's who you know." Well, to make headway in outsourcing, it's both. Work hard to build quality relationships, particularly with those working in careers of potential interest to you. Those relationships, in conjunction with your knowledge, skills, and experience, will be your ticket to a new career.

TIP To succeed in outsourcing, maximize networking.

You don't have to—nor should you—go it alone. Help is available everywhere in the form of career counselors and coaches, school career centers, mentors and teachers, and a host of other resources (including the Outsourcing Career Center, which we'll talk more about in a later chapter).

Tap into the career expertise that's all around you. You're going to need everyone—former employers, colleagues, competitors, suppliers, and employees—to make it in the outsourcing marketplace.

Strategy 9: Keep Your Eye on the Prize

Changing jobs is one of the most difficult things you will have to do; but it's also one of the most invigorating. Approached with the right attitude and by following these guidelines, the opportunities offered by outsourcing can revitalize your career. We conclude this chapter with some strategic guidelines:

- *Look for an outsourcing job in another field only after careful consideration.* Make sure that the "hot" outsourcing career field is a good fit for you. At the same time, stretch your perception of what might work for you.
- *Take time to consider your options.* Decide what you really want to do. Get thorough information about the outsourcing fields you're considering by networking, reading, and doing online research.
- *Network, network, network.* A poll by the Outsourcing Career Center recently found almost 95 percent of all new outsourcing jobs are not advertised publicly.[4] This, of course, will change as the demand for outsourcing professionals explodes.
- *Use placement agencies or search firms wisely.* Currently, very few search firms specialize in careers in outsourcing. The only international search firm currently devoted entirely to the recruitment and placement of outsourcing executives and professionals is the Outsourcing Career Center (www.outsourcingcareercenter.com).

CONCLUSION

Don't expect to switch to a fabulous outsourcing career path overnight. It typically will take a minimum of six months, though it frequently stretches to a year or more. Outsourcing industry recruiters want the most qualified, certified, credentialed, and experienced folks available, and will take the time necessary to find them.

NOTES

1. *Source:* http://www.forbes.com/investmentnewsletters/2004/02/18/cz_jd_0218advisor.html.

2. David M. Togut, CFA, Morgan Stanley CIO Survey Series: Release 4.5, December 8, 2003.

3. Kathleen Maclay, University of California-Berkeley UC Berkeley News: UC Berkeley study assesses "second wave" of outsourcing U.S. jobs, October 29, 2003, http://www.berkeley.edu/news/media/releases/2003/10/29_outsource.shtml.

4. The Outsourcing Career Center, "High Growth Outsourcing Executive and Professional Employment Opportunities in 2005," January 2005 newsletter, http://www.outsourcingcareercenter.com.

CHAPTER 13

LEARNING TO MARKET YOURSELF IN THE GLOBAL ECONOMY

Job hunting today requires much more than responding to a newspaper ad with a cover letter and resume and waiting for a phone call. To succeed in the global job marketplace, you need a sophisticated approach, one that includes well-researched knowledge of the digital (i.e., Internet) landscape. You must be prepared to:

- Conduct daily scans of online job boards in search of fresh postings.
- Create multiple versions of your resume in various digital formats.
- Research new employers in the outsourcing industry.
- Reinvent yourself, if necessary to prepare for the impact of outsourcing on traditional careers.

Sound challenging? We won't deny it: it is, especially if you haven't had to conduct a job search in recent years. America's jobless recovery is also making it tough. Though the economy is gradually improving, there are few new jobs. As companies continue to send more jobs overseas, mainly to India, Ireland, and the Philippines, competition for jobs that haven't been offshored, nearshored, or bestshored grows more intense. You can expect dozens, sometimes hundreds of other applicants for each position.

This chapter will shed some light on this dark scenario. It is intended for:

- Those already unemployed or underemployed due to the widespread use of outsourcing by American companies.
- Those entering the workforce again or for the very first time and looking for a realistic career path to take based on market conditions.

Note: Web addresses flagged with a (†) are author affiliated sites.

- Those developing outsourcing businesses, or entrepreneurs seeking resources for how to staff or build a vendor organization.
- Organizations buying outsourcing services or contemplating buying outsourced noncore services and planning to build an internal division.

GETTING BACK ON TRACK AFTER A LAYOFF

Jerry Arnold formerly worked in a New York-based company, Dunkirk Pharmaceutical Technologies, in Los Angeles, California, which provides Internet-related services to pharmaceutical industry clients. When the firm began moving jobs overseas, Jerry decided to go with the flow, rather than swim against the tide. He contacted international headhunters across the globe to promote himself, as well as some of his colleagues, as consultants on pharmaceutical IT projects in India. Jerry has 24 years of experience in the field; many of his colleagues are similarly well trained. They are ideal candidates to oversee and manage the work of less-experienced workers in India.

Like Jerry, you too can find a place for yourself in the changing employment market. Here are some suggestions for getting back on track:

- *Contact your former employer's outsourcing vendor.* This should be one of your first calls. Contact the head of the department that replaced your function and tell him or her directly about your experience. Believe it or not, your layoff may prove to be a blessing. You may stand a better chance of securing a raise or promotion in an outsourcing vendor corporation.
- *Investigate working for outsource vendors that serve your industry or are ancillary to it.* Your industry experience will be attractive to a business process outsourcing (BPO) professional in an allied profession because your skills are transferable—you will have to learn only a small piece of the business rather than start as a rookie. BPOs typically serve a wide variety of industries, and your niche experience in, say, oil and gas finance, may be a perfect fit for a related vendor organization.
- *Check out niche outsourcing vendors.* If you have been a top-level manager for a large organization, you'll be a prize catch for a small to midsize outsourcing company that can use your experience, which might be able to offer you a more appealing culture.
- *Become certified in either buyer outsourcing management or vendor outsource administration.* We've talked about this in Chapter 9, and we'll

discuss it further later in this chapter. Suffice to say, becoming credentialed will be your best qualification in this new job environment.

- *Contact outsourcing recruitment firms.* We recommend the Outsourcing Career Center (www.outsourcingcareercenter.com), the largest and only American firm dedicated to the placement of outsourcing personnel. That said, many other recruiters are expanding their services to include outsourcing as supplementary to their main practices.
- *Utilize online job search tools.* We talked about this in Chapter 12. When it comes to searching for outsourcing jobs both in the United States and abroad, there exists no better resource than the World Wide Web. You'll find myriad sites for job postings, resume postings, matching services, resources, and career self-improvement.
- *Access information portals.* Called *information access portals* or *outsourcing career portals* (OCPs), these are web sites that provide access to employment opportunities, recruiters, job site directories, and more. An OCP might, for example, include links to other web sites that will help expand your search for outsourcing employment. Several OCPs will also lead you to information regarding corporate and geographic cultures, travel, salary comparisons, and anticipated vacancies. Some offer broad ranges of opportunities, while others may focus on a specific job function or outsourcing BPO niche. Once you enter an OCP, look for:

  —*Job opportunity databases.* Typically allow you to enter location, job type, and posting date.

  —*Job bulletin boards.* Employers post positions currently available and anticipated vacancies.

  —*Resume banks and posting services.* Outsourcing employers scan candidates at these sites by keywords and experience. Your resume should be one of them. (Note: Some outsourcing posting sites charge a nominal annual fee to post your resume.)

  —*Outsourcer vendor directories.* Directories are places to gather information about organizations to tailor your resume and cover letters.

  —*Internet newsgroups.* From all over the world, dedicated to specific industries, niches, BPO types, geographies, and cultures.

  —*Directories of outsourcing professionals.* For both recruitment and networking purposes; for instance, www.ChiefResourceOfficer.com[†] and www.OutsourceManagementInstitute.com.

- *Tap into online outsourcing job databases.* A number of employment-related web sites have mushroomed over the past decade, but the largest sigle source of outsourcing jobs online is at www.outsourcecareercenter.com. Each job description specifies location, BPO sector, and career opportunities. The private sector has been the largest user group for these resources, but increasingly public agencies are using them as well. Job databases include ads from direct vendor organization employers, buyer organizations seeking outsourcing management personnel, and professional recruiters working on behalf of buyer organizations.

TIP You do not pay the recruiter for assistance in placement; that is typically an employer expense.

TWO APPROACHES TO THE SAME PROBLEM

Many techies and white-collar professionals in the United States have lost their once high-paying jobs and are struggling to locate another. Some have settled for less prestigious occupations in which they earn only a portion of what they did as IT professionals. In Chapter 12, we talked about the importance of having a forward-thinking attitude. Consider these two scenarios as you chart your new course.

Meet Perry Lewis: Perry has been looking for work for over two years, ever since his company's information systems (IS) division was outsourced. The father of two, he is worried about his mortgage, his kids' college tuition, his reputation, and his mental and emotional health. He is feeling defeated and angry and doesn't even know where to begin to look for a job anymore.

Meet Bill Hicks: Like Perry, Bill had been looking for work for two years, ever since his company's human resources division was outsourced. Bill, too, has a family, a mortgage, and mounting bills. Bill is a realist yet remains optimistic. Instead of making excuses and blaming everyone from the president of the United States to the bill collector who just called from the American Express call center in India, Bill decided to find a way to be successful again. He investigated the new career possibilities that are opening as a result of corporate outsourcing. Some required training and certification; others required experience; still others required a shift in thinking.

(Continued)

So Bill enrolled in online certification courses, volunteered a free month of service to an outsourcing vendor, and learned as much as he could about outsourcing management.

As a result, of his approach, Bill was hired as the chief resource officer for a corporation that is outsourcing many of its functions and needed a manager to oversee those processes. Bill's new position is challenging and well paid.

Sadly, Perry is still unemployed. He hasn't done much to adapt to the world of outsourcing. His current strategy is to hope some legislation or paradigm shift will occur to change things back to the way they were. In the meantime, he has exhausted his unemployment benefits.

CLIMBING THE MANAGEMENT LADDER

Kris Borowicz's job won't last much longer. She is a chief operations officer (COO) of Taylor Medical, in Pennsylvania, a distributor for hospitals and nursing homes. The start-up, whose workforce has shrunk to 8 from 30, has outsourced everything except its core functions of distributing medical supplies. Even the sales functions have been outsourced.

So the 40-year-old recently began job hunting among outsourcing companies abroad. "I definitely see opportunity over there in outsourcing management," says Borowicz. "I just don't have the credentials or precise experience yet to make the transition from COO to chief resource officer."

Kris Borowicz's prospects look extremely promising, however, as CROs are expected to be one of the fastest growing positions in American business management in the next five years. After posting her resume on several job sites with global reach in March, she received calls from 11 American corporations looking for a top-notch CRO. "They wanted to hear how I could apply my generalist management skills and experience over IT, finance, human resources, accounts payable, sales, and logistics and to a CRO position," Borowicz says. she added that American executives with outsourcing relationship and governance expertise can write their own ticket.

Recruiters say Americans are most avidly sought for both U.S. and foreign CRO positions, particularly those executives with experience in sales and finance or in positions involving technology—especially in Germany, Switzerland, France, and Scandinavia.

As Kris Borowicz's story demonstrates, the outsourcing of departments formerly reporting to traditional corporate officers (e.g., human resources, facilities, information systems, safety and security, finance, functional operations departments, hands-on service delivery, and other noncore competencies) will close the door on a number of traditional executive and management jobs, including:

- Chief operating officers
- Chief information officers
- Chief human resource officers
- Chief financial officers
- Human resource directors
- Assistant administrators
- Department heads and supervisory managers

Conversely, outsourcing is opening other management doors. For example, those previously or currently employed in smaller to medium-sized organizations know well how difficult it is to climb management ladders due to the smaller size of the departments. For instance, in human resources, the director position may be as far as one might expect to progress. In, contrast, in outsourcing organizations, an HR generalist or manager will find a multitude of new possibilities, still with an HR scope, such as:

- First-line supervision
- Consulting and consulting management
- Sales and sales management
- Vendor/buyer relationship management
- Account management
- Executive ranks/owners

Many human resources experts believe that, as outsourcing continues to alter the traditional employment landscape, the strategy of some companies will be to try to give valued employees opportunities along two different career paths. In outsourcing, it might be in your chosen field, such as accounting, human resources, or IT, or along a new career paradigm such as metrics administration, contract management, sales and relationship leadership, or quality assurance analysis.

This dual-ladder approach means that you could move up the outsourcing ladder and be paid at an equivalent level to a supervisor or a manager by being an outsource professional and bringing value through innovation, ideas, and leadership—essentially becoming a manager of ideas, technology, or intellectual capital, rather than of people. A dual career ladder enables outsourcing vendor employers and buyer organizations with outsourcing management departments to move their employees up through the company.

CERTIFYING YOUR KNOWLEDGE

As we explained elsewhere, as organizations become more sophisticated in their outsourcing initiatives, their need for chief resource officers (CROs) will become more critical. Hence the concomitant need for you to consider becoming credentialed—that is, certified. The demand for qualified, certified outsourcing management practitioners is your passport to a new career in the changing global economy.

How great is the demand? Outsourcing vendor and buyer organizations need qualified, certified outsourcing administrators, outsourcing support staff and personnel, outsourcing-credentialed officers, performance management analysts, outsourcing account specialists, contract managers and relationship managers, and outsourcing business development and sales staffs. And they need them *now*.

Outsourcing management is rapidly becoming the benchmark discipline for businesses determined to leverage their human and financial capital.

WHERE TO FIND SANCTIONED CERTIFICATIONS FOR OUTSOURCING PROFESSIONALS

Vendors: The Outsourcing Management Institute (OMI)
(www.outsourcingmanagementinstitute.com)

This is the only global organization for certified outsourcing administrators and certified outsourcing procurement professionals. It is also the only certification and training organization specializing in outsourcing vendor organization managers and support staff personnel in all trades and industries. The International Society of Outsourcing Business Professionals recognizes OMI as the only outsourcing education vendor to qualify for its "Presidential Distinction." They also sanctioned OMI as offering the "only comprehensive outsourcing career certification" and the only trademarked programming globally. (Note:

Certification must be renewed every three years.) It is the fastest growing and most demanded certification in the field of outsourcing globally.

Buyers: The Chief Resource Officer (CRO Institute)
(www.croinstitute.com)

This organization is rapidly becoming the benchmark provider of quality outsourcing governance and support staff training. It is recognized as the only source internationally for qualified outsourcing administrative and support personnel in buyer organizations. The CRO Institute is the fastest growing global training provider in the area of buyer outsource management credentialing/certification and the recognized leader in Buyer Governance staff training and education. The CRO Institute is the first, and only, full-service worldwide resource for outsourcing administrators and outsourcing organization management professionals and practitioners purchasing outsourcing services. (Certification is obtainable via online or on-campus coursework.)

Certified Professional Outsourcing
(www.certifedprofessionaloutsourcing.com)

A subsidiary of the CRO Institute, it offers certification and advanced training to individuals interested in the support governance roles in outsourcing buyer organizations. Typically, CPOs report directly to the CRO or are among the overseeing personnel in buyer companies. The certification is among the fastest growing of outsourcing governance professionals.

Certification signifies that you not only have an expert grasp on the fundamentals of the discipline, but that you have also proven that you can put that knowledge into practice to lead real-world outsourcing initiatives.

CONCLUSION

The analogy between marriage and outsourcing arrangement is often used by business experts when they describe how words, hard work, and attention to the little things are critical to a successful relationship. Still, there are going to be misunderstandings, difficulties, show downs and cooling off

periods along with the joy and successes. Think of the growing career opportunities as outsourcing marriage counselors.

As a result, a large number of companies are hiring certified chief resource officers, certified outsourcing administrators, and certified support
staff members to manage this sensitive relationship. Whereas in a marriage,
a counselor may be consulted when a problem arises, in an outsourcing relationship, a buyer company would rely on its CRO or certified governance staff, and a vendor company would rely on its COAs to prevent a
problem from erupting.

Executive placement experts agree that as more and more companies look
to outsource a wide range of their departments and/or division functions
it will be absolutely necessary for them to hire professionals who understand
how the outsourcing partnership will work—someone who will work to
apply consistent values and know-how to keep those relationships strong.

Through certification training, the certified chief resource officers, the
certified outsourcing administrators, and the outsourcing support professionals, when empowered as the focal point of all outsourcing strategy,
implementation and relationship management, can ensure that all outsourcing relationships live up to expectations from both buyer and vendor
perspectives.

Creating roles within companies will specifically serve to monitor and
mediate the outsourcing relationship, enabling both the buyer and the vendor to focus on their core responsibilities and job functions, with the reas-
surance of knowing that the line of communication is not only open but
being closely observed and scrutinized.

Outsourcing vendor and buyer organizations need qualified, certified outsourcing administrators, outsourcing support staff and personnel, outsourcing-
credentialed officers, performance management analysts, outsourcing
account specialists, contract managers and relationship managers.

The demand for qualified, certified outsourcing management practitioners is your passport to a new career in the changing global economy.
Outsourcing vendor organizations worldwide are zeroing in on leveraging
outsourcing knowledge which is innovative and foreign to most businesses
including those in outsourcing.

Outsourcing management is rapidly becoming the benchmark discipline
for businesses to leverage their human and financial capital. Certification
signifies that you not only have an expert grasp on the fundamentals of the
discipline; you have also proven that you can put that mastery into practice, to go forward and lead real-world outsourcing initiatives.

CHAPTER 14

HOT JOBS IN OUTSOURCING

The alarms being sounded about the loss of jobs to foreign countries are motivated by political need rather than by facts. Our report shows that foreign business creates far more jobs in the United States than are lost to overseas markets.

—Tom Donohue, president and CEO, U.S. Chamber of Commerce[1]

To identify the hot jobs in outsourcing, you have to know who's in demand in terms of skills and experience—that is, who companies see as hot prospects. In this chapter, we'll help you do that. First we'll tell you where to look online for information, then we'll tell you where the job market is heating up, broken down by job type. And at the end of the chapter, we compile that information into a directory, listing the hot jobs by category—accounting, planning, human resources, and so on.

TIP In addition to the information and resources contained in this chapter, we refer you to this book's companion web site: www.TheBlackBookOfOutsourcing.com. There you'll find complete updated career profiles on the hottest jobs in outsourcing, delineated by title, job summary, qualifications, typical duties, job expectations, and salary.

You'll also find information on: requirements, such as education, training, and certification; estimated annual earnings growth potential; anticipated job openings; opportunities nationally and internationally; outsource buyer and vendor job opportunities; self-employed/consulting opportunities; and short-term/temporary opportunities.

TAKING YOUR PROFESSIONAL TEMPERATURE

How "hot" are you in the job market? How do you take your professional "temperature?" Here's what Jane Fiona Cumming, a director with Article13, a global business consultancy specializing in corporate governance, social, and environmental risk, has to say: "Managers who are capable of getting the best out of a workforce that's becoming increasingly diverse, and are aware of the challenges that accompany [diversity], are in huge demand." Though international companies may not be using such outsourcing-specific terms as "cross-cultural management," "outsourcing administration," or "vendor relationship management" in their job ads yet, there's no denying they're desperate for managers with such skills. Those who have or acquire these capabilities will be singled out for hire, and advancement, possibly even for grooming for top leadership positions. "Transcultural competence" is, simply, the single hottest job qualification in the outsourcing industry.

Cross-cultural management skills come from working with a broad range of people over time. "It's about being aware of diversity in everything you do, from giving out a recruiting brief to selecting a team, to looking at suppliers. You always have to be asking, 'Is this the right mix for this project or the future?'" That's how Rob Young, business psychologist at Kiddy & Partners in London, and author of several management books (e.g., *The Ten Career Commandments: Equip Yourself with the 10 Most Important Skills to Move Up the Career Ladder,* London: How to Books Ltd., June 2002).

TIP You may be wondering if you'll need an advanced degree to secure a senior international management position with, say, a multinational company. It can't hurt, although you may have trouble finding a major university teaching outsourcing management principles. Peterson's Guide, available online at www.petersons.com /ugchannel/can direct your search.

FINDING VENDOR EMPLOYERS

Before we get into specific hot job categories, we want to give you some direct "hotlines" to vendor and employer resources.

Vendor identification sites that link buyers and sellers can provide invaluable information on companies with outsourcing career opportunities, but you must learn to dig deep into their sites. We recommend these sites to start the excavation process:

OutsourcingProviders.com
(www.outsourcingproviders.com)

OutsourcingInstitute.com
(www.outsourcinginstitute.com/oi_index/buyers_posied.html)

Outsourcing.org
(www.outsourcing.org)

And don't forget to refer to Chapter 10, which contains a comprehensive listing of vendor web sites.

Ironically, it's at some *anti-outsourcing* sites that you'll find a number of the most revealing lists and contact information of the top United States and international companies that are outsourcing functions and launching outsourcing initiatives. We recommend you tap into these while they continue to exist. They can direct you to the outsourcing buyers' web sites and employment links, as well as provide you with information on what buyers are outsourcing, the depth of the individual outsourcing initiatives, and subdivided indexes on industry types. Again, the more resourceful you are, the more useful these sources will be for you. Here are five to start with:

Lou Dobbs' List of Firms Exporting Jobs
(www.cnn.com/CNN/Programs/lou.dobbs.tonight)

Stop Selling America
(www.stopsellingamerica.com/WebForm_OUTSOURCERS.aspx)

Who's Offshoring/Who's Outsourcing/Who's Not Directories
(www.onshorealternatives.com/index4.html)

The IT Professionals Association of America "out" Outsourcers
(www.itpaa.org)

Who's Outsourcing.com (www.whosoutsourcing.com/news.htm)

GETTING HOT

In this section, we itemize for you the really hot job categories in outsourcing today.

Outsourcing Logistics Management

You won't find a hotter outsourcing job category than logistics management. The frenetic pace of global trade, coupled with outsourcing of manufacturing around the world, has transformed delivery into a complex engineering task. Thus, companies are enlisting logistics consultants to untangle supply chains and to monitor shipping lanes and weather patterns.

Outsourcing also puts more players on the supply and distribution fields, while product life cycles become shorter. A product introduced on one side of the world can quickly make obsolete an existing product across the ocean. A promotion that includes a 20 percent price reduction can raise demand tenfold. Corporate logistics departments are charged with getting desired products to respond to such rapid changes.

Indeed, these behind-the-scene functions are capturing the attention of executives who see a competitive advantage in fast and reliable delivery and potential for savings in squeezing the supply chain. It's a huge growth area for services providers and an important part of improving productivity in U.S. industry.

Outsourcing Governance, Administration, and Management

Employment with Outsourcing Buyers.   Outsourcing governance and administration is potentially the fastest-growing segment of U.S. and U.K. outsourcing-related positions, and holds the most promise for reemploying laid-off managerial workers whose original jobs were offshored. The demand for experienced and certified buyer governance professionals is forecasted by the CRO Institute to increase tenfold by 2007. However, currently these positions are rarely advertised, as most Fortune 2000 and Global 200 companies still tend to prefer internal candidates who demonstrate the skill set to succeed in outsourcing oversight. This is not surprising, given that untrained and inexperienced outsourcing administrators' errors account for more than 55 percent of outsourcing initiative failures.[2]

Therefore, boards and shareholders of buyer organizations are demanding qualified administrators, who have continued their business training, earned outsourcing certification, and/or have completed external training/courses in outsourcing management. New governance job postings that require certification or three-plus years of outsourcing management experience represent more than two-thirds of those seen on general job search sites such as Monster.com and CareerBuilder.com for outsourcing administrators.[3] The reason is simple: too many inexperienced, internal incumbents cannot handle the intricacies and idiosyncrasies of outsourcing service-level management, vendor relation, and or contract construction; they also lack an outsourcing big-picture vision.

For more on this hot-job category, go to the Outsourcing Career Center web site (www.outsourcingcareercennter.com). If you have limited experience, we encourage you to enroll in outsourcing governance certification coursework, such as that offered through The CRO Institute (www.croinstitute.com).

Operations Management Employment with Outsourcing Buyers. The number of outsourcing operations management positions is exploding, both in the United States and internationally. Managers at all levels are needed, from front-line supervision to senior executives in vendor organizations.

In an effort to assure corporate competency in their management ranks, many outsourcing suppliers have employed outsourcing education consulting groups such as the Outsourcing Management Institute to certify their management staffs concurrently so that all managers have the same base of outsourcing knowledge. Candidates looking for positions in outsourcing vendor management should complement their industry-specific experience (such as in HR, IT, marketing, engineering) with supplier administrator certification for the best and broadest outsourcing career opportunities. Then search job boards and the career sections of vendor web sites for openings.

Employment as a Consultant or Outsourcing Entrepreneur. Business process outsourcing firms (BPOs) comprise one of the fastest growing service industry sectors. The market is not yet near capacity for BPO services and start-up and implementation consultants; assessment consultants also are in high demand.

A new BPO consultant should possess extensive (five-plus years) industry experience, a thorough understanding of outsourcing processes and best practices, vendor or buyer professional certification, and preferably an advanced degree. (Read more about becoming an outsourcing entrepreneur and starting your own business in Chapters 16, 17, and 18.)

TIP Outsourcing entrepreneurs can speed the start-up process by contacting Outsourced VC Solutions (www.outsourcedvcsolutions.com) or First Outsourcing Group (www.firstoutsourcing.com).

Marketing

Employment with Outsourcing Buyers.   Businesses, large and small, have been outsourcing their advertising and public relations functions for some time. However, most organizations tend to keep community communications, particularly response communications, in-house. Therefore, buyer organizations generally prefer to hire outsourcing marketing, PR, and advertising specialists and managers to work *internally* to handle these sensitive issues. Because media relations specialists with outsourcing buyer know-how are hard to find, they are highly coveted.

Employment with Outsourcing Vendors.   Marketing specialists and generalists alike bring needed outsourcing experience to supplier organizations. It is not uncommon for professionals in this field to find themselves working for up to five or ten companies/clients at a time. The opportunities in this arena are in fast-growth mode in vendor marketing and sales departments, for all levels of staff.

Most vendor organizations advertise their openings on their own web sites when they first become available, before posting them more widely. Therefore, we recommend you begin your search in this area by clicking the careers link on vendor web sites.

Employment as a Consultant or Outsourcing Business Owner.   As niche industries in marketing and advertising develop, along with them come the opportunities for outsource PR, marketing, and advertising specialist firms/consultants. Differentiating yourself as an "outsourcer to the outsourcing industry" is critical to attracting long-term client opportunities in this field. Crisis management marketing and ad firms with critical response experience are currently doing well in this arena to support start-up outsourcing marketing firms that are beginning to make their move for market share.

Planning

Employment with Outsourcing Buyers.   Outsource planning associates and managers must be extremely adept at forecasting, modeling, and budget/financial and strategic analysis. As some corporations expand into outsourcing, and others experience operational and functional outsourcing failures, planning professionals will be in even greater demand. Currently, qualified experts in this area are very difficult to locate, making this a high-demand field.

Employment with Outsourcing Vendors. Sales support and strategic planners are needed to provide sales managers and executives with information and tactic options on business development opportunities, lead generation, and best practices.

Contracting

Employment with Outsourcing Buyers. A typical buyer's contractual agreement often fails to address outsourcing expectations, performance, oversight, and/or supplier management. Thus, contracting professionals familiar with outsourcing practices, terms and conditions, and certification status can demand top-dollar salaries in today's marketplace.

Employment with Outsourcing Vendors. As buyer organizations become more savvy about their contracts, they are demanding more from supplier performance. To gain parity, vendors need well-trained and/or experienced contracting professionals. Renegotiators and contract-selling add-on specialists are in particular demand.

Employment as a Consultant or Outsourcing Business Owner. Experts in RFP development, vendor selection, and contracting/SLA preparation and analysis are all finding consultancy to be a lucrative area of career growth.

Transition

Employment with Outsourcing Buyers. Internal consultants, particularly project managers with a successful track record of transition processing, are favored by buyers over their external counterparts. Internal consultants work very closely with vendor implementation specialists. Those who can adapt easily to different implementations and service types, and can integrate services seamlessly, are most desirable.

Employment with Outsourcing Vendors. Those looking for a temporary or interim gig, or who just enjoy change, may find employment with a transistion outsourcing firm to be their best move in the new global economy.

Employment as a Consultant or Outsourcing Business Owner. Short-term assignments with both vendor and buyer organizations are continually available because this is a high-growth area for consultants.

Implementation

There are several advantages for working for an outsourcing implementation (IT project management) vendor. These companies leverage the knowledge and experience of thousands of successful software implementations, customizations, and conversions to help clients rapidly create comprehensive migration/integration solutions. Your implementation skill base will augment their experience. Their result is a strategy that is linked to an organization's overall business strategy and is composed of methods and processes grounded in industry standards and corporate best practices.

Outsourcing implementation consultants offer their experience ranging from providing a complete conversion-delivery service and initial client assessments through implementation. Migrations or conversions are managed under the hiring company's project management and software engineering methodologies. Conversions can be to/from their corporate applications or to/from other third-party systems. Employees, often referred to as implementation or migration/conversion consultants offer resulting values such as reduced conversion costs.

Quicker outsourcing vendor conversion project cycles, maximized utilization of technical resources on mission-critical activities, and reduced project risk.

Legal

Employment with Outsourcing Buyers. In-house counsel specializing in contracts, and corporate litigation attorneys with outsourcing expertise, are actively sought by employers. Businesses carving out outsourcing services to focus on core competencies also need legal support services professionals.

Employment with Outsourcing Vendors. Vendors too are looking to write ironclad contracts, hence need specialists in this area (they generally prefer in-house staff). Notably, vendors tend to offer higher salaries; however, there is a greater risk of termination due to business failures or productivity decreases.

Employment as a Consultant or Outsourcing Business Owner. Only a handful of national legal firms currently focus on outsourcing exclusively, and most represent both buyers and sellers. Consequently, new firms are springing up to meet the demand in this area, and are targeting specific client types.

Human Resources

Employment with Outsourcing Buyers. Companies that have outsourced their HR functions still require governance to assure that their vendors are performing to employee and employer satisfaction. There also may be other segments of the HR operation not being handled by the general HR outsourcer. Thus, opportunities in these areas abound.

Employment with Outsourcing Vendors. High-growth positions in this area include: HR consultants, support staff, administrators, and executives. Transitioning to a vendor organization may mean an HR professional will serve 10 clients instead of generalist functions for one employer.

Employment as a Consultant or Outsourcing Business Owner. As an HR specialist, you know what employers need, so look for the opportunities in this area.

Information Systems and Technology

Employment with Outsourcing Buyers. CIOs and CTOs are still the captains of their companies' technology future, even those that outsource completely. Companies that do not maintain strategic management and oversight tend to fail. Position yourself as a leader in this field.

Employment with Outsourcing Vendors. Contrary to widespread news reports, many IT jobs are still available in the United States and the United Kingdom, as IT security, administration, and data management are often seen as too vulnerable to outsource entirely. It is true, however, that salaries have dropped due to increased international competition. Thus, IT professionals need to diversity their job skills to increase their marketability, and/or be open to extensive travel or relocation.

Employment as a Consultant or Outsourcing Business Owner. Unless you are interested in opening shop in a lower-wage country (and many outsourcing entrepreneurs are), the opportunities for U.S., U.K., Canadian, and Australian IT outsourcing firms are limited due to the salary expectations of their workers.

Finance, Accounting, and Audit

Employment with Outsourcing Buyers.   Outsourcing potential for these fields is high in buyer organizations. Positions range across the organizational accounting and financial cycles. Responsibilities for outsourcing governance accounting and finance professionals include working closely with the vendor's engagement team and service provider team to create a business case that supports service provider comparison and election; researching and understanding client and supplier budgets, P&Ls, and other financial reports, to perform activity-based costing; analyzing the financial mechanics of an outsourcing agreement; assessing the client's current situation and making recommendations; supporting the sales cycle effort by participating with due-diligence teams, and supporting creative pricing strategies; maintaining business model templates for analyzing potential deals; and supporting the engagement team during the delivery process.

Employment with Outsourcing Vendors.   Audit, bookkeeping, accounting, and finance have all been outsourcing staples for decades. Career tracks are available from entry level to partner.

Employment as a Consultant or Outsourcing Business Owner.   Consultants still command the lion's share of outsourcing finance and accounting positions.

Operations, Organizational Performance, and Analysis

Employment with Outsourcing Buyers.   A lack of leadership raises internal obstacles, causes contractual failures, and results in poorly planned outsourcing initiatives and uncontrolled/unmanaged expectations from vendors. Analysts of all types, particularly those with outsourcing oversight, governance, or consulting experience are widely sought by the Fortune 2000 and Global 500.

Employment with Outsourcing Vendors.   Vendors no longer are willing to accept changes demanded by buyers based on buyer analysts' support documentation. Vendors are sending in their own analysts to assess outsourcing operations by the buyer to optimize relations and outcomes. Thus, experience in operational analysis and QA/QI translates to opportunities here.

Employment as a Consultant or Outsourcing Business Owner. Objective, independent analysts are in great demand.

Consultants

Employment with Outsourcing Vendors. Typically, successful candidates have a strong strategy/management consulting background (two to four years of experience with a top strategic management consulting firm, vendor or buyer professional certification, and/or an extensive background in a segment, functionality, or niche industry). Proven quantitative, analytical, problem-solving, and conceptual thinking skills are also essentials for success in outsourcing consultancy. Consultant firms offer positions from entry level to partner, and both narrow- and broad-scope projects, depending upon your background and preferences. Consultant organizations often use external recruiters to fill senior- and management-level positions. Individual search firms and collective recruiter sites, which represent groups of recruiters, often list the top-paying career opportunities with consultant firms.

Sales, Business Development, and Relationship Management

Employment with Outsourcing Buyers. Even when large manufacturers and service companies option distributors or outsourcers to represent their sales functionality, an internal marketing/sales/business development governance responsibility is mandatory for successful sales processing management, goal setting, and outcomes. Vendor relationships must be managed as well. Governance teams in larger corporations are forming to manage all facets of buyer/vendor relationships.

Employment with Outsourcing Vendors. Buyers, manufacturers, and companies all are outsourcing their sales functions at a meteoric pace. Thus, outsourcing vendors need salespeople, plain and simple, and opportunities are plentiful. The caveat is that vendors want professionals with experience, certification, and/or training. Positions range from lead generation to business development to international sales executives. Sales support roles also need to be filled.

Furthermore, because accounts must be maintained, cultivated, and managed after the sale, business developers are needed worldwide, particularly in the United States, Canada, the United Kingdom, Australia, and other business capitals where prospective buyers are abundant.

In greatest demand are client relationship professionals. Several relationship failures have been blamed on the lack of professional expertise in arrangements, due to employers selecting a former employee as their account managers. Although these account managers are familiar with internal processes and procedures, they are often untrained, uncertified, and inexperienced in vendor/client relations.

Qualified candidates are scarce, so many vendors turn to the larger job search engines to help with their search. That said, the best strategy may be to visit the vendors' web site career pages on a regular basis, as they tend to get less traffic, which means less competition for jobs.

DIRECTORY OF OUTSOURCING INDUSTRY GROWTH POSITIONS

Here is an alphabetical compilation of growth positions in the various job categories discussed in this chapter. Though this list is not comprehensive, it is extensive enough, we believe, to demonstrate just how plentiful are the job opportunities wrought by the advent of outsourcing.

Account Management
Client service advisor
Senior account manager
Corporate accounts manager
Global accounts manager
Account manager

Accounting
Outsourcing accounting manager
Senior accountant, outsourcing

Audit
Vice president, outsourced internal audit
Senior manager, outsourced audit services
Manager, outsourced audit
Senior auditor
Outsourcing audit specialist
Quality control manager, outsourced internal auditing
Operational risk associate

Business Development
Vice president, business development
Director, business development

Business development manager
Client development manager

Change Analysis
Manager, change analysis
Change analyst
Implementation analyst
Project management analyst

Consultancy
Professional employer consultant
BPO consultant
Outsourcing design consultant
Consulting associate
IT sourcing consultant
Human resources outsourcing consultant
Indirect sourcing specialist

Contracting
Senior contracting specialist
Field contracts manager
Contract administrator

Finance
Tax manager
Outsourcing group controller

BPA transaction processing controller
Director, accounts payable outsourcing
Finance manager
Outsourcing actuary
Financial manager, outsourcing practice
business development

Governance, Administration, and Management

Certified chief resource officer
Certified outsourcing administrator
Managing director, BPO
Chief advisor, business process outsourcing
Outsourcing delivery group manager
Outsourcing site manager
Outsourcing services director
Outsourcing project administrator
Vice president, outsourcing
Director, outsourcing procurement
Sourcing/purchasing manager
Operations management
Cost control director
Director, global support services
Integration administrator
Director, strategic sourcing
Outsourcing risk/safety manager
Director, global sourcing
Vice president, global delivery
management
Outsourcing branch manager

Human Resources
Management
Manager, organizational performance
Director, outsourced human resources
Vice president, human resources
outsourcing
Recruitment
Technical recruiter
Outsourcing staff recruiter
Compensation
Compensation specialist
Benefits
Benefits administrator
Benefits operations manager
Payroll
Outsourcing payroll manager
Payroll specialist
Payroll shared services director
Training
Outsourcing trainer
Market learning specialist

Implementation
Business system setup manager
Director outsourcing solutions
Change process manager

Information Systems
Administration
Chief technology officer, outsourcing IT
IT outsourcing service delivery
executive
International IT executive
Security
Information security manager
Architect director, managed security
Project Management
Global project manager
Outsourcing project manager
Senior project manager
Project manager
Defined benefits ongoing project
manager
Technology
Global technology leader
Division manager
Decision support leader
Technical support specialist
IT outsourcing architect

Legal
Attorney, outsourcing specialist
Attorney, workforce management

Marketing
Marketing specialist
Director, outsourcing marketing
Manager, marketing
Manager, advertising
Director, creative services
Manager, communications

Organizational Performance
Manager, organizational performance
Senior analyst
BPO operations analyst
Business analyst
Financial analyst

Planning
Director, strategic planning
Supply chain planning manager
Strategy manager

Quality Assurance/Quality Control
Service quality control analyst
Quality assurance analyst
Workforce process analyst

Relationship Management
Manager, vendor relations
Senior relationship director
Relationship representative
Business relations supervisor
Client development manager

Sales
Outsourcing Services
Director, sales training
Inside sales
Sales support
Outsourcing presales support
BPO sales associates
Outsourcing sales executive/professional

Government
Government outsourcing
Director, government sales

Human Resources
Sales executive, professional employer
  organization outsourcing
Benefits outsourcing sales executive
Director, HR outsourcing sales

Information Technology
Sales executive

Strategic Analysis
Senior strategy analyst
Strategic financial analyst
Business system analyst
Outsourcing operations analyst

Transition
Transition manager
Outsourcing transition project control lead
Manager, business transformation

NOTES

1. A special report by the Chamber of Commerce of the United States, "Jobs, Trade, Sourcing and the Future of the America Workforce," April 2004, http://www.uschamber.com/media/pdfs/outsourcing.pdf.

2. The Outsourcing Management Institute, Global Outsourcing Leadership Conference Proceedings, August 2004.

3. The Outsourcing Management Institute, Global Outsourcing Leadership Conference Proceedings, August 2004.

CHAPTER 15

FINDING AN OFFSHORE, NEARSHORE, OR BESTSHORE JOB

If you've read this far in the book, no doubt you have begun to wonder whether you should consider working in another country—whether you have what it takes both personally and professionally. Do you really want to spend six months or more in another country if, say, you have poor language skills, or a family you don't want to leave or uproot, or simply are prone to homesickness? You'll have to do a lot of soul searching, as well as conduct a detailed skills self-assessment before you make such a life-altering decision. In this chapter, we start your thinking process, to help you decide whether you're cut out to, or want to, make the move to an international position in outsourcing.

TIP To work overseas, first you must find an employer willing to sponsor you and submit all the necessary paperwork. Once your documents are completed, in many countries, you will also then be required to check in with the municipality where you will be working before employment can officially begin.

Taking the Measure of Yourself

Employment experts agree that the two-step process of, first, identifying your current skills and, second, determining how they can be translated

---

Note: Web addresses flagged with a (†) are author affiliated sites.

277

to a position in outsourcing, is essential to a successful job search in this arena. It is even more important when it comes to international job searches. Without this knowledge, you won't be able to complete an application, write a resume, or answer interview questions to the satisfaction of potential employers. Think of your skill set as comprising three categories of skills:

1. *Job content skills.* These are skills specific to an outsourcing job or occupation. An administrative assistant is skilled in typing, word processing, answering telephones, doing company correspondence, and filing. An accountant's skills include managing accounts receivable and payable, preparing payroll, figuring taxes, using an adding machine, and computer accounting programs. A salesperson is skilled at customer service, record keeping, order processing, inventory management, billing, and product displays.

2. *Self-management skills.* These are the personal skills you used every day to get along with others, to deal with problems professionally, face challenges equitably, and so on. They also reflect your character and work ethic: sincerity, reliability, tactfulness, patience, flexibility, timeliness, and tolerance are all examples of self-management skills. Employers look for these skills in candidates as evidence of how they will fit into the organization.

3. *Transferable skills.* These are skills that can be transferred from one job or occupation to another. They may be either self-management or job content skills, and often are both; they may or may not have been developed through previous employment. Examples include auditing, global business development, sales management, contract development, and service level agreement administration. For most job seekers, it is very unlikely that they will find an outsourcing job that closely matches their previous employment; for many, in fact, their new outsourcing job will be totally different from their past experiences. Therefore, it is critical to be able to tell an employer how your skills translate to the job at hand, whether with a buyer organization or a vendor service supplier.

Everyone has skills, hundreds of them, many of which outsourcing employers are looking for in an employee. Yet, most people can only identify a few of their skills, and few can describe their skills to their own advantage on paper or in an interview situation. To help you do that, we suggest you follow this list:

1. List by title each job you have held. Start with your most recent employment and work backward.
2. Write a detailed description of the four to five major duties of each position.
3. Write down the skills you used to accomplish each duty you listed as they might relate to outsourcing functions and responsibilities (review the list on pages 315–318 to jump-start your thinking). Remember to include job content, self-management, and transferable skills.
4. Repeat the preceding steps for each outsourcing-relevant activity you anticipate describing to an employer on an application, in your resume, or in an interview.

TIP Use this process to identify skills you've acquired through hobbies, volunteer work, and community experience. They count, too.

---

5. Once you have completed this process, you should have a long list of skills—too long probably. So the last step is to go through the list and highlight only those skills that most closely apply to your outsourcing career path or job goal(s).

Once you are satisfied that you have identified, and can describe, your full range of skills that are transferable to an outsourcing position, you'll need to concern yourself with how to translate that skills list to a resume that you can submit to international employers. That's the subject of the next section.

REVAMPING YOUR RESUME FOR INTERNATIONAL DISTRIBUTION

Probably the first question everyone has when it comes to submitting their resumes (in many countries called a *curricula vitae* or CV) to international employers is whether to translate it into the language of the country. The short answer is: It depends. Usually, this will be answered for you in the job listing; and, as mentioned earlier, fortunately for Americans, English has become the international language of business. All that said, if you do find the need to have your resume translated, we recommend you use an accredited translator—unless you're fluent in the language in question and are confident you can do the job yourself.

TIP If you decide to have your resume translated into another language, be sure to hire an *accredited* translator. Translators are accredited only after passing a rigorous three-hour exam administered by the American Translators Association (ATA) in Alexandria, Virginia (703-683-6100).

Equally important is that your resume be translated by someone who works in the same discipline or industry as you, especially if you're in a scientific field. Most translators have a niche in which they become expert.

But it's more than language you need to be concerned about. It's style, too. The streamlined resume format that's popular in the United States may not be sufficient elsewhere. Recruiters in Europe, Asia, and the Middle East typically expect to see information normally not included on an American resume, such as citizenship and passport data, date and place of birth, and marital status.

Moreover, in contrast to the self-assured, self-confident presentation employers like to see from American candidates, resumes for a foreign market should take a more understated stance (sometimes to the point of being self-effacing), featuring substantive content rather than active verb constructions. Language skills are evaluated by hiring managers and are a prerequisite for just about any managerial job overseas.

Another difference between resumes created for foreign markets is that experience should be listed chronologically (as opposed to reverse-chronology in the United States), starting with your first job and ending with your most recent position.

Some European employers will request that you submit your resume in your own handwriting. This enables them to judge your neatness and proper use of language—two important criteria overseas. It may be used for handwriting analysis, to reveal the type of person you are.

TIP For lower level positions, if you send your credentials to staffing agencies via e-mail, keep the documents as short as possible. In addition to personal information, include only where you've worked, for how long, and just a few lines describing what you did. Executive-level candidates must, however, adhere to the traditional format described.

INTERNATIONAL RESUME WRITING SERVICES

A & A Resume Services (www.aandaresume.com)
These professionals have more than 50 years of cover letter and resume writing expertise with thousands of satisfied customers from every continent on earth.

Vault Resume Writing (www.vault.com)
Experts will write your resume from scratch to ensure that it stands out from the pack and gives you the best shot at your dream job.

e-Resume.net (www.eresume.net)
This company is a national resume writing service company that combines personalized attention with the speed of the Internet to deliver professional global resumes.

OUTSOURCING CANDIDATE RESUME POSTING

Outsourcing Career Center
(www.outsourcingcareercenter.com)
Exclusive resume posting for outsourcing job seekers and outsourcing employers (buyers for governance staff, and vendors for all positions).

GENERAL CANDIDATE RESUME POSTING

Hot Resumes (www.hotresumes.com)
Greatly expands the reach and range of opportunity. Thousands of recruiters and companies are subscribed and search the database on a daily basis.

Hot Jobs (www.hotjobs.com)
Employers and staffing firms search this database of resumes by keyword, experience level, job preference, salary, and qualifications.

Job.com (www.job.com)
Tools to enhance your career, like Awesome Resume, Personal Salary Report, Career Assessment Tests, and Resume Distribution services.

(Continued)

Monster (www.monster.com)
Set up job search agents and have your dream job e-mailed to you. Access More Career Tools, Advice, and Information.

Six Figure Jobs (www.6figurejobs.com)
No charge for accessing their job database. As long as you meet their criteria, you can become a member.

Worktree (www.worktree.com)
Instantly apply online and directly to the companies in your state and every major city. Most are never advertised elsewhere.

RESUME DISTRIBUTION SERVICES

Resume Rabbit (www.resumerabbit.com)
Fill out one simple form (about 10 to 15 minutes) and get posted on up to 87 major career web sites.

Resume Zapper (www.resumezapper.com)
E-mail your resume and cover letter into the e-mail boxes of America's top Search, Recruitment, and Placement firms.

ResumeXposure (www.resumexposure.com)
Distribute your resume directly to recruiters working in your field. This is targeted, proactive delivery of your resume to the professionals who represent thousands of companies with great jobs.

RESUME MAILING SERVICES

Resume Stork (www.resumestork.com)
Mass mail your resume and cover letter directly to employers, using the postal service.

USING THE INTERNET TO FOCUS YOUR JOB SEARCH

Once you've done your skills assessment and have "internationalized" your resume, you'll need to start focusing your job search. Here are guidelines for using online capabilities to expand your job choices and connect with people who can influence the hiring decision:

- *Have specific outsourcing job targets in mind.* Remember, outsourcing job targets are found where your skills and interests intersect. Identify these targets and find different ways to describe them. Then use relevant job-search Internet services listed in this book to identify work situations that fit your needs. It might, for example, be as simple as doing research for an employer, redesigning a web site, or helping to launch a product. Consider short-term outsourcing projects: these are good ways to make an impact, demonstrate value, and establish a relationship without a long-term commitment on either side.

- *Identify specific locations where you want to live and work.* Here, your most important search parameter is where you want to live. Choose as many locations as you wish, as long as they're viable options.

- *Get the names of all the employers, public and private, in each location, whether or not they have posted jobs.* In your search engine, enter the location and such keywords as "outsourcing," "career opportunities," "business directory," "laboratory," "small-business directory."

- *Find out more about outsourcing organizations that appeal to you.* Know their competitors, industry, products, and financial condition, as well as their mission, values, and relationship to the community. This information is easy to locate online. You can review journals, products, agencies, affiliations, directories, suppliers, "Who's Who" listings, investment-research groups, industry publications, and more.

- *Get up close and personal.* Check the companies' web sites for job postings. If you find a listing that matches your qualifications, instead of responding immediately, find a way to contact someone directly who can make or influence the hiring decision. On the web, it's easy to find names of personal contacts.

- *Make your own outsourcing job listing.* If you can't find an appropriate opening, make one: Draw a diagram containing what you already know about the firm and where you could make a contribution (growth, recovery, turnaround, bailout, merger). Send an e-mail to the right person (say, someone who would benefit from your problem-solving skills) and ask to meet to discuss ways you can add value to this area. Stress the benefits you bring to the enterprise. Be sure your resume is organized to reflect these.

Keep the preceding guidelines in mind during the next step which is to tap into as many of the sources listed that are relevant to your job search:

Outsourcing Resources on the Web

Governance Opportunities

Branham Group 300
(www.branhamgroup.com)
Each year, the Branham Group ranks the top 300 Canadian information technology (IT) companies.

Entrepreneur.com Franchise 500
(www.entrepreneur.com/franzone)
Includes several franchise-interested Top Ten lists and information on hot growth companies.

Forbes' Lists
(www.forbes.com/lists)
For employer rankings, this includes: 200 best small companies, 400 best big companies, Forbes 500, Forbes International 500, Global 2000, largest private companies.

Fortune 500
(www.fortune.com/fortune/fortune500)
The Fortune 500. You can browse the list by company, CEO, or industry.

Fortune's Global 500
(www.fortune.com/fortune/global500)
A ranking of the largest companies in the world.

The Inc. 500
(www.inc.com/inc500)
The top 500 small businesses according to Inc. magazine.

NASDAQ 100
(http://dynamic.nasdaq.com/dynamic/nasdaq100_activity.stm)
Representing 100 of the largest nonfinancial U.S. and non-U.S. companies listed on the national market tier of the NASDAQ Stock Market, the NASDAQ-100 Index reflects NASDAQ's largest companies across major industry groups, including computer hardware and software, telecommunications, retail/wholesale trade, and biotechnology.

Fortune's Best Companies to Work For
(www.fortune.com/fortune/bestcompanies)
Rated by best benefits, salary, training budgets, work/life balance, and stock performance.

Outsourcing Career Center
(www.outsourcingcareercenter.com)
Jobs exclusively in outsourcing suppliers, and in outsourcing buyer governance.

International Outsourcing Employment Resources

Outsourcing Career Center
(www.outsourcingcareercenter.com)
The only international and regional outsourcing job bank, placement service, and resource site for outsourcing and global career seekers.

Nearshoring Opportunities (Canada, Caribbean, Virgin Islands, and Mexico) ActiJob
(www.actijob.com)
Impressive, large job site for Canada.

Canadian Careers
(www.canadiancareers.com)
Online since 1996, offers career and employment information for Canadians.

Canadian Executive Recruitment
(www.cdnexec.net)
Primarily focused within the Canadian chemical, consumer goods, plastics, automotive, electronics, and heavy industries.

CanJobs
(www.canjobs.com)
Gateway to hundreds of jobs for Canadians.

Caribbean Employment
(www.crsitjobs.com)
Caribbean Resourcing Solutions Ltd. (CRS) is the first IT placement agency established in Trinidad and Tobago.

Latin America
(www.bolsadetrabajo.com/bolsadetrabajo)
Employment opportunities and resumes for Spanish-speaking professionals.

Sympatico
(www.sympatico.ca)
Canadian guide to information and news from all over the country.

Virgin Islands
(www.usvi.org/labor/index.html)
Includes employment services.

Workopolis
(http://globecareers.workopolis.com/index.html)
Canada's largest job site.

Offshoring Job Resources Worldwide

+Jobs
(www.plusjobs.org)
Collection of international sites for job postings covering the United States (+Jobs America), Canada, Australia, Denmark (in Danish), and the United Kingdom.

African Jobs
(http://regional.searchbeat.com/africajobs.htm)
An alphabetical listing of business and job/career Web pages covering much of the continent.

All Job Search
(www.alljobsearch.com)
With one query, helps you search 1,000-plus job sites, newspapers, and newsgroups.

American Chamber of Commerce in Russia
(www.amcham.ru)
The AmCham online directory of its membership is not available to nonmembers, but the calendar of events, news update for Russia and for the organization, and advice for living and doing business in Russia can be viewed by anyone accessing the site.

Asia Job Search
(www.asia-links.com/asia-jobs)
Welcomes job seekers across the United States and Asia.

Asia Net
(www.asia-net.jp)
Established in 1997, Asia-Net has been serving Asia/Pacific-Rim business communities by helping professionals locate job opportunities, while providing companies with an online recruitment service.

Asia Online
(http://asiadragons.com/employment/home.shtml)
General job and resume posting board for the many countries that make up Asia.

Atlantic Research
(www.atlanticresearch.com)
Clients include start-up firms, successful high growth medium-sized firms, as well as some of the world's most respected and dynamic multinational firms in the high-tech, manufacturing, and service industries.

Australian Job Search
(www.jobsearch.gov.au)
Comprehensive listing of over 100,000 Australian jobs, grouped from several job posting sites.

Avotek
(www.avotek.nl/jobs.htm)
This site includes information on the many books Avotek publishes on the international job search. It also provides links to international job banks, recruiters, and other sources.

Career Builder International
(www.careerbuilder.com/JobSeeker/Jobs/jobfindil.asp)

Career.com
(www.career.com)

CareerIndia
(www.careerindia.com)

CareerBuilder International Job Search
(www.careerbuilder.com/JobSeeker/Jobs/jobfindil.asp?sc_cmp2=JS_HP1_QSB_Intl)
Lists international sites where you can find opportunities or recruit in markets from Canada to the United Kingdom to Japan. Southeast Asia, Europe, and other areas.

Career One
(www.careerone.com.au)
Career opportunities in Australia.

CVOnline
(www.cvonline.cz)
Czech site bringing you the inside scoop on companies' recruitment policies, jobs, culture, and business.

Direct Employers' Employment Search Engine
(www.directemployers.com)
Formed in 2001 by a consortium of leading U.S. corporations to confront a variety of issues facing Internet recruiting; policies, practices, standards, privacy, vendor dependency, and overall industry cost containment initiatives.

Embassy World
(www.embassyworld.com/embassy/directory.htm)
Directory and search engine of the world's embassies and consulates.

Employers Online
(www.employersonline.com)
A one-stop site for employers, recruiters, and job seekers.

Employment 911
(www.employment911.com)
A premier provider of solutions for job seekers, recruiters, and employers.

EscapeArtist.com
(www.escapeartist.com)
Superb resource site, which includes these sections: Jobs Overseas, Living Overseas, Country Profiles, Articles, eBooks, Escape Artist magazine, Offshore Investing, International Real Estate, Overseas Retirements.

EuroJobs
(www.eurojobs.com)
Jobs in all European countries.

European Employment Services
(www.europa.eu.int/eures/index.jsp)
Database of living and working conditions in all member countries.

GisaJob Recruitment
(www.gisajob.com)
U.K.'s original free jobs web site.

Going Global
(www.goinglobal.com)
The Goinglobal.com team is composed of individuals representing many different nationalities who all have one experience in common: they have lived and worked outside their home countries.

International Jobs.org
(www.internationaljobs.org)
Weekly international employment newspaper for subscribers, with some job listings accessible to nonsubscribers, including "hot jobs," those employers are urgently seeking to fill. Register to get these via e-mail.

Israel Job Net
(www.jobnet.co.il)
Searchable database for employment leads in Israel.

JobAsia
(www.jobasia.com/home.shtm)
Middle- and senior-level positions. Hong Kong's premier job site, advertised jobs span over 30 organizational functions from the most popular information technology, accounting, investment analysis, marketing, sales, and engineering to graphic design, editorial, laboratory operation, and management trainees.

Job Pilot
(www.jobpilot.com)
Offers services in 11 European countries and also maintains jobpilot.com as a strong international platform for global presence.

Jobs at+.com
(www.jobs-at.com/front/scripts/default.asp)
Serves English-speaking countries of U.K., Scotland, Wales, Ireland, United States, Canada, South Africa, Australia, New Zealand, as well as the EU.

Jobs DB
(www.jobsdb.com)
Specific areas included are: Australia, Hong Kong, India, Indonesia, Korea, Malaysia, Philippines, Singapore, Taiwan, and Thailand.

JobServe
(www.jobserve.com)
The largest source of IT vacancies in the United Kingdom, Europe, Asia, and Australia.

Job Shark
(www.jobshark.ca/caeng/index.cfm)
Advanced targeted recruitment advertising company with unmatched technological superiority integrated with the largest Skill Set Profile database of job seekers in Canada.

Job Street Singapore
(www.jobstreet.com.sg)
Lists opportunities for Singapore.

Job Web
(www.jobweb.com)
A web site of career development and job search information for college students and new college graduates, owned and sponsored by the National Association of Colleges and Employers (NACE).

Lat Pro
(www.latpro.com)
The largest Hispanic and bilingual jobs and diversity career board in the Americas.

Links to the World's Newspapers
(www.escapeartist.com/media/media.htm)
Provides link information to the International Press and Media of the World.

Middle East Jobs
(www.gulfjobsites.com)
An independent directory and search engine covering job and employment-related web sites from the Arabian Gulf/Persian Gulf region, including Saudi Arabia, United Arab Emirates, Oman, Kuwait, Bahrain, Qatar, Iraq, and Iran.

Monster.Com
(http://workabroad.monster.com)
Job search and career advice for transitioning to positions around the globe.

Naukri
(www.naukri.com)
A comprehensive resource for job seekers and employers in India.

New York Times Job Market
(www.nytimes.com/pages/jobs)
Find a job, get career advice, search employment trends, and investigate innovative job tools.

Outsource UK
(www.outsource-uk.co.uk/clients.html)
Provides information on IT candidates ranging across a wide range of skills and applications from Help Desk Support through Development to Project Management.

OverSeas Jobs.com
(www.overseasjobs.com)
Features international job opportunities for professionals and expatriates.

Recruit.net
(www.recruit.net)
IT recruiters for the Asia Pacific region. Thousands of candidates and jobs in the Philippines, China, Japan, Malaysia, Singapore, and Hong Kong.

Russian and European Employment Institute
(www.indiana.edu/~reeiweb/indemp.html)
Opportunities in this region or requiring an extensive background in the languages and cultures OF the region.

Search Engine Colossus
(www.searchenginecolossus.com)
International collection of search engines by country. Offers links to search engines and directories from 195 countries and 47 territories around the world. Conduct extensive Web searches. Locate your new favorite search engines. Search the Web using language of choice.

Superpages.com
(www.superpages.com)
Verizon's SuperPages.com is the most accessed for information.

Total Jobs
(www.totaljobs.com/jobseekers/totaljobs.asp)
Thousands of jobs in many fields, primarily, but not exclusively, covering the British Isles.

U.S. Firms in Russia
(www.departments.bucknell.edu/russian)

Most of the jobs for Russian-speakers listed here are in Russia, the NIS states, and East Europe; however, there are jobs in the United States and Canada with companies operating in those areas.

U.S. State Department
(www.state.gov/aboutstate)
Passports, visas, government employment overseas, foreign service, dangerous countries advisories, publications, and resources for Americans working abroad.

Vietnam Works
(www.vietnamworks.com)
Recruiting web site in Vietnam.

Work Tree
(www.worktree.com)
The largest job search portal in the world, with over 50,000 links to all type of job and career resources.

Popular International Job Search and Expatriate Web Sites

Escape Artist
(www.escapeartist.com/jobs/overseas.htm)
Web site for expats interested in all aspects of living overseas, including employment.

Expat Exchange
(www.expatexchange.com)
Post resumes, read job ads, and find in-depth cultural and adaptation information on countries around the world.

Going Global
(www.goinglobal.com)
Features country profiles, employment trends, country-specific career information on more than 23 countries, resume/CV information, and more.

The American Foreign Service
(www.aafsw.org)
The Associates of the American Foreign Service Worldwide provides links to expat sites and information for the foreign service community.

Transitions Abroad
(www.transitionsabroad.com)
The guide to learning, living, and working overseas. This online magazine provides helpful suggestions for work abroad resources and overseas programs.

International Career Research Sites

Action without Borders from Idealist.org
(www.idealist.org/resources.html)
The Contact Center Network publishes a directory of contacts to nongovernmental and nonprofit organizations, which is arranged geographically and topically.

DirectEmployers.com
(http://state.directemployers.com)
Employment search engine that links directly into an employer's job listings. Links to domestic and international jobs. Search by keyword, country, state, company, industry, job category.

EscapeArtist.com
(www.escapeartist.com/jobs/overseas.htm)
An extensive listing of employment job search sites for every country in the world.

CareerBuilder International Job Search
(www.careerbuilder.com/JobSeeker/Jobs/jobfindil.asp?sc_cmp2=JS_HP1_QSB_Intl)
Lists international sites where you can find opportunities or recruit in markets from Canada to the United Kingdom to Japan. Southeast Asia, Europe, and other areas have localized versions of CareerMosaic geared to help job seekers and employers alike. CareerMosaic Asia, for example, offers opportunities in Singapore, Malaysia, Thailand, Indonesia, and Brunei.

Career Resource Center
(www.careers.org)
This huge site contains links to over 11,000 sites in the United States, Canada, the United Kingdom, Australia, Japan, and other countries.

Career Site
(www.careersite.com)
This comprehensive employment site for both job hunters and employers in all industries enables totally confidential job searching. It uses the power of virtual agents and virtual recruiters to find jobs or employees quickly, easily, and accurately.

Career Web
(www.cweb.com)
A global recruitment service, listing jobs that users can access for free worldwide. Employers and recruitment companies worldwide may post job openings for a fee per listing per month.

Career Women
(www.careerwomen.com)
Provides news, advice, resources, and interview tips, as well as a job bank, resume bank, and job posting bank.

The Embassy Page
(www.embassy.org/embassies)
Provides contact information for embassies around the world.

EXPAT Forum
(www.expatforum.com)
Job posting as well as information for individuals who are working, living, or doing business overseas. Contains such information as cost of living, using the telephone, time zones, and cultural differences. Check the Jobs and Careers section on the Expat Chat! message board. You will need to register to contribute or ask questions.

Flipdog.com
(www.flipdog.com/js/loc.html?_requestid=1318679)
You can find overseas job listings, as well as information on many countries and a listing of global companies and profiles.

Global Careers
(www.Globalcareers.com)
Job listings.

International Business Resources on the WWW
(www.globaledge.msu.edu/ibrd/ibrd.asp)
Directs you to hundreds of resources for international business news, newspapers, government resources, and company directories.

International Career Employment Weekly
(www.internationaljobs.org/contents.html)
A substantive list of international job databases, with links to job sites in every major job market, with a charted description of each link.

Monster.com International
(www.international.monster.com)
Job postings for the international market. Regions include Africa, Asia, Australia, Canada, Central America, Europe, Mexico, Middle East, and South America. Also check out globalgateway .monster.com.

Outsourcing Career Center
(www.outsourcingcareercenter.com)
This is the only exclusive listing of outsourcing positions for industry vendors and buyers, professionals, managers, and executives in all areas, including governance, administration, sales, analysis, and senior-level management.

Overseas Digest
(www.overseasdigest.com)
Contains resources for overseas jobs, an overseas employment guide, free monthly newsletter, and detailed information for Americans who are living abroad, plus e-zine materials.

Overseas Jobs
(www.overseasjobs.com)
Contains numerous listings ranging from summer positions to senior-level assignments, as well as links to articles, international recruiters, and job banks.

Saludos.com
(www.saludos.com)
Hispanic employment service.

Teaching Jobs Overseas: The International Educator
(www.tieonline.com)
News and job information resources for educators looking for overseas employment.

University of Indiana Center for the Study of Global Change
(www.indiana.edu/~world/gl_careers.html, www.jobpilot.net/index.phtml, or www.job-hunt.org/general.shtml)
International job market with offices in Germany, Poland, Spain, the United States, Thailand, Switzerland, Austria, France, and Sweden.

Regional Job Search Sites

AsiaCo
(www.asiaco.com/top50/job)
Top job sites for Asian employment.

Asia Employment Center
(www.asiadragons.com/employment/home.shtml)
Job postings from all over the world with emphasis on high-quality jobs in Asia. Jobs are organized as one long list.

Asia-Net
(www.asia-net.com)
Jobs for bilingual professionals with Japanese, Chinese, and Korean backgrounds.

Byron Employment Australia
(www.Employment.byron.com.au)
A near-comprehensive listing of positions in Australia and the United Kingdom, with occupational links.

Enlace Career Resource Links for Latin America
(www.lanic.utexas.edu/enlace/resources)
Comprehensive list of links to Central and South American employers, businesses and job openings.

Europe's Career Market on the Internet
(www.jobpilot.net)
Job Pilot offers Europe's career market on the Internet.

International Computer Professional Associates
(www.icpa.com)
Worldwide recruitment site for computer professionals, with emphasis on attracting candidates in the tech, marketing, and finance fields for jobs in Japan and other Pacific Rim countries.

Job Street
(www.jobstreet.com)
Enables job searching in the following countries: Singapore, India, Malaysia, the Philippines, Australia, Hong Kong, Indonesia, and Thailand.

LatPro.com
(www.latpro.com/USER/JOBS/search_by_country.php?1034354723)
Search here for jobs in Central America, Latin America, Spain, and Madrid.

StepStone
(www.stepstone.com)
Europe's leading independent online recruitment site, publishing "thousands of job opportunities across Europe every day, and offering recruiters a range of services to help fill their vacancies with quality people, quickly and efficiently."

Outsourcing Professional Recruiters and Business Trainers

Chief Resource Officer.com
(www.chiefresourceofficer.com[†])
For buyer organizations only. Largest site of global job offerings exclusively for CROs. Resources are available to help CROs hone their skills and to help novices become qualified candidates.

Outsourcing Career Center
(www.outsourcingcareercenter.com)
For both vendor and buyer organizations. Largest site of global job offerings exclusive to outsourcing. Includes employer-sponsored job searches and executive search firm postings.

Field-Specific Outsourcing Recruiters

Business.com List of International Executive Recruiters
(www.business.com/directory/human_resources/hiring_and_retention/recruiting_services
/executive_search_firms)
Executive Recruiters Listings, Recruiting firms focused on placing top-level executives.

Executive Agent
(www.executiveagent.com)
Enables you to confidentially send your resume—in its current format—directly to executive recruiters that specialize in your field.

Executive Direct
(www.bizwiz.com/executive/toprec.htm)
Provides a service that confidentially matches top level executives with job opportunities, provides confidential networking capability for candidates with incomes over $200,000, and assists
companies and recruiters with Human Resource functions.

ExecuSearch
(http://jobs.execu-search.com)
One of the tri-state's leading professional recruitment and temporary staffing firms, servicing
clients throughout the New York metro area.

*Global 200 Executive Recruiters: An Essential Guide to the Best Recruiters in the United
States, Europe, Asia, and Latin America*
(www.wiley.com/WileyCDA/WileyTitle/productCd-0787941395.html)
Profiles 200 of the world's most successful executive recruiters, providing in-depth information
on their backgrounds and specific areas of expertise.

GO JOBS
(www.gojobs.com)
The job distribution solution, choose from over 2,000 Job Boards.

Google Business Directory: Executive Recruiters
(http://directory.google.com/Top/Business/Employment
/Recruitment_and_Staffing/Recruiters)
Sponsored listing of hundreds of recruitment firms.

The International Directory of Executive Recruiters
(www.kennedyinfo.com/er/ider.html)
Published by Kennedy Information LLC, the Directory of Executive Recruiters has the contacts
whether an executive is seeking a position at a microbrewery or an SAP software consulting firm.
Known to insiders as the "Red Book," the 2003 edition contains detailed information on over
14,700 recruiters at more than 7,800 offices in North America, and lists full contact information
for 2,515 firm locations in 80 countries.

Kennedy Information
(www.kennedyinfo.com/wsj/ider_db.html)
Kennedy Information's Online Database of International Executive Recruiters gives you unique
access to hundreds of executive recruiters working in over 80 countries worldwide—custom selected according to your country, industry, and job function.

The Recruiter Network
(www.therecruiternetwork.com)
Maintains a database containing thousands of recruiters with open positions and thousands of job seekers' resumes. The job seeker may post his or her resume for free and be contacted by one of the many recruiters searching the database of resumes.

Recruiters Online Network
(www.recruitersonline.com)
Tools and technologies to help thousands of 3rd party recruiters, staffing companies.

Reed UK
(www.reed.co.uk)
Search the widest selection of jobs on one of the U.K.'s biggest and best job sites.

Top Echelon
(www.topechelon.com)
Provides unique and powerful services to independent recruiters to help you make placement revenue.

Yahoo Business Director: International Executive Recruiters
(http://dir.yahoo.com/Business_and_Economy/Business_to_Business
/Corporate_Services/Human_Resources/Recruiting_and_Placement
/Executive_Search_Firms)
Extensive Internet link directory of hundreds of executive recruiters.

International Management and Global Professional Executive Recruiters

Top outsourcing executive positions may be found at:

Allen & Associates (www.allenandassoc.com/home.php)

The Amrop Hever Group (www.amrop.com)

A.T. Kearney Executive Search (www.executivesearch.atkearney.com)

Battalia Winston International (www.battaliawinston.com)

Boyden (www.boyden.com)

Christian & Timbers (www.ctnet.com)

Egon Zehnder International (www.egonzehnder.com)

Executive Advisors (www.executive-advisors.com)

Hall Kinion International (merged with K Force in 2004) (www.kforce.com)

Heidrick & Struggles (www.heidrick.com)

International Executive Search (www.international-executive-search.com/about_executive_job_search.htm)

International Staffing (www.international-staffing.com)

JB Hunt Executive Search (www.jbhunt.net)

K-Force (www.kforce.com)

KMC International (www.kmcinternational.co.uk)

Korn/Ferry International (www.kornferry.com)

Lucas Group (www.lucasgroup.com)

Management Recruiters International (MRI) (www.brilliantpeople.com)

Manpower Professional (www.manpowerprofessional.com/procom/index.jsp)

Michael Page International (www.michaelpage.com)

Norman Broadbent (www.normanbroadbent.com)

Ray & Berndtson (www.rayberndtson.com)

Robert Half International (www.rhii.com)

Robert Walters (www.robertwalters.com)

Russell Reynolds Associates (www.russreyn.com)

Sanford Rose (www.sanfordrose.com)

Snelling (www.snelling.com)

Solomon-Page Group (www.solomonpage.com)

Spencer Stuart (www.spencerstuart.com)

Spherion Recruitment (www.spherion.com/recruiting_home.jsp)

SYNERGY International Recruitment (www.synergyindia.com /international_recruitment.htm)

TMP Highlands Executive Search (www.highlandsearch.com)

Whitney Group (www.whitneygroup.com/whitney)

Interim Outsourcing Management Sites

Four sites for those seeking interim positions are:

Outsourcing Career Center (www.outsourcingcareercenter.com)

SiCoTec (www.sicotec.com/EN_SOP_Interim.htm)

BHR Outsourcing (www.bhrgrp.com/outsourcing/interim.htm)

Pink Roccade (www.pinkroccade.co.uk)

PART THREE

THE INDISPENSABLE GUIDE FOR OUTSOURCING ENTREPRENEURS

CHAPTER 16

STARTING DOWN THE ENTREPRENEURIAL PATH TO OUTSOURCING

Judy Ranus was, understandably, upset when her small-business employer decided to outsource her office manager position; and, initially, she did what everyone does when they lose or are about to lose their job: she worried about being able to find another job—quickly. But rather than see outsourcing only as something that takes jobs away from Americans, Judy decided to dig deeper. What she found was that outsourcing might in fact offer her more options than she ever imagined.

And she was right. She soon learned that independent office administrators, specifically so-called virtual assistants (VAs), were becoming the leading worldwide suppliers of this service category, particularly to the small-business owner. Judy also learned that most VAs are American, some even working abroad to service U.S. companies back home. Judy and her husband (a French national), now empty nesters, packed up and moved from Cleveland to Paris, where Judy became an entrepreneurial VA. Ironically, most of Judy's clients are based in midwestern United States.

Judy Ranus is just one of thousands of Americans who are taking advantage of the widespread use of outsourcing to reinvent themselves as entrepreneurs. As you know by now, companies today all over the world are outsourcing everything from claims processing to creative services. And while outsourcers may belong to diverse business segments, they all have something in common: they have joined the revolution that is changing the way the world does business. Perhaps you too have been bitten by the entrepreneurial bug and are thinking about outsourcing your specialty, as opposed to joining another firm on a full-time basis. Then this chapter and the next are for you. In this one we cover fundamentals; in Chapter 17, we go into greater depth about how to take advantage of the many opportunities available now and in the near future for the independent-minded professional.

You'll find there are many opportunities for small, medium, and large outventures alike, particularly in the services segment. In fact, according to the CRO Institute/Outsourcing Management Institute, in the next three to five years, many U.S. businesses are expected to outsource their entire business processes, rather than just specific segments (see Table 16.1).

TIP New and exciting opportunities also are emerging for outsourcing entrepreneurs in animation, market and technical research, credit services, turnkey IT, knowledge management, and full HR management.

Along with these new areas in outsourcing has come a shift in the reasons companies choose to outsource. In addition to cost reduction, buyers are seeking these benefits from their outsourcing vendor relationships:

- Expertise
- Speed, productivity, efficiency
- Operations management

Table 16.1
Global Outsourcing Opportunity Overview

	Currently Outsourcing (%)	Planning to Outsource within Two Years (%)
Software maintenance/support	37.9	52.6
Hardware maintenance	34.5	56.4
IT development and integration	32.7	60.0
Consulting	24.7	41.7
Education and training	16.5	30.2
Business process/transaction management	14.5	28.2
Management services	9.3	19.2
Others	9.6	36.7

- Improved morale
- Ability to focus on core business
- Ability to reduce tasks/functions
- Improved customer service
- Improving capabilities
- Improved product development, time-to-market and market share

The bottom line is, for creative entrepreneurs today, the door is wide open to develop a profitable niche outsourcing business. But do you have what it takes to walk through that door? In the next section, we'll help you do the soul-searching necessary to answer that tough question.

HAVING WHAT IT TAKES

It takes more than just a fire in your belly and funding to chart an independent course in outsourcing. We recommend that you ponder these questions carefully—and honestly—before you plunge in:

- *Do you have a passion to outsource?* Do you have a compelling outsourcing business idea, one that you can't stop thinking about and imagining its realization? Successful entrepreneurs of all stripes have one thing in common: they have a powerful inner motivating force, a resolve that enables them to face the risks and challenges associated with starting an outsourcing business.
- *Are you a leader?* To make your outsourcing business succeed, you must have strong leadership qualities. Not only will you have to identify and attract the right kind of talent for your start-up, you'll have to motivate others to share your passion.
- *Do you have a game plan?* This is different from a business plan. To shape your outsourcing business idea, you'll first have to figure out such factors as scale of operations and whether you plan to cater to an entire market (e.g., general accounting) or a niche segment (e.g., hospital payroll).
- *Are you tenacious?* Unquestionably, along the way you're going to run into problems related to finance, personnel, the economy, and myriad others. You'll need a strong personal commitment and self-confidence, as well as the ability to adapt to changing—sometimes rapidly—circumstances.

- *Have you charted the outsourcing terrain?* It's important to draw a road map that will lead you to your business goals. To draw this map, you'll need to do your homework, in the form of substantive research, not just in your field of expertise, but in the outsourcing landscape as a whole.
- *Do you have a business plan?* Once your ideas have taken shape, you must then translate them to a well-prepared and detailed business plan so that you can secure seed money.
- *Do you have the seed money?* You'll need to raise the capital to start your outsourcing business, and you may not be able to count on venture capitalists to provide it. To date, worldwide, VCs have funded no more than 0.5 percent of entrepreneurs in outsourcing businesses.[1]
- *Can you manage the cash flow?* Many start-ups, no matter the business model, end up belly up simply because of bad cash flow management.

Remember that your entrepreneurial fortunes will be closely tied to those of your buyers/clients. So, plan your business model according to their requirements.

ENTREPRENEURIAL GUIDELINES

- Assess your individual skills and financial capabilities.
- Evaluate labor market.
- Choose a business with potential.
- Learn to negotiate (terms of contracts, payment and delivery schedules, etc.)
- If the outsourcing job is overseas, familiarize yourself with the law of the land.
- Never overcommit.
- Be reliable—meet delivery deadlines.
- Scale up cautiously.

SELLING YOUR OUTSOURCING VALUE PROPOSITION

Assuming you've concluded you have what it takes to join the outsourcing entrepreneurial revolution, next on your agenda is selling your value proposition. This is a fourfold process:

1. Demonstrating primary benefits.
2. Being a good partner.

3. Determining prospects' compelling reason to outsource.
4. Being a problem solver.

Demonstrating Primary Benefits

Though any value proposition can be viewed from different aspects, there are four fundamental value propositions—potential benefits—of outsourcing that your service company must be able to express to potential clients. You must be able to:

- *Assure customers that you will free them to focus on their core competencies.* You must be able to demonstrate that the service your company provides will better enable them to focus on those areas they regard as core to their success.
- *Give customers access to world-class expertise.* Whether in design, implementation, maintenance, or access to the latest technologies, you must leave no doubt that your company intends to provide the very best.
- *Guarantee staffing flexibility.* Your firm must be able to help its customers respond quickly and cost-effectively to changes in market demand.
- *Lower customer's total cost of ownership.* Because the ongoing operational costs of many systems are significant, and detract from core competencies, you must be able to demonstrate you can reduce other costs.

TIP The most important capability for an outsource provider is to be able to focus on noncore functions for the client.

Being a Good Partner

The most critical factor for success as an outsourcing entrepreneur is, ironically, the one most often overlooked: relationship management. Dun & Bradstreet research indicates that 20 to 25 percent of all outsourcing relationships fail after two years; and 50 percent fail after five years.[2] Don't become part of those gloomy statistics.

In an outsourcing relationship, both you and your clients will face risks. A client faces the risk of nonperformance or poor performance, which will quickly escalate into two problems for the buyer:

1. Delay to market for a product or service
2. Increased cost of development, to remedy nonperformance

Your inability to mitigate these risks will quickly deteriorate your reputation as a credible outsourcing vendor. To make sure that doesn't happen:

- *Keep your staff well trained.* They must know how the product/service works from both sides of the relationship.
- *Qualify the buyer.* Is the buyer financially viable? Are there contractual safeguards in place to make sure you are paid on a timely basis and that incentives are accurately computed?
- *Assign a top manager as your certified outsourcing administrator.* Recall what we said earlier, that many companies today are advocating the creation of a CRO, whose focus is on managing the outsourcing strategy, process, and relationships for the company. The

QUALIFYING OUTSOURCING PROSPECTS

Be able to answer the following questions before signing on to an outsourcing relationship:

- Do you fully comprehend your client's decision-making paradigm and time frames?
- Has your prospect ever outsourced before? The answer will impact how you position your company and services. If yes, was/is the experience a positive one? If no, realize you will probably face a longer sales process, as you will have to prove that outsourcing is a viable solution in the first place.
- Where is your prospect in the outsourcing buying process? They may not be ready to buy yet, which means your early sales efforts will have to focus on the merits of outsourcing, as opposed to the merits of your company.
- Do you know who is making the decision to select the outsource vendor? Depending on who that person is, position your solution to address, as appropriate, financial return, risk mitigation, strategic alignment, political situation, and so on.
- Do you have senior leadership buy-in? Ideally, you want the support from the chief resource officer or other operational executives looking to capitalize on the benefits outsourcing can offer.

counterpart in vendor organizations is the certified outsourcing administrator within the vendor organization.

- *Document the requirements.* Ascertain the legalities of operating your business, particularly in foreign locations. Strategize and develop a marketing plan with specific goals so you can document and measure your progress.
- *Develop an appropriate change process.* Especially if you have development occurring in multiple sites around the world, you will need to establish a clear change process to make sure only the changes the clients wants are made.
- *Select outsource projects with predictable requirements for first endeavors.* Minimize the uncertainities where possible.
- *Account for scope creep.* Expect any project to take longer and cost more, especially at the beginning of an outsourcing relationship. The rule of thumb is to increase the estimated time by 30 percent for the first project.
- *Keep the same team for the duration of a project.* This is not always in your control, as people may leave, but when possible, keep the same people assigned to a project, otherwise, the time you spend training the people will be wasted.
- *Be good to your word.* That is, assign the people you said you would to work on the client's project. Many non-U.S. outsourcing firms have earned a bad reputation for "baiting and switching" consultants and account management staff.

TRACK YOUR VALUE PROPOSITION

Prepare a track record against which your outsourcing buyers can evaluate and compare their in-house operations. It will provide excellent talking points when introducing your company's services to prospective buyers, include:

- Target markets (geographies)
- Technology and architecture
- Product size and complexity
- Product customers/users
- Application/field (if possible)

UNDERSTANDING YOUR PROSPECTS' COMPELLING REASON(S) TO OUTSOURCE

There are as many reasons to outsource as there are companies. When and why the decision to outsource is made will depend on the severity of existing problems or challenges, as well as the availability of an outsource solution and the in-house staff to implement the initiative. As an entrepreneurial outsourcer, you'll have to understand, one at a time, your clients' specific reasons for outsourcing.

Though each situation must be evaluated individually, there are a number of recurring reasons companies choose to outsource one or more of their business functions:

- Executives are not reaping benefits of internal department.
- The company is not keeping pace with changes in technology.
- Inventory costs are too high.
- Personnel turnover is too high.
- IT and operational department budgets are not predictable or are no longer affordable.
- Operational departments or managers do not have a strong grasp of company's objectives, critical success factors, and/or bottom line.
- Organization does not implement industry best practices, processes, and/or services to internal/external customers.
- Departmental strategies are not consistent with overall business strategy.
- The company has suffered the loss of senior or valuable managers.
- Too many delivery dates have been missed.
- There is an increased need to focus on core competencies and business units.
- An executive dictum has been handed down to increase earnings, growth, ROI, and/or shareholder value.
- There is no business continuity/recovery plan, leading to lack of focus.
- No documented, measurable, and/or repeatable business unit strategies are in place.
- The company is not ready for e-business.
- The company has poor-quality internal and/or external customer service.

BEING A PROBLEM SOLVER

To capture a piece of the outsourcing market, as an entrepreneurial outsourcing vendor, you'll have to prove yourself as a problem solver for your clients. To that end, you must learn to strategically position your solutions to fit their business needs. First you'll have to understand what the buyer/client is trying to achieve by outsourcing. Most commonly, it's one or more of the following:

- Improve productivity of department or function.
- Reduce operating cost.
- Upgrade, introduce, or transform skills.
- Better manage department or function.
- Free up resources for core area(s).
- Improve cash flow.
- Implement business change.

Conversely, you'll have to understand why companies choose *not* to outsource. The six top reasons are:

1. Loss of control over the process.
2. Loss of outsourcing competitive advantage.
3. Partnering with wrong supplier.
4. Costs not justified.
5. Company wants to integrate vertically.
6. Company does not understand the benefits of outsourcing.

CONCLUSION

If, at the end of this chapter, you've concluded that the entrepreneurial path is the one you want to take to outsourcing, come down it a little further with us in Chapter 17, where we tell you how to capitalize on what can only be described as a start-up boom.

NOTE

1. Outsourced Venture Capital Solutions, "Emerging VC Trends in Outsourcing," *VC Outsourcing Newletter,* Winter 2005, http://outsourcedVCsolutions.com.
2. Dun & Bradstreet, Dun & Bradstreet's Barometer of Global Outsourcing: "Dun & Bradstreet Sees 25 Percent Growth for Global Outsourcing in 2000," February 23, 2000, https://www.dnb.com/newsview/0200news6.htm.

CHAPTER 17

CAPITALIZING ON THE OUTSOURCING START-UP BOOM

Outsourcing companies around the world took in over $3 trillion during 2003, and the market for these services tripled from 2000 to 2003.[1] There are myriad types of outsourcing businesses in the global marketplace, each of which fills a specific outsourcing need. On the one hand, this is a positive because it virtually guarantees you can parlay your skills and experience into an outsourcing business. On the other hand, it may seem overwhelming to sift through all of the different possibilities and choose the right one for you. In this chapter, we offer some guidance to help you do that.

TIP In Chapter 15, we asked you to conduct a skills assessment to help you find a job in the international marketplace. Refer to that assessment before reading on here, because what you learned there will also help to determine where you are best qualified as an entrepreneur.

LAYING THE GROUNDWORK

We begin by sharing the five most important elements for success in this area, according to Outsourcing Entrepreneurs, Inc.'s (www.outsourcingentrepreneur .com[†]) consulting specialists who study outsourcing business start-ups:

1. Knowledge in the outsourcing field through both formal training and on-the-job experience.

Note: Web addresses flagged with a ([†]) are author affiliated sites.

2. Can-do attitude and willingness to work long hours for many months and sometimes years.
3. An outsourcing business plan—a business without a plan is like a ship without a rudder.
4. Capital, cash, and resources.
5. Tenacity and capability to follow through to implementation—a get-it-done determination.

In sum, make sure that you are willing and able to commit to whatever it takes to make your outventure a success. Answer—honestly—the following 10 questions:

1. Do you know what you want and understand what's involved to get it, including the personal sacrifices? Are you willing to devote long hours to see your plan through to fruition?
2. Have you done your research? You must conduct research to ensure that there is a need for your planned service offering and that market conditions can support your business. Researching your market thoroughly can prove to be the single most important factor in whether your outventure thrives or struggles. Therefore, it is worth taking your time and planning your research well. The first question to ask and to research is if there is adequate demand for your particular outsource service. You must ensure that you will have a steady flow of clients. Talk with friends, family, and advisors to obtain business information. Contact government agencies, trade associations, and other organizations that offer services and programs to help get your business started. Use the many resource listings throughout this book to get your research started.
3. Have you detailed how you will utilize your skills and compensate for your weaknesses? Refer to the skills assessment in Chapter 15.
4. Have you decided what form your outsourcing business will take— a corporation, partnership, sole proprietorship, or other?
5. Have you thought about how you will promote and market your outventure? How are you going to distinguish yourself from the competition or invoke a need for your outsourcing specialty?
6. Have you decided on a pricing strategy? What does the price say about your services (versus those of the competition)? Think about what you'll charge people for your outsourced services. Estimate your break-even point and revenues.

7. Have you prepared a detailed outventure business plan? We've said it before, this is an essential.
8. Do you know which funding sources will fuel your outsourcing enterprise? You must secure in advance sufficient financial resources for start-up and operations. More and more banks are making small business loans available for outsourcing start-ups. Venture capitalists are also looking to invest in outsourcing businesses with the capacity to grow.
9. Have you decided where you will locate? United States? Offshore? Pick a business location that makes sense for you and your customers.
10. Do you know how your outsourcing business will operate on a daily basis? How will you deliver your service and manage your business? Figure out what you'll need for the day-to-day smooth functioning of your business.

TIP The Outsourcing Management Institute (www.outsourcingmanagementinstitute.com) offers in-depth information on outsourcing management to set you on the right path to a successful outventure start up.

As these questions make clear, you will have many things to learn and problems to solve in starting your outventure. It is important—really, imperative—to maintain a positive attitude while at the same time being realistic. Typically, what differentiates a success and a failure is how problems and challenges are handled. When the going gets tough—and it will—remember, at the end of the rainbow is a large pot of money to be earned in outsourcing ventures, locally, regionally, nationally and globally. As Table 17.1 clearly illustrates, the pros outnumber the cons.

We can suggest a variety of strategies that, depending on your current situation, might help to ease your way up the learning curve:

- *Don't quit your day job—yet.* A strategic way to start a business is on a part-time basis, while continuing to work at your full-time job—assuming, that is, that it hasn't been outsourced already. This can give you the much-needed transition from employee to outsourcing entrepreneur.
- *Work for someone already in the outsourcing business you want to enter.* Working for a potential competitor can give you valuable insight, both on a personal and professional basis. (A word of caution:

Table 17.1
Pros and Cons of Starting an Outsourcing Business

Pros	Cons
Initial investment level is decided by you and your ability to attract investment.	Comparatively little hands-on help and advice are currently available.
Many organizations are available to offer support, subsidies, and funding.	You will have to climb a steep learning curve.
You have the ability to explore new business concepts and formulae.	You may fall in love with the business and forget the point—to make a profit.
All post-tax profits are your own.	Most business start-ups fail in their first year.
There are no restrictions on your business methods.	Venture capital for outsourcing business start-ups is difficult to find.
You can control expansion to suit yourself.	The acquisition of smaller outsourcers by larger corporations is creating some mega-suppliers to have to compete against.
You have the ability to adapt quickly to changing economic circumstances.	
You have the potential to sell, franchise, or list on the stock market once your outsourcing business has stabilized.	Outsourcing is still controversial (positive and negative aspects).
Great sense of achievement.	Labor, culture, work styles, and ethics with employees in foreign countries can be difficult for new outsourcing owners.
	Control, because of remote locations and multiple client sites, is logistically difficult.

Be careful about signing anything that includes a noncompete clause that would prohibit you from starting a similar business.)

- *Cover your bases—in advance.* Obtain any required licenses for your business or occupation. Register your business with the state and obtain a federal identification number. Familiarize yourself with zoning regulations and state and federal regulations for safety and health of employees; verify the eligibility of new employees with the Immigration and Naturalization Service. Purchase necessary business insurance to protect contents of your business in case of fire, theft, or other loss; consider business interruption insurance.
- *Consider working from home.* At least initially, this is a good idea to keep overhead low. Explore "incubators" for start-up businesses or suites that give access to needed business services as part of your rent. Incubators are pay-per-use office administrative services, which help start-ups limit their overhead.

- *Don't forget to promote your idea.* Start-up outsourcing business owners often forget they have to sell their idea or product. You can't stand back and wait for people to come to you. Every business owner should be able to give a 10-second, 30-second, or 1-minute description of what your business is and does. If marketing is not your thing, consult with a professional in this area.
- *Identify your money sources.* As a new business owner you will be putting money in the business, often for several years. So before you launch, review your personal finances: How are you going to pay the mortgage? Do you have an emergency fund? What about health benefits and insurance? If you are going into business with your spouse or a partner, one of you might continue working while the other starts the business. Start-up outsourcing business owners typically have to use their own savings and resources, such as credit cards and family and friends.

TIP When interest rates are low, home-equity loans can be an inexpensive way to raise money to start a business. The time to take out a home-equity loan is while you still have a job; banks won't look at you if you don't have a stable source of income.

- *Develop an outsourcing entrepreneurial mentality.* The common thread among successful outsourcing entrepreneurs is a passion and belief in what they are doing. You're going to need both.
- *Never underestimate the value of ethics.* A number of large corporations have gotten into trouble in recent years because they haven't adhered to ethical standards. What you do and how you do it will resonate throughout your company and with the public. Employees will follow your example. Keep in mind, outsourcing is under public scrutiny these days. Commit to operating above reproach.
- *Spend time determining just how "different" things will really be.* It's a common belief that international markets operate drastically differently from the United States—that laws, commercial customs, and so on are, by definition, strange and bewildering. Certainly that's true in some places—in Latin America, for example. But there are many other countries where the nuts and bolts of business are not that different. Seek out local guidance. Finding locally based competent advisors is absolutely critical. Whether attorneys or

bankers, make certain that they're located in the market where you want to set up shop.

- *Research the particulars of the market, specifically, the market for outsourcing.* Don't fall prey to the mistaken assumption that, by virtue of being American, your business will sell itself. It's imperative to understand the market conditions, such as overall potential, competition, and marketing channels.
- *Protect yourself and your intellectual property.* This is an important guideline whether you're setting up shop overseas or in America. If, for instance, your outsourcing operation is centered on a unique service or data software program or even a logo, be sure to secure the necessary trademark protection. Line up any necessary patents and trademarks—one by one, if need be.

Now that you have a clear-eyed view of what it will take to launch an outsourcing venture, let's discuss how you can take advantage of the many opportunities out there.

STAKING YOUR CLAIM

As business needs continue to change, outsourcing needs and opportunities are more numerous but also more complex. Business process outsourcing is, without question, a buyer-driven market; there is more demand than there are suppliers to meet it. In this section, we discuss some great ways an outsourcing entrepreneur can take advantage of this market.

TIP Some of the most astute outsourcing suppliers are those employees who came from the Big 5 accounting firms. Other new vendors find their target buyers among those who have trouble finding the right supplier and are about to abandon their outsourcing efforts. Many of these start-ups are initiated by former employees of these same companies.

Find a Niche

If you believe you have a "first-mover" advantage, capitalize on this opportunity. If you think a larger market will develop, you can create your own outsourcing company with 100 percent ownership. That said, creating your own outsourcing company works only if the board and the senior management clearly understand the outsourcing model. These groups must be willing to make the capital investment to generate the kind of leverage that makes outsourcing so attractive. When the management is enlightened, these new suppliers do extraordinarily well.

Bring in Outside Capital

If you have the process knowledge, find someone with the equity and form a partnership. This allows outside capital to flow to your process. Then select a seasoned management team that understands outsourcing principles and has experience in governance.

Form a Joint Venture

A variation of the preceding is to form a joint venture with an existing supplier or a consulting group that wants to become a BPO player. Adding your expertise to an existing consultancy or business can be the winning combination. Joint ventures work, however, only when a strong governance program is in place to act as the glue that holds the partnership together. Be wary that conflicts may arise if the process owner wants to own all the equity in the new supplier. Joint ventures can also have trouble sustaining capital formation, unless the partners have agreed in advance to these continuing expenditures for process improvement.

Consider a Gainsharing Arrangement

Gainsharing is the easiest route to success for a new supplier, and the fastest. In this scenario, the outsourcing buyer "owns" a portion of the outsourcing supplier's profits as compensation for shouldering some of the risks of the new venture. In this way, buyers can achieve their goals of lower costs and improved service much more rapidly. Good gainsharing partners are private equity firms and companies with a well-honed core process eager to enter the outsourcing world. These companies want to become suppliers by "wrapping" an outsourcing offering around their process.

GO GOVERNMENT

Did you know that the U.S. government is the world's largest buyer of products and services? Purchases by military and civilian installations amount to nearly $200 billion a year, and include everything from complex space vehicles to cancer research to janitorial services. In short, the government buys just about every category of commodity and service available.

By law, federal agencies are required to establish contracting goals, such that 23 percent of all government buys are intended to go to small businesses. In addition, contract goals are established as follows: for women-owned businesses (5 percent), small disadvantaged businesses (5 percent), firms located in HUBZones (3 percent), and service-disabled veteran-owned businesses (3 percent). The Historically Underutilized Business Zone (HUBZone) Empowerment Contracting program, which was enacted into law as part of the Small Business Reauthorization Act of 1997, provides federal contracting assistance and opportunities for qualified small businesses located in distressed historically underutilized business zones, known as "HUBZones." Furthermore, federal agencies have a statutory obligation to reach out to and consider small businesses for procurement opportunities. But it is up to you to market and match your business products and services to the buying needs of federal agencies.

Selling to the federal government is, in some ways, similar to selling to the private sector. While federal procurement procedures may have a different set of rules and regulations, many of the same marketing techniques and strategies you already employ may work here. Here are some guidelines:

- Get to know the agency and understand the context in which your product or service could be used.
- Obtain available information on past awards, quantities, costs, and awarders.
- Become known to potential purchasers.
- Take a close look at your company and consider what the government will look for when considering your company for a contract award. Financial status, staff capabilities, and track record are all of interest to the government.

Here's what the government gains:

- The private partner brings in specialized IT skills and other resources. Outsourcing helps the government, generally lacking in the knowledge of current and emerging IT technologies, to make the right choice of technology.
- By outsourcing, government services can be digitized with least penalty in time, cost, and other resources, because private

(Continued)

> vendors generally work more efficiently and effectively at a lower cost. Day-to-day tasks of running, maintaining, and managing the system can be left to the specialized private partner.
> - Outsourcing makes it possible to bypass inherent legacies of government systems.
> - As in the commercial sector, by outsourcing, government agencies can concentrate on their core competencies, thereby enhancing productivity.

GETTING IT RIGHT

Because entrepreneurial outsourcing is a relatively new phenomenon, there is little accumulated knowledge and information available for "getting it right." As a result, most entrepreneurs wishing to outsource cobble together a variety of techniques to develop their own tailored approach.

In the absence of any tried and tested formula, it's important to look for evidence of what has worked for some. In particular, a study of the outsourcing scene in India suggests that it pays to follow a well-thought-out, structured process, one that addresses all the issues that are part and parcel of the outsourcing cycle. Based on the experiences of a number of successful outsourcers, we have developed a comprehensive model that helps entrepreneurs identify all the issues involved in outsourcing business processes to India, reducing the risks and improving the chances of successful implementation on a time-bound basis.

TIP Resources, presence, and current capabilities will all factor into your choice of whether to offer a full-service business process outsourcing service line (e.g., human resources administration) or to focus on a very specific segment of the service line (e.g., exempt/professional recruitment).

From the time an organization begins to consider the idea of outsourcing to India, it may take 6 to 12 months to get top-level buy-in and decide the best way to proceed. Thereafter, vendor selection will take three to six months before the processes can begin to be migrated. Setting up a shared services center may take even longer. Depending on the complexity of the process, it can take anywhere from three to six months to establish a process and achieve target efficiency levels.

During the awareness phase, which may entail between 6 and 18 months, a few executives champion the concept and work to ensure that the executive group understands the key issues, including what their competitors may be doing. To help executive groups achieve such buy-in, it's important to present examples of organizations (preferably in the same field, especially direct competitors) that have successfully traveled down this road. Most organizations depend on Indian providers to act as information and consultancy resources for them, but these providers usually do not have the complete perspective to navigate organizations this extremely complex process. The formula, such as it is, becomes muddier depending on logistics. Are you going to locate your headquarters overseas or stateside? Your first research stop should be at the U.S. Department of Commerce (DoC) web site (www.commerce.gov), regardless whether you're moving abroad or just investigating the possibility. The DoC can provide a wealth of free information, covering such topics as overseas agents and tax ramifications.

TIP Make certain that any contracts you draw up contain a locally enforceable arbitration clause to settle any disputes that may crop up.

RULES FOR EFFECTIVE VENDOR-FOCUSED BPO AGREEMENTS

BPO agreements are frequently negotiated by executives not connected with the business being outsourced. To ensure that your company will obtain the service levels and cost benefits desired, it is necessary that the executives—say in HR or finance or other process being outsourced—understand the details of the outsourcing agreement so they can attempt to influence them before the contract is signed. The five "rules" delineated here address the operating requirements and infrastructures necessary for a successful relationship.

Rule 1: Get the Outsourcing Agreement Right

Even though the pertinent executives may not be "approvers" of a BPO agreement, they will play a key role in evaluating the competency of the provider and providing a framework of knowledge to ensure the interests of the company and the employees are well served.

The motivation companies have for outsourcing is frequently lost in the shuffle of due diligence, solution building, and contracting. To prevent this from happening, every negotiating team should establish a short list of its reasons for outsourcing (e.g., reduced operating costs, improved service, cost avoidance, head-count reduction) and then test vendor proposals against the list. This is not as easy as it seems. If there is a dedicated "deal team" in place, its idea of success and completion may be different from the executives who will have to manage the ongoing relationship.

Many executives discuss having a seat at the table—in this case, the negotiating table. The intent is to receive agreed-on services at an agreed-on price for a period of time. If services and price don't match, there will be unpleasant consequences later. And, remember, the provider also needs to make money. If the deal is too one-sided, then service or investment in new technology and processes will suffer. Executives with a longer term focus can validate the need for change and counsel the negotiating team if the cost focus overwhelms the service focus. The steps in contracting process are shown in Figure 17.1.

In addition to understanding the process, there must be a clear definition of roles and responsibilities. Identify decision makers, advisors, constituents, key staff, and the deal team. Each has a distinct role, but together they will ensure objectives are met and support the previously established

Figure 17.1
Steps in the Contracting Process

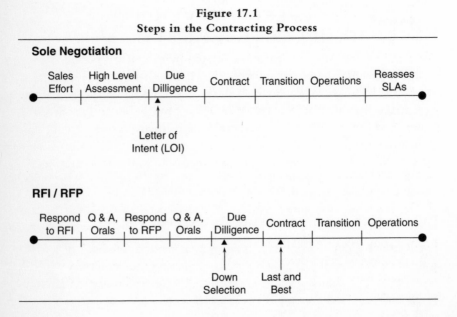

definition of success. In addition to the decision makers, a project management office (PMO) must be established to ensure work is done and deadlines are met. The PMO is established when it appears a contract is likely and continues throughout transition. Some organizations have the PMO established when requests for information (RFIs) are issued.

Rule 2: Institute Change Management Early

Change management is all about ensuring the buying organization supports the business initiative. It's also about leadership and communications. Many outsourcers refer to this period as "migration" or "implementation," but only the savvy outsourcers get involved in mitigating the fallout that many times accompanies change. The effort ideally should begin before any potential vendor is involved, but rarely begins until your staff actually appears onsite, post contracting. A shared communications strategy must be in place to ensure that the buyer's employees, especially those who may be at risk, understand the reasons and feel they will have some level of protection during and after the vendor selection. Your efforts in this process will reap huge benefits for both your client and your staff. This is not easy, and if your organization does not have the professional staff to support this effort, outside resources may be necessary.

TIP The term *change management,* as used here, refers to leadership change management. This is different from the change process that accompanies the actual operations. Once operations begin, there will be a change process with elements such as change orders and work orders. If there is a large IT component involved, make the distinctions early to reduce confusion.

Different constituencies have separate interests and needs. The change management process must include all of them. In HR outsourcing, for example, the most common alignment of the internal groups includes employees, human resources leadership, and senior/line management. External groups could include financial analysts, shareholders, unions/work councils, and current third-party providers. The internal program should work in tandem with the provider's program to ensure clarity and consistency of message.

Rule 3: Get the Transition Right

In the simplest definition, transition is all about getting processes and people from internal control to external control. For this process to work, internal resources must be a willing part of the process. This takes some effort if client employees' positions are at risk (see rule 2). It may be necessary to devise retention programs for key employees. Turnover during this phase must be controlled or an orderly transition to your outsourcing services company will fail.

Transition can be further defined as the detailed, desk-level analysis and documentation of all relevant tasks, technologies, workflows, and functions. It also covers the movement of people if they are "in-scope." If the process is to be moved as-is, the focus is on the current state; if the process is to be transformed, changed, or will use new technology, the focus is on the delta between current state and future state.

- *Process transition.* The provider will assign team leads to manage one or more processes. The teams will include staff from both client and vendor. The team members will be needed for significant amounts of time. During the transition process, documentation is created and assembled. "Job shadowing" may be part of the methodology. The client should sign off on the readiness of the provider before accountability moves to the provider.
- *People transition.* The scale will depend on the nature of the contract. If there will be employees moving to the provider, the usual process of interviews, job offers, and acceptance periods will follow. It may be necessary to devise retention plans for key employees, and severance plans and reassignment programs for impacted staff. Expenses for retention and severance plans are generally borne by the client. People issues must be a major focus of leadership during the critical transition process.
- *Technology transition.* If the provider will be assuming licenses or operations of client-owned systems, applications, or infrastructure, then all in-scope systems must be identified and documented. Licenses, maintenance agreements, hosting, LAN, WAN, and telecom are subject to review and may be part of the transition. If separate entities will manage applications and/or hosting, protocols must be established to ensure roles and responsibilities are clear.

The governance process will be finalized during transition (see Figure 17.2). This is the fundamental basis for managing the relationship during the "build" and "operate" phases of the relationship. There are

Figure 17.2
Sample Governance Model

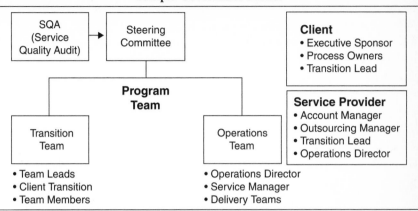

multiple models for this subject; the key point is to appoint individuals with sufficient authority to manage the relationship on a day-to-day basis. The governance methodology should cover the change process and issue resolution, as well as the actual contractual relationship. Web portal design and content also need to be part of the governance process.

Service level agreements (SLA) and key performance indicators (KPI) are determined as part of both the contract and transition period. They are generally finalized at the end of transition, although they may be reopened at an agreed time if new processes or technologies have been implemented. (One word of caution about SLAs: Don't overmeasure; instead, look for leading indicators.)

Rule 4: Love Your Client's Relationship Manager

Business process outsourcing agreements are long-term, complex, and personal relationships. Because end-to-end BPO is not commoditized, it takes care and feeding to make it work. Legally it is a client-vendor relationship, but it can and should work collaboratively as a partnership.

Both parties will have relationship managers. These individuals ensure that changes occur in a timely, orderly manner and that issues are resolved appropriately. Selection criteria for the client's manager should focus on relationship skills, knowledge of the organization, business case and analytic skills, and reputation within the organization. They should also be senior enough to make decisions in a timely manner, without further approvals, within defined boundaries.

Give a good reference where deserved. This is a very significant way to signify approval of the results and relationship. It's almost as good as paying invoices in a timely manner.

Rule 5: Let Outsourcing Be a Strategic Enabler

Moving a buyer to an outsourcing model successfully will not make them more strategic. What it will do, by eliminating large organizations and consolidating SLAs, is allow your clients more time to understand the needs of their organization. Understanding the basic business better allows you to propose and implement more creative and effective strategies. In addition, as the outsourcing provider, you will have more resources and access to best practices to support your multiple clients' business objectives. Outsourcing can be an enabler to becoming more strategic.

Outsourcing is based on outcomes. The client defines the outcomes and the vendor supplies the means. Once trust is established, the total team can create a true partnership to the betterment of all. As more and more organizations move to an outsourced model, choices and processes will improve and the journey will become easier (Figure 17.3).

Figure 17.3
New Project Implementation and Transition Framework

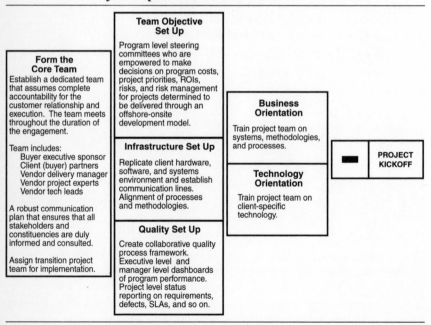

WHERE OUTSOURCING SELLS
AROUND THE GLOBE

NORTH AMERICA

The sectors experiencing the greatest growth in North America are accounting and finance, administrative support, marketing/sales, logistics, human resources, manufacturing, and new media. While the overall growth rate for outsourcing is 15 percent, outsourcing among smaller companies (those with $10 million to $50 million in sales) is expected to increase by more than 25 percent in both Canada and the United States.

ASIA

Outsourcing in Asia is expected to grow by nearly 50 percent again this year. Manufacturing constitutes nearly half the total, with information technology, financial expertise, legal assistance, and sales contributing the balance. American companies are increasing their outsourcing in Asia. Countries where they are most likely to search for outsourcing partners include Japan, China, India, and Taiwan.

EUROPE

Outsourcing throughout Europe continues to grow rapidly at 25 percent per year, with companies in the United Kingdom, France, Italy, and Germany most likely to outsource. They also look beyond Europe, in particular to China, Hong Kong, Japan, Australia, and the United States, with some minor outsourcing in Africa. Transportation outsourcing is the leading category, followed by financial services, information technology, and facilities management. New media, particularly the need for web site development, is also taking off.

AUSTRALIA

Australia has adopted outsourcing almost as completely as North America. The sector is very large relative to the size of the economy and is growing rapidly; information technology, financial support, and sales/marketing are the leading types of outsourcing. Australia also provides substantial outsourcing services to Asia.

(Continued)

SOUTH AMERICA

Companies in South America are still skeptical that others can perform internal functions better, and this attitude will probably not change in the next few years. While the 13 countries do little intercontinental outsourcing, many North American and European companies outsource work to them.

Source: Dun & Bradstreet, Dun & Bradstreet's Barometer of Global Outsourcing, February 23, 2000, https://www.dnb.com/newsview/0200news6.htm.

CONCLUSION

We'll conclude this chapter with one final piece of advice: Anticipate, and be prepared to meet, the changing needs of your chosen market. Successful business people know that their ability to satisfy the changing demands of customers has become increasingly important in recent years. Nowhere is change more noticeable than in the outsourcing marketplace. Anticipating future outsourcing market needs and managing the necessary changes is as important as satisfying current markets. New technology, growing international trade, improved communications, and increasingly sophisticated and demanding outsourcing buyers have all increased the pressures on suppliers to make continuous improvements in their service lines.

Given a choice of outsourcing suppliers, discerning customers will always go with the one that most completely meets their needs. These customers then, typically, grow to rely on that supplier, forming long-term and lucrative (for both) partnerships. Those companies best able to satisfy customer needs will become the most successful in their marketplace. Learn to be one of them.

NOTE

1. *Bulletin of the Federation of Indian Export Organizations,* vol. XXIV, 2004, http://www.fieo.com/fieonews.

CHAPTER 18

STARTING AN OUTSOURCING BUSINESS

No doubt you're aware that airline pilots are required to go through a checklist before they take off each time. To ensure that your outsourcing business "gets off the ground" without a hitch, we suggest you do the same thing. Here are the items we recommend you have on your checklist. (Add any items appropriate for your field of work.)

- Have I taken the time to gain practical outsourcing and job experience and learn the basics of my business by first working in the business for someone else? This is probably the best way to discover if you have made a choice that will be not only successful, but also satisfying to you.
- Have I completed my outsourcing management certification and training? For information on this, go to www.outsourcingmanagementinstitute .com.
- Have I focused on a specific outsourcing niche service? As a general rule, outsourcing specialists outperform nonspecialists. Or, will further specialization or focus improve my prospects for success? The more specialized the niche, the better.
- Is my outventure business plan complete and in written format? Does it include preopening, first-year, and long-range planning? This will play a key role in securing investors and will help uncover any weaknesses in the implementation process. A resource that can provide business plans for 400 different types of business is www.bplans.com /common/products/?affiliate=myownbusin.

- Have I budgeted adequately for prototypes, research, sampling, and trials?
- Have I successfully test-marketed my outsourcing service line? Was the response positive? If not, you need to redesign, rework, and retest.
- Do I have a marketing plan that serves my target niche? Do I understand the difference between finding a market niche and going against what the general business outsourcing buyer wants?
- Will my business be home based? Online? Storefront? Could I franchise?
- Do I know my competition?
- Do I know my strengths and weaknesses?
- Do I have a one-year cash flow projection prepared to ensure ongoing liquidity?
- Do I have the necessary e-commerce tools in place?
- Are all my insurance policies up to date and in force?
- If I plan to sell on credit terms, do I have a credit rating policy in place to prevent taking on high-risk customers? The last thing you need is to have clients who don't pay on time, and good customers will respect you for this policy.
- Have I focused on selling a great service line at a fair price rather than a fair product at a great price?
- Do I have all the communication, computer, and other business tools in place?
- Has my accountant fully explained the difference between hiring independent contractors and employees, and the importance of complying with IRS rules?
- Are the following elements of my business structure in place, as appropriate:
  __Is my accounting and bookkeeping system in place? Accountant selected?
  __Are my premises ready? This includes having a signed lease and tenant improvements completed.
  __Have I secured all necessary permits and licenses?
  __Has the business name been registered? Check with my attorney.
  __Are computers, telephones, cell phones, fax, and utilities operating?
  __Are graphics for advertising and promotional materials ready?
  __Is the web site name registered and web site online?
  __Is the infrastructure in place for e-business?
  __Are all security systems in place, including protection of premises, shrinkage control, and internal security?
  __Have I selected and trained the number of employees I will need?
  __Have I determined my personal work schedule?

Table 18.1
Causes of Outsourcing Business Failures

Lack of knowledge and experience in the outsourcing business

Poor control over costs and quality of product

Reluctance to seek professional services

Poor relations with employees

Failure to anticipate outsourcing market trends

Underpricing of services sold

Poor customer relations

Failure to promote and maintain favorable public image

Poor relations with suboutsourcers

Inability of management to reach and act on decisions

Failure to keep pace with management systems

Illness of a key person

Failure to minimize taxes through tax planning

Inadequate insurance

Loss of key personnel

Lack of staff training

Competition disregarded due to complacency

Poor control of assets

Insufficient working capital

Insufficient capital to take advantage of growth opportunities

Poor budgeting

Extended too much credit

Ignoring information on the company's financial position

Poor recordkeeping

Now that you know what you need to do to launch an outsourcing business, take a look at Table 18.1, which lists the most common reasons outsourcing businesses are sidelined.

PRICING AND PROMOTION

No matter how carefully you do the cost-benefit analysis we discussed earlier, pricing remains a somewhat amorphous process. There are no fail-safe formulas that we know of, and it sometimes seems what you really need is equal parts luck, creativity, and guesswork. Still, there are some basic guidelines we can share with you.

Don't Lowball Yourself

As you saw in Table 18.1, a common cause of outsourcing business fail-ure is underpricing. Most outsourcing entrepreneurs are far more likely to underprice than overprice. To avoid falling into this trap, research what others are doing with prices, percentages of gross margin, and related in-formation, and from this information estimate their pricing structure. Pricing resources you can experiment with online include direct tele-phone sales, interviews, and mock services, to see how prospective clients react. In the second half of this chapter you'll find an extensive listing of outsourcing-related business sites to help you do this research.

Price Strategically

Your pricing sends a message, so the best way to price your product is as part of your marketing strategy. Pricing is your most powerful tool in posi-tioning an outsourcing start-up. The first step is to consider pricing as the

---

TOP 10 COUNTRIES FOR OUTSOURCING

INDIA—Population: 1 billion

Telling statistic: India's IT software and services export market will grow from nearly $10 billion in 2002 to $60 billion by 2008.

Strengths: Low wages, favorable tax rates, quality of IT training and education, English language skills.

Weaknesses: Political and economic risk, poor infrastructure.

U.S. companies outsourcing there: Hewlett-Packard has 10,000 people in India doing everything from writing software code to managing other companies' IT needs.

CHINA—Population: 1.3 billion

Telling statistic: The population under age 18 in China is larger than the combined total populations of the United States and the U.K. In other words, think unlimited supply of people.

Strengths: Low wages, good educational system.

Weaknesses: Intellectual property piracy, bureaucratic red tape, English language skills.

U.S. companies outsourcing there: IBM opened three new IT/BPO (business process outsourcing) data centers last year—two in Hong Kong and one in Shenzen. Accenture has a 1,000-person software development unit in the northeastern city of Dalian.

MALAYSIA—Population: 23 million

Telling statistic: Malaysia has even less bureaucratic red tape than Canada.

Strengths: Low costs, high level of global integration, strong government support.

Weaknesses: Piracy, relatively small population will keep it from reaching India's scale.

U.S. companies outsourcing there: The government-backed "intelligent city" of Cyberjaya has become home to regional offshore service centers for Motorola and IBM.

CZECH REPUBLIC—Population: 10 million

Telling statistic: The offshore services market is growing at greater than 10 percent annually.

Strengths: Competitive infrastructure costs, good education system, stable business environment.

Weaknesses: Higher labor costs relative to Asian countries, small population limits market size.

U.S. companies outsourcing there: Accenture has IT and BPO operations; IBM and Sun Microsystems have IT and business support centers. Dell has a multilingual service center for European customers.

SINGAPORE—Population: 5 million

Telling statistic: On a purchasing power parity basis, Singapore has the second-highest income per capita in the world. Yet, it still attracts U.S. companies as a place for regional headquarters and increasingly, higher-end technology and services.

Strengths: Education system, infrastructure, intellectual property protection, stable political environment.

Weaknesses: Higher labor costs, small population.

U.S. companies outsourcing there: HP has a BPO (business process outsourcing) center and Eli Lilly has an R&D center.

(Continued)

PHILIPPINES—Population: 77 million

Telling statistic: Graduates an estimated 15,000 technology students annually—more than any other country in the index except the four largest: China, India, Russia, and Brazil.

Strengths: English language skills, low costs, cultural affinity for the United States.

Weaknesses: Overall business environment, political instability, infrastructure.

U.S. companies outsourcing there: Convergys, Time Warner, Chevron-Texaco, Procter & Gamble, all have call centers and/or BPO units.

BRAZIL—Population: 182 million

Telling statistic: Brazil's international call center workforce is expected to grow to 5,000 by the end of this year from just 700 last year.

Strengths: Low costs, large population, good business process outsourcing results.

Weaknesses: Education and English language skills.

U.S. companies outsourcing there: Ford Motor has a plant in the northeastern state of Bahia, and Flextronics International has a 172-acre campus in Sao Paulo state that makes cell phones and telecom infrastructure products.

CANADA—Population: 32 million

Telling statistic: Turnover at CGI, one of Canada's largest call centers, is just 6 percent versus 25 percent to 50 percent turnover at most U.S. call centers.

Strengths: Business environment, high-quality workers, infrastructure, language skills.

Weaknesses: Costs are higher than countries like China and India.

U.S. companies outsourcing there: EDS has more than 1,500 employees in Nova Scotia; services include a call center. General Motors announced last month it would move some white-collar jobs to Canada.

CHILE—Population: 16 million

Telling statistic: Santiago, Chile's capital, is among the least expensive cities in the world.

Strengths: Good infrastructure, including telecom networks, good business environment.

Weaknesses: More costly than other Latin American countries, lack of bilingual technicians, intellectual property protection.

U.S. companies outsourcing there: Citigroup has a software development group and fund advisory center.

POLAND—Population: 39 million

Telling statistic: The Polish Agency for Information and Foreign Investment aims to get 25 percent of foreign investment flows targeted on advanced technologies.

Strengths: Good education system, slightly lower costs than Czech Republic and Hungary.

Weaknesses: English language skills, infrastructure, business environment, and IP security inferior to Czech Republic's.

U.S. companies outsourcing there: IBM, General Electric, and Motorola all have BPO centers.

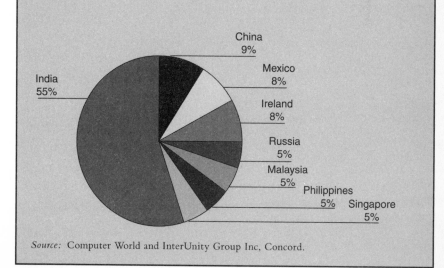

Source: Computer World and InterUnity Group Inc, Concord.

foundation of service line positioning. Some outsourcing vendors have been extremely successful with very high pricing and matching position. In addition to offering higher margins, high prices are an important part of the benefits they sell. These higher price points offer prestige and exclusivity and make others perceive these outsourced service lines as higher value.

Keep in mind, outsourcing buyers don't always want the least expensive vendor. As you work with pricing, refer back often to your positioning statements. If you believe that your outsourcing service line is the best, then consider pricing it above the competition. If, on the other hand, your business model calls for low prices and discounting, pull your prices down to match your positioning.

Understand Your Pricing Limitations

Before you think about pricing as strategy or positioning, take a good hard look at your actual outsourcing business situation. Not all businesses have the luxury of setting their own prices, such as government agencies and insurance companies. Similarly, some dentists and doctors can set their own prices, while others, based on their relationship with HMOs and insurance programs cannot. And some public agencies and utilities require government approval to change their prices.

Determine Your Price Point

To find your best price point, you must first determine both the highest and lowest price you can charge. Be sure you never charge more than the current budgeted amount expended for similar in-house services (unless you have considerable value-add-ons). Understanding your costs is a critical component in establishing the price for your outsourcing service line. Likewise, determining the cost "floor" for your service is an important step toward establishing the range of where your price should be (see the next guideline). This will help you understand where you can exercise pricing discretion to set your price point.

Know Your Price Floor

Pricing at the floor means that you are not making any money, or margin, on the services you sell. Therefore, the price of your outventure services must be greater than your total costs. This may seem like common sense, but many business failures are the result of not fully understanding the total costs they incur to provide the service to their customers. When the price of your outsourcing service is not contributing to your bottom line, you don't have the opportunity to "make it up in volume."

Calculate your costs as accurately as you can to find the price floor. This exercise will make certain that you don't price your outventures too low, thereby preventing you from making revenue from each client. As mentioned, another consideration in pricing too low is the risk of having a low price associated with low quality. This will be based on your customers' perceived value and its correlation to the price that they will pay to benefit from their purchase.

In addition to the cost structure, the price point may be determined by these factors:

- Level of demand for your outsourcing niche
- Degree of competitive threat
- Impact of government regulation by country
- Presence of substitute products or in-house options
- Product positioning
- Production and distribution capabilities
- Overall marketing strategy

MARKET NEEDS ASSESSMENT

With very few exceptions, every outsourcing business begins as a small business. Some stay small, others grow as the years go by. Profitability and future growth of an outsourcing business are based on the ability to understand business operations and make good decisions. Good business planning is focused on a vision of the future while recognizing current resources, intended activities, and financial realities. It also reflects foreseeable changes within and outside the outsourcing industry that will affect your business and its future vitality. These combined steps are often addressed in a Market Needs Assessment before embarking on your outsourcing business.

Given all those realities of business life, it's important to get off to a good start. Before diving headlong into setting up your own

(Continued)

outsourcing business, it's important to understand what is involved. This checklist provides some guidance for your initial business planning. Through your needs assessment, identify and carefully consider the advantages and disadvantages of owning/operating your own outventure.

New Suppliers and Programs

For a general understanding of the market for outsourced services
As input for the definition of a market strategy
To find out the type of services that clients wish to purchase
As a basis for investing in a new service
To get to know the competition

Existing Suppliers and Programs

As input for the definition of a revised market strategy
To find out the type of outsourcing that clients wish to purchase
To discover growth potential
To balance supply of and demand for services
To assess whether services provided are adequate
To obtain information on correct pricing of services

Our Clients and What They Want

How aware are clients of the potential benefits of outsourcing for their enterprise?
Which outsourcing services do clients want?
What kind of outsourcing do clients presently use?
How likely are clients to buy our services?
Are clients willing to pay for our services, and how much?
How do clients rate our services?
How attractive is the market?
How big is the market for different types of outsourcing?
How many potential clients are in the market?
Which types of services are already available?

What is the current outsourcing market turnover?

What are the market's prospects for growth?

Market Competition

Number and size of competitors

Market share of competitors

Services offered by competitors

Competitor pricing

Comparison of our position with that of competition

Outsourcing Business Web Sites

Outsourcing Entrepreneurs

Outsourcing Entrepreneur.com
(www.outsourcingentrepreneur.com[†])
This is the leading resource site for new outsourcing business owners and potential owners.

Venture Capitalists

Outsourced VC Solutions.com
(www.outsourcedvcsolutions.com)
VCs can find comprehensive resources on the impact of outsourcing on profitability, need for outsourcing on return on investment, and due diligence. Assessments and consultation services provide VCs with the information they need to make knowledgeable decisions on all types of new businesses.

Outsourcers for Outsourcers

First Outsourcing, Inc.
(www.firstoutsourcing.com)
This site provides how-to setup, advice and matching services for both new outventures and existing outsourcing organizations.

Outsourcing Brokerage

Outsourcing Providers
(www.outsourcingproviders.com)
At this site you can buy, sell, trade, barter, or broker services with other outsourcers and/or identify business development opportunities.

General Business Web Sites

Business Researcher's Interests
(www.brint.com/interest.html)
BizTech, search engines and directories, company and industry info, accounting, finance, marketing, telecom, law, international, job market, data mining, benchmarking, e-commerce, e-money, small business, intellectual property, and more.

Is It Any of Your Business?
(www.fdic.gov/news/conferences/consumerprivacy.html)
Consumer information, privacy, and the financial services industry. Includes transcripts and video files of speeches given on consumer privacy.

Krislyn's Strictly Business Sites
(www.strictlybusinesssites.com)
From Krislyn Corporation. Includes resources on most business topics, including: financial calculators, deposit and loan quotes, information on business barter, resources for developing a business plan, payment mechanisms, credit services, bankruptcy law, an inflation calculator, franchising, chambers of commerce, multilevel marketing, philanthropy, public speaking, ISO 9000 information, and venture capital.

Occupational Outlook Handbook
(www.bls.gov/oco)
Career information for many different occupations, including a brief review of important features and "what workers do on the job, working conditions, the training and education needed, earnings, and expected job prospects."

Wharton School of Business Sites
(http://oldsite.library.upenn.edu/resources/subject/business/guides.html)
Web sites for all areas of business, including nonprofits. Excellent research helper for business students.

International Business

Asia Business Center
(www.asiadragons.com/business_and_finance/home.shtl)
Information on doing business in Australia, China, Hong Kong, India, Indonesia, Japan, Korea, Malaysia, Philippines, Singapore, Taiwan, and Thailand.

European Union Internet Resources
(www.lib.berkeley.edu/GSSI/eu.html)
Award-winning site from University of California, Berkeley. Provides links to EU servers and institutions, EU documents on the Web, and other items of interest from EU universities, documentation centers, newspapers, and journals.

Federation of International Trade Associations, Internet Resources
(www.fita.org/webindex/noaccess.html)
A metasite useful for research in international trade. Includes trade leads, investment info, currencies, taxation, translation services, international law, treaties and conventions, trade barriers, resources for expatriates, and more.

globalEDGE
(www.globaledge.msu.edu/ibrd/ibrd.asp)
Feature articles on international business and links to resources chosen by the Center for International Business Research at Michigan State University.

GLOBUS and NTDB
(www.stat-usa.gov/tradtest.nsf)
Contains trade opportunity leads, foreign exchange rates (updated twice daily), market research and reports, agricultural trade leads, and export and import price indexes.

Rutgers, Resources for International Business Research
(www.libraries.rutgers.edu/rul/rr_gateway/research_guides/busi/intbus.shtml)
Especially good for country and regional information. Includes full-text documents, country studies, and economic information from international and intergovernmental organizations.

Virtual International Business and Economics Sources (VIBES)
(www.library.uncc.edu/display/?dept=reference&format=open&page=68)
Provides over 1,600 links to international business and economic information, in English and free of charge. Links include recent articles and research reports, statistical tables and graphs, and meta pages.

Virtual Library on International Development
(http://w3.acdi-cida.gc.ca/virtual.nsf)
In English and French, from the Canadian International Development Agency. Resources to help those interested in developing business connections in a wide variety of countries.

BASIC ECONOMIC ANALYSIS

In looking at the prospects for business in the country of choice, it is essential to look at the basic economic condition of that country. Some of the key factors are listed here:

- Population (totals, growth rates, geographic distribution, age, sex, etc.)
- Economic statistics and activity (GNP/GDP, growth rate, inflation)
- Personal income per capita; average family income; distribution of wealth
- Principal industries
- International trade statistics, balance of payments, countertrades
- Exchange rates
- Labor force (size, unemployment rates, trends)
- Science and industry
- Current technology available (computers, machinery, tools, etc.)
- Percentage of GNP/GDP invested in research and development
- Technological skills of the labor force
- Infrastructure
- Telecommunications
- Transportation
- Utilities

(Continued)

- Channels of distribution
- Middleman availability
- Customary markups (wholesale and retail)
- Retailers: number, typical size
- Role of chain stores, department stores, specialty stores
- Rural and urban markets
- Media
- Availability and cost of media: television, radio, print, other
- Percentage of population reached
- Cost of advertising

Four sites to visit for information gathering are the Department of Commerce, for news and economic indicators (www.osec.doc.gov); the Monetary Fund (www.imf.org); Stat-USA, which maintains international statistics from the U.S. Department of Commerce (www.stat-usa.gov); and World Bank Economic and Sector Reports (www.worldbank.org)

International Resources for Start-Ups

Country Profiles

CIA World Factbook
(www.odci.gov/cia/publications/factbook)
The best one-stop shop for planning an international outventure. Descriptions, maps, geographical, economic, and communications data and transnational issues.

International Market Audit and Competitive Markets

BizEurope
(www.bizeurope.com)
Europe's leading import and export directory

British Companies
(www.britishcompanies.co.uk)
A directory of British companies and their governing bodies, associations, and institutes.

Bureau of Export Administration
(www.bxa.doc.gov)
Governs export licenses from the United States, commodity classifications, commodity jurisdiction.

Cross-Border Tax and Transactions
(www.crossborder.com)
Focuses on international tax planning and transactions. Choose United States, Canada, or International.

ECeurope.com
(www.eceurope.com)
Post and view B2B trade lead messages in this fast-growing e-marketplace connecting companies in Eastern, Central, and Western Europe with international buyers and sellers around the world.

EUbusiness.com
(www.eubusiness.com)
European business community for news, tenders, economic data, factsheets, Web links, and documents, categorized into EU topic sectors.

ExecutivePlanet.com Business Culture Guides
(www.executiveplanet.com)
Guides to international business culture and etiquette.

Federation of International Trade Associations
(www.fita.org)
Focuses on the role of local, regional, and national associations engaged in international trade.

International Political Economy Network Site for the International Political Economy Community
(http://csf.colorado.edu/ipe)
IPENet joins students, faculty, professionals, community workers, international bankers, trade unionists, development workers, and other people around the world interested in the workings of the global political economy. Maintains a moderated discussion list.

The Internationalist
(www.internationalist.com)
The source for books, directories, publications, reports, and maps on international business, import/export, and more.

International Trade Administration
(www.ita.doc.gov)
Mission: To encourage, assist, and advocate U.S. exports; to ensure that U.S. business has equal access to foreign markets; to enable U.S. businesses to compete against unfairly traded imports, and to safeguard jobs and the competitive strength of American industry.

Journal of International Business Studies
(www.gsb.georgetown.edu/prog/jibs)
A refereed journal that publishes the results of social science research and other types of articles that advance the understanding of business.

Management International Review
(www.uni-hohenheim.de~mir)
Presents insights and analyses that reflect basic and topical advances in the key areas of international management. Its target audience includes scholars and executives in business and administration.

Russian Business Directory
(www.rusmarket.com)
Directory of business resources for Russia and other newly independent states.

Trade Information Center
(www.trade.gov/td/tic)
Go to "Country Information" and look by region for business travel and etiquette documents found under some country listings.

Working Abroad: Country Profiles
(www.careerjournal.com/myc/workabroad/countries)
Career Resources from the Wall Street Journal.

World Bank
(www.worldbank.org)
Offers loans, advice, and an array of customized resources to more than 100 developing countries and countries in transition.

World Trade Organization
(www.wto.org)
The only international organization dealing with the global rules of trade between nations. Its main function is to ensure that trade flows as smoothly, predictably, and freely as possible.

Asia

AsiaOne
(www.asia1.com.sg)
Asia's news, business, and lifestyle channel.

Asia-Pacific.com
(www.asia-pacific.com)
Provides timely strategic business information on the region, with access to data, experts, news, analysis, books, journals (with full-text articles), and other resources.

eThailand.com
(www.ethailand.com/express)
Thai news and information, business and economy, and more.

Hong Kong Trade Development Council
(www.tdctrade.com)
The statutory organization set up to promote Hong Kong's trade in goods and services.

Japan External Trade Organizations (JETRO)
(www.jetro.go.jp)
A nonprofit, Japanese government-related organization dedicated to promoting mutually beneficial trade and economic relations between Japan and other nations.

Keidanren
(www.keidanren.or.jp/A2J)
Access to Japan List of Contact Points for Procurement.

Mizuho Securities Research & Links
(www.mizuho-sc.com/english/ebond/index.html)
Research and links to English-language resources on Japanese finance, economy, politics, and law.

Singapore Online
(www.singapore.com)
Provides a one-stop link for all businesses interested in Singapore.

U.S.-China Business Council
(www.uschina.org)
The principal organization of U.S. companies engaged in trade and investment in the People's Republic of China. Founded in 1973, the council serves more than 250 corporate members through offices in Washington, DC, Beijing, and Shanghai.

U.S.-Thailand Business Council
(www.ustbc.org)
Provides U.S. companies with an opportunity to build long-term relationships with key members of the Thai public and private sectors.

Web India
(www.webindia.com)
Doing business with companies in India.

Europe

Business in Poland
(www.poland.com/modules.php?name=Business)
The Internet guide to business in Poland.

Finfacts
(www.finfacts.ie)
Extensive information on Irish finance and business.

Latin America

Latin Trade
(www.latintrade.com)
Business source for Latin America.

Middle East

Middle East Business Information
(www.ameinfo.com)
Headquartered in Abu Dhabi. Provides complete business information on the Middle East.

International Trade Associations

Agency for International Trade Information and Cooperation (AITIC)
(www.acici.org/aitic/index.html)
Focuses on reinforcing the capacity of less advantaged developing countries and economies in transition to lead a more effective trade diplomacy, to benefit from the multilateral trading system.

America-Asian & Associates
(www.america-asian.com)
A consulting firm providing international business management services to North American companies interested in doing business in China and the Asian marketplace.

American Australian Association (AAA)
(www.americanaustralian.org)
Focuses on trade between the United States, Australia, and New Zealand. Includes information on membership, events, and related links.

American Importers Association
(www.americanimporters.org)
Brings exporters worldwide together with American importers and wholesalers.

American-Russian Business Council
(www.russiancouncil.org)
Based in the United States, with offices in Russia, dedicated to promoting trade and investment between the two countries and assisting companies with their international business needs.

APEC-CHINA
(www.apec-china.gov.cn)
International symposium and exhibition on fruit and vegetable processing technology and industrialization.

Asia Pacific Foundation of Canada
(www.asiapacific.ca)
Canada's think-tank on Asia brings together people and knowledge to provide current and comprehensive information, research, and analysis on Asia and Canada's transpacific relations.

Association of Forfaiters in the Americas, Inc. (AFIA)
(www.afia-forfaiting.org)
Promotes forfaiting (trade finance/discounting of trade receivables). Events, news, member list, and contact information.

Association of German Australian Industry
(www.germany.org.au/html/default.htm)
Promotes bilateral trade between Germany and Australia, assists members and the public in finding trade partners.

Atlanta British American Business Group
(www.babg.org)
Dedicated to facilitating trade, investment, and business opportunities for both large and small companies in the United States and the United Kingdom.

Australia Arab Chamber of Commerce
(www.austarab.com.au)
Nonprofit association promoting and assisting bilateral trade and investment between Australia, the Middle East, and North Africa.

Australian Business Network in Italy
(www.australianbusiness.it)
Local forum where Australian organizations that do business in Italy, and Italian organizations that do business with them or in Australia, can meet and network.

Brazil Chamber of Commerce and International Business
(www.braziltampa.org)
International source for business to provide a strong link between U.S. business and Brazil, English, and Portuguese information.

Brazil-U.S. Business Council
(www.brazilcouncil.org)
A bilateral trade organization that provides a high-level private sector forum for the business communities of both countries.

The British-Caribbean Chamber of Commerce
(www.britishcaribbean.com)
Includes information on trade links between Britain and the Caribbean, events, trade missions, news, contacts, and how to join the group.

Business Council for International Understanding
(www.bciu.org)
BCIU is a U.S. business association dedicated to promoting dialogue and action between the business and government communities for the purpose of expanding international commerce.

Canada New Zealand Business Association (CANZBA)
(www.canada-nz.org.nz)
Promotes trade between Canada and New Zealand. Includes mission, history, executive, services, newsletters, and activities of the association.

Coalition of Service Industries
(www.uscsi.org)
Business organization dedicated to the reduction of barriers to U.S. services exports and to the development of constructive domestic U.S. policies. Events, publications, and membership.

Consuming Industries Trade Action Coalition (CITAC)
(www.citac.info)
Advocates trade policy and relief that is consistent with the needs of America's consuming industries.

The Danish American Chamber of Commerce in New York
(www.daccny.com)
A membership organization designed to promote commerce between Denmark and the United States.

Dominican-American Chamber of Commerce
(www.amcham.org.do/english)
A binational business organization concentrating on fostering mutually beneficial trade, investment relationships, and an interchange of ideas between the Dominican Republic and the United States.

Federation of International Trade Associations
(www.fita.org)
A network of companies belonging to international trade associations in the United States, Canada, and Mexico.

Fédération Internationale des Déménageurs Internationaux
(www.fidi.org)
FIDI is a global organization representing fully qualified professional international moving companies around the world.

Foreign Trade Association
(www.fta-eu.org)
Represents the foreign trade interests of European commerce, with headquarters in Brussels. Features membership information.

Foundation for Russian-American Economic Cooperation
(www.fraec.org)
A nonprofit organization with membership and government grants making efficient, positive changes in business relations between the United States and Russia, focusing on the U.S. West Coast and Russian Far East.

The G77 Trade & Information Network
(www.g77tin.org)
Organization provides access to markets in the developing world through a network of chambers of commerce, trade organizations, and government contacts; offers discussion groups, training resources, and workshop information.

International Accreditation Forum, Inc.
(www.iaf.nu)
World association of conformity assessment accreditation bodies. Its primary function is to develop a worldwide program of conformity assessment that will promote the elimination of nontariff barriers to trade.

International Agency for Economic Development
(www.iaed.org)
Charitable organization for businesses working with the United Nations.

International Association of Administrative Professionals
(www.iaap-hq.org)
Worldwide association for administrative support staff.

International Chamber of Commerce
(www.iccwbo.org)
The only representative body that speaks with authority on behalf of enterprises from all sectors in every part of the world.

International Executives Association
(www.ieaweb.com)
An elite business networking organization founded to share business leads and information among its member firms.

International Import-Export Institute
(www.expandglobal.com)
Internationally recognized body that certifies the proficiency of import-export trade professionals worldwide.

The Italian Chamber of Commerce and Industry in Australia Inc.
(www.italchambers.net)
The main activity of the Italian Chamber of Commerce is to promote trade and commerce between Italy and Australia, part of a worldwide network of similar organizations located both in Italy and internationally.

The Moroccan American Business Council Ltd.
(www.usa-morocco.org)
A not-for-profit organization to foster trade and investment, between the Kingdom of Morocco and the United States of America.

National Association of Foreign-Trade Zones
(www.naftz.org)
A nonprofit organization composed of public entities, individuals, and corporations involved in the U.S. Foreign-Trade Zones program.

New Zealand German Business Association Inc.
(www.germantrade.co.nz)
Promotes trade between Germany and New Zealand and is New Zealand's local representative of the German Chamber of Commerce network, which helps promote and facilitate bilateral trade.

Polish Economic and Business Association (PEBA)
(www.peba.org.uk)
United Kingdom-based organization that facilitates awareness of economic and business developments in Poland. Site provides news, calendar of events, membership information, and a members-only networking forum.

Puerto Rican Chamber of Commerce of South Florida
(www.puertoricanchamber.com)
Working to enhance the business environment in the community. Also active in promoting expanded trade and commerce between the markets of South Florida and Puerto Rico. Based in Miami.

Research Unlimited
(www.wheretodoresearch.com/Assns.htm)
List of links to the official sites of over 150 major professional associations, trade associations, and trade groups in the United States.

Swiss Australian Chamber of Commerce and Industry (SACCI)
(www.sacci.com.au/sacci/sacci_home.nsf)
Provides business contacts both in Australia and Switzerland for small, medium, and large organizations.

Sweden Trade Council
(www.swedishtrade.com)
Formed to help Swedish companies achieve substantial and lasting improvements in their North American sales.

Tradeco Export Import Industries Development Association
(www.tradecoexportimport.net)
Nonprofit association provides advisory services for exporting and importing. Site features multilingual access in English, Italian, German, French, Portuguese, and Russian.

TransAtlantic Business Dialogue
(www.tabd.com)
Offers a framework for enhanced cooperation between the transatlantic business community and the governments of the European Union and United States.

World Federation of Direct Selling Associations
(www.wfdsa.org)
Mission is to support direct selling associations in the areas of governance, education, communications, consumer protection, and ethics in the marketplace. News, legal compendium, and position papers.

World Technology Network
(www.wtn.net)
Encourages emerging technologies by bringing together key players from diverse disciplines: technology, finance, marketing, government. Events and membership.

GLOSSARY

Backsourcing   The expiration or termination of an outsourcing arrangement and the recapture in-house of the formerly outsourced function.

Barriers to outsourcing   Companies often experience resistance, especially from inside the organization, to outsourcing. The most common ones re: fear of loss of control, viewing an activity as too critical to outsource, loss of flexibility, concern over potential customer issues, and concerns over potential employee issues. All can be overcome and turned into positives through properly structured and managed outsourcing relationships.

Benchmarking   A method of comparing contract services to market services or other independent standards. Used by public sector organizations, charities, and private companies alike for gauging their performance by comparing it with the performance of other organizations, typically of a similar size and nature.

Best practices   Those practices and procedures that, followed regularly, reflect the wisdom and experience at leading-edge companies. The collection, interpretation and assembly, and redefinition and updating of best practices have been historically performed by management consultants working in many industries and analyzing common threads. One commentator, in an article in the *Wall Street Journal,* dated October 20, 1998, said that best practices are what consultants see while working at one company, repackage it, and sell it to other corporate clients, touting it as their own.

Brokering outsourced services   Many firms turn to outsourcing brokers to match their needs to the capabilities of vendors, whether through a request for proposal (RFP) or other selection process.

Business process outsourcing (BPO)   Puts together two powerful business tools: business process management and outsourcing. Business process management uses technology to break down barriers between traditional functional silos, such as those found in finance, order processing, and call centers. The goal is to redesign the process, reduce unnecessary steps, and eliminate redundancies. Outsourcing uses skills and resources of specialized outside service providers to perform many of these critical, yet noncore, activities. BPO does both at the same time, thereby speeding implementation and ensuring that the intended benefits really hit the bottom line. In short, BPO means examining the processes that make up the business and its functional units, and then working with specialized service providers to both reengineer and outsource these at the same time.

Business process reengineering   Represents planned change in the manner of conducting a business function, such as information collection and reporting, manufacturing, finance, compliance, or administration.

Captive center   A company-owned offshore operation. The activities are performed offshore, not outsourced to another company.

347

Certified Chief Resource Officer   Outsourcing buyer organizational executive with earned certification through the CRO Institute.

Certified Outsourcing Administrator   Outsourcing vendor professional certified through the Outsourcing Management Institute.

Chief resource officer (CRO)   The governance executive in buyer organizations charged with leading the outsourcing and outsourcing governance initiatives.

Commercialization   Outsourcing often provides an opportunity for an organization to "commercialize," that is, generate incremental revenue dollars or equity value, from its internal operations. This can be done in many ways, such as selling existing internal assets to the provider, licensing intellectual properties, and entering into a strategic alliance or joint venture with a provider.

Competitive insourcing   A process whereby internal employees engage in bidding to compete with competitive, third-party bidders for a defined scope of work. See also *insourcing*.

Contract manufacturing   The outsourcing of a manufacturing job to an onshore or offshore third party with the necessary infrastructure and know-how to perform the job.

Core competencies   The unique skills and knowledge sets that define an organization's competitive advantage. For example, Microsoft's core competencies are software design, development, and marketing. Chrysler's are product design, process design, and marketing. Core competencies also are areas of special expertise unique to a company. Core competencies are critical to business success, and will change over time. Typically, such items as strategic planning and project management skills are considered to be core competencies, and are not outsourced.

Cosourcing   When a business function is performed by both internal staff and external resources, such as consultants or outsourcing vendors, with specialized knowledge of the business function.

Critical versus core operations   Operations critical to a company's operations but that do not represent a differentiating competitive capability; that is, they are not core competencies. A classic example is payroll. Processing payroll accurately and timely is critical to the success of any organization, but is a core competency of very few organizations—mainly those that provide this service to other companies.

CRO Institute (www.CROInstitute.com)   The ISBOP (International Society of Business Outsourcing Professionals) and IACRO (International Association of Chief Resource Officers) sanctioned provider of outsourcing buyer organization and outsourcing governance professional certifications.

Customer relationship management (CRM)   A marketing and fulfillment system that usually includes a call center, databases, software, and marketing strategy. CRM initiatives are complex, involve redesign of internal business process, and retraining. Successful contracting for CRM outsourcing requires attention to business as well as technology and legal issues.

Downsizing   Reducing a workforce (by firing or laying off employees) for the purpose of reducing the size of a company.

Facilities management   The solution by which the customer entrusts to an external service provider the responsibility for operations and software applications and for managing the associated instrumentalities (hardware, software, applications programming personnel, etc.), while retaining general oversight and supervision of its information technology. In broader terms, facilities management may apply to other fields, such as applications maintenance, updating, or revision.

Financial outsourcing   Also known as facilities management, when a company subcontracts all or part of its financial function.

Functional process outsourcing   A company's business processes end at its true customers, the people paying the bills. There are, however, many internal processes that exist to support people within the company, and are often performed within a single department. Human resources, finance and accounting, travel, and facilities services are examples. When these functional processes are outsourced, along with the supporting technologies and supply chains that feed into them, it is referred to as functional process outsourcing.

Gainsharing   A contract structure wherein both the customer and provider share financially in the value created through the outsourcing relationship. One example is when a service provider receives a share of the savings it generates for its client.

Global BPO value equation (GBPOV)   The expanded value model for outsourcing, where: GBPOV = (Business case) × (Acceleration + Flexibility) = Innovation, is the full value of global business process outsourcing is the traditional business case multiplied by the improvement to the organization's acceleration and flexibility, all raised to the power of innovation.

Global outsourcing   Global outsourcing (meaning globally inclusive in nature) involves the wholesale turnover of IT management to a contractor, whether the contractor is a vendor or another state agency. All aspects of IT are provided by contract services to the organization, and in-house resources remain only to oversee the contract and provide input on business and technology alignment.

Governance   The oversight and management of all aspects of an outsourcing relationship. Areas of focus include: change management, communications management, performance management, operational management, risk management, strategic management, and others.

Heresourcing   Describes local outsourcing, or outsourcing within the same country. The term is used to distinguish same-country outsourcing from insourcing (see next).

Insourcing   The transfer of an outsourced function to an internal department of the customer, to be managed entirely by employees. As organizations became more experienced with IT and their business needs, some processes that had been outsourced were moved back in-house, giving rise to the term.

Just-in-time sourcing   When an organization adopts a continuous sourcing planning process that takes place on a project-by-project basis. Sourcing decisions are considered to last only as long as the projects that created the need for them. Shared services centers are often managed this way, with the organization's internal customers free to take their business on a project-by-project basis to the source they believe can best contribute to the outcomes they seek, whether that source is inside or outside the organization.

Make versus buy Outsourcing is often referred to as a "make versus buy" decision on the part of the customer, to answer the question: Is it in the organization's best interests to continue to (or start to) perform the activity itself using its own people, process expertise, and technology or to "buy" the activity from the service provider marketplace?

Market-driven sourcing A market-driven approach to sourcing means that the organization's decisions are in direct response to the capabilities of the available providers. Where the organization's internal capabilities are superior to that of providers, the activity is performed internally; where they are not, the activity is outsourced.

Massive outsourcing The process whereby a majority of business support processes are outsourced in one transaction or a small number of related transactions. The purpose of massive outsourcing is to drive shareholder value through shifting to others the operational responsibility for critical operations that do not deliver comparative advantage, or in which the company chooses not to invest due to comparatively low returns on investment.

Nearshoring Offshore outsourcing to a nearby territory, one in the same or neighboring time zone.

Offshoring Performing or sourcing any part of an organization's activities at or from a location outside the company's home country. Companies create captive centers offshore, where the employees work for them, or outsource offshore, where the employees work for the outsourcing provider.

Offsourcing The restructuring of a supply chain wherein one company relies on its supplier for functions that were previously performed in-house. The offsourced functional unit is able to generate greater value as a part of the supplier's business than in the customer's business. The supply chain is tightened by the improved functioning of the offsourced employees in the new environment.

Outsourcing The transfer or delegation to an external service provider the operation and day-to-day management of a business process or function. The customer receives a service that performs a distinct business function that fits into the customer's overall business operations. Sometimes the process is one that historically has been performed by a vertically integrated enterprise, such as data processing. More recently, outsourcing defines the sector for those services that were not part of the vertically integrated enterprise, such as telecommunications, web site hosting, transportation services, logistics, and professional services of regulated professionals.

Outsourcing at the customer interface A provider assumes responsibility for direct interaction with an organization's customers. This interaction may be in person, over the telephone, via e-mail, mail, or any other direct means.

Outsourcing framework A structure for mapping all of the activities of an organization in a way that allows consistent evaluation, planning, implementation, and management of sourcing decisions.

Outsourcing process A repeatable, multistage, management procedure for identifying outsourcing opportunities and moving those opportunities from concept through implementation and ongoing management.

Outsourcing teams Multidisciplinary working groups that are formed for specific purposes throughout the outsourcing process.

Outsourcing Management Institute (OMI)   Globally renown center of outsourcing education and certifications, primarily directed toward vendor organizations and professionals.

Out-tasking   An emerging concept. Generally refers to the turning over of a narrowly defined segment of business to another business, typically on an annual contract, or sometimes a shorter one. This usually involves continued direct or indirect management and decision making by the client of the out-tasking business. Out-tasking is typically implemented to indicate to a workforce that it is being evaluated for possible outsourcing.

Request for information (RFI)   A document that asks prospective service providers for general information on their capabilities and overall business functionality. An RFI provides material for first cut, shows vendor interest, and sometimes is used as a "tire-kicking" effort to validate the need to outsource.

Request for proposal (RFP)   A document detailing a customer's outsourcing requirements and the evaluation criteria that will be used for selecting a provider. An RFP is typically sent to a limited number of potential providers, around three to five, that have been previously qualified as capable of delivering the needed services.

Scope   Identifies what is available for sourcing from external service providers.

Sectional outsourcing   The strategic outsourcing of certain aspects of IT management (e.g., disaster recovery services, applications development, or data center operations) as a result of determining that the business goals and objectives are not best served by providing these services in-house.

Service-level agreement (or SLA)   A document of specifications for services to be delivered. SLAs define the type, value, and conditions of the outsourcing services to be provided. SLAs define the overall relationship by establishing parameters for quality of service.

Smartsourcing   A euphemism for the basic challenge of outsourcing as a management technique.

Sourcing-as-strategy   A powerful way to improve an organization's capability to serve customers, compete in its markets, and grow. It's a strategic approach to outsourcing that involves mapping the markets the organization plans to serve, the competitive advantages it seeks in each market, and then identifying the sources of those competitive advantages—whether they come from inside or outside the organization.

Strategic outsourcing   Outsourcing to achieve better return on investment and accelerated growth. Strategic outsourcing is approached as a redirection of the organization's resources toward its highest value-creating activities—its core competencies.

Subcontractor   A service provider who is responsible directly to the general contractor, and who may not be privy to the contractual relationship with the outsourcing customer.

Supply chain   A network of facilities and distribution options that performs the functions of procurement of materials; transformation of these material into intermediate and finished products; and distribution of these finished products to customers. A supply chain essentially has three main parts: the supply, manufacturing, and distribution. The supply side concentrates on how, where from, and when raw materials are procured and supplied to manufacturing. Manufacturing converts these raw materials to finished products; and distribution ensures that these finished products reach the final customers through a network of distributors, warehouses, and retailers. The chain can be said to start with the suppliers of your suppliers and end with the customers of your customer.

Supply chain management   An integrated process for managing all levels of the flow of information from an enterprise to its suppliers and customers, including its own internal manufacturing resources.

Tactical outsourcing   Outsourcing to achieve operational efficiencies. Tactical outsourcing is approached as a competition between existing internal operations and outside service providers.

Transformational outsourcing   Outsourcing that takes advantage of innovation and new business models. Transformational outsourcing is approached as a way to reposition the organization for competitive advantage.

Transitional outsourcing   Outsourcing that occurs when a vendor or another company is hired to oversee or manage technology change for an organization. The vendor is brought in to provide needed expertise in technologies, project management, and knowledge transference. Once the transition has been accomplished, in-house resources manage the system.

Value proposition   The benefit the organization is looking to gain through outsourcing. Overall, approximately half of organizations state that reducing costs is their primary reason for outsourcing. This means that something other than cost savings is the primary value sought by the other half. The other reasons most frequently cited are: focus on core competencies, enable a more variable cost structure, gain access to needed skills, grow revenue, improve quality, conserve capital dollars, increase innovation.

X-sourcing   Used to denote the extensive list of prefixes attached to the word "sourcing" to identify a specific approach to or type of outsourcing—co-sourcing, smart-sourcing, e-sourcing, insourcing, business process outsourcing, strategic sourcing, strategic outsourcing, and multi-sourcing, to name just a few.

Zero-based sourcing   An approach whereby the sourcing decision for each and every aspect of a business operation is rejustified every planning cycle from an assumed base of zero. This ensures that the organization is consistently and objectively retesting its internal operations against the best available external solutions.

INDEX

A

Accenture, 153, 159, 164, 165, 167, 168, 169, 170, 171, 329
Accenture HR Services, 167, 171
Accidental transformation, 29
Accolo, 169, 171
Accord Human Resources, 167, 172
Accountability, 144
Accounting and audit, 3, 7, 8, 9, 41, 108–109, 121, 122, 157, 164, 168, 259, 263, 272, 274, 278, 301, 313, 323, 326, 336
Accounts payable, 157, 164, 259
Accounts receivable, 157, 164, 278
ACS, 164, 167, 169, 170, 172
Acxiom Corporation, 166, 168, 172
Adecco Recruitment Management Solutions, 169, 170, 172
Administaff, 167, 173
Administrative and management support services, 157, 164
ADP Employer Services, 161, 165, 167, 173
ADP TotalSource, 161, 169, 173
Advanced Business Fulfillment (ABF), 166, 167, 173
Advantec, 167, 170, 174
Advertising, 103, 153, 268, 275, 288, 326, 338
AFFINA, 166, 173
AIG Technologies, 174
Ajuba Solutions, 165, 167, 174
All States Technical Services, 164, 174
Allenbrook, Inc., 168, 174

AlphaStaff Group Inc., 165, 167, 169, 175
American Association of Chief Resource Officers, 151
American Customer Care, Inc., 169, 175
AMG Logistics, 168, 170, 175
Amisys Synertech, 167, 175
Amnet Systems Private Limited, 167, 175
AMR Research, 4
Anderson, Stuart, 90
Anti-outsourcing web sites, 265
Aon Consulting, 167, 170, 175
API Outsourcing, Inc., 164, 176
AppLabs, Inc., 170, 176
Application development, 157, 164
Application maintenance and reengineering, 157, 164
Application management, 157, 164
Applications, 158, 168
Aquarian Group, 164, 167, 177
Aquent Inc., 164, 165, 167, 170, 177
Arambh Network, 168, 176
ArchiLog, 168, 176
Architecture and engineering, 157, 164
Argentina, 5
Ariba, 169, 170, 176
ARINSO International, 165, 167, 169, 177
Artemis PR and Design, 166, 177
Arthur, Sir Michael, xiii
Assess to expertise, 87
Assessment team, 75–76
Asset transition, 129
AT&T Solutions, 169, 170, 178

353

Atos Origin, 161, 167, 169, 178
Auburn University, viii
Australia, 48, 58, 272, 274, 285, 288,
    291, 292, 293, 323, 336, 341, 342,
    343, 344, 345
Avaya, 170, 178

B

Backoffice outsourcing, 52, 101, 154,
    164
Backsourcing, 347
Bangalore, xiii, 3, 238
Banking and financial solutions, 158,
    165
Banking industry, 2, 286, 310, 312
Banking jobs, 2
Barry-Wehmiller International
    Resources (BWIR), 166, 167,
    178
BearingPoint, 166, 167, 168, 170, 179
Benchmark audits, 59
Benchmark Electronics, 169, 179
Benchmarking, 2, 59, 72, 79, 133, 260,
    261, 262, 336, 347
Benefit Information Services, Inc.
    (BIS), 165, 179
Benefits administration, 158, 165
Benefits of outsourcing, 70, 73–86,
    125, 153, 258, 275, 283, 304, 334
Best practices, 34, 51, 134, 139, 140,
    141, 151, 269, 270, 306, 322, 347
  employing, 34
  implementing, 140–141
Bestshore Outsourcing, 49
  finding jobs, 277–296
Birch Group, 169, 179
Birlasoft, 168, 179
Black Book Model of Successful
    Outsourcing, 26
Blogs, 247
BlueStar Solutions, 168, 180
Booz Allen Hamilton Inc., 168, 180
BrassRing, 169, 180

Brazil, 330, 342
Bridgestone/Firestone Information
    Services (BFIS), 168, 180
Brokering outsourced services, 347
Bundling, 123–125
Bush, President George W., 4
Business continuity services, 158, 165
Business plans, 325
Business Process Outsourcing (BPO):
  attitudes toward, 7
  benefits from, 8
  common categories, 89
  definition, 20
  finance and accounting, 3, 89
  global growth, 3
  growth in India, 3
  human resources, 89
  IT growth, 3
  logistics, 89
  payment services, 89
  revenues, xi
  sales and marketing, 89
  satisfaction with, 8
  usage, 7
  worldwide market, 9
Business process outsourcing (BPO)
    management, vii, 2, 158, 165,
    347
Business process reengineering, 347
Business Roundtable, The, 19, 28
Business services reengineering, 158,
    165
Business support systems, 158, 165
Buyer characteristics, identifying, 52

C

Call centers, 41, 158, 165, 238, 257,
    330
Canada, 4, 48, 49, 274, 285, 286, 288,
    291, 292, 323, 329, 330, 338, 342,
    343
Canned contracts, 149
Capggemini, 159, 167, 168, 180

Capital business management, 158, 165
Capital funds, 46
Captive centers, 347
Career ladders, 259
Career opportunities emerging,
    150–156, 246, 251, 252, 254, 268,
    285, 291, 292
CareerSoar, 165, 169, 181
Caresoft Inc. Software Quality
    Assurance Labs, 170, 181
Castellani, John, 19, 28
CCR Services, 165, 181
Celent, 2
Cendian Corporation, 168, 169, 181
Cendris, 166, 167, 181
Ceridian Centrefile, 161, 166, 167,
    181
Certifications:
    buyer professional, 151–152
    in outsourcing, 151, 249
    vendor professional, 151–152
Certified Chief Resource Officer, 151,
    262, 275, 348
Certified Outsource Administrator,
    151–152
CGI, 160, 164, 167, 168, 182
Change management, 146
Channel Solutions, 158, 165
CheckPoint HR, 167, 182
Chief Resource Officer, 57, 59, 69, 70,
    125, 126, 138, 150, 151, 152, 153,
    154, 258, 260, 261, 262, 267, 293,
    300, 304, 348
Chief Resource Officer, training
    courses, 151–153
Chile, 48, 331
China, vii, 3, 10, 48, 58, 289, 323,
    328, 330, 331, 336, 340, 341
CIC Enterprises, 170, 182
CISCO, 166, 169, 182
CJR's Campaign Desk, 30
ClientLogic, 166, 169, 183
CNN, *Lou Dobbs Tonight,* 30
Coalition for Economic and American
    Jobs, 28
Coase, Ronald, 48
CoEfficient Back Office Solutions, 183

Cognizant Technology Solutions, 160,
    164, 168, 170, 183
Collections, 158, 165
Commercialization, 348
Communications, 56
Communications management, 158,
    165
Compass Technology Management,
    165, 166, 183
Competitive, 348
Competitive process, 138–139
Complete HR, 167, 183
CompuCom, 168, 183
Computer Enterprises Inc., 166, 184
Confidentiality, 146–147
Construction, 158, 166
Consulting outsourcing versus, 27
Content solutions, 158, 166
Contingency planning, 86
Contract:
    drafting, 141–145
    guidelines, 144
    key elements, 142
    management, 145–149
    manufacturing, 348
    measurements, 141
    negotiation, 141–145
Contract boilerplate, 145
Contracting, jobs in, 269
Contracts:
    outsourcing, 137–139
    renegotiations, 3
Control, 64–66
Convergys Corporation, 159, 165, 166,
    184
Convergys Employee Care, 167, 184
Corbett, Michael, 8
CoreBriX, 169, 184
Core competencies, 6, 7, 33, 36–37,
    41, 45–46, 51, 54–57, 60, 67, 70,
    74, 77, 80, 113, 118, 146,
    155–156, 234, 262, 270, 301, 303,
    306–307, 316, 348
Core competency screen, 74
Corporate cultures, comparative,
    119–120
Cosourcing, 348

Cost(s), 2, 5, 10, 11, 14, 34, 39, 42, 47, 49, 50, 51, 52, 54, 60, 61, 65, 70, 71, 72, 74, 75, 77, 79, 80, 81, 82, 83, 84, 85, 121, 128, 134, 142, 148, 149, 156, 235, 236, 238, 270, 303, 306, 307, 315, 318, 322, 327, 329, 330, 332, 333
  assessing, 73–86
  benefit analysis, 41, 80–82, 85
  control screen, 74
  determination, 118–119
Council of Economic Advisors, 29
Covansys, 161, 164, 167, 168, 185
Creative sourcing, 68
Creditability, 39
Credit services, 158, 166
Critical versus core operations, 74, 348
CRO Institute, 348
CSC:
  Credit Services, 160, 166, 185
  Financial (Computer Sciences Corp.), 160, 164, 165, 166, 167, 185
CTG, 164, 166, 185
Customer First Call Centers, 165, 186
Customer Relationship Management (CRM), 97, 158, 166, 322, 348
Customization, 68
Cybersecurity and infrastructure support, 158, 166
Czech Republic, 329

D

D&B Receivable Management Services, 165, 186
Daksh (IBM), 159, 164, 165, 167, 186
Dartmouth College, 12, 33
Database management, 158, 166
Databases, job, 256–257
Data center management, 158, 166
Data Infosys Ltd., 168, 186
Datamatics, 162, 164, 170, 187

Data return, 164, 187
Data security, 236
Decision drivers, 45–47
DecisionOne Corporation, 168, 187
Deloitte, 5, 163, 164, 167, 170, 187
Design and multimedia, 158, 166
Diamond Cluster International, 5
Digica Ltd., 166, 188
Direction Inc., 170, 188
Diversified Information Technologies, 188
Dobbs, Lou, 30, 265
Document creation and management, 158, 166
Document processing, 158, 166
Donohue, Tom, 263
DOW Networks, 165, 188
Downsizing, 348
Dual ladder approach, 259
Due diligence, 59

E

EADS (European Aeronautic Defense and Space Company), 167, 188
Earnest John Technologies (EJTL), 164, 189
Eastco Building Services, 166, 189
Eastern Europe, 9, 48
eBenX, Inc., 165, 189
Ebix Inc., 170, 189
EchoData West, 167, 189
Eclipsys, 190
Economic analysis, 337–338
eDATA Infotechp Ltd., 164, 190
Edcor, 170, 190
EDS, 162, 164, 165, 167, 190
Educational training, 104
eFunds Corporation, 159, 164, 165, 166, 167, 190
E-Learning and education solutions, 158, 166
Electronic Data Systems. See EDS
Emerging opportunities, 91–110

Employee contact and service centers, 158, 166
Employment solutions, 158, 166
emr Technology Ventures, 164, 191
End-of-contract options, 148
Energy analytics, 158, 166
Engineering, 104
Enterprise Resource Planning (ERP), 158, 166
Enterprise storage solutions, 158, 166
Entrepreneurial, opportunities in government, 314–316
Entrepreneurs, 249
  outsourcing market, 14
Entrepreneurship, 308–324
Environmental management, 158, 166
EonBusiness, 170, 191
Epicenter, 165, 169, 191
Equitant, 166, 170, 191
Ernst & Young LLP, 159, 164, 170, 192
ERP Outsourcing Asia Pte Ltd., 166, 192
Espire Infolabs Inc., 164, 192
Estco Medical, 169, 192
Estonia, 5
ETelecare, 165, 192
Eurobase Limited, 170, 192
Europe, xi, 3, 6, 7, 11, 48, 143, 154, 280, 286, 287, 289, 293, 294, 323, 324, 336, 338
EXL Service, 164, 193
Expatriate, 290–291
Expense management, 158, 166
Exult, Inc., 160, 166, 167, 170, 193. *See also* Hewitt

50 best managed outsourcing vendors, 159–163
Finance, outsourcing, 3, 5, 7, 8, 52, 76, 115, 123, 126, 145, 249, 255, 258, 272, 274, 301, 317, 323
Finance accounting and audit jobs in, 272
Finance and financial services, 158, 167, 272
Financial:
  benefits, 52–53
  management, 101
  outsourcing pros and cons of, 54
  ratios, 38
  services outsourcing, 95, 349
First Mover, 313
1st Odyssey Group, 167, 171
firstoutsourcing.com, 59, 116, 132, 193
First Outsourcing, 168, 193
Flexibility, 158, 168
FOCUS AMC, 164, 194
Forms Processing, Inc. (FPI), 167, 194
Forms processing/BPO, 158, 167
Forrester Research, 3, 11
Fortune Infotech, 167, 194
Foundations, 53–55
Framework, 350
Full-time equivalents, 39
Functional process outsourcing, 349
Functional pros and cons of outsourcing, 54

G

Gain sharing, 314, 349
Galbraith, John K., 73
Gartner, 3, 4, 125
Gateway TechnoLabs, 164, 194
GE Capital International Services, 165, 194
Gelco Information Network, 166, 195
Geller & Company, 167, 195
GENCO, 170, 195

F

Facilities management, 104–105, 158, 166, 349
Failures, cause of, 327
FBD Consulting, Inc., 165, 193
Feasibility study, 73–75

Getronics, 161, 167, 168, 169, 170, 195
Getting started, 53–72
Gevity HR, 165, 167, 196
Glassman, James, 30
Global BPO value equation (GBPOV), 349
Global Business Services, 166, 196
Global delivery:
  models, 3
  and sourcing, 158, 167
Globalization, 2, 12, 244
Global outsourcing, 349
Global Outsourcing Partnership, 2, 169, 196
Goals, 147
  screen, 74
Governance:
  jobs in, 266–267
  outsourcing buyer, 2, 43, 57, 64, 74, 75, 116, 120, 125, 129, 138–140, 149, 151–154, 236, 239, 258, 262–266, 271–275, 281, 291, 314, 321, 349
  sample model, 64, 321
Government:
  contractors, 247
  regulations, 237
  services, 94
  sourcing, 158, 167
Greenspan, Alan, vii, xii
GTL Limited, 165, 196
Guidelines for effective outsourcing, 70–72

H

HCL BPO, 160, 164, 165, 167, 168
Healthcare information, 95
Henderschott, Robert, 5
Heresourcing, 349
Heritage Environmental Services, 166, 197
Hewitt Associates, 160, 165, 167, 170, 197
Hewlett-Packard (HP), 159, 164, 165, 167, 197
Hexacta, 168, 198
Hidden costs, 235–236
Hinduja TMT Ltd., 165, 167, 168, 198
Hiring professionals, 152–153, 155
Homeshoring, 49
Hospital, clinical, and medical services, 158, 167
Hot jobs, 263–276
HRCentral, 167, 198
HR XCEL, 165, 167, 198
Hudson Resourcing, 169, 170, 198
Hughes BPO Services, 165, 168, 170, 199
Human Resources, 97, 109–110, 158, 167
  administration, 10
  jobs in, 270
Hungary, 48
Hyrian, 169, 199

I

IBM, x, 159, 164, 165, 167, 168, 199
ICG Commerce, 170, 200
ICICI OneSource, 159, 165, 168, 170, 200
IDC, 3
i-flex Solutions, 161, 200
iGATE, 162, 164, 201
IKON, 166, 200
Implementation, 158, 166
  jobs in, 270
  transition framework, 322
India, vii, xii–xiii, 328
  BPO growth, 3
  Ministry of Education, xii
  Ministry of Information Technology, xiii
  1991 statement on industrial policy, xii
  outsourcing market, xii–xiii
India Life Capital, 165, 201

Industrial Revolution, viii, 10
Infocrossing, 162, 168, 201
Information Management Systems,
    Inc., 169, 202
Information retrieval, 158, 167
Information systems, jobs in, 271–272
Information technology, 97–101, 158,
    167, 259, 271, 275
Information Technology Association of
    America (ITAA), x
membership list, 10
Informed outsourcing, 67
Infosys Technologies Limited, 161,
    164, 165, 167, 169, 170, 202
    Progeon BPO Division, 164, 165,
        202
Infrastructure set up, 322
Insourcing, 349
    benefits, 13
    and intersourcing, 158, 168
Insurance Data Services, 168, 202
Insurance systems, 158, 168
Intellectual property, protecting, 313
Intelligroup, 161, 170, 201
Interactive messaging, 158, 168
Interim management resource sites, 296
Internal capabilities, 62
Internal management, 134
International Association of Chief
    Resource Officers, 151
International network administration,
    170, 202
International Smart Sourcing (ISS),
    169, 203
International Society for Business
    Professionals, 151
Internet job searching, 282–296
Interpro Global, 164, 203
Intetics Co./Web Space Station, 166,
    203
Investment Administration Sciences
    Inc., 164, 203
Ionline Outsourcing Resources,
    284–296
Ireland, 48, 331
ISeva, 169, 203
ISP Help Desk Services, 158, 168

Israel, 48, 288
Issues in outsourcing, how to
    prioritize, 77–78
(i)Structure, Inc., 168, 169, 204
IT:
    infrastructure management, 158, 168
    mainframe and server management,
        158, 168
    performance and organizational, 158,
        168
    storage management, 158, 168
    strategy and planning, 158, 168
    support services—embedded systems,
        158, 168
    support services and enterprise, 158,
        168
    systems:
        and data hosting, 158, 168
        development, 158, 168
        integration, 158, 168
i-Vantage Inc., 168, 204

J

Jacobson Companies, 168, 204
Japan, vii–ix, xi, 289, 291, 293, 323
Jargon, outsourcing, 49
Jobless recovery, vii
Job listings, electronic, 250
Job losses, by category, 11
Job search, 246, 254–263, 283
Job seekers, 14
Johnson Controls—Facilities
    Management, 166, 204
Just-in-time sourcing, 349

K

Kanbay International, 167, 205
Kawin Interactive Inc., 170, 205
Kaye-Smith, 170, 205

Keane, Inc., 160, 165, 167, 169, 170, 205
Keane Worldzen, 160, 165, 167, 206
Kenexa, 166, 169, 170, 206
Knowledge transfer costs, 238
KPMG LLP, 167, 178, 206

L

Labor:
  high cost, 48
  low cost, 48
Larsen & Toubro (L&T) Infotech, 164, 166, 206
LASON, 164, 167, 168, 206
Layoffs, 5
  getting back on track after, 255
Lead Dog Design & Development, 170, 207
Legal, 103
Legal services, jobs in, 270–271
Legislation, state specific outsourcing, 90–91
Liability, 149
Liberata, 165, 207
LiveBridge, 165, 207
Loan processing, 158, 168
Logisteon supply chain solutions, 170, 207
Logistics, 158, 168
Logistics management outsourcing, 265
Long list, 114

M

MachroTech, LLC, 208
Mahindra-British Telecom (MBT), 168, 208
Make versus buy, 350

Making an informed outsourcing decision, 67–70
Malaysia, 329
Managed application systems, 158, 169
Managed service providers, 158, 169
Management recruiters, general, 295–296
Mankiw, Gregory, 1, 29
Manpower, 167, 170, 208
Manufacturing, 4, 106
Manufacturing and engineering, 158, 169
Market-driven sourcing, 350
Marketing, 96
  jobs in, 268
  program management, 158, 169
Market needs assessment, 333–335
Marlborough Stirling, 169, 208
Massive outsourcing, 350
Mastek, 164, 208
MBS, 169, 209
Measuring performance, 79–85
Medicine, 92–93
Mellon HR Solutions, 167, 209
Mercer, 167, 209
Meridian, 164, 209
Meta Group, 2
Mexico, 3, 48
Michaels, James, W., 243
Miller, Harris, 10
Mistakes, 233–239
Mitigating risk, 45
Morgan Stanley Dean Witter, 44
Morneau Sobeco, 165, 210
Mortgage banking, 158, 169
Motif, Inc., 164, 210
Mphasis, 159, 164, 167, 168, 210
MSS★Group, Inc., 170, 210
Myths of outsourcing, ix–xi

N

NAFTA, 6, 90
NASDAQ, 44

National Foundation for American Policy, 90
NCO Group, 166, 167, 211
Nearshore outsourcing, 49
Nearshoring, 350
NEC, 168, 211
Needs assessment, 44
Network Management, 158, 169
Niche Vendors, 255
NIIT SmartServe Ltd., 164, 165, 211
Nine strategies for success, 244–251
Non-core activities, outsourcing, 70
Non-exportable careers, 248
Northrop Grumann, 161, 166, 211

O

Office solutions and document conversion, 158, 169
Office Tiger, 162, 164, 167, 169, 170, 211
Offshore:
  job resources, 285–290
  migration, 10
  outsourcing (see offshoring)
Offshoring, vii, 49, 135, 350
  benefits, xi
  positive impact, vii
  savings, x–xi
Offsourcing, 350
OKS Group, 164, 165, 212
Olive Optimized e-Business Solutions, 164, 212
Online resources, 63
Onshore outsourcing, 49
Operations, 102
Operations management, jobs in, 267
Oracle On Demand, 160, 166, 195, 212
Organizational analysis, jobs in, 272–273
Outsourced Venture Capital Solutions, 170, 213

Outsource Management Group, 167, 212
Outsource Partners International, Inc., 164, 170, 213
Outsourcing:
  to acquire better management, 37
  to acquire new skills, 37
  agreements, 128
  to assist a fast-growth situation, 38
  back office transaction processing, 22, 38
  barriers to, 347
  benefits, 20
  best choices, 33–34
  BPO revenues, 2002–2008, xi
  budgets, 4
  bundling, 123–125
  business failures, causes of, 327
  business process, vii
  business starting, 325–346
  business web sites, 335
  buying services, 13
  careers, high growth, 274–276
  categories of, 74–75
  challenges, 2, 29
  complexities, 6
  considering, 7
  consulting, jobs in, 267
  contribution to U.S. economic growth, 12
  cost of managing, 135
  critics of, xii
  customer interaction services, 23
  decision making process, 33–43
  decisions, critical factors, 48
  definition, 20–21
  elements of, 22–23
  employment process, 22
  employment resources, 284
  to enhance credibility, 39
  in Europe, 3
  European market, 6
  evaluation process, 75–83
  evolution, 27
  finance and accounting, 7
  to focus on core functions, 37

Outsourcing *(Continued)*
  to focus on strategy, 37
  global market, 6
  to handle overflow situations, 38
  history of, viii–ix
  human resources, 7
  to improve financial ratios, 38
  to improve flexibility, 38
  to improve overall performance, 39
  Indian market, xii–xiii
  information technology and
      software, x–xiii, 23
  informed, 67
  jobs lost to, 5
  knowledge and decision services, 22
  lack of governance, 2
  to launch a new strategic initiative,
      39
  levels of, 20–21
  main drivers, 47
  marketing services, 22
  matching needs, 27
  maximizing opportunities, 9
  most common challenges, 29
  myths, ix–xi
  needs, identifying, 36–37
  offshore, vii
  operational support services, 22
  operations finance and accounting,
      23
    jobs in, xi–xii
  options, 85–110
  payroll, 7
  phases of, 120–125
  pricing guide, 2
  process, 19–32, 350
    phases of, 25
  procurement, 7
  project plan, 68–70
  project management, 41–42
  pros and cons, 54, 310
  providers, 26
  qualitative considerations, 83–84
  quantitative considerations, 83, 84
  real estate, 7
  reasons for, 21, 37
  recruiters and trainers, 292–295
  recruitment process, relationships, 5,
      127–134, 140–141
  to reduce costs, 39
  relationships scope of, 24
  research and development, 5
  rise in financial sector, 5
  satisfaction with, 8
  savings, 11
  shopping bids, 39
  silver lining perspective, 1–3
  software services, x–xi
  spending, 6
  staffing issues, 86
  starting, 40–43
  talent and human capital, 22
  teams, 350
  terminology, 20
  third generation, 24
  three stages of negotiations, 137–141
  top ten countries, 328–331
  traditional, 24
  typical legal factors, 138–139
Outsourcing Career Center, 256
Outsourcing Career Portals (OCPs),
    256
Outsourcing Management Institute
    (OMI), 72, 351
Outsourcing Partnership, The, 59
Outsourcing Solutions, Inc. (OSI),
    165, 213
Out-tasking, 27, 351
Outventures, 14
  how to price and promote, 327–333

P

PacificNet Communications, 165, 213
PAR Computer Sciences (Int.) Ltd.,
    164, 214
Patents, 313
Patni Computer Systems Limited, 162,
    168, 214
Payroll, 158, 169
People transition, 320

Performance measures, 55
Performance measuring, 79–85
Perimeter Technology, 165, 214
Perot Systems, 164, 167, 168, 214
Perot Systems Corporation, 162, 170, 214
Personal goal setting, 14
Peterson's Guide, 264
PFSweb, Inc., 165, 215
Pharmaceuticals, 94, 158, 169
Philippines, 10, 330
Pitney Bowes, Inc., 165, 166, 215
Placement agencies, search firms, 252
Planning, jobs in, 268–269
PlanTech, Inc., 169, 215
PlatformOne, 167, 216
Point solutions, 158, 169
Poland, 331
Polaris Software Lab Limited, 216
Power Logistics, 216
Preprocess questionnaire, 50–52
PricewaterhouseCoopers (PwC), 164, 170, 216
Pricewaterhouse Coopers decision-makers study, 2–8
Pricing, 121–122
Primary reasons for outsourcing, 77
PrintGPO, Inc., 169, 216
Printing and fulfillment, 158, 169
Problems, 41–43
Process transition, 320
Procurement and outsourcing matching, 158, 169
Professional employer organizations, 158, 169
Project management, 158, 169
Promotion, 327, 332–333
Prosero, 169, 170, 217

Q

Qualitative costs, 42
Qualitative outsourcing considerations, 83

Quality, 51
Quinn, James Brian, 33

R

Raytheon Professional Services (RPS), 170, 217
Real estate, 102
Real estate management outsourcing, 158, 169
Reasons to outsource, identifying, 37–40
Recruitment process outsourcing, 158, 169
Redix Web Solutions, 166, 217
Re-engineering benefits, 45
Regulatory compliance, 107–108
Relationship manager, 322
Relationships, buyer/vendor, 2, 3, 5, 34–35, 41–44, 53, 55–57, 60–62, 65–67, 72–79, 85, 112, 114, 116, 118, 120–121, 125, 127, 132, 135, 137–142, 147, 149–156, 233, 235, 239, 251, 259–262, 273, 276, 283, 303, 305, 317, 321, 332
Reliable Integration Services, 168, 217
Request for information (RFI), 115–117, 351
Request for proposal (RFP), 351
  example, 113
Research and analytics, 158, 169
Research and development, 107
ReSourcePhoenix.com, 166, 218
Resume distribution services, 282
Resumes, 279–282
Resume writing services, 281
Retail, 158, 169
Retail services, 94
RightNow Technologies, 166, 218
Risk:
  assessing, 73–86
  buyer considerations, 85
Roth, Zachary, 30

RSM McGladrey Employer Services,
    167, 218
Ryan, Jim, viii

S

Safety, 158, 169
SAIC, 169, 218
Sales and business development, jobs in,
    273–274
Sales and marketing, 93–94, 96, 158,
    159
Sand Martin, 164, 219
SARCOM, 166, 219
Satyam, 160, 164, 165, 166, 169, 219
Scholarship Management Services, 170,
    219
Scientific and engineering business,
    outsourcing, 158, 169
Scope, 351
    screen, 74–75
    of work, definition, 130
Score card, outsourcing decision
    making, 35–36
Sectional outsourcing, 351
SEEC Software, 168, 220
Self marketing, 254–262
Service-level agreement (SLA), 45, 52,
    59, 60, 66, 112, 113, 122, 127,
    130, 133, 139–140, 154, 269, 278,
    318, 321, 322, 351
Service level requirements, 59
Shared vision, 55
Siemens Building Technologies, Inc.,
    166, 220
Siemens Business Services, Inc., 161,
    168, 169, 220
Singapore, 48, 329
Siri Technologies Pvt. Ltd., 164, 168,
    220
Skills assessment, 277–280
SLA's buyers view, 139–140
Slaughter, Matthew, 2
SmartSource Corporation, 168, 221

Smartsourcing, 351
Smith, Adam, xiv
Softtek, 168, 221
Software quality assurance/testing,
    158, 170
Solutions, outsourcing development, 42
SourceNet Solutions, 163, 166, 169,
    221
Sourcing-as-strategy, 351
South America, 324
South Korea, 10
Spherion, 161, 166, 221
SSI Inc., 165, 222
Staffing:
    issues, 86–87
    and workforce, 158, 170
STA International, 165, 222
StarTek, Inc., 170, 222
Startup checklist, 325–326
Startups, international resources,
    338–345
Staubach Management Services (SMS),
    167, 222
Steps to launch, 70–72
Strategic Alliances LLC, 166, 222
Strategic enabler, outsourcing as, 322
Strategic IT partnership outsourcing,
    158, 170
Strategic outsourcing, 21, 351
    business, 308–313
    customized, 61–62
    implementing, 60–63
    pros and cons, 311
StratSource, 166, 223
Sub-contracting, 10
Subcontractor, 351
Success factors, 48
Successful offshoring, 135–136
Success strategies, 243–252
Sundaram Finance Group, 167, 223
Supplier relationships, outsourcing
    versus, 27
Suppliers, candidate research, 71–72
Supply chain, 3, 10, 108, 266, 275,
    351
    administrative, 10
    information, 10

management, 158, 170, 352
physical, 10
transformation, 4
Supply Chain Dynamics Inc., 170, 223
Sutherland Global Services, 160, 165, 166, 169, 223
Syntel, Inc., 161, 164, 165, 223
Systems integration and consulting, 158, 170

T

Tactical outsourcing, 21, 352
Taiwan, 10
TalentFusion, 166, 224
TATA Consulting Services, 161, 166, 167, 168, 224
TATA Infotech Ltd., 161, 166, 224
Tax services, 158, 170
TechBooks, 162, 166, 225
Tech Central Station, 30
Technology transfer, 134–135
Technology transition, 320
Tecnovate eSolutions, 165, 225
Telecommunications, 5, 158, 170
Telelink, The Call Center, Inc., 165, 225
Telephony and B\business communications, 158, 170
Ten key drivers, 45–47
Term sheet, example, 112
Terra Solutions, 166, 225
TGA Sciences, Inc., 169, 225
Thinksoft Global Services, 165, 170, 226
Tim Kirker Creative, 170, 226
TMA Resources, 168, 226
Top ranked vendors, 159–163
TopSource Global, 164, 226
Top ten outsourcing countries, 328–331
TowerGroup, 4
Training and staff development, 158, 170

Trammell Crow Company, 169, 227
Transaction processing, 158, 170
Transferable skills, 278
Transformational outsourcing, 24, 158, 170, 352
Transformational versus traditional outsourcing, 24
Transition:
management, jobs in, 269
process, 36, 46, 48, 55, 57, 60, 72, 86, 128, 129, 130, 148, 149, 155, 235, 245, 258, 269, 276, 310, 318, 320, 321, 322
responsibilities, 128–129
TriActive, Inc., 169, 227
Trinity Partners, 165, 227
Trowbridge Group, 167, 169, 227
TSi Logistics, 168, 227
Tuition and scholarship services, 158, 170
24/7 Customer, 160, 165, 171

U

Ukraine, 49
UNICCO, 166, 228
Unisys Corporation, 160, 165, 167, 168, 169, 228
Unisys Managed Application Services, 169, 228
United Customer Management Solutions (UCMS) Inc., 166, 228
United Kingdom, xi, xii, 58, 271, 274, 285, 323, 342
United States Labor Department, 5
United Systems Integrators Corporation (USI), 168, 229
Unseen costs, 81–82
USA-BPO, 169, 229
U.S. Bank, 169, 229
U.S. Chamber of Commerce, 263
U.S. Federal Reserve Board, vii, xii
U.S. Government, 4
U.S. Personnel, Inc., 167, 229

V

Value proposition, 352
VCustomer, 165, 166, 168
Vedior, 230, 170
Vendor:
    employers, finding, 264–265
    expectations, 120
    fit, 131–132
    focused agreements, rules for,
        317–323
    management, 127–136
    relationships, defining, 76–79
    selection, 111–126
        criteria, 117
    and suppliers directory, 157–232
Venture Capital Outsourcing Services,
    158, 170
Veritude, 170, 230
VMC, 165, 166, 168, 169, 230

W

Walsh, Paul, 111
Wealth of Nations, xiv
Web development, 158, 170
Web publishing, 158, 170
When not to outsource, 233–235
Where outsourcing sells, 323–324
White collar jobs, 247
White House Council of Economic
    Advisors, 1
Wipro Spectramind, 159, 166, 230
Wipro Technologies, 165, 168, 230

WNS Global Services, 163, 165, 166,
    169, 231
Workforce consulting and management,
    158, 170
Work force quality, 48
Workscape, Inc., 165, 231
World Trade Organization, 90
Worldwide forecast database, 89
Worldwide sourcing, 28

X

Xansa, 160, 168, 231
Xchanging, 169, 231
Xerox, 169, 231–232
X-sourcing, 352

Y

Yale Center for the Study of
    Globalization, xiii
Yankelovich Partners, 7
Young, Rob, 264

Z

Zenta Technologies, 165, 232
Zero-based sourcing, 352